The Ancient Maya of the Belize Valley

Florida A&M University, Tallahassee
Florida Atlantic University, Boca Raton
Florida Gulf Coast University, Ft. Myers
Florida International University, Miami
Florida State University, Tallahassee
University of Central Florida, Orlando
University of Florida, Gainesville
University of North Florida, Jacksonville
University of South Florida, Tampa
University of West Florida, Pensacola

Maya Studies
Edited by Diane Chase and Arlen Chase

The books in this series focus on both the ancient and contemporary Maya peoples of Belize, Mexico, Guatemala, Honduras, and El Salvador. The goal of the series is to provide an integrated outlet for scholarly works dealing with Maya archaeology, epigraphy, ethnography, and history. The series will particularly seek cutting-edge theoretical works, methodologically sound site reports, and tightly organized edited volumes with broader appeal.

Salt, White Gold of the Ancient Maya, by Heather McKillop (2002)

Archaeology and Ethnohistory of Iximché, edited by C. Roger Nance,
Stephen L. Whittington, and Barbara E. Borg (2003)

The Ancient Maya of the Belize Valley: Half a Century of Archaeological Research,
edited by James F. Garber (2004)

The Ancient Maya
of the Belize Valley

Half a Century of Archaeological Research

Edited by James F. Garber

University Press of Florida

Gainesville · Tallahassee · Tampa · Boca Raton
Pensacola · Orlando · Miami · Jacksonville · Ft. Myers

09 08 07 06 05 04   6 5 4 3 2 1

Library of Congress Cataloging-in-Publication Data
The ancient Maya of the Belize Valley: half a century of archaeological research /
edited by James F. Garber
p. cm. — (Maya studies)
Includes bibliographical references and index.
ISBN 0-8130-2685-7 (cloth: alk. paper)
1. Maya—Belize River Valley (Guatemala and Belize)—Antiquities.
2. Excavations (Archaeology)—Belize River Valley (Guatemala and Belize)—History.
3. Belize River Valley (Guatemala and Belize)—Antiquities. I. Garber, James. II. Series.
F1445.A63 2004
972.82—dc21   2003054096

The University Press of Florida is the scholarly publishing agency for the State University
System of Florida, comprising Florida A&M University, Florida Atlantic University,
Florida Gulf Coast University, Florida International University, Florida State University,
University of Central Florida, University of Florida, University of North Florida,
University of South Florida, and University of West Florida.

University Press of Florida
15 Northwest 15th Street
Gainesville, FL 32611-2079
http://www.upf.com

Dedicated to the memory of Gordon R. Willey

(1913–2002)

Contents

List of Figures   xi
List of Maps   xv
List of Tables   xvii
Foreword   xix

Introduction

1. The Archaeology of the Belize Valley in Historical Perspective   1
Arlen F. Chase and James F. Garber

2. Retrospective   15
Gordon R. Willey

The Central Belize Valley

3. Middle Formative Prehistory of the Central Belize Valley:
An Examination of Architecture, Material Culture, and Sociopolitical
Change at Blackman Eddy   25
*James F. Garber, M. Kathryn Brown, Jaime J. Awe,
and Christopher J. Hartman*

4. Archaeological Investigations at Blackman Eddy   48
*James F. Garber, M. Kathryn Brown, W. David Driver, David M. Glassman,
Christopher J. Hartman, F. Kent Reilly III, and Lauren A. Sullivan*

5. Major Center Identifiers at a Plazuela Group Near the Ancient
Maya Site of Baking Pot   70
James M. Conlon and Terry G. Powis

6. Ancient Maya Settlement in the Valley of Peace Area   86
Lisa J. Lucero, Scott L. Fedick, Andrew Kinkella, and Sean M. Graebner

The Upper Belize Valley

7. Cahal Pech: The Middle Formative Period   103
Paul F. Healy, David Cheetham, Terry G. Powis, and Jaime J. Awe

8. The Role of "Terminus Groups" in Lowland Maya Site Planning:
An Example from Cahal Pech   125
David Cheetham

9. Buenavista del Cayo: A Short Outline of Occupational and Cultural
History at an Upper Belize Valley Regal-Ritual Center   149
Joseph W. Ball and Jennifer T. Taschek

10. Xunantunich in a Belize Valley Context   168
Richard M. Leventhal and Wendy Ashmore

11. The Royal Charter at Xunantunich   180
Virginia M. Fields

12. Buenavista del Cayo, Cahal Pech, and Xunantunich:
Three Centers, Three Histories, *One Central Place*   191
Jennifer T. Taschek and Joseph W. Ball

The Belize Valley: Neighboring Connections

13. The Ancient Maya Center of Pacbitun   207
Paul F. Healy, Bobbi Hohmann, and Terry G. Powis

14. Defining Royal Maya Burials: A Case from Pacbitun   228
Paul F. Healy, Jaime J. Awe, and Hermann Helmuth

15. Integration among Communities, Centers, and Regions:
The Case from El Pilar   238
Anabel Ford

16. The Classic Maya Trading Port of Moho Cay   257
Heather McKillop

The Belize Valley: Integration

17. Problems in the Definition and Interpretation of "Minor Centers"
in Maya Archaeology with Reference to the Upper Belize Valley   273
Gyles Iannone

18. The Emergence of Minor Centers in the Zones between
Seats of Power   287
W. David Driver and James F. Garber

19. The Terminal Classic to Postclassic Transition in the
Belize River Valley   305
James Aimers

20. Polities, Politics, and Social Dynamics: "Contextualizing" the
Archaeology of the Belize Valley and Caracol   320
Arlen F. Chase

Conclusion

21. Diverse Voices: Toward an Understanding of Belize Valley
Archaeology   335
Diane Z. Chase

References Cited   349
List of Contributors   403
Index   407

Figures

1.1. Plan of Barton Ramie 6
3.1. Blackman Eddy Structure B1 profile 26
3.2. Radiocarbon dates from Blackman Eddy 28
3.3. Blackman Eddy artifacts 32
3.4. Plan map of bedrock beneath Structure B1 at Blackman Eddy 34
3.5. Blackman Eddy Middle Formative vessels 36
3.6. Structures B1-4th and B1-5th at Blackman Eddy 39
3.7. Structure B1-3rd subphases at Blackman Eddy 43
4.1. Map of Blackman Eddy site core 50
4.2. Artifacts from Burial 4 on Structure B1, Blackman Eddy 53
4.3. Anonal Buff-polychrome vessel from Burial 4, Structure B1, Blackman Eddy 53
4.4. Structure B1-2nd, Blackman Eddy 55
4.5. Drawing of upper east mask facade, Structure B1-2nd-b, Blackman Eddy 56
4.6. Formative and Classic examples of bowls with supernatural entities 57
4.7. Stelae drawings 63
5.1. Map of Baking Pot, showing location of Bedran Settlement Cluster 71
5.2. Plan of the Bedran Settlement Cluster 73
5.3. Plan of the Bedran Group plazuela 73
5.4. PSS glyph band on Orange Walk Incised bowl recovered from Burial 2, Structure 2, Bedran Group 77
6.1. Land classes in the VOPA area 89
6.2. Saturday Creek 92
6.3. Yalbac 97
7.1. Plan of Cahal Pech 104
7.2. Plan of Cahal Pech Plaza B 105
7.3. Plan of the Tolok peripheral settlement group, Cahal Pech 111

7.4. Late Middle Formative circular platforms 112

7.5. Reconstruction of Cunil phase ceramic vessels from Cahal Pech 113

7.6. Select motifs from Cunil phase ceramics, Cahal Pech 114

7.7. Formative period hand-modeled ceramic figurine heads from Cahal Pech 115

8.1. Terminus group site plans 128

8.2. Plan of the Zopilote Terminus Group 131

8.3. North-south profile of pyramidal Structure A-1, Zopilote Terminus Group, Cahal Pech 132

8.4. Ceramic vessels from Tomb 1, Structure A-1, Zopilote Terminus Group 134

8.5. West-face profile of "Stela Chamber" 135

8.6. Stela 9 from Tomb 2 136

8.7. Idealized evolution of a "multiple nuclei" Maya center 143

9.1. Buenavista del Cayo 150

9.2. Middle Preclassic (Kanluk phase) twisted biface, Guerra locality 152

9.3. Terminal Middle/Initial Late Preclassic (Umbral phase) structural cache, Buenavista 154

9.4. Footprint plans of Buenavista del Cayo center 155

9.5. Stucco statuette of hunchbacked dwarf from primary centerline cache, Structure BVc-3 159

9.6. The "Buenavista Device" 160

9.7. The Buenavista "Palace School" 161

10.1. Final map of central area of Xunantunich 172

11.1. Architectural friezes on Xunantunich Structure A6-2d 183

11.2. Chak Xib Chak on the Cosmic Plate 184

11.3. Limestone panel from Palenque 184

11.4. Vessel from Seibal Burial 14 186

11.5. Quirigua Stelae A and C, north faces 188

11.6. Quirigua Stelae A and C, south faces 189

12.1. The upper Belize Valley Late Classic "Jade Hearth" 192

12.2. Xunantunich 193

12.3. Cahal Pech 195

12.4. Late Classic (Paloverde ceramic phase) polychrome bloodletting bowl from Cahal Pech 200

12.5. Stela 9, Cahal Pech 201

13.1. Plan of Pacbitun Core Zone 209

13.2. Plan of the elite residential court zone at Pacbitun 211

13.3. Artist's rendering of the Pacbitun ballcourt (Early Classic and Late Classic) 212

13.4. Stela 6 at Pacbitun (reconstruction), dated to ca. A.D. 475 214

13.5. Plan of the Middle Preclassic structures below Plaza B at Pacbitun 223

14.1. Stylized plan of Pacbitun BU 1–9 (tomb) interior 230

14.2. Ceramic vessels from Pacbitun BU 1–9 231

14.3. Artifacts from Pacbitun BU 1–9 232

14.4. Hollow, cut bone tubes from BU 1–9 232

15.1. Belize River Archaeological Settlement Survey area with regional transect surveys, test excavations, and full-scale excavations 240

15.2. Map of the greater extent of the major regional center of El Pilar (Belize)/Pilar Poniente (Guatemala) 242

15.3. A large ridgeland residential unit excavated in 1992 by the BRASS project 246

15.4. The regional location of El Pilar 249

15.5. The El Pilar transect just south of the center of El Pilar 252

16.1. Map of Moho Cay 259

16.2. Feature 4 burial in Unit 2a 263

16.3. Feature 9 burial in Unit 2b 263

16.4. Feature 3 burial in Units 2c, 2d, and 2f 264

16.5. Feature 5 burial in Unit 8a 265

16.6. Feature 8 burial in Unit 22 included a bichrome, round-side dish, similar to others found offshore 266

16.7. Manatee bone midden in Units 6–6c 267

18.1. Site plan of Floral Park 294

18.2. Site plan of Esperanza 295

18.3. Site plan of Nohoch Ek 296

18.4. Site plan of Ontario 298

18.5. Site plan of Ontario settlement zone 299

19.1. Paxcaman Red grater bowl 309

19.2. Augustine Red collared jar 312

19.3. Augustine Red tripod dish 315

20.1. City of Caracol 326

Maps

1. The Belize Valley 2
2. The east-central Maya lowlands 127
3. The central Maya lowlands with Maya centers indicated 239
4. The Belize Valley with 9.9-km "districts" 290

Tables

3.1. Middle Formative construction sequences by phase from Structure B1 at Blackman Eddy 27

3.2. Radiocarbon dates from Blackman Eddy 29

4.1. Construction phases of Structure B1 at Blackman Eddy 51

4.2. Earliest dated monuments and the development of the ISIG 65

4.3. Summary of Stela 1, Blackman Eddy 66

6.1. Soil attributes and land capability classes 90

6.2. VOPA soil classes 91

6.3. Residential unit density by soil class in the upper Belize River area 98

6.4. Average structure/residential unit per km² 99

7.1. Middle Formative radiocarbon dates from Cahal Pech site core and settlement zone 106

7.2. Identified fauna from Formative period Cahal Pech 117

8.1. Morphological data of select terminus groups from the east-central Maya lowlands 129

13.1. Settlement of the Periphery Zone of Pacbitun 218

13.2. List of identified taxa from Pacbitun 219

Foreword

Archaeologists are a persistent and conscientious group of individuals, and persistence was especially necessary to see this volume through to fruition. The idea for this book began at the Society for American Archaeology meetings in St. Louis, Missouri, in April 1993, at a session titled "Recent Developments in the Archaeology of the Belize Valley." This was a first attempt to get the plethora of researchers with an interest in the Belize Valley together to share and discuss the archaeological data they had been gathering.

In the 1990s and continuing to this day, the many different projects (and subprojects) in the valley were being undertaken by individuals from many different universities and institutions. All of these researchers not only hold different methodological and theoretical backgrounds but also have varied personalities, backgrounds, and training. There is also an element of competition among these individuals, even though many of them have been working side by side for twenty years. The long-term nature of these multiple projects also means that most see "next season" as providing them with crucial missing data. All of this means that it is often difficult for other researchers to obtain information and to see any broader picture of the Belize Valley. This volume, therefore, is the first presentation of the diverse data collected over several decades in the Belize Valley in a single compilation. Because the valley is one of the most intensively worked regions in the Maya area, these data form an important baseline for other interpretations.

Gordon Willey first brought attention to the Belize Valley some 50 years ago by restarting Harvard University's presence in the field of Maya archaeology after an absence of nearly 50 years (since that institution's cessation of work at Copan, Honduras, at the end of the 19th century). By using an academic program as the launching pad for an archaeological project, Willey was at the forefront of the integration of Maya studies into academic curriculums following World War II. In the 1950s, a series of universities (Harvard University at Barton Ramie, Belize; the University of Pennsylvania at Tikal, Guatemala; and Tulane University at Dzibilchaltun, Mexico) actively sought research programs in the Maya region and integrated them into their graduate programs in anthropology. The continuation of university-sponsored research involving undergraduate and graduate anthropology programs has prospered at the sites reported on in this book and has exposed a whole new generation of students to the archaeology of the Belize Valley.

Whereas Willey et al. (1965) was able to publish a synthesis of his archaeological data less than 10 years after the close of his three-year excavation project, with a few exceptions (Bullard and Bullard 1965), there have not been any published synthesis or site reports on the more recent work undertaken in the Belize Valley. There are few remaining outlets for the publication of research data in the form of site reports. Yet site reports and recorded artifactual and contextual data retain their value long after theoretical interpretations and "breakthroughs" become old and hackneyed. We sincerely hope that the monograph part of our Maya Studies series will begin to alleviate this very real publication problem by providing an outlet for well-prepared final site reports. As an edited volume, this book represents an intermediate step in the long-term production of final site reports. While researchers may quibble with some of the current interpretations and theoretical frameworks used in this volume, the archaeological data presented are timeless and will be used and cited by future generations of archaeologists.

Arlen F. Chase and Diane Z. Chase, series editors

1

The Archaeology of the Belize Valley in Historical Perspective

Arlen F. Chase and James F. Garber

Half a century ago, Gordon Willey instituted the first formal settlement pattern work in the Maya area. Trained by Julian Steward in cultural ecology and already having successfully carried out similar work in the Viru Valley of Peru (Willey 1953), he selected the Belize Valley as the locus of investigation for demonstrating how settlement pattern archaeology could be applied to the Maya area (chapter 2; Willey et al. 1965:15–16). His focus on small unassuming housemounds rather than on a large spectacular Maya center revolutionized the field of Maya archaeology by causing researchers to examine non-elite remains. This work also indirectly produced questions concerning the organizational scale of ancient Maya society: chapters 17 and 18 (this volume) address these issues as they relate to the function and variability of "minor ceremonial centers" as defined in Willey's initial study; chapters 9 and 11 (this volume) address these questions as they relate to "major ceremonial centers" as originally defined by Willey.

The Belize Valley

The Belize Valley may be defined in terms of its waterways. It includes two topographical subregions. The first zone is referred to here as the "upper Belize Valley" and consists of the upland area characterized by hills and steep slopes above (west of) the convergence of the Macal and Mopan Rivers in western Belize. The second zone is referred to as the "central Belize Valley" and consists primarily of broad alluvial flatlands and bordering hills that occur along the western sector of the Belize River from the

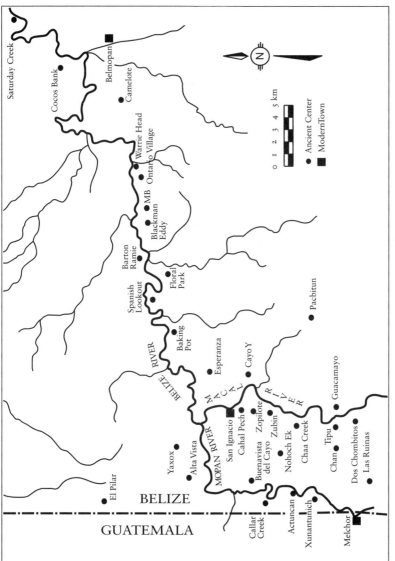

Map 1. The Belize Valley (drafted by James F. Garber). The upper Belize Valley, characterized by hilly terrain, extends from the modern town of Melchor on the west to the conjunction of the Macal and Mopan Rivers to form the Belize River on the east. The central Belize Valley, characterized by settlement on flatter alluvial terraces, starts at the conjunction of the Mopan and Macal Rivers and extends to the marshy area just east of Cocos Bank. Note that El Pilar and Pacbitun are technically not in the Belize Valley.

juncture of the Macal and Mopan to an area south of the modern capital of Belmopan, where the river begins its descent into the low-lying marshy swamps and savanna that stretch another 30 km to the Caribbean Sea (map 1). In terms of landmarks on the river, the Belize Valley extends from the modern town of Benque Viejo del Carmen in western Belize to the eastern ruins at Cocos Bank.

Ancient Maya settlement in central-western Belize was conditioned by the Belize River and its surrounding terrain. The lowest part of the Belize River (east of Cocos Bank and Saturday Creek) runs through savanna and swamp that were not conducive to either large or small Maya settlements. Agriculture was not only difficult in the coastal plain immediately adjacent to the Caribbean, but also some 30 km inland, where poor soil conditions still prevailed. Only the alluvial soils along rivers that flooded and carried upland soils into these areas could readily support settlement. To some extent, these ecological conditions determined one of the areas where the ancient Maya would settle—in the flatter, sometimes flooded, areas along rivers where rich alluvial soils had been deposited. Thus, the densest ancient Maya settlement occurs along the banks of the Belize River above the point where it spills into the broad savanna plain.

During the rainy season from May through December, the level of water in the rivers associated with the Belize Valley occasionally rise as much as 12 m, causing severe flooding and depositing alluvium on the river terraces. Willey and colleagues (1965:23) reported that "the alluvium of the upper terraces seems to be at least 10 m. deep." Limestone foothills dominate the western part of the Belize River Valley, essentially ending where the Macal and Mopan join to form the Belize River. The limestone foothills of the Maya Mountains also intermittently form the southern boundary of the Belize River between Floral Park and Cocos Bank. However, the zone between the modern town of San Ignacio and Floral Park is characterized by broad alluvial terraces on both sides of the river.

Probably because of the location of the modern road and the effect that this road has had on modern settlement, the majority of the sites known from the Belize Valley lie to the south of the Belize River (map 1). Apart from the work done by Willey et al. (1965) at Barton Ramie and the transect surveys carried out by Ford (1990) in the western part of the valley north of the Belize and Mopan Rivers, there has been little archaeological reconnaissance on the northern side of the river. Undoubtedly, other sites and settlements will be found there in the future.

Maritime trade was always of importance to the ancient Maya (McKillop and Healy 1989). Along with the Hondo River (D. Chase and A. Chase

1989) and New River (Garber 1989), the Belize River is one of the natural transportation and communication routes between the Caribbean Sea and the Petén heartland of Guatemala. The portage of long-distance trade goods would have been greatly facilitiated by the use of the Belize River. Given its position, the Belize Valley would have served as the last gateway for the transport of goods into the Maya interior. The archaeological record correspondingly exhibits exotics from throughout the Maya area— much of it material that had been transported up or down the Belize River (Jackson and McKillop 1989). At the other end of the Belize River, Mojo Cay served as a trade entrepôt (chapter 16).

While river traffic is possible up both the Macal and Mopan Rivers in the upper Belize Valley, rapids are encountered in each, making travel more difficult. South of the modern town of San Ignacio, the Macal River is characterized by steep sides with relatively little in the way of flat alluvial areas. Thus, the sites of Cahal Pech and Cayo Y effectively form the gateway community for the eastern extent of the Macal River throughout most of the Belize Valley's history (being replaced by Negroman-Tipu [Graham et al. 1985] in the Postclassic and Colonial eras). Interestingly, the jump-off station for travel to points in the interior remained on the Macal River throughout the Historic period with the town of San Ignacio, situated at the juncture of the uplands and plain, serving until relatively recently as the off-loading point for most travelers coming by boat (including archaeological projects; see pictures in Black 1990).

The Mopan River, characterized by rapids but also by a more direct interior route, appears to have had more settlement along its banks than did the Macal, probably because the terrain was gentler. This settlement, however, is not as dense as that documented at Barton Ramie, Baking Pot, or Spanish Lookout, all located along the Belize River in the central Belize Valley. Whereas Cahal Pech was the gateway community for the Macal River, a cluster of three sites seems to have served this purpose on the Mopan River—Actuncan in the Preclassic, Buenavista del Cayo in the Classic, and Xunantunich in the Terminal Classic. Ball and Taschek (chapter 9) explore the shifting political dynamics of this portion of the valley.

There are important compositional differences between the sites on the Belize River in the central Belize Valley and those above the confluence of the Macal and Mopan in the upper Belize Valley. Most of the settlement in the central Belize Valley is clustered on the sides of the Belize River and consists of many small mounds widely distributed over the landscape, much like Barton Ramie and Spanish Lookout. The sites at the Belize headwaters, on or between the Macal and Mopan Rivers in the upper Belize Valley, appear to be more concentrated in their settlement and to consistently exhibit larger scale architecture; this phenomenon is addressed by Driver and Garber (chapter 18). Cahal Pech (chapters 7 and 8), Xunantunich (chapters 9 and 11), Buenavista del Cayo (chapter 10), and even El Pilar (chapter 15), all form fairly compact sites with clear focal centers. In the central Belize Valley, Baking Pot (chapter 5) mimics this focus, but its settlement and its habitation mounds are relatively numerous and more widely dispersed (consistent with other ancient occupation on the flatland alluvial terraces).

Gordon Willey and Barton Ramie in Historical Perspective

Although Willey and his colleagues (1955, 1965; Willey and Bullard 1956) excavated at several sites (Barton Ramie, Spanish Lookout, Baking Pot, Melhado) in the Belize Valley between 1954 and 1956, the bulk of their archaeological work focused on the site of Barton Ramie, where 65 out of 262 mounds were investigated, 13 of them intensively. Barton Ramie was seen as being typical of the settlement found in the Belize Valley (Willey et al. 1965:561); "so dense are these mounds that they form a ribbon strip of virtually continuous settlement for many kilometers along the alluvial flats and higher banks of the stream." Few archaeological remains were located by Willey's project at any distance from the river; most (like the site of Floral Park) were no more than 1 km distant.

Barton Ramie (fig. 1.1) was a fairly unassuming site best characterized as a settlement zone located on the floodplain of the Belize River approximately 5 miles from the Belizean district capital of San Ignacio. Unlike other sites that had been investigated before 1950 by the Carnegie Institution of Washington and the University of Pennsylvania, Barton Ramie was not characterized by large temple-pyramids, carved stone monuments, or standing stone architecture. Instead, the site consisted primarily of raised earthen mounds that upon excavation revealed stone facings and other architectural remains. Also revealed in these tumuli was a rather lengthy sequence of occupation. Initially, at least, these investigations were fit into a preexisting paradigm that dictated an uncomplicated village development with eventual abandonment of the site and valley at the time of the Maya collapse (Willey 1956a; Willey et al. 1955). More recent research has shown both greater complexity and time depth to this initial occupation (chapters 3 and 7).

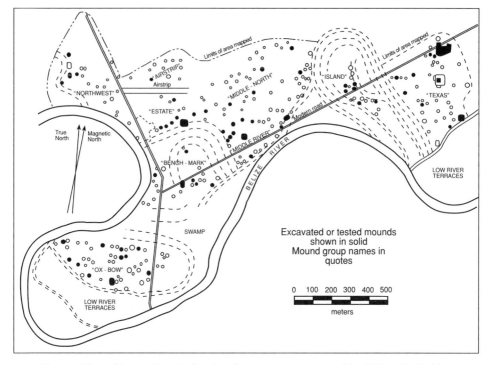

Fig. 1.1. Plan of Barton Ramie showing the structures excavated by Willey (drafted by James F. Garber after Willey et al. 1965:277).

Rather than fitting neatly with what was already known about the Maya elsewhere, however, the Barton Ramie ceramic sequence was found to be related to, but still peripheral to, the developments in the central Petén (Gifford 1976). The ceramics were not simply copies of those already known from Uaxactun (Smith 1955) or San José (Thompson 1939). The temporal faceting of these materials was also different from that assigned to central Petén ceramics (Gifford 1976).

Regional Chronology

Archaeological research undertaken in the Belize Valley in the half century since Willey et al.'s (1965) original work at Barton Ramie has served to confirm and broaden the cultural historical sequence that he initially established—with only slight changes. The original ceramic sequence defined by Gifford (1976:23) spanned "at even a conservative estimate, perhaps two thousand years." With the potential exception of its earliest and latest archaeological remains, the Belize Valley cultural sequence accords

6

well with developments known from elsewhere in the southern lowlands. The earliest part (Middle Preclassic or Middle Formative) of the Belize Valley sequence dates back to approximately 1000 B.C. (in spite of radio-carbon dates that indicate a potentially even earlier dating; Hammond 1977:62) and is characterized by variability in the ceramic remains. Some of these ceramics, called the Kanocha and Cunil Ceramic Complexes, have led to the postulation that there may have been non-Maya populations in the Belize Valley at this early date (Ball and Taschek 2000, 2003). Other early remains, termed the Jenney Creek Ceramic Complex and dated to approximately 600–900 B.C. at Barton Ramie (Gifford 1976), are quite different from the Mamom-related materials (Smith 1955) excavated throughout the central Petén of Guatemala, but still could be related to early Maya groups. The more recent archaeological work has recovered the Cunil Ceramic Complex from basal deposits at Cahal Pech (chapter 7), Xunantunich (LeCount et al. 2002:42), and the Kanocha Complex at Blackman Eddy (chapter 3).

By 300 B.C. (the onset of the Late Preclassic or Late Formative), how-ever, the valley had been subsumed into broader ceramic traditions found in the southern lowlands and most of the centers in the Belize Valley had been established. However, a Late Classic florescence of Xunantunich is argued for, based on "the overall paucity of evidence for occupation from the Late Preclassic to Early Classic" (LeCount et al. 2002:43). The integra-tion of the Belize Valley with the broader southern lowland area, at least ceramically, continued from the Late Preclassic through the Early Classic to the early part of the Late Classic period (A.D. 600–700).

Originally, the Barton Ramie archaeological data loomed large in con-siderations of the transition from the Late Preclassic to the Early Classic period. A ceramic complex (named Floral Park) was defined that was viewed as being intrusive into the area (Willey and Gifford 1961), and arguments were made for an influx of people into the Belize Valley at the end of Late Preclassic. These migrants were viewed as being refugees from a volcanic eruption in the El Salvadoran region. They were also believed to have introduced a new style of pottery into the Maya low-lands and to have helped usher in the Classic period with the introduc-tion of new social and political systems (Sharer and Gifford 1970). The postulated ceramic connections between Belize and El Salvador were later forcefully refuted (Demarest 1986:173–186; Demarest and Sharer 1986), but the appearance of a new style of ceramics in the archaeological record, especially in burial contexts, at the onset of the Classic period has yet to be adequately explained (see also Brady et al. 1998).

During the Late Classic period, the Belize Valley ceramics became increasingly regionalized, focusing on types and forms generally not found in surrounding regions. A better understanding of the Late Classic ceramic relationships for the Belize Valley probably would be gained through clarification of the archaeological picture at Naranjo, Guatemala, and a definition of that site's ceramic sequence. Terminal Classic ceramics show widespread variability at the sites in the valley and could not be faceted in the original Barton Ramie sample (Gifford 1976:226). Both Xunantunich (in terms of architecture) and Buenavista del Cayo (in terms of ceramics) exhibit ties to the northern lowlands, raising questions about the possible presence of "foreign" populations.

While most of the upper Belize Valley sites were largely abandoned after the Terminal Classic (e.g., Xunantunich; LeCount et al. 2002), the extensive riverine settlement in the central Belize Valley is almost uniformly characterized by Postclassic peoples who used ceramics that are similar to those found around the many lakes in the central Petén of Guatemala. This could be interpreted as indicating that the Belize Valley was integrated into broader sociopolitical and economic systems throughout the Postclassic era. Colonial period remains, including a Spanish visita church and ceramics that are very similar to the Postclassic remains in the central Belize Valley, have been extensively documented from the upper Belize Valley site of Negroman-Tipu (Graham et al. 1985). When viewed in conjunction with the modern town of San Ignacio, the archaeological data from the Belize Valley provide evidence of almost 3,000 years of continuous human settlement.

Like its early remains, the latest ceramics from Barton Ramie were problematic. Initially, the Postclassic occupation of Barton Ramie was considered to be minimal. In an early synthesis of the Barton Ramie data, Willey (1956a:781) noted that "not a single one of the numerous test excavations in the Belize Valley has brought to light ceramic or other evidence that would demonstrate a Postclassic period occupation of any of the village house mounds." Subsequent ceramic analysis actually revealed it to be widespread, occurring in 62 of the 65 mounds investigated (Gifford 1976:288; Willey et al. 1965). The relatively abundant Postclassic artifactual material and construction levels were not recognized during the fieldwork (possibly because no interments with recognizable Postclassic pottery were recovered) but instead were recognized during the subsequent ceramic analysis. Thus, the contextual linkages of this material are not secure and even the exact relationships among the Barton Ramie Postclassic ceramics are still largely unresolved (Bullard 1973; Cecil 2001;

A. Chase 1982; A. Chase and D. Chase 1983; D. Chase and A. Chase 1988; Graham 1987; Rice 1985, 1987; Sharer and Chase 1976). Even though more recent archaeological data relating to the Terminal Classic and Early Postclassic remains in the Belize Valley have been recovered (e.g., chapter 19), the problematic interpretation of the sequences, dating, and meaning of the latest Barton Ramie "New Town phase" material serves as a cautionary note for modern researchers to conjoin laboratory and field operations as fully as possible.

History and Retrospection

The excavations at Barton Ramie did not actually define the entirety of that site's settlement patterns. What they did define was the form and longevity of Maya structures and groups that were interpreted as being common households and living areas. This alone was a major advancement for Maya archaeology (see Taylor 1948). Thus, the value of Willey's work at Barton Ramie lay in its emphasis on Maya remains that were considered to be typical households of the lower stratum of Maya society. These were not elite remains. This was a level of people about whom little was known. Only a few earlier researchers had bothered to even investigate this class of remains (see chapter 2). Thompson (1931) had excavated a series of test excavations within residential groups located in the Mountain Cow area of the Vaca Plateau; he (1939) had also investigated larger palacelike structures that were clearly residential at San Jose. Limited samples of housemounds also had been intentionally excavated at Uaxactun (Wauchope 1934), but these had been located in fairly close proximity to the large central architecture of that site (Ricketson and Ricketson 1937; Smith 1950).

The excavations at Barton Ramie, however, did not address issues of how these structures and groups physically articulated with more elite remains—even those at Barton Ramie itself, as Coe and Haviland (1966) pointed out. This type of research was later attempted with the settlement work undertaken at Tikal, Guatemala (Puleston 1983). Barton Ramie was assumed to have been a small "rural" village within "a large but well-integrated network of theocratic stations and substations" that included three identified "ceremonial sites of middling size (Banana Bank, Banking Pot, Cahal Pech . . .)" and "one impressive ceremonial center at Xunantunich" (Willey 1956a:778)—"the nearest ceremonial or organizational center of consequence . . . some 20 kilometers upriver to the west" (Willey 1976:vii). But how this articulation actually worked was not specified and still engenders considerable debate (see chapters 9, 11, 17, 18, and 20).

The concentration of settlement at Barton Ramie is substantial (Ford 1990; Fry 1990) and much denser than settlement around the larger architectural concentrations of Cahal Pech or Xunantunich in the upper Belize Valley (but not as dense as ridgetop settlement outside of the valley proper [chapter 15]). The comparative implications for this density were never fully explored by Willey or others. Was Barton Ramie independent? Was it a cluster of nonrelated households? Was it a tightly organized group of people? Did it have different societal levels and an elite stratum? How were these people organized socially, politically, and economically? When Willey and his colleagues excavated Barton Ramie, Maya archaeology was not ready to answer these questions. Rather, the collected data were important in establishing the existence and dating of Maya residential groups. However, Willey's work also presaged many other questions that continue to plague Maya researchers. For example, exotic remains were found in association with the simple constructions at Barton Ramie and such remains were fairly widely distributed (Willey et al. 1965). Willey (1956a:778–779) himself contemplated what this meant for interpretations of how complex ancient Maya society was and for how it was organized, but could come to no firm conclusions regarding site or regional organization. Since Willey's study, the site of Blackman Eddy (chapter 4), located less than 3 km from Barton Ramie, has been discovered and investigated, providing new clues to the integration of the Barton Ramie settlement into the valley system.

All of the projects that have worked in or near the Belize Valley have followed Willey's tradition of emphasizing the study of ancient settlement. This is specifically seen in research undertaken at Xunantunich, Cahal Pech, Baking Pot, Buenavista del Cayo, and Valley of Peace. Where the more modern projects have diverged from Willey has been on their almost universal focus on large architectural concentrations. The majority of recognizable architectural concentrations or "site centers" on the south side of the valley have been investigated. Yet with the exception of the Xunantunich Project (Ashmore 1998) and the work done in the western part of the valley (Ford 1990; Fedick 1994), most of the archaeological projects have not attempted to systematically record and test settlements between centers or to block-map broad areas as Willey et al. (1965) did at Barton Ramie and Spanish Lookout (see also Caracol; A. Chase and D. Chase 2001a).

The Barton Ramie research undertaken by Willey and his colleagues (1965) was heralded as a breakthrough in methodology for Maya archaeology (Sabloff 1994:68–72). It was multidisciplinary and regional in scope and examined non-elite Maya settlement. Of particular note, it was fully published with relative speed. All of these were goals aspired to by later long-term Maya archaeological projects. Willey's work firmly entrenched settlement pattern studies in Maya archaeology (e.g., Ashmore 1981). Yet it is only with the more extensive, often small-scale, research projects that have been carried out subsequent to Willey's work that we have actually started to gain a sense of the broader settlement patterns of the Belize Valley.

The Belize Valley in Current Archaeological Perspective

It is rare in Maya archaeology, especially in the southern lowlands, for large areas to be mapped and surveyed so that the various settlement nodes, locales, and distributions situated in a given region can be compared and contrasted. This is possible in the southern lowlands with the sites of Tikal (Puleston 1983), Calakmul (Folan et al. 2001), and Caracol (A. Chase and D. Chase 2001a; A. Chase et al. 2001). Laporte (1994, 1996a, 2001) also has provided much regional data for the southeast Petén. The Belize Valley is the only other part of the southern lowlands that has comparable areal coverage. Thus, the true value of the Belize Valley archaeological data lies in the continued, incrementally additive regional research that has ensued in this location since Willey's Barton Ramie Project in the 1950s.

It was fortuitous that Willey (chapter 2) selected the Belize Valley for his settlement research. While the settlement and farming activities in the valley can be destructive, they also can be conducive to archaeological survey. Willey and colleagues (1965:15) noted that "the bulldozer-made clearings" at Barton Ramie were "worth thousands of man-hours to the archaeologist" and "too good to pass up." Since Willey's research, development in the Belize Valley has kept pace with the modern world, revealing (and destroying) more sites and Maya settlement (as testified to by many of the chapters in this volume). But the proximity to modern urban communities has also lured archaeologists to the Belize Valley because of the ability to maintain some semblance of modern creature comforts rather than having to effect an "Indiana Jones–Early Explorer" mode of archaeology of the kind still found in archaeological camps in the more undeveloped parts of the southern lowlands. Given this proximity to "civilization," the Belize Valley has become one of the most intensively worked areas in the Maya lowlands.

Even before Willey (1998) had relaxed in the Stork Club and the Western Club in San Ignacio, others had already sought temporary haven in these refuges (chapter 2). But none of the other early researchers had carried out a long-term project in the Belize Valley. Rather, their efforts were fleeting. Linton Satterthwaite (1950, 1951) of the University Museum (University of Pennsylvania) had gotten Willey interested in doing archaeology in the Belize Valley and had carried out limited work at both Cahal Pech and Xunantunich. J. Eric S. Thompson (1940), no stranger to jungle fieldwork, had worked briefly at Xunantunich (Pendergast and Graham 1981). Gregory Mason (1940:98) had popularized the ruins in the area by writing about a spur-of-the-moment excavation at an undesignated site 4 km south of San Ignacio. Two Harvard students also carried out short-lived excavations in the upper part of the Belize Valley, specifically at Nohoch Ek in 1949 (Coe and Coe 1956).

In the midst of this earlier work, however, two focal sites emerged. Xunantunich on the Mopan River was repeatedly investigated from both a research and a tourist perspective (chapter 11; Ashmore 1998; LeCount et al. 2002; Leventhal and Ashmore, this volume; MacKie 1961; Thompson 1940; Willey et al. 1965:315–316) with its stucco facade receiving early attention and restoration (Satterthwaite 1950). Another focal site was Baking Pot, first excavated by Ricketson (1929), then by Anderson (Willey et al. 1965:304), then by Willey (et al. 1965:305), then by a Royal Ontario Museum expedition (Bullard and Bullard 1965), and most recently by the Belize Valley Archaeological Reconnaissance Project (Awe, personal communication, 2002; Moore 1997).

Subsequent projects have added significant coverage to these two focal sites, both inside and immediately outside the Belize Valley. In the upper Belize Valley, research has been undertaken not only at Xunantunich and its immediate settlement area (Ashmore 1998) but also at the major sites of Buenavista del Cayo (chapters 9, 12; Ball and Taschek 1991) and Arenal (Las Ruinas; Taschek and Ball 1999), as well as at Negroman-Tipu (Pendergast et al. 1993) and Chaa Creek (Connell 2000). Cahal Pech has been the subject of more research than any other upper Belize Valley site, actually having been excavated by two different projects. One project focused on earlier remains and outlying settlement (chapters 7 and 8; Awe and Grube 2001; Awe and Healy 1994; Healy and Awe 1996). The other focused on the excavation and stabilization of the site's palace compounds (Ball 1993). Settlement has also been examined north of the Mopan River (Fedick 1994; Ford and Fedick 1992) with most research focusing on the site of El Pilar (chapter 15; Ford 1990:chap. 15) just outside the Belize Valley proper. In the valley itself more work has been undertaken at Baking Pot (Awe, personal communication, 2002; Moore 1997), and the site of Blackman Eddy has also been a locus of major research (chapters 3 and 4; Garber et al. 1998). Investigation immediately south of the valley has focused on the sites of Ponces (Morris, personal communication) and Pacbitun (chapters 13 and 14; Healy 1992, 1999; Healy and Awe 1996). To the east, salvage work has been undertaken in the Valley of Peace (chapter 6; Awe and Topsey 1984; Morris 1984). Taken together, this research permits a better understanding of regional development and spatial relationships in the Belize Valley that both complements and supplements that gathered for Barton Ramie by Willey and his colleagues (1965) some 50 years ago.

Summary

Fifty years of research have expanded our knowledge about the archaeology of the Belize Valley. Based on the continued excavation of unassuming housemounds and smaller sites in the valley, we know much more archaeologically about this part of the Maya world than we do about most other regions. The Belize Valley exhibits a continuous occupation history from the dawn of Maya civilization to the present. Its riverbanks are lined with almost solid ancient settlement. The larger nodes of settlement that have been identified in the valley display a uniformity in their distribution that seems to be consistent with central place theory; we have no answer for exactly why this is. In spite of all the data that have been collected and all the sites and transects that have been mapped, the ancient organizational systems and internal and external relationships that must have existed in the Belize Valley are still a matter of debate. To some extent the debate is due to the use of conflicting models in an attempt to answer broad anthropological questions. And, to some extent there is simply healthy disagreement over the interpretation of the extant archaeological data. In spite of the disagreements, the archaeological data that have been gathered as a result of 50 years of research in the Belize Valley are key to understanding Maya social and political organization both here and elsewhere. When Willey undertook his initial settlement research at Barton Ramie so long ago, he could not have foreseen that he was laying the groundwork for such long-term regional archaeology.

Acknowledgments

We would like to thank Diane Chase, Norman Hammond, and an anonymous reviewer for comments on an earlier version of this chapter. Hammond also kindly related details (which he attributes to Joseph Ball) about why Gordon Willey did not find Buenavista del Cayo, one of the largest sites in the Belize Valley: "According to one of Willey's local informants from the 1950s in the Western Club, he 'asked about little mounds like those at Barton Ramie, but he didn't ask about big mounds, so nobody told him.'"

2

Retrospective

Gordon R. Willey

The Belize Valley and its archaeology are associated in my mind with my beginnings in Maya archaeology. As it happened, these beginnings did not come about until I was well into my career. I had spent some years in the archaeology of the Southeastern United States; I had gone to Peru for two long field seasons, the earlier of which resulted in my doctoral dissertation and, subsequently, had carried out two expeditions in Panama. The second of these Panamanian adventures had been run out of my base at Harvard University, where, since 1950, I had been Bowditch Professor of Mexican and Central American Archaeology. I was set to continue my Central American investigations by digging my way northward in Panama and on into Costa Rica when my distinguished predecessor at Harvard, Alfred M. Tozzer, told me that I should stop fooling around down in "no man's land" and work in the "Maya Area," which was what Mr. Bowditch really had in mind when he bestowed his professorship on Harvard (see Willey 1988). I took his advice on this, as I usually did on other matters, and I am glad that I did. Although defining archaeological phases and working out culture sequences in Panama and Costa Rica would have been useful, lowland Maya archaeology had gone beyond the basics of culture history and presented more interesting challenges to me.

I was, though, admittedly awed by these Maya challenges. To begin with, there was a vast literature on the ancient Maya. While I could, through reading, assimilate much of the more routine "dirt" archaeological information such as ceramics, artifacts, and architecture—I would need more time than I had to master the more arcane aspects of the old Maya—such as their hieroglyphics, calendrics, art, and iconography. Given my background, what could I do that would contribute most effectively to the field in the time that I had? In this frame of mind I was struck that I should lead from my strengths. In the second season of my Peruvian field researches, I had tackled the problem of "settlement patterns," in effect, total archaeological site layouts, not only temples, palaces, and public buildings, but residences, their natures, numbers, and distributions. In such patterning and their changes through time we inevitably had clues to the ecological adaptations and to the social and political formations of ancient societies. My monograph on this Peruvian fieldwork carried out in 1946, had just been published (Willey 1953) as I was contemplating my first foray into Maya studies. As I began to review the literature of Maya archaeology, it struck me that settlement study would also be a useful contribution.

Until that time, Maya field research emphasis had been upon the great sites—Tikal, Uaxactun, Piedras Negras, and Chichen Itza. This was in no way surprising: such centers or cities, with their impressive architecture, monuments, and arts justifiably captured the archaeological imagination, as they still do. Early archaeological explorers in the area would have been considered out of their minds if they had ignored these glories to concentrate on small residential structures scattered through the forests. However, now I thought a reasonable argument could be advanced that the glories of the mysterious lost cities of the jungle might be better understood if archaeologists were able to view them in what had been their more complete social and demographic settings. In brief, a king, to be properly appreciated, must be viewed in a context that also includes his subjects.

When I turned to experienced Mayanists, they were not very enthusiastic about my "settlement research" proposals. Professor Tozzer said yes, he could remember seeing little, presumably residential, mounds in the jungle as he had ridden mule back along trails near Tikal in his youth. They seemed to turn up more or less everywhere, as everyone knew. Search for such things was hardly something to build a Maya research career around. Other very distinguished Mayanists—Eric Thompson, Tatiana Proskouriakoff, and Harry Pollock—who were in the building of the old Carnegie Institution of Washington's Historical and Archaeological offices, in those days just across the alley from the Peabody Museum, also knew about these small mounds scattered through the Petén and Yucatecan bush, but they didn't seem very interested in them. To be sure, they were then beginning to map such small residential mounds within the encircling walls of the site of Mayapan, but this was a site proper, defined by a wall. Thompson pointed out that he had excavated a small Maya ceremonial center in

British Honduras (Thompson 1939), at San Jose. It had been interesting, but he didn't feel that more research was necessary in this particular direction, at least for the present. In general, all of these experienced Mayanists were essentially of the same opinion. I would be wasting my time on any all-out, long-term "settlement pattern" approach to Maya archaeology. In retrospect, I can understand their feelings. They had devoted the prime years of their research lives to specialized, and highly important, aspects of Maya archaeology: hieroglyphic studies, calendrics, art, iconography, and elaborate architecture. What I wanted to do seemed of minor importance and without interest to them.

Fortunately, I finally did get some encouragement—and from a very respected Maya source. I turned to Linton Satterthwaite, at the University of Pennsylvania. He had had years of experience in the Maya field at Piedras Negras and elsewhere. After listening to my plans, Satterthwaite told me that he thought I was on the right track. Indeed, he said that if he were a young man, starting out on a career in Maya archaeology, he would set about doing just what I said I wanted to do: investigate and obtain knowledge of the ancient Maya settlement arrangements, from individual households up through lesser centers to major centers. Moreover, Satterthwaite offered some practical help to get me started. He had been carrying out fieldwork in British Honduras, and he was returning there that winter of 1953. While he was planning to excavate at the large, and at that time little known, major center of Caracol in the southern part of the colony, he would be glad to show me a small Maya center, a place called Cahal Pech, near the town of El Cayo (now San Ignacio), in the Belize Valley of British Honduras. He had been working at Cahal Pech in the previous season, and he thought it might be the place to begin my research.

Taking advantage of Satterthwaite's kind offer, I began by inviting a graduate student of mine, Bill Bullard (see Willey 1988) to go along with me on my introductory "settlement survey" field trip. Bill had worked the previous winter-spring season with Harry Pollock and the Carnegie group at Mayapan and he was planning to return there in the present winter. So I asked him if he would be willing to precede this with a month with me in British Honduras. We could look things over down there and hopefully, make plans for long-term settlement pattern research beginning in 1954. After arranging with the Carnegie for his late arrival at Mayapan, Bill accompanied me to Belize City where, by appointment, we met up with Satterthwaite and a graduate student of his, Jerry Epstein, also destined to become a Maya archaeological researcher in the upcoming years.

After a short time in Belize City, where Satterthwaite introduced us to the governor and other officials of the colony, including Hamilton Anderson, the archaeological commissioner, we went on up to the town of El Cayo, the capital of the colony's Western District and located only a dozen kilometers or so from the border of the Guatemalan Petén. We hired a car to drive from Belize City to El Cayo, a relatively easy three-hour journey with this mode of transportation. In so doing, we had it easy compared to the way the trip was made in earlier years when archaeologists came into the Petén bush via British Honduras. Back then, after a ship's landing in Belize City, one transferred yourself and your gear, plus the mountain of food supplies you purchased there in the city, to a small river steamer. This mode of transportation went back to Tozzer's and Morley's time, and Harry Pollock, who was with Ricketson and other Carnegie archaeologists at Uaxactun, told me about it. There were sleeping accommodations of a sort on the steamer, although some, and Harry remembered the late George Vaillant in this select group, who would sit up all night and play poker. This kind of journey, although nonstop, took three days and three nights. On arrival in El Cayo, they were then met by an efficient agent, a gentleman of Chinese-Maya parentage by the name of Leocandio E. Hopun. Hopun organized the mule trains there, and he would have these in readiness for his archaeological patrons. After a night's sleep in El Cayo, you were ready to go next morning, with personnel and bundles of supplies mounted on mules, for what then was to be another three-day journey, this time with night camps along the way, to Uaxactun.

This same Hopun, who still lived in El Cayo and was still dedicating his services to archaeology, met us when we arrived there after our relatively brief auto journey. He had been employed by Satterthwaite in previous seasons, and he agreed to help our Harvard party if we decided to work in the Belize Valley. El Cayo then having no hotel, Hopun had arranged for the four of us to sleep in the Church of England Rectory, a then uninhabited building there in the town. After a night in these quarters, we breakfasted in a nearby restaurant that had been recommended to us by Hopun. While so doing, a member of the Black Colonial Constabulary appeared at an open window of the dining room, calling a fulsome welcome to Linton Satterthwaite. After going over to the window for an amiable exchange with this representative of the law, Linton returned to the table with the remark "Swell fellow! It is always good to keep in with these boys, it's something for you to remember if you're going to work around here."

Ten minutes or so passed as we worked our way through the eggs, frijoles refritos, and tortillas. Then, once more, Satterthwaite's policemen friend came to the window. "Doctor," he said, addressing Satterthwaite, as he pulled a small slip of paper from his shirt pocket, "this is a parking violation ticket from last year when you left your Jeep in an unauthorized zone here in El Cayo. It's a two dollar fine, Doctor. You can take it over to the Police Station to pay it, but I thought it would be more convenient for you just to pay me."

I mused then upon El Cayo's parking and traffic problems. In the short time we had been there, I didn't think I had seen more than one other vehicle in addition to our rented one, at least in what might be called "the downtown business district." Nevertheless, it was a lesson to me that parking violations would not be tolerated if we should decide to base ourselves here in the capital of the Western District.

Breakfast over, we drove out of town, up the hill for a short distance to Cahal Pech. This small Maya ceremonial center, aptly named in that language as "the place of the tick," was on the hilltop, which overlooked El Cayo and the Macal branch of the Belize River. As I recall, it numbered two or three plazas, had a sizable pyramid, and a single plain stela. Satterthwaite had done some digging there in the previous season, but as will be revealed by the chapters in this volume, his knowledge of the place was still superficial. It appeared to him to be a minor center, presumably drawing its support from a sustaining area of residences stretching for a few kilometers along the river and quite probably being subordinate to the much larger center of Benque Viejo (now known as Xunantunich and discussed elsewhere in this volume) located several kilometers to the west. In any event, Cahal Pech appeared to Satterthwaite to be a suitable place from which to begin a settlement pattern survey.

Two workmen, armed with machetes and dispatched there by Hopun, awaited us at the site. Satterthwaite outlined his plan of action. We would begin on the lower slopes of the Cahal Pech hill and cut a *breccia*, or path, through the bush in an easterly direction from the center, down toward the river, which was about a kilometer away. In this way we would begin to get some idea of how densely or sparsely residential mounds were grouped around a center and, eventually, how far out they extended. Did they, for example, continue right along, more or less evenly distributed until we came to another ceremonial center? So we set to our task. It was about 8:00 in the morning, and the fog had not yet burned off when we began. Satterthwaite had not only arranged through Hopun for the workmen but had borrowed machetes for the four of us. The use of the machete, Linton advised, was absolutely essential for anyone aspiring to be a Maya archaeologist, and this was especially so in my case given my "settlement pattern" ambitions. How else would I find all the little mounds, and so comprehend "total settlement," except by its use. So I took my turns on the *breccia* and swung away uneasily with my unfamiliar weapon. Bullard, by way of contrast, enjoyed it thoroughly, with a display of swordsmanship that alternated between low, close-to-the-ground sweeps and overhead slashes. The sun came out. We continued to whack away. Satterthwaite, although more experienced than I, was also a good bit older. The two of us began to spend more time at the rear of the column than on the front line. By about 11:00, we had progressed 200 m or so into the thicket that seemed to grow more overwhelming as we penetrated it. By this time we had discovered two or three little mounds. I wondered aloud if maybe we shouldn't stop and reflect on all of this for a bit. After all, we didn't want to discover everything on the fist day. Bullard was for going on, but Linton and I overruled him. Linton suggested that we might go back in town for a little while where we could have a cold beer and reflect on the whole question of Maya settlement survey. Besides, as he told us, Hamilton Anderson, the colony's archaeological commissioner, who was driving up from Belize should be in town shortly, and we ought to be on hand to meet him. This settled, we retreated to city life in El Cayo.

Linton took us to a bar known as the Western Club. In El Cayo, at least in those days, one didn't just patronize a bar, one "belonged" to a "club." Satterthwaite assured us that he was a member in good standing at the Western, that we would be welcomed there as his guests, and that there would be no trouble in "putting us up for membership" if we so desired. The Western was located at one end of the town's main thoroughfare, actually not far from the restaurant where we had eaten breakfast only a few hours before. The other club in town was the Stork, situated at the opposite end of the same street. Despite the more fashionable associations of the Stork's name, we were given to understand that the Western was really the "in" place in El Cayo.

The Western's interior was quite dark, especially as one entered from the bright sunlight. Light came in only from two open windows at the front whose wooden covering had been raised and propped up by sticks. Window glass, in those days anyhow, tended to be rare in El Cayo. A bar ran along the back of the room. In the row of bottles behind the bar, I saw one with a sign on it: Have a Drink on Dr. Satterthwaite. Linton told me that, yes, he was the "sponsor" of this particular bottle and that it dated from last year's season at Cahal Pech. It was a good "public relations" idea, he said. I noticed that the bottle was empty so his "public image" must have benefited for a time, however brief. There were some tables in front of the bar, and we found our way through the gloom to one. The bartender or proprietor—or as the principal functionaire of the club he may have been known as the "steward"—came over and exchanged greetings with Satterthwaite that were as hearty as those that had passed earlier that morning between Linton and his lawman friend. They had some conversation about replenishing the Have a Drink on Dr. Satterthwaite bottle, then our new friend took our order for four cold beers and went back to the bar to see to it.

As we sat there drinking our beers, which turned out to be so good that we ordered seconds, and mused over the future of cutting *breccias* through the undergrowth in search of housemounds and the mysteries of old Maya settlement—two members of the club showed up and took a table next to ours. They were English and very amiable fellows, one a labor foreman and the other an accountant, both from the Barton Ramie Estate Project of the British Colonial Development Corporation. The Barton Ramie Estate was located a few kilometers down river, to the east of El Cayo. It was then in its third year of operation. We were told that ramie was a very tough tropical fiber plant of southeast Asiatic origin, whose long fibers were used for making such things as fire hoses or fishing lines. The ramie had been planted on the extensive alluvial flats near the Barton Creek tributary of the Belize River and the hope was that it would become an important factor in vitalizing the British Honduran economy. Unfortunately, the enterprise was failing because it was found that the ramie would not grow to its appropriate height without annual costly fertilization that would exceed the profits to be made from the sale of the fibers.

On our side, we kept the conversation going by identifying ourselves as archaeologists and describing our interests of the moment. We were, we said, not so much concerned, with big Maya pyramids or fancy sculptures: instead, what we were really looking for were the small, simple mounds that marked ordinary household residences. We suspected that such were around in great numbers although because of the jungle growth they were hard to find. At that point, our new clubmates assured us that if that was what we were looking for we had better come back to Barton Ramie with them where, they exclaimed, "There were more bloody little mounds than you could count." At about that time, Hamilton Anderson showed up at the Western; he had just driven up from Belize. He, too, knew of the Barton Ramie mounds, and he wanted to see more of them. So we all went out and, following our new English friends in the Barton Ramie Estate Land-Rover, made the short trip out to Barton Ramie.

We were met there by Marcus Chambers, the estate manager, who was our courteous host for the rest of the day and, as it turned out, for the following season when we began our surveys and excavations of the Barton Ramie "little mounds." These were, indeed, impressive in their numbers. The agricultural clearing was about 2 km² in extent, and the mounds were seen everywhere. The ramie plants were then, in their stunted condition, only about knee high, disastrous commercially, but ideal for archaeological survey. The mounds averaged about 2 m in height and 20 to 30 m in diameter. They were located, on the average, perhaps 50 to 60 m apart. Eventually, we were to map and count 264 of them in the cleared agricultural area. There were a few larger ones, and one unit, in particular, consisted of a little plaza group that included a small pyramid mound about 12 m high. This unit, thus, had the appearance of a ceremonial center of a very minor sort but one much smaller than, say, Cahal Pech.

After this view of Barton Ramie, we spent the rest of the week looking at sites in the Belize Valley. We saw Xunantunich, then called Benque Viejo, where Thompson (1940) had once done some digging and where, later, Anderson had carried out some excavation-restoration work. We also looked at a number of other sites in the region, including Baking Pot, where Ricketson (1929) had dug before going into Uaxactun. Baking Pot was only about 6 km upriver, to the west of Barton Ramie. It had a larger ceremonial center than the little one at Barton Ramie and was also surrounded by numerous small, residential-type mounds, although the Baking Pot clearing was not as large as the one at Barton Ramie.

Before leaving El Cayo, I had an argument with Satterthwaite about my plans for subsequent seasons. I had made up my mind, I said, that I would begin with mapping and excavations at Barton Ramie. Linton thought this was a grave mistake, a setting off down the wrong path in settlement pattern research. If I did that, he warned, I'd be beginning "in the middle of nowhere." The Barton Ramie tiny ceremonial unit was too small to even qualify as a "minor center." In his opinion, I should begin with some place like Cahal Pech and work out radially from there. In this way, I could get some idea of the size and nature of the "sustaining area" for a reasonably well-defined center. I countered by saying that Maya settlement pattern studies were so little developed that we didn't know where we were anyway. Why not begin with Barton Ramie and take advantage of the huge clearing? Satterthwaite responded that I was "afraid of the bush," that I didn't like to cut *breccias*. I'm afraid I couldn't deny that I would like to bypass as much machete work as possible. Later, I talked the matter over with Bill Bullard. After all, he would be a key figure in our project. What did he think? He agreed that Satterthwaite had a logical point that conceptually, anyway, we had to work and think "from center outward." At the same time, he agreed with me that we couldn't afford to pass up the practical advantages of the Barton Ramie clearing.

So we began our intensive instrument surveys and excavations at Barton Ramie in the early winter of 1954, and we continued there, as well as at nearby Spanish Lookout and Baking Pot, through the winter of 1956. In addition to Bullard and myself, we had three other graduate student supervisors over the three seasons so we were able to dig several of the Barton Ramie residential mounds in detail. In addition, we test-pitted almost 60 others. Bullard, I might add here, was particularly effective a this work. He had a sense for structures and the stratigraphic complexities of structures plus refuse that enabled him to get a maximum amount of information from the clay, plaster, and rough stone levels of the little mounds. It is of interest to note that of the mounds excavated or test-pit sampled, all had been occupied in the Late Classic period. Significant numbers of these also had Early Classic and Late Preclassic levels, and in a few cases evidence of Middle Preclassic construction levels and refuse was found. In the chapters of this volume, the reader will find substantiations of this domestic mound sequencing at other sites in the valley.

In addition to our Barton Ramie and nearby digging, we also traveled around on weekends and in this way began to get some overall picture of the archaeology of the valley, with its several ceremonial centers, their geographical spacing and their relationships to small, residential mounds. We wondered about Maya occupation of other types of terrain, especially the hills lying back from the river bottoms. Had these been occupied by the ancient Maya? We didn't have time to explore these to any extent, but it seemed reasonable to assume that the Maya also had occupied them. Still, it was our opinion—or perhaps I should qualify this and say my opinion for I think Bullard may have had his doubts—that the immediate valley floor was where most of the residential mounds, as well as the ceremonial centers, were to be found. In writing about this at the time, however, I did add a little cautionary note, which is amusing in retrospect. In the concluding section of the Willey et al. (1965) monograph, I said, "This probably should not be taken to mean that the hills and hillsides were unsuited to residence for if we had extended our survey several kilometers north or south of the Belize Valley we might have come upon clusters of house mounds in hill terrain" (591).

Now, in the light of Anabel Ford's surveys of those uplands lying back of the river flats (chapter 15), we do, indeed, know that we would have come upon "clusters of house mounds" if we had moved farther into the hills. For while the immediate foothills at the edges of the valley bottom in the vicinity of Barton Ramie were not heavily occupied, the higher ridge-lands behind these foothills have turned out to be thick with residential mounds. In addition to these, Ford also has discovered an important ceremonial center, El Pilar, which lies in the ridgelands 10 km north of the river. El Pilar is a site that compares favorably in monumental architectural size with centers nearer the river, such as Xunantunich, Buenavista, and Baking Pot. It is also surrounded by a dense settlement of residential units.

In brief, as the chapters in this volume make abundantly clear, there is a universe of Maya settlement in the Belize Valley of which we were unaware when my colleagues and I began our work there in the 1950s. The reader will find this volume an exciting record of work in progress. As will be seen, none of the authors feels that he or she has answered all of the questions with which they began their respective researches. Rather, they all point to new questions and problems that lie ahead. Nevertheless, I am amazed and gratified by the ground that has been gained. I shall not attempt to summarize it. Diane Chase does that very ably in the concluding chapter of the book. I will only point, again, to the Belize Valley's importance as a sector of the Maya lowlands. It is fully a part of that story of the Maya rise from Preclassic beginnings, through Classic achievement, into the Postclassic decline that we know, in general, from other parts of the area; and yet, as these chapters indicate, it displays peculiarities unique to the region. James Garber, the editor of the volume, as well as a significant contributor to Belize Valley archaeology, is to be commended for focusing our attention upon this very important portion of the Maya past.

3

Middle Formative Prehistory of the Central Belize Valley

An Examination of Architecture, Material Culture, and Sociopolitical Change at Blackman Eddy

James F. Garber, M. Kathryn Brown, Jaime J. Awe,
and Christopher J. Hartman

Archaeological investigations conducted in the central Belize Valley at the site of Blackman Eddy have revealed a stratified sequence of occupations starting at the end of the Early Formative (ca. 1100 B.C.) and extending to the Late Classic period (A.D. 900). Prior to the 1990s, the bulk of our knowledge of the Formative prehistory of the Belize Valley derived almost exclusively from data collected by Willey's investigations at Barton Ramie in the 1950s (Willey et al. 1965). In the decades following Willey's investigations, numerous researchers have conducted investigations in the valley, making it one of the most intensively studied regions in the Maya lowlands. Most of these projects focused on questions pertaining to Classic period (A.D. 300–900) elite, agriculture, monumental architecture, settlement patterns, sociopolitical organization, ritual and cosmology, and Postclassic (A.D. 1000–1500) occupation. Although these research efforts have made significant contributions to our understanding of the Maya in this region, our understanding of the Formative occupants of the valley remained limited. The situation is compounded by the Mesoamerican tradition of building new structures on top of older ones. The earliest buildings are deeply buried under massive subsequent constructions. Due to the logistical problems of investigating deeply buried deposits, our knowledge of the earliest constructions is limited at best (Culbert 1977:28; Hester et al. 1983:13).

The Texas State University–San Marcos Belize Valley Archaeology Project (BVAP) was initiated in 1990. The primary goal of the project was to assess the sociopolitical role of Blackman Eddy relative to the larger valley centers to the west (map 1). Unusual circumstances redirected the project objectives. Unauthorized bulldozing activity in the mid-1980s cut a structure in half, revealing a profile that illustrated a construction history spanning approximately 2,000 years (fig. 3.1). Because of the damage and the danger of extensive collapse, the Belize Department of Archaeology decided in 1994 that the damage was too severe to repair and the best solution was to initiate an intensive excavation program to excavate the remaining portions of the structure to bedrock. The focus of the project shifted in 1994 to fully document the construction history and thus provided a unique opportunity to conduct an extensive horizontal excavation on a series of Middle Formative constructions. As a result of these efforts, the investigations have revealed considerable information on the Formative prehistory of the valley. The sequence starts with a Formative bedrock-level occupation (ca. 1100 B.C.) overlain by plaster and masonry platforms of increasing size.[1] Blackman Eddy is situated 200 m south of the Western Highway on a hill overlooking the valley below (map 1 and fig. 3.1). (See chapter 4 for information pertaining to the Late Formative and Classic period investigations.)

The Middle Formative remains were encountered in Structures B1 and B2 in a single horizontal block excavation covering an area of approximately 150 m². Thirteen distinct Middle Formative construction phases were revealed (five domestic, seven public), some of which had subphase modifications as well (table 3.1). Extensive ritual deposits were associated with the buildings.

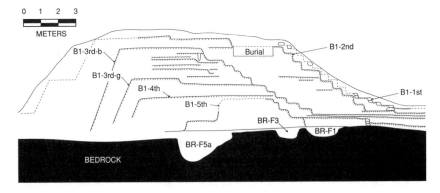

Fig. 3.1. Blackman Eddy Structure B1 profile.

Table 3.1. Middle Formative construction sequences by phase from Structure B1 at Blackman Eddy

Period	Phase	Structure
Early Middle Formative (1100–900 B.C.)	Kanocha	B1-13th
	Kanocha	B1-12th
	Kanocha	B1-11th
	Kanocha	B1-10th
	Kanocha	B1-9th
	Kanocha	B1-8th
Early Middle Formative (900–700 B.C.)	Early facet Jenney Creek	B1-7th
	Early facet Jenney Creek	B1-6th
	Early facet Jenney Creek	B1-5th
Late Middle Formative (700–350 B.C.)	Late facet Jenney Creek	B1-4th
	Late Facet Jenney Creek	B1-3rd-g–e

The Kanocha Phase (1100–900 B.C.)

The Kanocha phase represents the initial occupation of Blackman Eddy. Two wares are present in the Kanocha Complex, one utilitarian with calcite and quartzite temper and the other a dull-slipped ware characterized by ash temper. Major forms include lugged and strap-handled jars with short necks, tecomates, colanders, bowls of various forms, and flat-bottom plates with out-curving sides and wide everted rims. Decoration techniques include appliqué fillets, post-slip incising, and differential firing techniques. The predominant utilitarian ware shows strong parallels to unslipped Jocote types of Jenney Creek and appears to be its developmental precursor. Some of the dull-slipped types show strong developmental ties to the succeeding Mars Orange group as well.

The closest stylistic parallel to the Kanocha ceramic material appears to come from the southeast in Honduras. The Chotepe phase (1100–900 B.C.) ceramic material from the site of Puerto Escondido in Honduras exhibits a coarse paste group and a fine-paste group with volcanic ash temper (Joyce and Henderson 2001). The fine-paste ceramic group has stylistic similarities to the Kanocha dull-slipped ware group, both of which have incised and carved motifs on flat-bottom, flaring wall bowls, and also use differential firing techniques to produce dark fire clouding on cream or white slipped vessels.

Several aspects of these ceramics such as dating, origins, and relationship to subsequent complexes have been the subject of considerable discussion and debate. The radiocarbon dates from Blackman Eddy (fig. 3.2 and

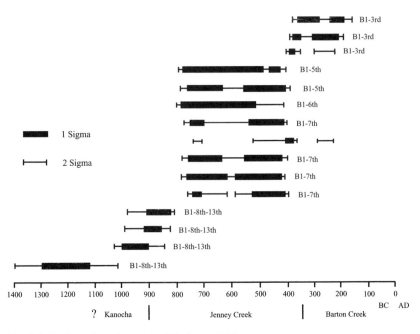

Fig. 3.2. Radiocarbon dates from Blackman Eddy.

table 3.2) support the proposed beginning date for the appearance of these ceramics at ca. 1100 B.C. and may have made their first appearance earlier. The same is true for the Cunil Complex at Cahal Pech (chapter 7). Prior to these discoveries, the earliest deposits of the valley were those of early facet Jenney Creek at 800 B.C. (Gifford 1976) and thus, the Kanocha phase at Blackman Eddy and Cunil phase at Cahal Pech both predate Jenney Creek. These early ceramic types have also been recovered at Xunantunich (Strelow and LeCount 2001), Pacbitun (Powis, personal communication 2000), and in the BVAP excavations at Floral Park.

The issue of origins is more complex. There are four basic possibilities: (1) these ceramics were developed in situ with no, or little, outside influence; (2) the underlying concepts of ceramic production were introduced into the valley from Maya groups in adjoining regions; (3) ceramics and/or the underlying concepts of ceramic production were introduced into the valley from non-Maya groups in adjoining regions or beyond through interaction; and (4) this portion of the Maya lowlands was settled by non-Maya groups, bringing with them the concepts of ceramic production.

The iconography and general quality of the Kanocha phase ceramics represent a well-developed technology, not a first attempt at producing ceramics. There is no evidence for ceramic experimentation. The first

Table 3.2. Radiocarbon dates from Blackman Eddy

Location	Phase	Beta #	Radiocarbon age b.p.	Radiocarbon age b.c.	Calibrated 1 sigma b.c.	Calibrated 2 sigma b.c.
BR-F3	Kanocha	122281	2990 ± 60	1040 ± 60	1295–1120	1395 (1215) 1015
BR-F5b	Kanocha	162573	2800 ± 40	850 ± 40	1000–900	1030 (930) 840
BR-F5a	Kanocha	159142	2750 ± 40	800 ± 40	920–830	990 (900) 820
Bedrock	Kanocha	122282	2730 ± 50	780 ± 50	910–820	980 (845) 805
BR-F2	EJC	162571	2420 ± 40	470 ± 40	740–710 and 530–410	760–620 and 590 (420) 400
BR-F1	EJC	162570	2460 ± 40	510 ± 40	760–620 and 590–420	780 (740, 710, 530) 410
BR-F4	EJC	159144	2450 ± 40	500 ± 40	760–640 and 560–420	780 (520) 400
B1-7th	EJC	162572	2340 ± 60	390 ± 60	410–380	740–710 and 530 (400) 360 and 290–230
B1-6th	EJC	159146	2430 ± 40	480 ± 40	750–700 and 540–410	770 (500, 460, 430) 400
B1-5th	EJC	122279	2500 ± 50	550 ± 50	780–515	795 (760, 635, 560) 410
B1-5th	EJC	103956	2440 ± 60	490 ± 60	760–635 and 560–405	785 (505) 390
B1-4th	LJC	103959	2480 ± 50	530 ± 50	775–485 and 465–425	790 (755, 685, 540) 405
B1-3rd	LJC	159141	2290 ± 40	340 ± 40	390–370	400 (380) 350 and 300–220
B1-3rd	LJC	159145	2240 ± 40	290 ± 40	380–350 and 310–210	390 (360) 190
B1-3rd	LJC	159147	2190 ± 40	240 ± 40	360–280 and 240–190	380 (340, 320, 210) 160

Notes: All samples are wood charcoal. Dates in parentheses indicate calibration curve intercepts. EJC = early facet Jenney Creek; LJC = late facet Jenney Creek.

possibility above can reasonably be ruled out on the basis of clear iconographic ties to other regions of Mesoamerica. Moreover, nonlocal exotics were encountered within the Kanocha phase at Blackman Eddy and the Cunil phase at Cahal Pech (Awe 1992) suggesting interaction with outside regions. With ceramic producing populations surrounding the Maya lowlands it seems logical that the early inhabitants of the valley would have had an understanding of ceramic technology. The fact that cultigens and associated technologies were spreading all over Mesoamerica is ample evidence of considerable interaction even at an early date.

The second possibility, that the underlying concepts of ceramic production were introduced into the valley from Maya groups in adjoining areas, flows from "conventional wisdom" among Mayanists in a very simple general working assumption that if something occurs in the Maya lowlands it must be Maya. We would expect to find preceramic deposits in the valley indicating an earlier lifeway more dependent on wild resources. Such finds are present, but scarce, and the density and significance of these Archaic valley populations has not been determined. Compelling evidence that the early settled villagers were well adapted to the local environment of the valley lends support to this possibility.

Distinct external influences on the Classic, Postclassic, and Historic periods are well documented and thus the third and fourth possibilities, both of which involve non-Maya groups, should be given careful consideration. Ball and Taschek (2000, 2003) present an intriguing reassessment of the Middle Formative ceramics of the valley that may shed some light on this issue. They suggest that the earliest permanent settlers of the valley were not Maya or at least not the Maya of the Classic period. Furthermore, they suggest that the ceramics in use between 950 and 500 B.C. in the valley are not of a single complex, the result of a "closed-system" but represent multisystem composites:

> While the Kanluk [Cahal Pech Jenney Creek] and Jenney Creek ceramic complexes as defined are based on stratigraphic depositional associations, they do not represent one-to-one equivalents of local Middle Preclassic production-consumption assemblages but depositional composites made up of locally manufactured and used pottery plus additions resulting from local exchange, long-distance trade, possible gifting, the curation of heirlooms or antique vessels, and other processes. The evidence for some of these processes is easily recognized, that for others is not. However, what should be realized is that the compositional character of a Middle Preclassic complex like Jenney Creek or Kanluk really is no different from that of a

central lowlands Terminal Classic complex that includes fine orange, plumbate, or thin-slate ceramics, or a northern lowlands Late Complex with inclusions of Palmar or Petkanche group polychromes or fine-paste wares from outside the immediate region of archaeological discovery (Ball and Taschek 2000:6).

According to their argument, what has been regarded as a single complex may actually be made up of two distinct production systems, one Maya, the other non-Maya. The ceramic groups that make up these complexes appear to be a part of a "generic Middle Preclassic" ceramic tradition with a wide distribution that extends across the isthmus as opposed to a "Maya Middle Preclassic" tradition. This pattern would be analogous to the situation in the Copan Valley, where the earliest ceramics (Rayo and Gordon Complexes) have been linked to complexes of Chalchuapa (Demarest 1987; Fash 1991), and Xe ceramics linked to Mixe-Zoque groups most likely from eastern Chiapas or the northern highlands of Guatemala (Andrews 1990). In these models, the Mixe-Zoque groups were absorbed or replaced by Maya groups expanding from Mamom-based ceramic systems that had developed out of Petén-based or Swasey pre-Mamom roots. The validity of this model for the Belize Valley ultimately rests on a comprehensive analysis of the ceramic material coupled with a thorough comparison to neighboring areas and beyond. Such an analysis is currently in progress (Joseph Ball, personal communication 2001).

In the initial description of the Cunil phase at Cahal Pech, Awe (1992) describes a set of motifs and elements of the incised types as well as those on greenstone artifacts of the same phase. Subsequently, these motifs were the subject of a more detailed analysis (Cheetham 1998). The kan cross and avian-serpent have been identified on the Kanocha phase ceramics at Blackman Eddy and on the contemporaneous Cunil phase ceramics at Cahal Pech (see fig. 7.6). Both are part of a widespread generic Middle Formative system found in several regions of Mesoamerica, including Chiapas, Pacific Coast, Gulf Coast, El Salvador, Morelos, Valley of Mexico, and Oaxaca. The Kanocha (fig. 3.3d,e) and Cunil phase figurines are stylistically similar to examples from the northern Guatemalan highlands, western El Salvador, and central Chiapas and are quite unlike those from the Gulf Coast and the southeastern Pacific Coast (Awe 1992; Cheetham 1998).

The distribution of these motifs indicates that the iconographic program was not Maya in origin but rather was a part of a larger pan-Mesoamerican Middle Formative symbol system. These symbols, are not a part of the Swasey Complex in northern Belize (Kosakowsky 1987; Kosa-

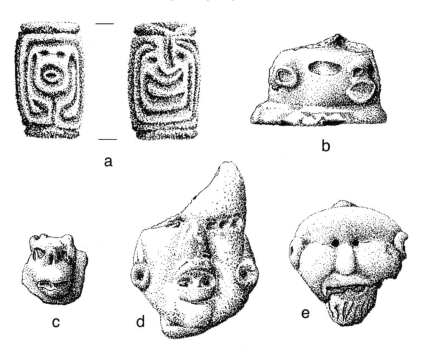

Fig. 3.3. Blackman Eddy artifacts: (a) late facet Jenney Creek roller seal; (b) early facet Jenney Creek anthropomorphic ceramic bottle fragment; (c) early facet Jenney Creek ceramic vessel lug; (d) Kanocha phase figurine; (e) Kanocha phase ocarina fragment.

kowsky and Pring 1998). Furthermore, they are not a part of Jenney Creek at Barton Ramie or Blackman Eddy, Kanluk (Jenney Creek at Cahal Pech), Mamom, or Bolay. Cheetham (1998) believes these pan-Mesoamerican motifs were adopted by the resident Maya population of the valley. Although we do not reject this hypothesis, we leave open the possibility that the earliest settlers of the valley (Maya or other) arrived with these iconographic concepts as a part of their cultural baggage. Given the above reassessment by Ball and Taschek and the possible problems with our current understanding of who the earliest settlers of the valley were, where they might have come from, and what groups they may have been influenced by, we reserve judgment on the possible explanations for the origin of the early ceramics of the valley pending further analysis and excavation.

Kanocha artifacts include retouched flakes, scrapers, drills, burins, chert macro-blades, hammerstones, quartzite and granite manos, tecomate stone bowls, polished greenstones, marine and freshwater shell disk beads, bone needles, bone rings, stingray spines, stone pendants, ceramic ocarinas, and molded ceramic figurine fragments (fig. 3.3d,e). From the establishment of their initial settlement, the Terminal Early Formative and early Middle Formative inhabitants of the valley were involved in long distance trade. Exotic goods include greenstone, obsidian, and marine shell. The presence of greenstone from the Blackman Eddy Kanocha phase and Cahal Pech Cunil phase (Awe 1992) is one of the earliest uses of greenstone in the Maya lowlands. The marine shells are predominantly *Strombus*, available on the Caribbean coast. The early occurrence and diverse origins of these exotic goods imply that an extensive system of long distance trade and exchange had been established in the Maya lowlands by the beginning of the first millennium B.C.

The initial Terminal Early Formative/Early Middle Formative sequence at Blackman Eddy consists of a bedrock-level occupation evidenced by a series of postholes cut into bedrock and low apsidal tamped-earth platforms that supported pole and thatch buildings. These are designated Structure B1–8th to B1–13th (fig. 3.4). All appear to be circular or apsidal in outline. A piece of pole-impressed daub plaster with a trace of a red hematite stripe was recovered in the excavations. A Cunil phase building at Cahal Pech, B4 10c-sub, was decorated in a similar manner (Awe 1992). The function of the Blackman Eddy pole and thatch buildings appears to be domestic and represents the earliest occupation of the site. These first occupants modified bedrock by leveling and filling in low areas. In some areas bedrock was used as a living surface. Midden material immediately to the south, associated with what was probably the final phase of the postholes, contained lithic debris, ceramics, and numerous freshwater shells.

Although the construction sequence of Structures B1–8th through B1–13th could not be determined with absolute certainty, B1–10th through B1–13th probably preceded the construction of B1–8th and B1–9th, both of which are elevated platforms representing a relatively higher input of labor. B1–10th to B1–13th are bedrock-level buildings (fig. 3.4). Structures B1–8th and B1–9th are probably contemporaneous. Both platforms are circular or apsidal in outline, approximately 6.0 to 8.0 m in diameter and up to 0.45 m in height. The platform edges consisted of roughly trimmed limestone blocks set in marl. The fill of the platform was composed of untrimmed limestone chunks, marl, and soil and the surfaces were composed of tamped marl. As can be seen in figure 3.4, the excavations only revealed a portion of these platforms and thus overall size and function could not be determined. B1–8th has a series of posthole patterns representing two successive pole and thatch buildings. No postholes were observed on Structure B1–9th but only a portion of the platform was ex-

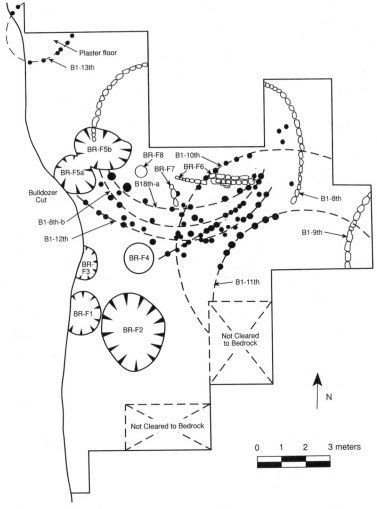

Fig. 3.4. Plan map of bedrock beneath Structure B1 at Blackman Eddy.

posed in the excavation. Like B1–8th, it too probably supported a pole and thatch building.

Similar early deposits have been found at Cuello, Colha, Nakbe, and Cahal Pech (Awe 1992; Powis 1996; chapter 7) and Pacbitun (Hohmann et al. 1999; Hohmann and Powis 1999; chapter 13). At Cuello, the initial occupation is marked by cultural debris mixed and impacted into the old ground surface associated with postholes excavated into bedrock (Gerhardt and Hammond 1991). The earliest architectural features found at Nakbe consist of hard-packed earthen floors overlying a buried paleosol level (Hansen 1998). Postholes carved into bedrock were also associated with these early constructions. Like the initial occupation at Blackman Eddy, these constructions were built directly on the ground surface. In the case of Blackman Eddy, low areas of the ground surface were filled in. Radiocarbon samples from the initial occupation at Nakbe consistently range between 1400 and 1000 B.C. calibrated (Hansen 1998). These dates are consistent with the radiocarbon data from Blackman Eddy (table 3.2).

A two-chamber *chultun* had been dug into the soft bedrock (BR-F5a and BR-F5b in fig. 3.4). This was probably associated with Structure B1–9th, -10th, or -11th and could not have been associated with B1–8th or B1–12th as can be seen in figure 3.4. Each chamber measures approximately 1.5 m north-south by 2.5 m east-west and 1.2 m deep. A complete colander vessel (fig. 3.5b) was found nestled in a depression at the base of the chultun. The interior basal surface of the vessel in and around the area of the drain holes was encrusted with a layer of white lime. Colanders probably functioned as containers to rinse off lime soaked corn in the preparation of maize gruel or to soften maize prior to grinding. The original function of the chultun is not clear but it may have been dug to catch and store water. Laminate fine slits and clays were present in the bottom as a result of sediment settling out of water that had collected in the chultun. Other artifacts from the lower levels of the chultun include bone needles, manos, marine shell beads and detritus, chert drills, a stone tecomate, and a possible nutting stone. Two radiocarbon dates were obtained from the chultun (Beta-162573 and Beta-159142, table 3.2).

The initial architectural constructions at Blackman Eddy are quite modest. It is a hilltop settlement overlooking the floodplain below. These early constructions consisted of simple pole and thatch buildings at or slightly above ground level. Subsequent Kanocha phase buildings consisted of low stone-edged tamped marl platforms upon which perishable buildings were constructed. These buildings were clustered and had associated tamped earth patio surfaces. Immediately following this phase, lime plaster floors and simple stone masonry make their appearance. The increased complexity of architecture and the associated increased labor investment coupled with the presence of exotics and the ceramic vessels that carry iconographic information are indicative of the emergence of social differentiation toward the end of the Kanocha phase.

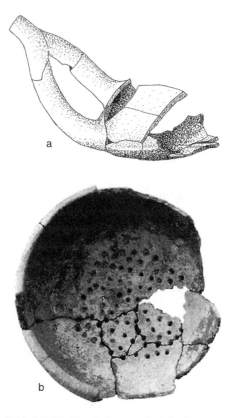

Fig. 3.5. Blackman Eddy Middle Formative vessels: (a) stirrup spouted ceramic vessel; (b) Kanocha phase colander vessel.

Artifacts include a wide range of chipped stone tools and a variety of ceramic vessel forms, including jars, bowls, and plates. The presence of grinding tools and colanders indicate the use of maize. The evidence of feasting suggest communal ritual activities possibly functioning as integrative activities to form social bonds and allow redistribution of goods through local giftgiving and exchange networks. A rich faunal assemblage demonstrates the use of a wide range of animal foods as well. Exotics include obsidian, marine shell, and greenstone, indicating that these early settled groups were a part of an extensive system of exchange. The iconographic motifs indicate participation in a pan-Mesoamerican symbol system. The collection of new data, as well as continuing analysis of existing data, should prove productive in answering questions about the origins and interregional relationships of this early period as well as the role of these villagers in shaping subsequent phases.

Early Facet Jenney Creek Phase (900–700 B.C.)

Several important changes occur at Blackman Eddy at the beginning of this phase. Most notable are the extensive use of lime plaster and trimmed block masonry, the construction of public architecture, the common occurrence of dedicatory and termination deposits, and the appearance of several new ceramic types. At the beginning of this phase there was a shift in building form. This is evidenced by the construction of a low rectangular platform (B1–7th) covered in thick plaster rising approximately 25 cm above its associated plaza surface. Exposed dimensions are 6.16 m north-south by 7.10 m east-west. The overall dimensions are not known at this time. Construction fill consisted of a wet-laid dark gray matrix intermixed with small limestone cobbles. The southern face of the platform was partially removed in antiquity. Only the basal course of the wall was in place consisting of small roughly shaped limestone blocks. This southern wall would have been three courses high. Numerous marine shell fragments and various faunal remains were scattered in the fill.

A dense midden deposit reflects a ritual feasting event (BR-F1 and BR-F2 in fig. 3.4) associated with the initial construction of B1–7th. This deposit consisted of two basin-shaped depressions cut into bedrock and then layered with over 10,000 freshwater shells, including bivalve, *Jute*, and *Pomacea*. Several marine shell fragments were also encountered. Lithic material, ceramics, and faunal remains were dispersed throughout.

The lithics in this deposit were quite varied and included 307 flakes, over 200 irregular fractured chips, 48 utilized pieces, two distinctly retouched flakes, 33 cores, seven broken biface fragments which appear to have been smashed, two complete bifaces, and one hammer stone. Fourteen of the cores exhibited evidence of severe battering. A complete mano, several metate fragments, approximately 15 smooth river cobbles, and 11 unusual elongated stones were dispersed throughout the BR-F1 deposit. Several of the elongated stones appear to have been modified and exhibited use wear. Two of the elongated stones also had scored bars on one end. The varied lithic material is somewhat perplexing, although it may reflect a number of different food processing activities as well as possible ritual destruction of tools. Ritual destruction of cultural material is common in Late Preclassic and Classic dedicatory termination rituals (Garber 1983) and is recited in the Quiche Maya Creation story, the Popol Vuh (Tedlock 1985). Most of the shells were whole and intact, which indicates that the deposit was not trampled or left exposed for any significant period of time. It was most likely covered over shortly after the feasting event, possibly to eliminate the smell from the rotting debris. This deposit does not resemble other domestic middens, which generally appear to have been left exposed and exhibit evidence of trampling within the material culture remains.

Structure B1–6th directly overlaid B1–7th reaching a height of 50 cm. The exposed area of the platform extended 7.10 m north-south by 7.70 m east-west. The hard plaster summit was in excellent condition. The southern frontal wall was partially dismantled in antiquity, however, the basal course was still in place. This southern wall was probably six courses high. As with Structure B1–7th, high densities of marine shell fragments were found in the fill. Other artifacts included marine shell beads, a partial ceramic figurine, obsidian blades, chert bifaces, unifaces, and retouched flakes.

Similar low rectangular platforms have been found elsewhere in the Belize Valley at Nohoch Ek (Coe and Coe 1956), Pacbitun (Hohmann and Powis 1999) and in Guatemala at Nakbe (Hansen 1998). Platforms of this kind are present at Nakbe around 800 B.C. and consist of masonry walls three to five courses high reaching a height of approximately 50 cm.

Structure B1–5th, a three-structure complex, was significantly more elaborate than the previous construction phases, indicating an expansion in labor investment and an increased emphasis on ceremonial activity (fig. 3.6). Evidence of feasting, reverential termination, and dedicatory activities related to the subsequent construction phase was observed. The excavations revealed two structures of the complex and traces of a third were observed in the scar of the bulldozer cut (fig. 4.1). Structure B1–5th was a linear triadic complex consisting of a central platform flanked by two lower platforms to the west and east. The central component rises 1.48 m above the associated plaza surface. It is approximately 5.5 by 5.5 m. The eastern platform had two low tiers reaching a height of 0.68 m. The dimensions of the lower tier are 7.10 m north-south by 8.63 m east-west. The platforms were covered with a layer of hard lime plaster. The central and eastern components (and presumably the western component as well) had a wet-laid rubble core. The southern frontal wall was constructed of small trimmed limestone blocks.

At the onset of construction, a ritual deposit was placed at the basal level of the platform within the confines of the supporting walls. This deposit appears to be the remains of a feasting event associated with the construction of the central platform, possibly a dedicatory act to the building. Artifacts included sherds, lithic debris and tools, marine shell frag-

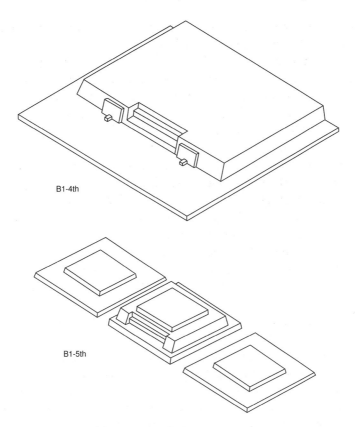

Fig. 3.6. Structures B1-4th and B1-5th at Blackman Eddy.

ments, marine shell beads, a worked greenstone fragment, obsidian blades, mano fragments, riverine shells, carbon, and faunal remains.

A deposit of ritual debris was encountered in the alley between the central and eastern components. This deposit was associated with the termination of use of the building and also appears to reflect feasting activities. It consisted of smashed ceramics, faunal remains, riverine bivalve and jute shells, lithic debitage, and carbon. One complete miniature Jocote Orange-Brown bowl was also uncovered. Ceramic analysis and radiocarbon data (Beta-103959) from this deposit suggests a transitional date between the early Middle Formative and late Middle Formative (ca. 600 B.C.) (table 3.2). A polished deer metapodial bone bloodletter was recovered at the base of the deposit, as well as several small marine shell beads, obsidian blades, and a bone bead fragment. Several faunal remains have been identified, including domestic dog, rabbit, white-tailed deer, brocket deer, peccary, armadillo, and a passerine bird, possibly parakeet (Norbert Stanchly, personal communication 1997). The small passerine bird specimen does not appear to have been used as a food source and may represent some form of ritual use. The presence of dog and deer further supports the ritual nature of the deposit as these species are typically restricted to elite contexts (Pohl 1983). Evidence for the inclusion of dog in feasting was found in a Late Preclassic elite context at Kichpanha, Belize (Shaw 1991). The faunal remains from the Middle Formative construction phases of Structure B4 at Cahal Pech also indicate high percentages of dog, deer, and rabbit (Awe 1992; Cheetham 1998). The Blackman Eddy deposit was covered with a layer of white marl followed by a layer of peach-colored marl. A deposit that may have been associated with this same feasting event was encountered to the east along the eastern edge of the east building. This deposit was in a thick gray clay matrix immediately on top of the platform and contained several obsidian blades and a ceramic roller seal (fig. 3.3a).

An additional feasting event was encountered above the layers of marl capping the alley and extended onto the lower terrace of the eastern component of B1–5th. It appears to be the remains of a feasting event dedicated to the construction of the subsequent building, Structure B1–4th. The cachelike deposit consisted of a small greenstone subspherical bead placed on a fractured partial plate, several whole and partial vessels, including two Savana Orange partial stirrup spouted vessels (fig. 3.5a), a Joventud Red bowl, and a Jocote Orange-Brown jar. Other remains included a deer mandible and scapula, numerous chert items, marine conch columella, freshwater shells, faunal remains, and carbon. The material culture from this deposit was spread over a wide area and may represent offerings brought to the communal building from the surrounding community during the final phase of construction activities. The feasting debris was left in place and then covered with a layer of white marl. In an ethnographic and ethnohistoric cross-cultural study of nine platform mound-using groups, Elson (1996) identified a correlation between the use of platform mounds and redistribution/feasting. He also notes a correlation between increasing mound size and increasing social complexity. The feasting evidence and increasing elaboration of the Middle Preclassic platform constructions at Blackman Eddy support this association.

A support population for the early Middle Formative public architecture has not been identified in the immediate vicinity of Blackman Eddy. However, 18 of the 65 housemounds investigated at Barton Ramie show evidence of occupation during the Jenney Creek phase (Willey et al. 1965: 279). Only three of these have evidence of possible platform constructions. The remainder appeared to be occupied directly on the original ground surface (Willey et al. 1965:279). No public architecture dating to this period was encountered at Barton Ramie. Given the relative close proximity (2.0 km) of Barton Ramie, the inhabitants of that site were likely tied to the ritual/sociopolitical system at Blackman Eddy.

The ceramic phase for this period shows close affinities with early facet Jenney Creek at Barton Ramie (Gifford 1970, 1976; Willey et al. 1965). Barton Ramie terminology is used for the Blackman Eddy sequence because of the close physical proximity of the two sites. Jenney Creek witnessed the appearance of several new pottery types most notable being Jocote Orange-Brown and Mars Orange, both of which evolve from types of the Kanocha phase and became the predominant types of early facet Jenney Creek. Other new ceramic types also make their appearance (fig. 3.3b,c). These include types with close affinities to the Ramgoat Group from Colha and the Quamina Group of the Bladen Complex at Cuello. The former is represented by modeled bottle fragments, and the latter is present in two varieties of Tower Hill Red-on-Cream. Additionally, there is an increase in vessel forms and decorative techniques. Jenney Creek had been originally assumed to be a "closed-system" of production and consumption. However, in a recent reassessment, Jenney Creek now appears to be composed of two separate production systems—one local (Jocote) and the other based in northern Belize or the Petén (Ball and Taschek 2000, 2003. Alternatively, both systems may be local, the Jocote Group emerging from a pre–Jenney Creek base, and the other a result of developing contacts to the west, south, and north.

Early facet Jenney Creek ceramics were recovered from several of the housemound groups at Barton Ramie, 2.0 km to the northwest (Willey et al. 1965). The more widespread occurrence of early facet Jenney Creek ceramics, relative to pre–Jenney Creek ceramics may be indicative of increasing populations at this point in time. Alternatively, the lower frequency of pre–Jenney Creek remains may be a function of limited sampling and the logistical problems associated with exposing significant areas of deeply buried deposits.

During the early facet Jenney Creek phase, external contacts were maintained along lines established in the Kanocha phase. Evidence for long distance trade is apparent. Excavations produced over one hundred examples of marine shell from the Caribbean coast and obsidian and greenstone are present as well. Social stratification is more evident in the valley during early Jenney Creek times than in the preceding phase. This is marked by the construction of relatively large public function masonry architecture at Blackman Eddy (Structures B1–7th, B1–6th, B1–5th, and B1–4th). The architectural complexity and material culture remains suggest that differences in status and wealth were more pronounced during this phase and that they were probably increasing along established family lines as evidenced by continued occupation and elaboration at the same location.

The early facet Jenney Creek architecture at Blackman Eddy witnesses a substantial increase in the use of coursed stone masonry and lime plaster. Furthermore, building size, associated plastered plazas, artifacts, and ritual activity are indicative of a public function and the emergence of monumental public architecture with its implied social stratification. These early expressions of monumental architecture immediately overlie simple low platforms. Their construction demonstrates the ability of an emerging elite to marshal increasing amounts of labor.

Late Facet Jenney Creek Phase (700–350 B.C.)

The late facet Jenney Creek phase witnessed some of the most notable changes at Blackman Eddy. The construction activity on Structure B1 at Blackman Eddy is substantial. There is also a notable increase in domestic activity at the nearby site of Barton Ramie. The earliest indication of sculpted architectural decoration is seen at the beginning of this phase, Structure B1–4th (fig. 3.6). It is a single-tiered, 1.58-m-high rectangular platform oriented 8 degrees west of true north, with an inset staircase and an extended basal platform. Structure B1–4th is 9.75 m north-south by approximately 16.4 m east-west. The upper portions of the southern platform wall and central stair were torn out in antiquity. The summit was severely burned over much of its surface. A highly fragmented mask armature flanked the staircase (fig. 3.6). The nose armature of the mask was still in place and rested directly on the low basal platform. This is the earliest facade mask found in the Maya lowlands to date (Brown and Garber 1998).

Structure B1–4th was desecrated in antiquity. The summit surface was severely burned and the middle and upper portions of the mask facade had been intentionally pulled from the front of the platform. Postholes in the summit indicated the presence of a perishable superstructure. The massive burning and destruction of this building suggests probable warfare activities in the valley at this early date (Brown and Garber 2003). This conflict may be related to the "Mayanization" of the non-Maya settled population of the valley postulated by Ball and Taschek (2000, 2003).

The late Middle Formative period reflects another shift in architectural style as seen in the construction of Structure B1–3rd (fig. 3.7). This shift in style occurs immediately after what appears to be a hostile event at the site as evidenced by the massive destruction carried out on Structure B1–4th. The style did, however, continue the linear triadic form es-

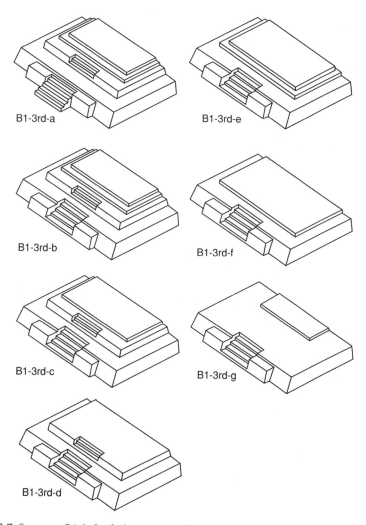

Fig. 3.7. Structure B1-3rd subphases at Blackman Eddy.

tablished earlier, as evidenced by the construction of Structure B2, which flanks Structure B1 to the east (fig. 4.1). Structure B2 has an early phase that is associated with the initial construction of B1–3rd. The style of architecture, as well as construction techniques, changed substantially with the construction of B1–3rd. This phase had six additions to the original building, four of which date to the Late Preclassic period (fig. 3.7). The earliest three subphases, B1–3rd-g, B1–3rd-f, and B1–3rd-e, date to the Late Middle Formative period. The subsequent modifications doubled the height of the building. An outset staircase was added to the final phase, B1–3rd-a.

The initial construction, B1–3rd-g, consisted of a large rectangular platform with an inset staircase. The building was oriented eight degrees west of true north and rose to a height of 1.74 m above the associated plaza surface. The north-south basal dimension is 11.0 m. The east-west dimension is estimated to be 20.8 m. Flanking the staircase, the structure had outset platforms, which were constructed of tightly fitted large cut limestone blocks. Interestingly, a similar shift in construction techniques is seen at Nakbe during the late Middle Formative period, where large cut limestone blocks are utilized for the first time (Hansen 1998). A centerline dedicatory cache consisting of a Joventud Red bowl was recovered just south of the B1–3rd basal platform. Although the upper tier of the building underwent many revisions, the basal tier remained unchanged with the exception of the above mentioned addition of an outset staircase to its final configuration. The summit of the original construction, B1–3rd-g, was heavily burned, perhaps due to desecratory termination activities related to warfare during this period as well. Several of the later additions also showed evidence of extensive burning, perhaps indicating the continuation of conflict in the valley.

Mamom sphere ceramics appear, including types of the Joventud, Chinhinta, and Pital Groups but types of the older local Jocote Group and the Savana Group dominate. Trade during this phase is evident by the presence of greenstone, obsidian, and marine shell. The picture that emerges for late Jenney Creek phase culture in the valley is one of a precocious society. There is evidence for an increase in population and settlement, craft specialization (Hohmann 2002), and for the construction of monumental public architecture. An expansion of existing exchange networks and interregional contact is manifested by changes in the procurement of obsidian (chapter 7; Awe 1992) and by the introduction of new exotic goods. Taken as a whole, these factors are indicative of an increased level of cultural complexity.

Conclusion

Primary objectives in the recent investigations at Blackman Eddy were to augment the emerging Formative period database of the upper Belize Valley region (Awe 1992). At the start of these initiatives, what was known of Formative occupation of the area was essentially what Willey and his colleagues (1965) had discovered in the 1950s. More recently, Ball and Taschek (1986), Ford (1990), Ford and Fedick (1992), and Healy (1990a) recorded evidence of Formative occupation at Buenavista del Cayo, Pacbitun, and the area to the northwest of the Belize River, but these data were represented by little more than ceramic remains. Collectively, the information gained from these sites indicated that Jenney Creek pottery represented the earliest ceramic tradition of the region. These ceramics however, had not been isolated stratigraphically and its early Middle Formative date had been determined solely by seriation (Willey et al. 1965:562–563; Gifford 1976). In his discussion of early facet Jenney Creek pottery, Sharer acknowledged this problem: "It should be stressed that the following facet definitions are minimal, that is, further excavations in the Belize Valley area should add to and refine this picture of the initial pottery tradition in the eastern Maya Lowlands" (Sharer 1976:61).

Prior to the excavations at Blackman Eddy (Brown and Garber 1998) and Cahal Pech (Awe 1992; Cheetham 1995, 1996) there were no data on securely dated Jenney Creek phase architecture, no evidence for settlements or construction prior to 800 B.C., and no monumental architecture dating to the Formative period recorded at Barton Ramie or other neighboring sites. Data regarding interaction spheres or the procurement of exotic goods were limited as well. The earliest occurrence of obsidian had been dated to the late Jenney Creek phase. Jade or greenstone first appeared in the later Barton Creek phase (Willey et al. 1965). In part due to this limited database, Willey et al. (1965), Gifford (1970), and Sharer and Gifford (1970) initially suggested that sociopolitical complexity did not develop in the upper Belize Valley until the terminal Late Formative, and they argued that this development was probably sparked by outside highland influence.

The excavations at Blackman Eddy have revealed a developmental sequence of architectural construction initiated at approximately 1100 B.C. with the construction of pole and thatch domestic buildings built on and slightly above bedrock. Through time, the buildings increased in complexity. By the beginning of the early Jenney Creek phase (900 B.C.), the inhabitants of the valley were constructing lime-plastered, cut masonry, monumental public architecture. Participation in a far-reaching interaction sphere has been documented for these earliest settled groups. Evidence for the importation of exotic goods from the Guatemalan highlands, the Motagua Valley, and the Caribbean coast predate the late Middle Formative record for these activities at Barton Ramie (Willey et al. 1965).

The presence of dedication and termination offerings, feasting debris, figurines, carved greenstone, and the incised elements and motifs of the early ceramics, indicate the importance of symbolism and ritual ideology at an early date in the Maya lowlands. The iconographic motifs of the Kanocha phase at Blackman Eddy indicate that the earliest settled groups of the Belize Valley participated in a pan-Mesoamerican symbol system. This is evident in the Cunil phase at Cahal Pech as well (Awe 1992; Cheetham 1998; chapter 7).

The investigations at Blackman Eddy have revealed Jenney Creek phase material in sealed stratigraphic context. The associated radiocarbon dates for these remains confirm the early Middle Formative date (900–700 b.c.) for early Jenney Creek ceramic remains (table 3.2). Stratigraphically beneath, and thus predating, these remains at Blackman Eddy are deposits of the Kanocha phase in place by at least 1100 b.c. and possibly beginning earlier. There are several important questions about this phase that remain unanswered. These concern the origins of the ceramic types, their developmental relationships to Jenney Creek, and their relationship to the early ceramics of the Petén and northern Belize.

Note

1. The numbering of Structure B1 architecture presented here differs from and supersedes earlier presentations of these data.

Acknowledgments

Collection of the data for this chapter occurred during the 1990 to 2002 field seasons of the Belize Valley Archaeology Research Project, Department of Anthropology, Texas State University–San Marcos. The authors would like to acknowledge the Department of Archaeology, Belmopan, Belize, for their continued support of this project. Figure 3.3 was drafted by Erich Fisher. Figure 3.5a was drafted by Amy Duckworth. We would also like to thank our project staff, student participants, and Belizean assistants for their dedicated efforts. The friendship and hospitality of the people of Blackman Eddy village and San Ignacio made our work especially enjoyable. Special thanks go to the Bob Jones and Busman Arnold families for all of their generosity and help. Financial support for the BVAP project was provided by the Department of Anthropology and Office of Sponsored Projects of Texas State University–San Marcos, and the Foundation for the Advancement of Mesoamerican Studies, Inc. (FAMSI) grant numbers 96052 and 00090.

4

Archaeological Investigations at Blackman Eddy

James F. Garber, M. Kathryn Brown, W. David Driver, David M. Glassman,
Christopher J. Hartman, F. Kent Reilly III, and Lauren A. Sullivan

The Texas State University–San Marcos Belize Valley Archaeology Project
(BVAP) was initiated in 1990 to investigate the site of Blackman Eddy and
surrounding areas. Blackman Eddy is located in the central portion of the
Belize Valley on a ridge overlooking the valley (map 1). During the first
years of the project, the primary objective was to examine the role of
Blackman Eddy relative to larger centers to the west. Subsequently, the
objective was modified to conduct a thorough investigation of Structure
B1 (chapter 3).

Willey et al. (1965) listed three major ceremonial centers in the valley:
Benque Viejo (Xunantunich), Cahal Pech, and Baking Pot. All are located
in the upper portion of the study area near the confluence of the Mopan
and Macal Rivers. They are characterized by sizable, steep-sided temple
mounds, lower palace platforms, two or more plazas, stelae, and at least
one ballcourt. These architectural features are the physical representations of rulership and authority and provided the site's rulers with the
necessary architectural instruments of elite ritual and access to supernatural power. Although Willey suggests that it is unlikely that additional
ceremonial centers of this class are present in the valley (Willey et al.
1965:561), a resurgence of investigations in the area revealed several previously unknown major centers. Five have been identified in the western
end of the valley. These are Buenavista del Cayo (Ball and Taschek 1991;
chapter 9), Las Ruinas (Ball and Taschek 1991), El Pilar (Ford and Fedick
1992; chapter 15), Pacbitun (Healy 1990a; chapter 13), and Actuncan

(McGovern 1993). In the central portion of the valley (east of Baking Pot), where Willey noted that public architecture appeared to be limited to minor centers, two major ceremonial centers, Blackman Eddy and Camelote, have been identified. BVAP made an initial map of the Camelote site core, but no excavations have been conducted at that site.

Although Blackman Eddy is smaller than major centers to the west, it does have all the architectural features that define a major center. Blackman Eddy is significantly larger and more complex than minor centers such as Floral Park or Warrie Head in Willey's second-tier category, which he called minor ceremonial centers. The presence of a complete inventory of ceremonial architecture at Blackman Eddy and Camelote indicates greater size diversity within the category of major ceremonial centers than originally defined and includes centers with all of the complexities, but not the scale, of the larger sites in the valley. Additionally, the presence of sites with architectural manifestations of authority in this portion of the valley alters our understanding of sociopolitical organization in the Belize River area as a whole and has important implications for our understanding of other components of the system as well. Even as efforts toward centralization intensified during the Late Classic with massive growth in the upper valley, site size and complexity continued to remain small as one moved farther east down river, as implied by Willey.

The Blackman Eddy site core is 200 m north-south by 95 m east-west, covering an area of approximately 1.9 hectares (fig. 4.1). Plaza B is located at the northern portion of the site and has been severely damaged by bulldozing activity (chapter 3). The final configuration of the site core was attained in the Classic, although many structures have Preclassic building phases. Twelve of the structures in the site core have been investigated. At this point, however, it appears that the Middle Formative building activity is restricted to the north end of Plaza B in Structures B1 and B2 (chapter 3).

The site core is situated on a fingerlike ridge that overlooks and extends into the valley below. These fingerlike ridges are found to the east and west of the site core and have plazuela groups on them that, like the site core, have a commanding view of the valley below (Garber et al. 1998). Test excavations demonstrate that these were constructed during the Late Classic period. Several mound clusters have been observed in the hilly regions to the south of the site core. Dense mound concentrations have been recorded within the floodplain regions of the site as well. Barton Ramie is located approximately 2 km to the northwest. The earliest occupation at

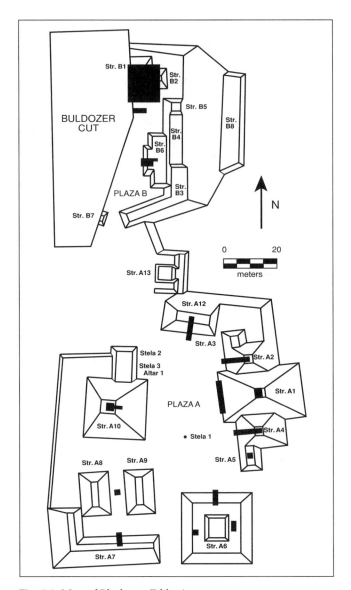

Fig. 4.1. Map of Blackman Eddy site core.

Barton Ramie dates to the Middle Preclassic (Jenney Creek, 850 B.C.) and extends into the Early Postclassic (New Town, A.D. 1000–1200). Blackman Eddy is the closest ceremonial center to Barton Ramie and appears to be the administrative center for that settlement zone. The next closest major center is Baking Pot, approximately 8 km to the southwest of Barton Ramie.

Plaza B Excavations

Structure B1

Plaza B was severely damaged by bulldozing activity in the mid-1980s. Most of the western half of Plaza B was bulldozed to bedrock. Traces of foundations and construction fill are present indicating that Plaza B was more or less symmetrical. Structure B1 is the dominant architectural feature of Plaza B. Facing south, the temple mound rises to a height of 3.5 m. Of all the structures in the site core, Structure B1 was thus situated for the best view of the valley below (fig. 4.1). Structure B1 has been extensively damaged by the aforementioned bulldozing activity as its entire western half has been removed. The resulting cut has provided a profile of its central axis (fig. 3.1). This complex profile illustrates much of the Structure B1 construction history. Excavations to bedrock have revealed thirteen major building phases as well as numerous revisions. These phases and their construction dates are shown in table 4.1. The Preclassic phases are discussed in chapter 3.

Table 4.1. Construction phases of Structure B1 at Blackman Eddy

Structure	Period	Ceramic phase	Date
B1-1st	Late Classic	Tiger Run	600 A.D.–900 A.D.
B1-2nd-a	Early Classic	Hermitage	300 A.D.–600 A.D.
B1-2nd-b	Early Classic	Hermitage	300 A.D.–600 A.D.
B1-3rd-a	Late Preclassic	Barton Creek	350 B.C.–300 A.D.
B1-3rd-b	Late Preclassic	Barton Creek	350 B.C.–300 A.D.
B1-3rd-c	Late Preclassic	Barton Creek	350 B.C.–300 A.D.
B1-3rd-d	Late Preclassic	Barton Creek	350 B.C.–300 A.D.
B1-3rd-e	Middle Formative (late)	LJC	700 B.C.–350 B.C.
B1-3rd-f	Middle Formative (late)	LJC	700 B.C.–350 B.C.
B1-3rd-g	Middle Formative (late)	LJC	700 B.C.–350 B.C.
B1-4th	Middle Formative (late)	LJC	700 B.C.–350 B.C.
B1-5th	Middle Formative (early)	EJC	900 B.C.–700 B.C.
B1-6th	Middle Formative (early)	EJC	900 B.C.–700 B.C.
B1-7th	Middle Formative (early)	EJC	900 B.C.–700 B.C.
B1-8th	Middle Formative (early)	Kanocha	1100 B.C.–900 B.C.
B1-9th	Middle Formative (early)	Kanocha	1100 B.C.–900 B.C.
B1-10th	Middle Formative (early)	Kanocha	1100 B.C.–900 B.C.
B1-11th	Middle Formative (early)	Kanocha	1100 B.C.–900 B.C.
B1-12th	Middle Formative (early)	Kanocha	1100 B.C.–900 B.C.
B1-13th	Middle Formative (early)	Kanocha	1100 B.C.–900 B.C.

Notes: EJC = Early Jenney Creek; LJC = Late Jenney Creek.

Several obsidian blades, human phalanges, and human teeth were recovered in the humus layer overlying the Structure B1–1st stair treads. The
presence of the phalanges and teeth on the central axis may be due to the
disturbance of a burial. Alternatively, the obsidian blades, teeth, and phalanges may result from ritual activity conducted on the central axis. The
murals at Bonampak (room 2 north wall) depict a bloodletting ritual in
which captives are shown with blood dripping from their fingertips (Miller
1986). Possibilities include bloodletting and fingernail or finger removal.
One individual is depicted holding an obsidian blade (Miller 1995). Depicted on an inset of the bench along the south wall of the same room,
three captives are shown on the battlefield with mangled hands, some possibly missing finger digits.

From the Zopilote group, an outlier of Cahal Pech, a broken Late
Preclassic stela was recovered inside a Classic period vaulted tomb (Awe
et al. 1995; Awe and Grube 2001; chapter 8). The fill of the chamber also
contained obsidian blades, incisors and 259 bowls that contained over
200 phalanges. The obsidian blades, incisors, and human phalanges recovered on Structure B1 at Blackman Eddy may be the result of a bloody
sacrificial ritual conducted on the central axis of the structure. Additionn-
ally, a concentration of heavily eroded sherds was recovered at the base
of the mound. This vessel, or vessels, may relate to the possible ritual
described above or they may relate to an abandonment or termination
ritual. Ritual remains of this sort have been observed at Blackman Eddy
Group 1, Ontario Village, and Floral Park (Garber et al. 1998). Because
these remains were recovered in the humus zone overlying the final Late
Classic construction phase, they reflect one of the last activities conducted
at the site.

Due to its proximity to the surface, Structure B1–1st was poorly preserved. Nonetheless, it was clear from the excavations that the structure
was oriented to the south, had a central staircase, and was probably two-
tiered. Excavations on the summit revealed the presence of a Late Classic
burial with associated high-status grave goods that included a polychrome
slab-foot cylinder jar (Anonal Buff-polychrome), carved bone and shell,
a slate mirror back, and a large jade bead (figs. 4.2 and 4.3). The human
remains consisted of one primary interment and three secondary interments, all within a stone slab crypt. This burial is intrusive into Structure
B1–2nd and may postdate the construction of B1–1st as well.

The positioning of the architectural features in the site core is significant

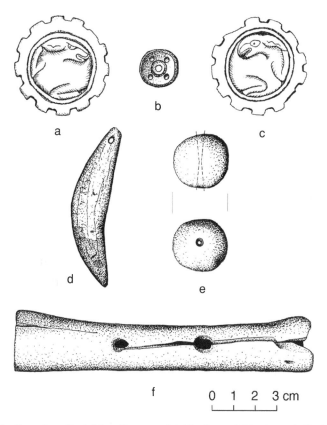

Fig. 4.2. Artifacts from Burial 4 on Structure B1, Blackman Eddy: (a–c) shell adorno; (d) drilled jaguar canine; (e) greenstone bead; (f) bone tube.

Fig. 4.3. Anonal Buff-polychrome vessel from Burial 4, Structure B1, Blackman Eddy.

and relates to a model of architectural arrangement proposed by Ashmore (1991). In this model, the principles of architectural arrangement are derived from cosmology and concepts of directionality. Structures, ceremonial centers, and settlements are microcosms that replicate a multilayered universe (Ashmore 1991, Freidel et al. 1993, Garber et al. 1998). Directions, and their associated structures, dictate the functions of structures and relate to symbolically portrayed statements of world order, royal ancestors, power, and authority. Authority can be marked by position and/or architectural adornment. Additionally, political and religious leaders and their associated rituals are situated in locations that convey authority and supernatural power. North is associated with sky themes and royal ancestors. Ashmore (1991:201) cites the Twin Pyramid Complexes at Tikal as examples of ruler portraits (stelae) located in the northern position of the Twin Pyramid Complexes and that this position equates sky and ancestors. Additionally, she notes that at Copan the ritual themes of the North Group are sky, royal ancestors, sacrifice, immortality, perpetuation, and resurrection. The themes (discussed below) represented in the iconographic program on Structure B1–2nd at Blackman Eddy show strong parallels to the "northern" themes at both Copan and Tikal.

The function of Maya ceremonial precincts was to replicate the cosmic order and provide a sanctified location for rituals that reenacted creation or provided the staging for shamanic performance. These structures were multitiered platforms topped by temples and were sometimes embellished with facades serving to fuse cosmology and myth into an architectural display of supernatural and political power. The Structure B1–2nd facades display iconographic attributes associated with power and authority.

Structure B1–2nd was well preserved and is shown in figure 4.4. Structure B1–2nd faces south and is a two-tiered structure reaching a height of 3.4 m. Due to the bulldozing activity its exact east-west basal dimensions could not be determined. Structure B1–2nd-b was constructed toward the end of the Late Preclassic. The structure was modified in the Early Classic with summit additions and the addition of ancillary staircases flanking the main staircase on the east and west (fig. 4.4). A dedicatory cache consisting of an Early Classic plate (Santa Elena Orange-polychrome: Dos Arroyos Variety) was found in the fill of the ancillary eastern upper-tier staircase. These modifications are designated Structure B1–2nd-a.

A large posthole, approximately 1.5 m in diameter and 3.5 m deep, was present in the southeast corner of the summit. The depth and diameter of this hole indicate that it would have contained a massive pole, similar to those on Structure 5C-2nd at Cerros (Freidel 1995, 1986b). A cache was

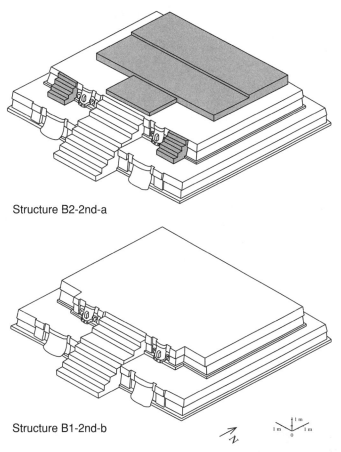

Structure B2-2nd-a

Structure B1-2nd-b

Fig. 4.4. Structure B1-2nd, Blackman Eddy.

found at the base of the hole that consisted of an obsidian blade and a portion of a Late Preclassic bucket. Because the western half of the structure was bulldozed, the presence of a corresponding posthole on that side could not be confirmed. If the posthole was part of a perishable superstructure, then there should have been a similar hole in the northwestern corner of the platform. This was not the case. Assuming the presence of a hole in the southwestern corner, these poles may have been part of a massive scaffolding used in accession ceremony. Placing the ruler in the sky, at this northern location in the site, is consistent with the Ashmore (1991) model and would have accomplished the same symbolic objective as the placement of ruler portrait stelae in the Twin Pyramid Complexes at Tikal. Such scaffolds are represented in stone on the roof combs of Late Classic buildings as seen in the Cross Group at Palenque and in stucco on the frieze at Xunantunich (chapter 11).

The preserved portions of the Structure B1–2nd mask and panels had traces of red paint. On the lower mask only the armature remained. Portions of preserved plaster were present on the panels adjacent to the lower mask but did not have iconographic detail (fig. 4.5). The upper mask, although also poorly preserved, did have sufficient detail to determine the ritual theme of the iconographic program. The upper panel, with a low bench along its base, consists of a mask flanked by panels. The panels immediately adjacent to the central mask each had partially preserved circular elements that represent earflares. The flanking panel has preserved plaster elements at its base that closely resemble the panels that flank all four masks on Structure 5C-2nd at Cerros (Freidel 1977, 1985, 1986b). These panels represent a zoomorphic supernatural being shown in profile. The preserved portions of the Blackman Eddy example represent the snout and protruding mouth elements of that entity (fig. 4.5).

No preserved plaster was present on the face of the mask except at the very base, but certain details can be discerned from the armature. Clearly, the mask had some kind of helmet or headdress as evidenced by the double course of outset stones above the face area. The most significant preserved portion, however, is at the base of the upper mask. It consists of an outwardly flaring bowl, shown in profile, adorned with three large dots. Re-

Fig. 4.5. Drawing of upper east mask facade, Structure B1-2nd-b, Blackman Eddy.

cent hieroglyphic and iconographic decipherment have underscored the importance of the three-dot symbolism in Maya ideology. When functioning as a symbolic motif, the three dots represent the three stone place, which the gods established at the cosmic center at the beginning of the present creation (Freidel et al. 1993:64–71). Thus, the damaged face on Structure B1–2nd is depicted emerging from a ritual bowl identified with creation. The mask represents a head in a bowl and symbolically conveys aspects of creation mythology. Similar renderings of bowls, with their emerging supernaturals, are found throughout Mesoamerica (fig. 4.6).

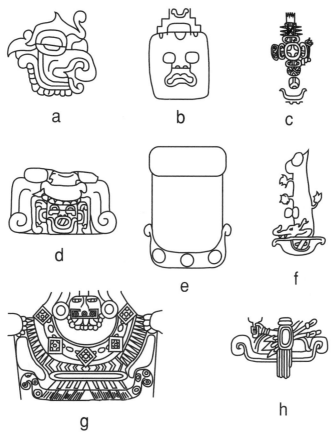

Fig. 4.6. Formative and Classic examples of bowls with supernatural entities: (a) headdress detail from La Mojarra (redrawn from Winfield Capitaine 1988: fig. 1); (b) Tzutzuculi (redrawn from McDonald 1983: fig. 12); (c) Humboldt Celt (redrawn from Reilly 1994: fig. 3.52); (d) Uaxactun (redrawn from Freidel et al. 1993: fig. 3:9); (e) Blackman Eddy facade mask (drawn by J. Wiersema); (f) Lowland Maya vessel (redrawn from Freidel et al. 1993: fig. 1:5); (g) Teotihuacan (redrawn from Taube 1983: fig. 3); (h) Teotihuacan.

Such bowls have been identified for the Classic and Late Preclassic periods as mirror or bloodletting bowls (Taube 1983). Preclassic and Classic period examples of the sacrificial bowl are found both inside and outside the Maya lowlands.

Excavations at the Pacific Coast, Middle Formative site of Tzutzuculi, clearly demonstrates that the facade masks of Blackman Eddy, Cerros, Uaxactun and other Maya sites are not unique and are, in fact, the product of an architectural tradition of great antiquity. The Tzutzuculi facade masks were constructed by a non-Maya people in the Olmec style, as early as 650 B.C. (McDonald 1983:37). Like the facade masks of the later Maya, those at Tzutzuculi are placed on a large, multitiered building, flanking a central staircase.

For the Classic period Maya and their contemporary Yucatecan-speaking decedents the Lacandon (McGee 1990:49–53), bloodletting bowls were the *Ol* or portal to the supernatural other world (Freidel et al. 1993: 213–219). Functioning as the *Ol* or portal, the bloodletting bowl itself constitutes liminal space standing between the natural and supernatural worlds. Bloodletting bowls were perceived by Mesoamericans as objects that could ritually generate the interface between the natural and supernatural realms. As sacred ritual instruments, Classic period examples of the bloodletting bowl often have their interiors incised or painted with important ideological symbolism. Such representations could take the form of the head of the maize god placed in a bloodletting bowl or the writhing bodies of the supernatural vision serpents who disgorged from their gaping maws the ancestors of the ruling elite (Freidel et al. 1993:216–217).

The presence of these facade masks indicates that the Terminal Late Preclassic and Early Classic elites of Blackman Eddy constructed their ceremonial precinct to replicate the cosmic order and provide a sanctified location for those rituals that either reenacted creation or provided the performance mechanism by which participants opened a portal to the otherworld. Undoubtedly, this ceremonial complex not only provided rituals essential to visual validation of social, political, and religious power, but also linked through a shared ideology the emerging stratified elites who controlled the complex political landscape.

Structure B2

Structure B1 is flanked on the east by a small mound, Structure B2 (fig. 4.1). Traces of a similar structure on the western side of Structure B1 are present in the bulldozer cut. In its final Late Classic configuration, B2–1st was a 3.0-m-high two-tiered building with a narrow staircase on its southern face. Along the primary axis, a simple cache of two manos was placed in the construction fill of the upper tier, behind the staircase. Structure B2–2nd may have supported a perishable building, but this could not be confirmed. The initial construction, Structure B2–2nd, was a single-tier 2.0-m-high building constructed during the Late Preclassic/Early Classic transition.

Structure B6

Structure B6 is a 23-m-long rectangular structure on the east side of the plaza. Structure B6 was built directly in front of two modified range structures, B3 and B4 (fig. 4.1). Excavations revealed two construction phases. The final phase, B6–1st, was poorly preserved and thus interpretation of its form is problematic. Associated ceramics indicate a Late Classic date for this final phase. The earliest construction phase, Structure B6–2nd, is represented by an outset staircase, which was centrally placed along the front (west) wall. The four steps abutted a 1-m-high wall. The staircase led to a poorly preserved plaster surface that was located at the top of the structure and perhaps once supported a perishable superstructure. A red-slipped Early Classic vessel, placed face down, was recovered on this floor. This vessel was located approximately 25 cm north of the staircase on the medial axis. Its placement on the summit floor suggests that it was associated with the abandonment or termination of this phase.

The location of the building in the site core, and the artifacts associated with the structure, support the interpretation of Structure B6 as an elite residence. These artifacts include a number of mano and metate fragments as well as a number of ceramic forms that are typically associated with a utilitarian use. The continuity of artifact types associated with Structure B6 suggests that the function of the building remained the same throughout its history.

Plaza A Excavations

Structure A1

Structures A1 and A10 are the tallest structures at the site, each reaching a height of approximately 10 m. Structure A1 had been severely damaged by looting activity. Excavations revealed the two basal-most stair treads of the final construction phase, A1–1st. Ceramic analysis indicated a Late

Classic date for this construction. An Early Classic staircase (A1–2nd) was encountered approximately 2 m behind A1–1st. Three superimposed plaster surfaces for Plaza A were present immediately to the west of the basal tread. Plaza A is approximately 1.8 m thick at this location.

Oddly, preservation was considerably better at the structure summit than at the base. Excavations revealed the presence of two construction phases that, in all likelihood, correspond to the two noted at the base. Two construction phases for the uppermost riser of the substructure were noted in one of the looter's trenches as well. The summit of Structure A1 consists of a solid rectangular platform approximately 80 cm in height atop the flat-topped, tiered substructure. This summit platform is faced with well-dressed limestone. A simple dedicatory cache was found on the centerline under the substructure summit platform immediately to the west of the summit platform western wall. This cache, associated with Structure A1–2nd, consisted of six worked marine univalve shells that were probably strung as a necklace. Careful examination of the looter's trenches did not reveal the presence of any vaulted rooms or construction phases other than those noted above.

Structure A10

This structure is located directly opposite Structure A1 and is of comparable size and shape (fig. 4.1). The summit excavations extended to a depth of 3.2 m below surface. No caches or additional construction phases were revealed, although the ceramic sample from construction fill indicates a Late Classic construction date. Earlier phases are probably present in the core of the mound.

Structure A12

This range structure defines the northern edge of Plaza A (fig. 4.1). The excavations revealed the presence of two construction phases, the outermost designated Structure A12–1st and the innermost Structure A12–2nd. Structure A12–1st was composed of six stepped risers on its southern face formed from moderate- to well-dressed limestone blocks and slabs. A centerline cache consisting of two Early Classic vessels was recovered in the construction fill of Structure A12–1st, establishing an Early Classic date for the construction. Ceramic sherds in the overlying fill indicate that it was utilized into the Late Classic. Structure A12–2nd was composed of four stepped risers composed of similar materials. No caches were recovered for this phase but ceramic analysis indicates a probable Preclassic date for its initial construction.

Structure A6

This structure is a large quadrangular platform, 2.4 m in height, which defines the southern limits of Plaza A, and is approximately 30 m on each side (fig. 4.1). The summit of the platform is edged by small linear range structures creating a sunken patio in the center. The quadrangle form of the platform provides a high degree of privacy. This, and the associated dark greasy midden debris with high sherd densities, indicates a probable elite residential function for this complex. An outset central stairway on the north face provided access to the plaza.

The excavation on the northern face indicated two major building episodes. The earliest was associated with the earliest surface of Plaza A. This platform appears to have been at least 1.6 m tall. Due to the limited exposure of this phase, it is unclear whether it had already been established as a quadrangular platform at that time. Sometime in the Late Classic, the platform was extensively enlarged. A 5-m-wide stairway on the north face led up to the summit, which supported either a low summit platform or perishable superstructures with low coursed stone foundations.

Structure A4

This mound is a secondary structure attached to the southern face of Structure A1. A similar feature is attached to the northern face of Structure A1 as well (fig. 4.1). Structure A4 has been severely damaged by a looter's trench and tunnel. The trench was approximately 2 m wide and cut into the western face of the structure. Approximately 5 m into Structure A4, the trench terminated and the tunnel began. This tunnel extended into the central core of the structure at the level of the Plaza A surface. Examination of the terminal end of the tunnel revealed the presence of several well-trimmed upright limestone slabs capped off with large trimmed slabs. This appeared to be a crypt burial, although careful examination of the looter's backdirt did not reveal the presence of bone. A small Early Classic vessel was recovered in the crypt. The central location of the feature suggests that the interment of this individual may have been the primary reason for the construction of Structure A4. While cleaning the northern wall of the looter's trench, a human cranium was observed in the sidewall. This cranium was enclosed on the top and sides by stone slabs indicating the presence of another crypt. The burial was of an adult and the body position was extended with the head pointing south. There were no associated grave goods and the bone preservation was poor. The crypt was narrow and composed of roughly trimmed slabs of limestone. Immediately to the east of this burial, two secondary burials were encountered. One is a poorly preserved subadult consisting of a skull with four long bones passing through it. No other remains of this burial were present. The other is an adult and consisted of a skull and long bone fragments. The relationship between these three burials and the postulated main burial could not be determined but the inclusion of secondary burials with the main interment may be a form of ancestor veneration. A similar pattern was observed on Structure B1 where three secondary burials were included with the principal interment.

Structure A5

Excavations were carried out on the summit of Structure A5. The purpose of this excavation was to locate possible burials, as was the case with adjacent Structure A4. No such burials were encountered. Like several of the other Plaza A structures at Blackman Eddy, Structure A5 has two major construction phases. The bulk of the mound was constructed during the final phase. Both phases date to the Early Classic.

Structures A7, A8, and A9

Test excavations were carried out in the playing alley of the ballcourt, Structures A8 and A9. The excavation unit was excavated to bedrock encountered at a depth of 80 cm. The profile of the unit revealed three distinct soil strata, but no preserved plaster surfaces. A centerline trench was excavated into Structure A7, the southern "end zone" building of the ballcourt. The northern end zone is formed by the south side of Structure A10 (fig. 4.1). The long axis of Structure A7 runs east-west and faces north into the ballcourt. The excavation of the centerline trench revealed three construction phases for Structure A7. The final phase, Structure A7–1st, was poorly preserved. It is a long low platform with four steps on its northern face. Each step was composed of roughly cut limestone blocks, three courses high. The east-west extent of these steps is not known. Ceramics in the fill of Structure A7–1st indicate a Late Classic date for this construction. Structure A7–2nd is also a low platform. Its final plastered surface had been heavily burned. Structure A7–3rd is a very well preserved platform constructed during the Late Preclassic. The southern wall consisted of well-trimmed large limestone blocks, some of which were 50 cm long. The associated plaza floor to the north of the wall was thick and well preserved. It also showed signs of having been burned. The large block masonry and thick plaster are both characteristic features of Preclassic constructions in the valley. In its final Late Classic phase, Structure A7 functioned as an end zone building for the ballcourt. Although it is clear that there is a Late Preclassic phase for Structure A7, it is not known if there are also Late Preclassic phases for the buildings of the ballcourt proper, Structures A8 and A9.

Stela 1

Three stelae and one altar were found at Blackman Eddy, all within Plaza A. Stela 1 is made of hard limestone and was found on the surface with its carved face up. It is 71.0 cm wide, 29.0 cm thick, and 61.0 cm long. It is broken on both the top and bottom. The preservation of the carved panel varies from moderate to poor. The inscription was done in low relief and was accomplished by the incision of a series of grooves, most of which are straight or nearly so. It has a centrally located incised panel with straight parallel sides.

A complete reading of the inscription is not possible due to weathering and the absence of clearly marked place notation (fig. 4.7a). The inscription includes an Initial Series Introducing Glyph (ISIG) followed by an 8 in the baktun position and a 17 in the katun position. This would fall between A.D. 376 and 396 (GMT correlation). An obsidian blade and a severely fragmented Early Classic bowl were recovered in the plaza fill be-

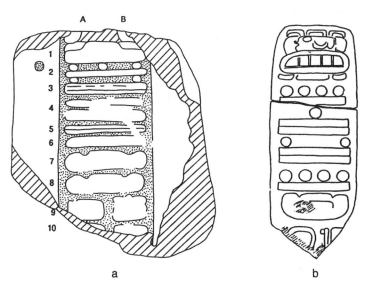

a   b

Fig. 4.7. Stelae drawings: (a) Stela 1, Blackman Eddy; (b) Pestac Stela, Tonina (after Blom 1935).

neath Stela 1. No evidence of a stela pit was observed and the association between the stela and the bowl/blade cache could not be established with certainty.

The inscription is similar to the Pestac stela from Tonina (Blom 1935) and Stela 6 from Pacbitun in that it is presented in an atypical style and format for the Maya lowlands that closely resembles Cycle 7 and early Cycle 8 Initial Series inscriptions from adjoining regions (figs. 4.7 and 13.4). All three have horizontally oriented bar-dot numbers without associated baktun, katun, tun, uinal, or kin-period indicators.

The inscribed panel of Stela 1 is illustrated in figure 4.7a. The A1–B1 position is composed of elements that make up an Initial Series Introducing Glyph (ISIG). This includes a tun sign and portions of the lateral elements of the ISIG trinary superfix. The tun sign is very similar to the ISIGs on Stela 5 at Abaj Takalik (Graham et al. 1978). From the midway point of Cycle 8 onward, the ISIG typically consists of the trinary superfix, an infixed month patron, and the tun sign, as exemplified by the Hauberg stela (Schele and Miller 1986), Stela 29 at Tikal (Shook 1960), and the Leyden Plaque (Morley and Morley 1938). Comb-shaped affixes do not become standard features until Cycle 9. The presence of a fully developed tun sign, a trinary superfix, and the absence of an infixed month patron and lateral comb elements is typical for an ISIG in Cycle 7 and the first half of Cycle 8 (table 4.2).

Stela 1 at Blackman Eddy, the Pestac stela from Tonina, and Stela 6 from Pacbitun, closely resemble non–lowland Maya Cycle 7 and early Cycle 8 Long Count inscriptions in style, presentation, and content. They are atypical for the Maya lowlands. There are problems in reading the Blackman Eddy inscription beyond those caused by heavy weathering. The coefficients are not grouped to clearly indicate place notation. The dots of the coefficients touch the bar elements of the preceding number. This is not a problem with numbers that include dots, as it is clear that the dots initiate the next coefficient. The lack of blank spaces between places does, however, become a problem in correctly grouping a set of consecutive bars. A similar situation can be observed in the Initial Series inscription of the Tuxtla Statuette, where spaces do not exist between coefficients, but in this case consecutive bars do not occur so the grouping of coefficients is not problematic.

In the baktun position (A2–B2) immediately below the ISIG is the number eight represented by a horizontally oriented bar and three dots. In the katun position (A3–B3) is a horizontal bar and two dots. The bar element

Table 4.2. Earliest dated monuments and the development of the ISIG

Inscription	Reading	Correlated date	Trinary superfix	Tun sign	Month patron
Chiapa de Corzo Stela 2	(7.16.)3.2.13	36 B.C.	?	?	?
Tres Zapotes Stela C	7.16.6.16.18	32 B.C.	Yes	Yes	Yes
El Baul Stela 1	7.(19.15.)7.12	A.D. 36	No	No	No
Abaj Takalik Stela 2	7.?	235–18 B.C.	Yes	Yes	No
Dumbarton Oaks Celt 1	(8.)4.	N/A	N/A	N/A	
Abaj Takalik Stela 5	8.4.5.17.11	A.D. 126	Yes	Yes	No
	8.(2 or 3).2.10.5	A.D. 83 or 103	Yes	Yes	No
La Mojarra Stela 1	8.5.3.3.5	A.D. 143	Yes	Yes	Possibly
	8.5.16.9.7	A.D. 156	Yes	Yes	Possibly
Tuxtla statuette	8.6.2.4.17	A.D. 162	Yes	Yes	Possibly
Hauberg stela	12(13) Xul-3 Ahau	A.D. 199	Yes	Yes	Yes
Tikal Stela 29	8.12.14.8.15	A.D. 292	Yes	Yes	Yes
Leyden plaque	8.14.3.1.12	A.D. 320	Yes	Yes	Yes
Blackman Eddy Stela 1	8.17.?.?.?	A.D. 376–396	Yes	Yes	No

has a series of horizontal, heavily weathered, parallel grooves (fig. 4.7a). These grooves are shallow and narrow relative to the grooves that separate bars farther down in the inscription. Due to weathering, the extent of these grooves could not be fully discerned but appear to have originally been two parallel grooves across the length of the bar. These grooves would have divided the bar into three thin bars of equal length making the katun 17. Although a katun reading of 17, as opposed to 7, seems more likely because of these incisions, this would place the Initial Series date in the second half of baktun 8, a time when period glyphs occur with vertically oriented coefficients as exemplified by Stela 29 at Tikal. A reading of 7 for the katun would make Stela 1 the earliest Initial Series Long Count date in the Maya lowlands, predating Stela 29 (8.12.14.8.5) at Tikal. A reading of 17 for the katun would make it one of the earliest in the Maya lowlands. Curiously, similar incised grooves occur on some of the bars on Stelae 2 and 5 at Abaj Takalik and do not function to create multiple bars (Graham et al. 1978:pls. 2 and 3).

A definitive assessment of position A4–B4 is impossible due to heavy weathering on this area of the stela. The lower portion of the A4–B4 position seems to be a bar that may or may not have been incised. Position A5–B5 and A6–B6 are represented by bars. The A5–B5 bar has a groove that extends across most of its length, similar to the grooves observed in position A3–B3.

Positions A7–B7 and A8–B8 are occupied by elongated elements with rounded ends. Each is incised with semicircular notches. The meaning of these is not readily apparent. These elements are unique in the Mesoamerican corpus with the exception of a glyph on the Pestac stela from Tonina where it functions as a zero in the kin position (fig. 4.7a). A similar element is present on Stela 6 from Pacbitun (fig. 13.4). Interestingly, the Pestac, Blackman Eddy, and Pacbitun stelae are the only known lowland Maya stelae that are presented with horizontally oriented bar-dot numbers in an Initial Series. Additionally, unlike all other lowland Maya stelae, they do not have glyphic period indicators. In positions A10, B10, A11, and B11 are glyphs that are incomplete or eroded beyond recognition. The components of the inscription are summarized in table 4.3.

Stela 1 at Blackman Eddy, the Pestac stela, and Stela 6 from Pacbitun

Table 4.3. Summary of Stela 1, Blackman Eddy

Position	Reading
A1–B1	ISIG
A2–B2	Baktun position—8
A3–B3	Katun position—17
A4–B4	Unknown
A5–B5	10
A6–B6	5
A7–B7	Unknown
A8–B8	Unknown
A9 through B10	Unknown

exhibit strong similarities to all known Cycle 7 and early Cycle 8 Long Count inscriptions. These include Stela 2 at Chiapa de Corzo (Lowe 1962), Stela C at Tres Zapotes (Stirling 1940), Stela 1 at El Baul (Waterman 1924), Stelae 2 and 5 at Abaj Takalik (Graham et al. 1978; Lehmann 1926), Stela 1 at La Mojarra (Winfield Capitaine 1988), and the Tuxtla Statuette (Covarrubias 1947; Washington 1922).

The characteristics of Stela 1 at Blackman Eddy are consistent with features observed on Cycle 7 and early Cycle 8 Long Count inscriptions found outside of the Maya lowlands. Specifically, these include: a single column format for the numerical coefficients, horizontal orientation of the numbers, an absence of period glyphs, and central location of the inscription on the carved panel. Additionally, the ISIG on Stela 1 is consistent with the developmental sequence established for the Introducing Glyphs from these early inscriptions.

The format of Blackman Eddy Stela 1 is a radical departure from what is typical of the Maya lowlands and closely resembles early Initial Series inscriptions from adjoining areas. A Late Preclassic stela from Zopilote also shows strong ties with regions to the south (Awe et al. 1995; Awe and Grube 2001; chapter 8). Thus, it appears that these adjoining regions influenced this portion of the Maya lowlands. Interestingly, influence from these regions is also seen in the earliest occupation levels at Blackman Eddy as well (chapter 3).

Summary and Conclusion

At the time of Willey's classic study (Willey et al. 1965), Blackman Eddy was unknown and did not come to the attention of archaeological investigators until the mid-1980s. Blackman Eddy is approximately 2 km from the intensively occupied area of Barton Ramie, one of the focal points of Willey's study. In all likelihood, Blackman Eddy was the administrative center for the Barton Ramie settlement zone. Willey describes a more or less continuous ribbon-strip of settlement along the river. Ceremonial centers such as Baking Pot, Blackman Eddy, and Camelote are evenly strung out within this ribbon-strip of settlement (chapter 18). Research in the upper valley demonstrates an increasing trend toward centralization in that portion of the valley into the Late Classic period (chapter 12). This does not appear to be the case in the central portion of the valley with the regular linear distribution of ceremonial centers along the river from Baking Pot to Cocos Bank.

Excavations in Plazas A and B at Blackman Eddy chronicle the construction history of the site core. The intensive excavation of Structure B1 revealed a building sequence spanning 2,000 years (chapter 3). The site was initially occupied at the end of the Terminal Early Formative (ca. 1100 B.C.), when the inhabitants constructed low apsidal- or circular-shaped platforms, hunted and gathered local resources such as freshwater mussels, *Jute,* and deer, as well as practiced maize agriculture. The first public structures were also constructed during the early Middle Preclassic (ca. 750 B.C.) and consisted of low rectangular-shaped platforms covered in thick lime plaster. Evidence of long distance trade and early craft specialization is also present.

By the late Middle Formative, larger more elaborate platforms appear, indicating increased labor investment and the emergence of social stratification. Larger architecture begins to appear at a number of sites in the valley during the transition from the Middle to Late Preclassic as seen at Actuncan, Cahal Pech, Pacbitun, El Pilar, and Buenavista del Cayo. At the end of the Late Preclassic, the occupants at Blackman Eddy erected a pyramidal building with grand mask facades flanking the central staircase. Architectural decoration in the form of mask facades is intricately tied to the institution of kingship. Blackman Eddy had an earlier mask tradition (chapter 3), which suggests that the site was a seat of power in the valley during the Middle Formative. The iconographic theme from the B1-2nd mask shows a head emerging from a bowl. This figure may represent the severed head of the father of the hero twins emerging from a blood bowl. This emergence or rebirth reflects the transformation of the severed head into the maize god. Maize god insignia is tied to kingship and is seen throughout the Classic period on a variety of media. The inhabitants also erected stelae during this time, one of which was carved in a foreign tradition. The political and social landscape of the valley was transformed during this time period as a number of powerful centers emerged and erected substantial monumental architecture.

During the Late Classic, Blackman Eddy witnessed a flurry of construction within Plaza A. The focus of the site shifted to the southern section of the site core. Structure B1 was modified one last time (Structure B1–1st) during the Late Classic. It is apparent that by the Late Classic, Blackman Eddy was eclipsed by larger centers to the west (chapter 12). Although diminutive in size, its full complement of monumental architecture and close proximity to Barton Ramie shed new light on the organizational principles of the "ribbon-strip" settlement of the central portion of the valley.

Acknowledgments

Collection of the data for this chapter occurred during the 1990 to 2001 field seasons of the Belize Valley Archaeology Research Project (BVAP), Department of Anthropology, and Texas State University–San Marcos. Figure 4.2 was drafted by Sean Goldsmith, and figure 4.5 was drafted by Jason Weirsema. The senior author drafted the remaining figures. The authors would like to acknowledge the Department of Archaeology, Belmopan, Belize, for their continued support of this project. We would also like to thank our project staff, student participants, and Belizean assistants for their dedicated efforts. We also thank Joseph Ball for his assistance with some of the ceramic type identifications. The friendship and hospitality of the people of Blackman Eddy village and San Ignacio made our work especially enjoyable. Special thanks go to the Bob Jones and Busman Arnold families for all of their generosity and help.

Financial support for the BVAP project was provided by the Department of Anthropology and Office of Sponsored Projects of Texas State University–San Marcos, and the Foundation for the Advancement of Mesoamerican Studies, Inc. (FAMSI) grant numbers 96052 and 00090.

5

Major Center Identifiers at a Plazuela Group Near the Ancient Maya Site of Baking Pot

James M. Conlon and Terry G. Powis

Archaeological investigations have been conducted by a number of researchers at the major center of Baking Pot (map 1) (Bullard and Bullard 1965; Ricketson 1931; Willey et al. 1965). The site consists of two groups connected by a raised causeway or *sacbe*. Although both groups have been tested, the site still remains relatively unexplored (Bullard and Bullard 1965:7). Recent research by the Belize Valley Archaeological Reconnaissance (BVAR) Project has augmented our knowledge of the site (Moore 1999; Piehl 1997). In particular, the excavations conducted at a small plazuela group, known as the Bedran Group, located in the western periphery of the site core have provided data regarding the social, political, and economic organization of the Baking Pot community during the Late Classic (A.D. 500–900) (fig. 5.1).

Minor Center Morphology and Function: Microcosms and Macrocosms

Settlement hierarchy remains one of the primary means for describing and assessing settlement organization at the regional level. The surface morphology of settlement in the region of the upper Belize Valley has been described as tripartite, consisting of major ceremonial centers, minor ceremonial centers, and housemound groups (Willey et al. 1965:561). These community units correspond to ascending foci of authority with minor leaders in minor centers and paramount rulers governing from major centers (Willey et al. 1965:580).

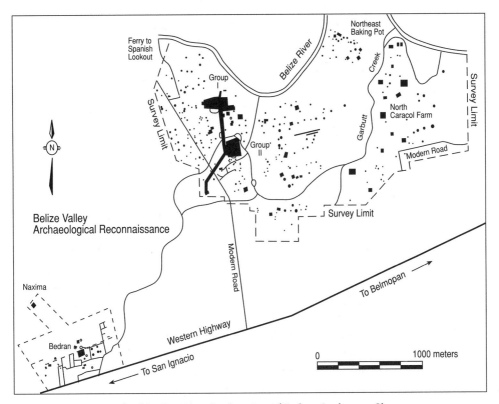

Fig. 5.1. Map of Baking Pot, showing location of Bedran Settlement Cluster.

The middle level of the settlement hierarchy, minor ceremonial centers (Bullard 1960:359–360; Willey et al. 1965:561), or, more simply, minor centers (Coe and Coe 1956; Ford 1981:57; Hammond 1975; Haviland 1981; Willey 1981:399) have remained poorly understood (Iannone 1996: 31; Willey et al. 1965:572–573; chapters 17 and 18).

Minor centers of the valley appear highly variable, like those initially identified in the northeastern Petén of Guatemala (Bullard 1960). This variability is reflected in site morphology, size, spatial location, structure type, artifact content, and surrounding support population. The newly accumulated knowledge concerning valley minor centers emphasizes the significance of comprehensive site-level settlement studies for assessing regional dynamics and facilitating interregional comparisons (chapters 17 and 18; A. Chase and D. Chase 1987:58).

If site variability is a factor in understanding regional settlement organization then it follows that a focus on the variability within groups of mounds of major centers, such that minor centers are one component, is also important. The surface morphology of minor centers is characteristically a copy, or "miniature version" (Culbert 1974:67; see also Bullard 1960:359; A. Chase and D. Chase 1987:54; Hammond 1975:42), of the architectural conventions employed in major centers. Thus, minor centers may be referred to as a "microcosm of the macrocosm" whereby they have the architectural appearance of being a "special ceremonial unit set within the field of smaller habitation mounds" (Willey et al. 1965:572). Minor centers were inhabited by minor leaders (Willey et al. 1965:580), more specifically, elite personages, though arguably less wealthy and powerful than those residing in major centers (Ford 1981:158).[1]

The identification and function of minor centers in the Maya lowlands has not been clearly defined (chapter 17). Did minor centers function as more than simply a place for elites to reside? Is it possible to discern a role other than "residential" for the elite inhabitants of minor groups? It is our contention that minor centers functioned not only as a place of residence but also as a place where elites assumed or performed some role, or combination of roles, within the social, political, and/or economic institutions of their community and region (Ball and Taschek 1991:158; Bullard 1960:368; Culbert 1974:67; Willey and Bullard 1965:369; Willey et al. 1965:562). Thus, determining where elites resided has a different meaning than what elites were doing where they resided. Both social affiliation and the organizational role performed in the larger community must be addressed when assessing intrasite relationships of not only minor centers, but by extension, any given circumscribed mound grouping.

The Bedran Group: Elements of the Macrocosm

The Bedran Settlement Cluster is located 2.27 km southwest of Group II at Baking Pot.[2] (figs. 5.2 and 5.3). The Bedran Group, the focus of the settlement cluster, approximates configurations known as "plazuelas" (Ashmore 1981:49; Thompson 1931), Plaza Plan II at Tikal (Becker 1971, 1983:169), and East Structure-Focus Groups at Caracol (A. Chase and D. Chase 1987:55). Within the settlement hierarchy of the Belize Valley the Bedran Group resembles the plazuela groups that are included in Bullard's (1960:359) "housemound" configurations and the "larger plazuela mounds" that fall between housemound and minor center at Barton Ramie (Willey et al. 1965:572). The larger plazuela mounds, also known as "lesser order" minor centers, are considered to represent a different, elevated social status compared with residents of other lower order housemounds (Willey et al. 1965:572). In addition to its plazuela configuration the Bedran Group also demonstrated architectural characteristics of minor ceremonial centers. In particular, the presence of an eastern pyramidal structure, typically identified with minor centers (Bullard 1960:360; Culbert 1974:67; Ford 1981:158), made the Bedran Group an ideal component for analysis. One of the most important characteristics concerning the assessment of the Bedran Group as a minor center and the role it played with the civic center of Baking Pot revolved around the evolution of this plazuela from its inception to abandonment (Ford 1981:151; Willey et al. 1965:581).

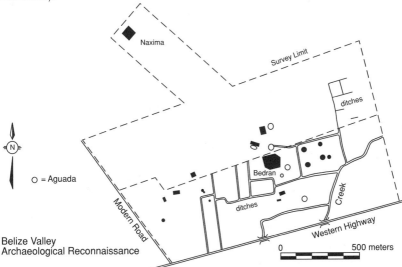

Fig. 5.2. Plan of the Bedran Settlement Cluster.

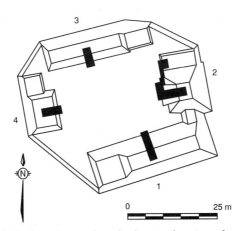

Fig. 5.3. Plan of the Bedran Group plazuela showing location of excavation units.

Inception (ca. A.D. 500–599)

Evidence in the first 100 years of the Bedran Group's existence is characterized by construction activity on the eastern and southern sides of the plazuela. The principal structure in the group was a round structure located on the east side of a plastered patio, bordered by Structure 1–1st on the south. The round structure, designated Structure 2–1st, was approximately 5.0 m in diameter, 1.5 m high, and had a large, centrally located burned area on the plaster platform summit. On the south side of the patio, Structures 1–1st and 1–2nd were low platforms, 15–25 cm high each, and likely represented residential buildings.

Rise (ca. A.D. 600–649)

Structure 1–3rd's plaster platform was raised approximately 85 cm above the coevally constructed first plaster plaza floor (90 cm above the old ground surface), and roughly 20 cm higher than Structure 2–1st that rose 60 to 65 cm above this same surface. The plaza extended north to the newly constructed Structure 3–1st, a 50-cm-high plastered platform (above plaza). No interments were recovered from this occupational period but one dedicatory cache, an Aguacate-Orange: Privaccion Variety vessel (Gifford 1976:129, 135), was recovered from Structure 2–2nd.

Fluorescence (ca. A.D. 650–799)

This phase is marked by ritual, continued architectural growth and an increase in the surrounding support settlement. The terminal phase plaza floor was constructed 20 cm over the first plaza floor, and extended west to incorporate Structure 4–1st. Structure 4–1st underwent several minor constructions during this period (4–2nd to 4–4th). Excavations in Structure 2–3rd revealed a "shrine inset," flanked by stairs leading to the summit. These stairs were subsequently modified into a single stairway. This stairway was then flanked by a basal platform that covered the shrine inset and was appended to the front of Structure 2–3rd's base. It extended roughly 2 m east-west and 5 m north-south, overlying the terminal plaza floor. At the time the basal platform was constructed there were two smaller structures added to both the north and south sides of Structure 2–3rd.

The maximum height of each structure was achieved during this phase. Structures 1–11th, 2–3rd, 3–3rd, and 4–4th are, respectively, 2.03 m, 1.96 m, 1.20 m, and 0.70 m. Orange alluvial clay found throughout the Bedran Settlement Cluster area became the preferred construction fill.

The exclusive reliance upon clay construction fill correlates with the inception of the ditched fields that run throughout the Bedran Settlement Cluster area. The clay removed during the digging of the ditches was subsequently used in the construction of the terminal phase of architecture. The recovery of only Spanish Lookout phase sherds from test excavations in the ditched fields indicates that they were dug sometime between A.D. 700 and 900.

Denouement (ca. A.D. 800–900)

Human remains from a disturbed burial (Burial 8), along with evidence for an abandonment ritual (Cache 8), were found just above the terminal plaza floor near the western base of the appended basal platform of Structure 2–3rd. Cache 8 is described as a "sherd cluster" and consisted of numerous sherds from different vessel types. The cache also contained an eccentric flint. Similar sherd clusters have been found at nearby Blackman Eddy (Garber et al. 1998), Cahal Pech, and Xunantunich (S. Chase 1993:42). They were all associated with either termination rituals or abandonment practices (see also Garber 1989:47–50). Only one early facet Postclassic period sherd, Daylight Orange type (Gifford 1976:300), was recovered. This sherd came from the surface of Structure 4 and represents an ephemeral reoccupation sometime after the Bedran Group was abandoned ca. A.D. 900.

Architecture

At first glance, the Bedran Group does not seem to indicate much in the way of status markers except for the inclusion of the eastern pyramidal structure. The architectural pattern of Structure 2 does, however, display two other elements indicative of authority. First, the architectural characteristics (pyramidal structure flanked by two smaller mounds on the north and south ends) of Structure 2–3rd strongly resemble the E-Group configuration identified at major centers across the Maya lowlands, including Baking Pot. Such replication, even at this smaller scale, is significant for its communicative power as a "standard grammar," expressing status differentiation (Ashmore 1992:173; Kurjack 1974:8).[3] The second element indicating authority is the feature referred to as a "shrine inset." The inset is similar in configuration to Room 1 of Structure II-A in the Baking Pot site core (Bullard and Bullard 1965:37). The Baking Pot rooms are unlike the typically vaulted "throne rooms" found in Structure A-1 at Cahal Pech (Awe 1992:74), which most often contain benches. The Baking Pot "rooms" could more appropriately be described as very large niches. Like Rooms 1 and 2 of Group II at Baking Pot, the shrine inset is indicative of a ritual focus for a powerful local elite.

The largest mound volumetrically, Structure 1 on the south, is also a significant communicator of structure function. It has been suggested by Ashmore (1992:178, 179) that the southern position is representative of the underworld and that the person who occupies such a locale "controls access to supernaturals" and is a "deliberate reiteration by the sovereign of his authority." A large central posthole through Structure 1–9th indicates that a substantial perishable superstructure once existed in the Late Classic (ca. A.D. 800). This posthole is apparently an interior support defining a large interior space with restricted access to certain areas, indicating a function other than domestic (Hendon 1991:906). Together, the ritual deposits that are present (see the section on Caches below), volumetric dominance within the group, physical attachment to Structure 2, and quality of construction materials all suggest that Structure 1 had an elaborated importance relative to the small, Late Classic period domestic Structures 3 and 4. We surmise that Structure 1 was the dwelling of the Bedran Group's lineage leader and also served as a meeting place for conducting administrative activities in relative privacy.

Burials

Interaction and integration with the civic center of Baking Pot are further supported by the burial data. There was a total of 12 Late Classic (ca. A.D. 600–900) period burials located along the primary axis of Structure 2. Both simple burials and cist burials (Welsh 1988:16–17) were recovered. The burials followed a chronological progression from the top of the structure late in the Tiger Run phase (ca. A.D. 650–700), to under the stairs early in the Spanish Lookout phase (ca. A.D. 700–800), to below the plaza floor late in the Spanish Lookout phase (ca. A.D. 800–900). Only one other interment was recorded at the Bedran Group, consisting of a simple grave of a one-year-old child placed in the terminal phase architecture of Structure 3. No grave goods were associated with this burial.

Two interments of the Tiger Run phase (ca. A.D. 600–700) were located under the terminal phase platform of Structure 2–3rd. Burial 2 (adult male), and 4 (adult female), were both cist burials (Welsh 1988:17). Both are similar in context to the male and female recovered from the cists located under the plaza at the base of Mound E of Group I at Baking Pot (Piehl 1997:64–66). One of the five vessels contained in Burial 2 of Struc-

Fig. 5.4. PSS glyph band on Orange Walk Incised bowl recovered from Burial 2, Structure 2, Bedran Group.

ture 2–3rd at Bedran was an Orange Walk Incised-type bowl incised with a Primary Standard Sequence (PSS) glyph band (fig. 5.4). The PSS glyph band on this vessel refers to "his drinking cup . . . tree-fresh cacao," which is similar in style and form to cacao vessels typically recovered from tombs of high-status individuals within site cores (Hall et al. 1990). Additionally, a large eccentric flint recovered from Burial 2 also indicates that the male interred here was of high status (Iannone and Conlon 1993:82).[4]

Burial 7, dating to A.D. 700–800, consisted solely of the complete skull of an adult female whose dentition showed evidence of filing. The skull was covered by an inverted McRae Impressed-type vessel (Gifford 1976: 259). The skull rested directly upon the plastered platform of the shrine. Incomplete or disarticulated skeletal remains are not necessarily evidence of lesser-status individuals. Burial 48 at Tikal was of a headless "elite" (Becker 1993:55) and demonstrates that not all incomplete skeletal remains represent sacrificial, lesser-status victims. As data summarized by Welsh (1988:tables 36, 37) indicate, burials of heads placed within, between, and under bowls are often associated with elite individuals.

Other interments were located beneath the terminal plaza floor at the base of Structure 2–3rd, including Burials 9 (juvenile male, 4–6 years of age), Burial 11 (adult male, 40–45+ years of age), and Burial 12 (adult). All were placed along the primary axis of the structure. Two burials (Burials 9 and 12) were placed directly above and below Burial 11, respectively. Placed on the right elbow of Burial 11 were the fragments of two long bones, a tibia and a fibula, belonging to the individual of Burial 9. The adolescent remains of Burial 9 may be considered grave goods associated with Burial 11. Other grave goods found in Burial 11 included two partial vessels and one miniature vessel. The location of Burial 9 atop Burial 11 suggests a possible association of a sacrificial victim subordinate, and possibly directly subservient, to the individual interred in Burial 11 (Welsh 1988:168–169). The adolescent of Burial 9 shares similarities to the types of sacrificial victims interred in Burial 160 at Group 7F-1 at Tikal (Becker

1993:61), more indicative of behavior associated with site center tomb interments (Haviland 1981:105; Laporte and Fialko 1990:52).

Caches

The data on caches also indicate status differentiation within the group as well as similarities to the epicentral practices of Baking Pot. Few caches were recovered from the primary axes of Structures 1, 3, and 4 at Bedran. They consisted mainly of metate fragments placed in Late Classic plaza construction fill at the base of the structures. However, a single, dedicatory partial-vessel-cache was recovered from beneath the platform modification of Structure 1–9th. The presence of this cache along with the remains of a small patch of cinnabar upon Structure 1–8th further indicates differential activity at this structure from the residences of Structures 3 and 4. Clearly, the majority of dedicatory deposits at Bedran were concentrated along the primary axis of Structure 2. A total of 25 caches were recovered from Structure 2 indicating that it was the main focus of the Bedran Group's ritual activities. Two of these caches are discussed below.

A cache (Cache 3) of 48 chert and obsidian eccentrics was found above, and likely associated with, Burial 5 (adult male, 35–40+ years of age). Both deposits were located under the central stairs of Structure 2–3rd near the shrine inset. Cache 3 is similar in content and location to a cache of 34 eccentrics found in Room 2 of Structure II-A at Baking Pot (Bullard and Bullard 1965:17). The architectural similarities between the shrine inset of Structure 2–3rd at Bedran and Rooms 1 and 2 at Baking Pot, were noted earlier. The similar occurrence of a large number of eccentrics in similar architectural locales of Bedran and Baking Pot further suggests a solidification of elite ritual practices between the epicenter and peripheral groups (Iannone 1992:253–254; Iannone and Conlon 1993:86).

Cache 16, a fragment of an effigy censer, was found directly in front of the shrine inset of Structure 2–3rd in the appended basal platform. Similar effigy censors have been recovered from burials 35 and 162 in front of Structure 7F-30 at Tikal (Becker 1993:56), and, when recovered at Santa Rita Corozal, correlates directly with "high-status groups" (D. Chase 1992:123; see also Rice 1999:38). The inclusion of a shrine inset for the specific purpose of "housing" ritual paraphernalia, such as effigy censors representative of gods or ancestors, or even the human heads of the ancestors themselves (Tozzer 1941:130; Welsh 1988:196), which Burial 7 represents, was an important feature in major site epicenters and, similarly, peripheral groups with high-status individuals (D. Chase and A. Chase 1998:319).

Ditched Fields

We now turn to an examination of why there was social affiliation between the inhabitants of Baking Pot and the peripheral dwelling elite at Bedran. Ultimately, as demonstrated at Copan and Seibal by Hendon (1992:35), the exercise of initial classification of potential elite residences may be less productive in the end than understanding the role that the inhabitants of large plazuela groups played in defining intrasite interaction and integration (see also Ashmore and Wilk 1988:3; Pendergast 1979:25). The ditch field system of the Bedran Settlement Cluster defines an important agricultural zone and its repercussions for the developmental sequence evidenced at the Bedran Group.

The term "linear indentation" was coined by Kirke (1980) to refer to shallow ditches in the field in which the Bedran Group is situated (fig. 5.2). The survey program performed by the BVAR Project has recorded a total of 1,300 linear meters of ditches with spot elevations indicating depths ranging from 15 cm to 180 cm below the modern surface (40 cm deep on average). The clay excavated from the ditched fields for use in construction activity at the Bedran Group provided significant water-holding capabilities. Test excavations in the ditches yielded broken "bifacial choppers" typically associated with agricultural activity (Willey et al. 1965:426), fragments of obsidian blades, and Spanish Lookout phase ceramics (A.D. 700–900). These data confirmed the temporal assignment of inception and use of the ditched fields. Furthermore, these ditches align exactly with the north-south axis of the terminal phase architecture of Structure 2 (approximately 10 degrees west of magnetic north).

The ditches extend beyond our surveyed limits of the Bedran Settlement Cluster (39.79 hectares) but encompass an area of roughly 64 hectares (Kirke 1980:283). The ditches that define this agricultural zone include an area large enough to have supported an estimated 330 people with a single crop of maize. The terminal phase population is estimated at roughly 105 people and thus a significant surplus was produced.[5] This surplus could have been destined for the Baking Pot epicenter and core (Harrison 1990:110) as either consumables or tribute. It is also possible that commercial crops could have been grown in this zone that may have been destined for redistribution elsewhere in the valley by elite residing in the epicenter of Baking Pot.[6] In either case, the Bedran Settlement Cluster inhabitants were producers of a substantial agricultural surplus beginning ca. A.D. 700 that coincided with the increased ritual caching and burials of the Bedran Group.

The Bedran Group data suggests that it became increasingly involved in elaborate ritual behavior over the period of its developmental history. Social unification and political interaction of the Bedran lineage leader(s) with the ruling elite of Baking Pot occurred sometime late in the Tiger Run phase (ca. A.D. 600–700). This social alliance is reflected by the relationship of the individuals of Burials 2 and 4 of Structure 2–3rd. The timing of this alliance corresponds with, and also accounts for, the proliferation and elaborateness of caches and burials at the Bedran Group. The high degree of ritual activity manipulated by the lineage leader(s) of the Bedran Group suggests its inhabitants were closely linked to the elite of Baking Pot, fully equipped for performing rituals of the "Great Tradition" (Gossen and Leventhal 1993:211). Their ability to perform high-status ritual acts demonstrates the reinforcement of ties with elite members of the Baking Pot community (Demarest 1992:143). However, the Bedran Group data suggest that its inhabitants did not enjoy total social inclusivity within the upper elite society until ca. A.D. 700, when the ditched field system was constructed. The construction of these ditched fields enabled the production of a substantial agricultural surplus, making the zone and its inhabitants economically important to the community of Baking Pot. Both social integration and economic interdependence with the epicenter of Baking Pot bore significant implications for supporting the Bedran Group's mimicry of architectural, burial and cache elaborateness and complexity.

Regional Implications for the Belize Valley

The late development of the Bedran Group follows the trend in the growth of plazuela groups from the Early Classic (ca. A.D. 300–600) onward in the valley (Willey et al. 1965:293, 566). The profusion of this community unit type in the Belize Valley of the Late Classic (ca. A.D. 600–900) also coincides with the Bedran Group's social integration and economic interaction with the Baking Pot epicentral elite. The emergence of minor centers in the Early Classic likely corresponds to a rapidly increasing stratified elite (Potter 1985:142; see also A. Chase and D. Chase 1992:13; Tourtellot et al. 1992:80), and a trend toward more definitive territorial claims through the direct control by a centralized authority (Haviland 1968:112; Willey et al. 1965:579; see also D. Chase and A. Chase 1992a:309). The data from Bedran conform to the observed trend of Late Classic primary elites attempting to assert direct control over the land and labor in their expanding realms (Lincoln 1985:75).[7]

We use the words "attempting to assert direct control" at centralization in deference to an alternative viewpoint of hierarchical relations between primary and secondary elite. However, heterarchical relations suggest a different organizational complexity wherein "relative ranking forms a basis for joint action" (Hendon and Joyce 1993:32). The interrelationships of the Bedran Group with the civic center of Baking Pot may best be viewed as a limited partnership whereby the primary and secondary elite best served their community in a cooperative, heterarchical, manner (Pendergast 1979:25; 1992:61). On a community level, the alliance of Bedran with Baking Pot was forged partly for purposes of effectively administrating the expanding Late Classic communities of the valley. It also enabled access to more distant resources that were locally owned, mainly those falling outside the immediate realm of the epicentral primary elite control.

That the administrative affairs of state likely befell the peripheral dwelling secondary elite is not a new insight (Culbert 1974:60, 66–68; Ford 1981:150, 1991a:40; Scarborough and Robertson 1986:174). Neither is the possibility that they were rank subordinates to primary elite dwelling in the central precinct of a major center (D. Chase and A. Chase 1992a:309; D. Chase et al. 1990:499; Haviland 1981:117; Willey et al. 1965:579). It has been suggested the "lesser magnates" of the periphery possessed their own power bases that could compromise primary elite power through elite internal competition (Potter 1985:142; Webster 1992:154–155). Following heterarchical lines of interrelationships, the economic peculiarities of the Bedran situation did not evolve separately from the need for political unity in the community (Willey 1953:381). Social unification provided a modicum of balance, "maintained through close and loose kinship ties" (Awe et al. 1991:29), between site control by epicentral elite and ancestral lineage kin-group autonomy at Bedran.

The political unification of the community through social integration underscores our impression of economic interaction superceding social affiliation in warranting greater accumulation of prestige items and associated ritual behavior. This also brings to mind our contention that minor centers were the loci where elite functioned. Defining territory is one function that minor centers performed (chapter 18), and has political ramifications for defining a civic center's realm. This may be why Nohoch Ek (Coe and Coe 1956), morphologically more elaborate and complex than the Bedran Group plazuela, was not endowed with an overwhelming array of caches and burials. This passive role was very likely primarily a prestige-based function and provided for only meager opportunities to access and acquire high-status items. In contrast, the active participation in economic exploitation at the Bedran Settlement Cluster allowed for a greater pre-ponderance of prestige items and behavior because of the significant im-plications for the Baking Pot community (Fried 1967; see also Sanders 1992:278). We are not advocating that the lineage leaders of the Bedran Group were of an elevated rank in status in comparison to the elite inhab-iting more morphologically complex minor centers. Rather, situations of social and political integration coincide with one aspect of rank within the elite stratum, but economic interrelationships placed individuals, even those of lesser rank within the elite stratum, in an advantageous position for warranting both the practices of high ritual and the acquisition of high-status items and signatures. In this circumstance the morphologically sim-plistic "larger plazuela" group of Bedran outdistanced the "minor center" of Nohoch Ek in archaeological signatures of elite integration.

Conclusion

The inability to readily recognize the Bedran Group plazuela as a "minor center" by its surface morphology alone has implications for correlating settlement hierarchy with social hierarchy. As microcosms of the macro-cosm, minor centers functioned variably within the social, political, and economic spheres of a community. We maintain that any group displaying characteristics more typically associated with the core of major centers is a strong indication of any group's integration and inclusion within a similar social stratum. While the overall pattern of behavior reflects the Bedran Group's inhabitants placement in the upper levels of ancient Maya soci-ety, this was achieved only partly through social integration. Its economic role heightened the Bedran Group's significance in the Baking Pot com-munity above and beyond its base social affiliations. When the role is simply sociopolitical, such as defining territory, then elite-status markers may not be so abundant as expected in an architectural complex of minor center stature.

Notes

1. A. Chase and D. Chase (1992:3) note the term *elite* is generally imprecisely defined but can be related to people of power and control (also see Hirth 1992:19; Kowalewski et al. 1992:136; Sanders 1992:278). We ascribe to Webster's defini-tion of *elite* (1992:136) as those people of prestige whose power and control

affected wider administrative spheres of politics, economics, religion, and warfare.

2. We employ Bullard's (1960:367–370) cluster, zone, and district terminology of settlement organization with an additional "group" designation. Thus, the plazuela Bedran Group is the focus for the Bedran Settlement Cluster that defines a zone in the southwestern district of Baking Pot.

3. Sites outside of major centers in the Belize Valley can display significant architectural conventions, such as ballcourts (e.g., Ferguson et al. 1996; Garber et al. 1994; McGovern 1994:110), more typically considered hallmarks of the civic centers in the region. Similar civic center architectural conventions, such as E-group "variants," are also commonly found in smaller centers of the Belize Valley. The Bedran Group E-Group variant replication, though nonfunctional as an observatory, denotes social standing and authority in the Baking Pot community and the region of the Belize Valley (also see Freidel 1981:190; Laporte 1993:299; von Falkenhausen 1985:127).

4. Iannone (1992; also see A. Chase and D. Chase 1992:11) presents a cautionary note regarding associating eccentric flints with elite individuals owing to a potentially skewed database through a focus within the major centers of the Maya. We are in concordance with Haviland (1982:429; also see Sabloff 1983:419–420; A. Chase and D. Chase 1992:11), who suggests a myriad of variables need to be considered before associating material remains with elite personages. However, as eccentrics are typically identified with "a charter of power" (Freidel 1986c:93; see also Iannone and Conlon 1993:84), we are confident the Bedran Group eccentrics represent the interaction between individuals of the elite social stratum.

5. The surveyed extent of Baking Pot presently represents 349 ha and 320 mounds (0.92 mounds/ha). Total mound count has been utilized to generate a population estimate (mounds × 5 people per mound) of 1,600 residents in the terminal phase of occupation for Baking Pot. In order to cross-check this population estimate, agricultural production potential and population consumption requirements were estimated closely following the method employed by Spencer et al. (1994). If all of the 349 ha surveyed extent of Baking Pot were employed in maize cultivation, an estimated population of between 1,799 and 2,855 people could have been supported. Although this range suggests the estimated population of 1,600 people may have been self-sustained in the environs of the Baking Pot civic center, the minimum production-consumption level (1,799) provides a clue to the role the Bedran Settlement Cluster played in agricultural production in the Baking Pot community. The 64 ha the ditched field system at Bedran covers could have produced enough crops to support 330 to 524 people, 225 to 419 more than the 105 people (21 mounds × 5 people per mound) estimated to have resided there in its terminal occupation phase. Agricultural production potential of two to four times more than that required by the Bedran Settlement Cluster inhabitants suggests a calculated plan for producing surplus foodstuffs. In the instance of minimum production levels at Baking Pot (1,799 people), Bedran

would have been an important supplier of consumable foodstuffs. At maximum production for Baking Pot (2,855 people), Bedran would have been free to produce commercial crops.

6. Willey et al. (1965:573) concluded that maize cultivation was likely restricted to hill slopes in the Belize Valley and was not extensively pursued in the alluvial flats. The alluvial flats may have been more advantageously exploited for the production of a commercial crop such as cacao (Willey et al. 1965:574). It is our impression, however, that the ditches of the Bedran Settlement Cluster zone, given their drainage and irrigation function, and the potentially diminished production and consumption capability of Baking Pot, especially within 500 m of the epicenter, more likely accommodated the cultivation of maize.

7. Webster (1992:136) makes the distinction of primary, ruling administrators, and secondary, occupational elite. Our use of the terms *primary* and *secondary* elite does not strictly conform to Webster's upper and lower ranking of elite. Instead, we use the term *primary elite* only to distinguish those elite residing within the monumental architectural complexes of the civic center and *secondary elite* for those elite residing outside these complexes. Our spatial distinction of primary and secondary elite is not meant to preclude the possibility of higher-ranking elite inhabiting zones or districts outside of the immediate civic centers.

Acknowledgments

We would like to thank the staff of the Department of Archaeology in Belize, including Commissioner John Morris, for the continued support of our research during the three seasons of investigations at the Bedran Settlement Cluster. The 1992 and 1993 field seasons were conducted under the auspices of the Belize Valley Archaeological Reconnaissance Project, directed by Jaime Awe. The 1994 field season of investigations were conducted under a permit held by Paul Healy, who, along with Jaime Awe, directed the Trent University Belize Valley Preclassic Maya Project. We would also like to thank Señor Abdala Bedran for permitting us access to the ancient mounds on his land. Survey at Baking Pot was greatly facilitated by the assistance of Mark August, Shawn Brisbin, Jennifer Ehret, Charles Golden, Cameron Griffith, and Gabriel Wrobel. Reconnaissance over a wider area was further enhanced by Angela Keller and Gyles Iannone. Iannone also performed the analysis of the eccentrics recovered from the Bedran Group. Other analyses were provided by Rhan-Ju Song (human remains) and Norbert Stanchly (faunal assemblage). Initial epigraphic analysis of the hieroglyphic vessels recovered from the Bedran Group were kindly provided by Nikolai Grube, Stephen Houston, and Dorie Reents-Budet. Our thanks are also extended to the excavation supervisory team, largely responsible for the success of the Bedran investigations: Grant Aylesworth, Joe Dantona, Kerri Finlayson, and Bobbi Hohmann. Kent Reilly provided editorial comments on a preliminary draft of this chapter, as did other anonymous reviewers, for which we are indebted. Any inaccuracies or omissions remain our sole responsibility.

6

Ancient Maya Settlement in the Valley of Peace Area

Lisa J. Lucero, Scott L. Fedick, Andrew Kinkella, and Sean M. Graebner

In their seminal book on Barton Ramie and the Belize River Valley, Gordon R. Willey and his colleagues (1965) asked several questions about ancient Maya society that are still relevant today. They realized that to reveal anything about ancient Maya social structure, it was necessary to move away from major centers to smaller settlement systems. As the chapters in this volume illustrate, this strategy continues to yield significant information. The major contributions of the Valley of Peace Archaeology (VOPA) project are twofold: we have expanded survey east beyond Cocos Bank, the eastern edge of Willey's survey area, and we address their question regarding where and why the Maya settled where they did and how they interacted with their physical and social surroundings.

Settlement decisions and density are largely related to agricultural potential of the soils. In the Belize River area there are two distinct resource zones, alluvial terraces and uplands. In the former, one finds minor centers and dispersed settlement (e.g., Barton Ramie, Saturday Creek). In the latter, one finds diverse settlement, from major centers to solitary farmsteads. In this chapter, we present results of a land evaluation and survey project conducted in the Valley of Peace area, situated north of the Belize River in central Belize. We first describe a predictive settlement model and mapping methods. We then describe seven surveyed areas selected based on their agricultural potential. We discuss the relationship of agricultural potential, settlement patterns, and social organization by briefly comparing results with those from the Belize River Archaeological Settlement Survey (BRASS) of the upper Belize River area where Fedick originally developed and applied the model (Fedick 1995, 1996; Fedick and Ford 1990; Ford and Fedick 1992).

Archaeology of the Valley of Peace Area

The VOPA research area is located in central Belize (40–120 m asl) north of the Belize River. The only previous archaeological research carried out in the VOPA area was a salvage operation conducted in 1982 when the Valley of Peace Village was founded (Awe 1984; Awe and Topsey 1984). Ceramic analysis indicates occupation from at least the Early Classic (ca. A.D. 250–550) through Terminal Classic (ca. A.D. 850–950) periods (Morris 1984).

The major goals of the VOPA project, initiated in 1997, were to assess a settlement pattern model devised by Fedick (1988) based on the agricultural potential of soils and to establish an initial regional chronology.

Land Evaluation and Predictive Modeling

An evaluation of land resources in and surrounding the Valley of Peace study area was conducted by Fedick prior to initiation of the VOPA project (Fedick 1988). Soil type definitions, properties, and mapped distributions are based on earlier, independent studies of soils in the Belize Valley (Birchall and Jenkin 1979; Jenkin et al. 1976). The soil maps used in the evaluation (Birchall and Jenkin 1979) were originally compiled at a scale of 1:50,000, a level of mapping intensity that distinguishes soil-type areas (mapping units) larger than about 10 ha in extent (Fedick 1996). The goal of the evaluation was to characterize the agricultural capability of soils from the perspective of hand-cultivation technology by farmers concerned with the potential for intensification (see Fedick 1995, 1996:121–122). The evaluation quantified limitations to cultivation as indicated by effective root zone, susceptibility to erosion, workability, drainage, and inherent fertility. Each evaluated soil type was then assigned to one of five capability classes (I–V), with Class I having the fewest limitations and Class V having the greatest limitations.

The resulting land evaluation also serves to predict ancient Maya residential settlement distribution. The model assumes that people will choose to reside in resource zones that are most capable of supporting intensive hand-cultivation and home gardens. Less intensive forms of cultivation, such as slash-and-burn milpa farming, would be conducted in lands surrounding the settlement (Fedick 1996).

A few qualifying statements are necessary in applying the land evaluation for the VOPA study area as a predictive model for settlement distribution. First, since the scale of the soil maps will not distinguish soil areas less
that 10 ha in extent, there will be cases where specific patches of land may
not conform to the generalized land evaluation as depicted on the map. In
the case of the BRASS study, this problem was resolved through detailed
mapping of soils within the archaeological survey transects (Fedick 1988,
1995; Ford and Fedick 1992). The refinement of the map data has not yet
been conducted in the VOPA survey areas. Second, the predictive model
identifies classes of land that are most likely to contain ancient settlements,
but not the specific location of a settlement within a patch of land. Third,
the model works best at predicting the locations for communities where
intensive gardening was practiced. Isolated farmsteads were likely to have
been established as secondary residences for farmers conducting seasonal
milpa cultivation in less desirable lands at greater distances from their primary residence. Fourth, and perhaps most important, the predictive model
is based on locational decisions most likely to have been made by independent farming households. Decisions to locate settlement in areas not
suitable for agriculture would require alternative explanations, such as
unequal access to land, specialized household activities other than agricultural production, or locational decisions dictated or restricted by administrators higher up in the political hierarchy.

Archaeological Fieldwork, 1997–2001

The 1997 VOPA survey was designed to investigate accessible locations as
per Fedick's predictive model. Modern roads and trails provided access to
the full range of land Capability Classes, where modern farmsteads and
recently cleared fields were examined for evidence of ancient settlement.
Visibility in the cleared fields was typically adequate. Tape and compass
maps were generated for each exposed site, and their UTM coordinates
were determined using a GPS unit. When possible, we collected diagnostic
ceramics from mound surfaces. Ceramic analysis was conducted using the
ceramic chronology developed for Barton Ramie (Gifford 1976), located
about 20 km to the southwest. In general, analysis indicates the ancient
Maya occupied the area from about the Middle Preclassic (ca. 900–400
B.C.) through at least the Late Classic (ca. A.D. 550–850), if not later (ca.
1200+).

In 1998 we mapped and collected ceramic data from one test pit and
several looter's trenches in structures located at Cara Blanca Pool 1 in the

north part of the project area. We also explored the pool for ritual offerings (Kinkella 2000; Osterholtz 1999). Finally, we mapped the minor river center of Saturday Creek and collected surface ceramics. In 1999, we test excavated 10 mounds at Saturday Creek to collect chronological data. In 2001, we conducted extensive excavations at Saturday Creek and mapped Yalbac, a major center 19 km northwest of Saturday Creek.

Results: The Agricultural Landscape

The land evaluation (table 6.1) and resulting map (fig. 6.1) represent a landscape viewed from the perspective of agricultural capability under hand-cultivation technology. The VOPA study area is 308 km², 300 km² of which has been classified (table 6.2). The other 8 km² of the area (3 percent) are bodies of water, land outside of the original soil-mapping project area, or land outside of the VOPA study area on the south side of the Belize River.

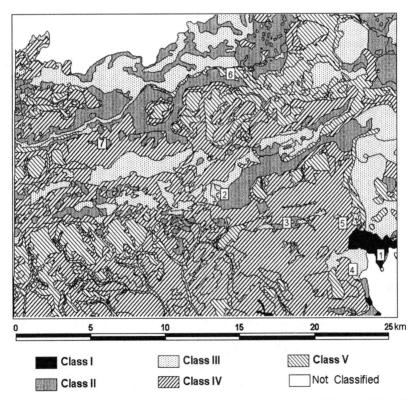

Fig. 6.1. Land classes in the VOPA area: (1) Saturday Creek; (2) Old Tom's Milpa; (3) Terrence Flowers' Pasture; (4) Three Sisters; (5) Milpa 1; (6) Cara Blanca; (7) Yalbac.

Table 6.1. Soil attributes and land capability classes

Soil series (phase)	Fertility	Erosion	Root Zone	Workability	Drainage	Rating total	Capability class[a]
Young Girl	1	1	1	1	1	5	I
Listowel	2	1	1	1	1	6	I
Chorro	1	2	2	1	1	7	II
Piedregal	1	2	3	1	1	8	II
Barton Ramie	1	1	3	1	3	9	II
Banana Bank	1	1	4	1	2	9	II
Seven Mile	1	1	3	3	2	10	II
Mumble de Peg	1	1	4	3	1	10	II
Seven Mile (Shallow)	1	2	3	3	2	11	III
Meditation (Pale)	2	1	4	1	3	11	III
Tambos (Shallow)	2	1	3	3	2	11	III
Banana Bank (Wet)	1	1	4	3	4	13	III
Piedregal (Hill)	1	4	4	2	2	13	III
Rancho Delores	2	1	4	4	2	13	III
Tambos	2	1	4	4	3	14	IV
Spanish Lookout	2	2	4	4	3	15	IV
Beaver Dam	3	1	4	4	4	16	IV
Iguana	3	3	3	3	4	16	IV
Cara Blanca	4	1	4	3	4	16	IV
Norland	3	3	3	4	4	17	V
Cadena Creek	2	3	4	4	4	17	V
Akalche	4	1	4	4	4	17	V
Akalche (Sand)	4	1	4	4	4	17	V
Garbutt (Sand)	1	1	1	2	1	6	V[b]
Pucte	?	1	4	?	4	9+	V[c]

a. Class limitations: I, few or none; II, some: reduces plant choices or may need to use conservation techniques; III, severe: above, even more so, or both; IV, very severe: restricted plant choices or management, or both; V, generally not suited for agriculture unless major reclamation and conservation techniques used.

b. In addition to the rating factors used, this soil is subject to annual or nearly annual flooding by the Belize River.

c. Swamp soil not suitable for habitation without substantial modification.

The most likely sites for the location of ancient communities are within land Capability Classes I and II. Class I lands are restricted in extent (1 percent), and are found only in the fertile, well-drained alluvium adjacent to the Belize River. Class II lands (16 percent) are fertile well-drained soils of the uplands that are well suited for communities practicing intensive

Table 6.2. VOPA soil classes

Class	Percentage of study area
I	1
II	16
III	19
IV	44
V	17

cultivation in home gardens and adjacent fields. Class III lands (19 percent) have agricultural limitations related primarily to steep slopes or impeded drainage. Class III lands are less suitable for residential construction, although hilltops, or better-drained locations within low areas, are potentially habitable. Class III lands are suitable for swidden cultivation and can be intensified through terracing on hill slopes or improvement of drainage in low areas. Class IV lands are the most common type in the study area (44 percent) but are not well suited for residential locations, as the soils are generally poorly drained. The Class IV lands are marginally suitable for swidden cultivation and are not favored by Maya farmers of the area today. Field houses or secondary residences may be established in Class IV lands in areas far from more suitable residential locations. Class V lands (17 percent) are very poorly suited as either residential sites or for agricultural production. A total of seven discrete areas were surveyed, each of which is described below.

Saturday Creek

Saturday Creek is a minor river center on the north side of the Belize River (map 1), and is similar in layout to Barton Ramie. It includes solitary mounds, patio groups, range structures or palaces, and temples over 10 m in height and a ballcourt of uncut stone facades with clay fill (fig. 6.2). Site layout does not appear to have been planned (Arie 2001). The core area of Saturday Creek rests upon an expansive terrace, which likely has been modified. Analysis of surface ceramics collected demonstrates a Middle Preclassic through Postclassic occupation (ca. 900 B.C.–A.D. 1200).

Saturday Creek is located within the only expanse of Class I lands (Young Girl and Listowel series) in the VOPA study area, consisting of rich alluvial soils. Seventy-nine structures were mapped in a 0.81 km² area bounded by roads on the north side of the river. Most of the site is located in a plowed field. It is currently intensively cultivated by Mennonite farmers and plowed at least twice a year to plant maize, beans, and water-

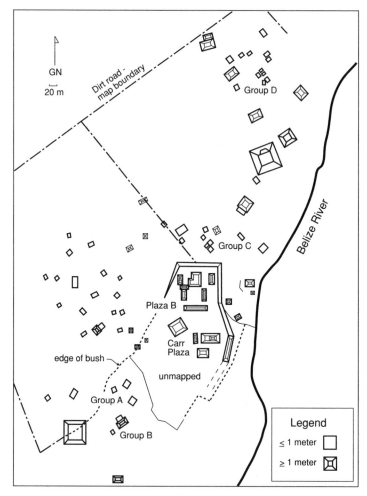

Fig. 6.2. Saturday Creek (map produced by A. Kinkella and L. J. Lucero).

melon. Consequently, mounds in the plowed field have been reduced in height and spread in areal extent. A large portion of the site (ca. 350 × 300 m), including the center core, has not been plowed. The core area has not been mapped in its entirety due to dense secondary growth. Adjacent to the settlement area is an expanse of Class V lands (Garbutt series), which are of high fertility, but are considered risky for cultivation and unsuitable for settlement due to annual or nearly annual flooding. While it was impossible to wade through the deep, soggy soils of this low-lying terrace in 1998, the area was dry in 1999, and survey did not indicate the presence of any cultural remains.

There are 53 solitary mounds (67 percent) that likely represent raised foundations for thatched wattle-and-daub structures. Surface artifacts such as plain and decorated ceramic bowls and jars, grinding stone fragments, chert tools, obsidian cutting blades, and daub indicate a probable domestic function (Lucero 2001). The four plazuela groups mapped at Saturday Creek (A–D) each consist of four to five mounds for a total of 15 mounds (19 percent). Surface artifacts differ from those at solitary mounds (e.g., ceramic figurine fragments, decorated vase sherds, and obsidian cores) and suggest higher social status.

Old Tom's Milpa

Old Tom's Milpa consists of a series of hills and the surrounding flat-lying area (fig. 6.1). The area surveyed was approximately 200 × 100 m. Due to time constraints, we only mapped the one mound on the top of a large hill. This mound was over 8 m in height with two major looter's trenches. At the base of the hill were other mounds about 1.5–2 m in height extending out from the side of the hill. No additional mounds were observed in the 200 × 100 m survey area, although visibility was difficult due to dense secondary growth. Surface sherds were too eroded for chronological assessment.

The mapped area of Old Tom's Milpa is situated at the southwest end of a large expanse of Class II soils. The tall, pyramidal mound is located on the summit of a hill with Class III agricultural land (Piedregal series, Hill phase). The smaller mounds at the base of the hill are within Class II soils (Chorro series).

Terrence Flowers' Pasture

Terrence Flowers' Pasture is approximately 620 × 230 m and is located on the crest of a hill in the northeast part of the Valley of Peace village (fig. 6.1). Modern construction includes a house, corral, and pigpens. Prehispanic settlement consists of solitary mounds (N = 4) and mound groups (N = 3, ranging from 14 × 12 m to 5 × 5 m and 5 m to 1 m high) on Class II soils (Chorro series). The mounds cluster east-west along the hillside and/or natural or artificial terraces. A larger mound, (14 × 12 m, 4+ m high) on top of a platform is constructed with cobble and boulder fill, plaster floors, and faced boulders. The other structures do not have standing walls. Preliminary ceramic analysis indicates Middle Preclassic through the Late Classic occupation. No settlement is present in the flat, low-lying expanse below the hillside, which comprises Class IV soils (Spanish Lookout series), which are particularly clayey.

Three Sisters

This floodplain site is located about 2 km southwest of Saturday Creek and about half a kilometer west of the Belize River (fig. 6.1). Three Sisters is a small monumental complex surrounded by dispersed settlement. This is the site that Willey et al. (1965:13) refer to as Cocos Bank, the easternmost extent of their survey area:

> Cocos Bank is about 20 km. northeast of Barton Ramie air line distance, but over 40 km. via the river. The terrain is flat alluvial soil. The ceremonial group is raised on a square, probably earth-filled, basal platform which is about 100 m. across and about 5.00 m. high. . . . Four rectangular mounds are placed on the edges of the basal platform so as to form a plaza group. The highest of these, on the east side, rise 4.00 to 5.00 m above the plaza and is thus 9.0 or 10 m above the ground level. A bulldozer cut at one corner of this highest mound shows rubble and earth fill with boulder retaining walls. The other mounds are one meter or so high and have signs of smaller superimposed platforms. Traces of stone pavement, at ground level, can be seen adjacent to the east side of the Cocos Bank group. On the north, west, and south sides of the group are deep pits from which soil was probably obtained for the construction of the mounds. These depressions now form small ponds. In addition to the ceremonial group, housemounds and occasional "plazuelas" are scattered on the flat alluvial terrain both at Cocos Bank and at the nearby Banana Bank.

The current landowner, John Carr of Banana Bank Ranch and Lodge, renamed the site Three Sisters based on local stories about three Maya sisters being entombed in the largest structure, TS-1. The large architectural features cluster near an aguada on top of a large artificially flattened hilltop approximately 195 × 180 m. The largest structure, TS-1, has at least four corbel arch rooms and is ca. 35 × 15 m, 5 m high. While there is evidence for further settlement between the complex and river, the dense secondary growth made survey difficult.

The dispersed settlement located west of the complex has been intensively plowed by Mennonite farmers. We mapped nine solitary mounds ranging from 0.5 (plowed) to 1.5 (unplowed) m in height, and 35 × 30 m (plowed) to 9 × 9 m (unplowed) in size. Surface collections suggest that prehistoric occupants had access to a variety of prestige or exotic goods, including Pachuca obsidian and hematite ornaments. Ceramic types indicate Early Classic (ca. A.D. 250–550) and Late Classic (ca. A.D. 550–850) occupation.

Three Sisters is situated in a large expanse of Class III lands (Banana Bank series, Wet phase). Field observations indicate that the Three Sisters site is not located in a Wet phase zone, and would accurately be classified as Class II (Banana Bank series).

Milpa 1

Milpa 1 is located in the eastern sector of the project area and is about 500 × 170 m (fig. 6.1). It includes various architectural types from solitary mounds (N = 4) to multimound platform groups (N = 3). The solitary mounds range in size from 12 × 12 m (1.33 m high) to 5 × 4 m (0.57 m high). The three-structure group mounds range in size from 11 × 9 to 7 × 7 m (heights range from 1.1 to 0.2 m). Preliminary ceramic analysis indicates Early Classic (ca. A.D. 250–550) and Late Classic (ca. A.D. 550–850) occupation. We also collected obsidian and polychrome pottery from the larger structures. While it is not clear in figure 6.1, Milpa 1 is situated in a patch of Class II lands (Piedregal series) that is bordered on the north by poorer agricultural soils of Class IV. While Class III land (Piedregal series, Hill phase) is indicated on the 1:50,000 maps, on site observation indicates that structures are on relatively level areas of Piedregal soils (not Hill phase) or Class II lands.

Cara Blanca

Cara Blanca consists of 22 pools extending east-west along the base of limestone cliffs/ridges (up to ca. 80–100 m high) in the northern section of the VOPA area (fig. 6.1). This is an uninhabited expanse of primary forest currently owned by a logging and citrus company. Of the six pools investigated in 1998, four have been distinguished as springs/wells (vs. rain-fed pools). The source of springs/wells consists of a subsurface cave and river system. All are surrounded by Class V land (Cadena Creek series) with black, poorly drained clay soils that flood during the rainy season.

The only pool associated with settlement is Pool 1, defined as a spring/well. The pool measures approximately 100 × 61 m and is surrounded by seven mounds. Looter's trenches show that the largest structure (Str. 1, 22 × 15 m, 4 m high) is a multiroomed vaulted building. Test excavations yielded mostly jar rims (63 percent of total rims) largely dating to the Late

Classic (79 percent, A.D. 700–900) (Kinkella 2000), which the Maya may have used to collect sacred water. In 1998, two scuba divers explored the pool. The sheer pool walls, relatively poor visibility (c. 10 m) and depth (40 m), however, prevented them reaching bottom (Osterholtz 1999). Consequently, we still do not know if the Maya made offerings in this particular pool, though we expect they did.

We only briefly visited five other pools. Pool 2 is located about 1 km west-southwest of Pool 1. This pool is known as Cara Blanca or "white face," aptly named for the steep cliff above (about 80–100 m in height). Also near Pool 1 is Pool 3, a clear, teal blue pool with good visibility and a steep drop-off. East of Pool 3, following the base of the ridge, is Pool 4, east of which is Pool 5 and Pool 6.

The limited survey we conducted north of Pool 1 in the surrounding ridges and cliffs also did not reveal any obvious settlement. These areas consist of Class III land (Piedregal Hill series) with relatively severe restrictions regarding intensive agriculture.

The Cara Blanca area is unique. Although there is plentiful water, steep cliffs and swampy/clayey soils present considerable limitations. The structures at Pool 1 are located on soils poorly suited for agriculture (Class V), as well as a seemingly undesirable location for residences. It seems clear that the structures built in association with Pool 1 were not located with consideration for agricultural activities, at least not for home gardens. Apparently, there were other reasons why the Maya built at Pool 1.

Yalbac

The medium-sized major center of Yalbac is located in the uplands along a perennial stream, Yalbac Creek, in central Belize. There are at least 19 monumental core structures and 28 looter's trenches (not all shown on fig. 6.3). The core consists of five major temples, several range structures, a ballcourt, possible causeways, three large plazas, and an acropolis over 20 m tall. We also excavated 1 × 2 m test pits in the centers of Plazas 2 and 3 to collect chronological information. They each had at least six construction phases consisting of plaster floors and cobble ballasts that date from 300 B.C. to A.D. 900.

Plaza 2 is ca. 70 × 49 m, around which are seven monumental structures, two of which comprise a temple ballcourt (Structures 2B and 2C). Plaza 3 is ca. 52 × 48 m, around which are six large buildings. Plaza 1 is the smallest (37 × 35 m), and is ringed by five structures, one of which is the

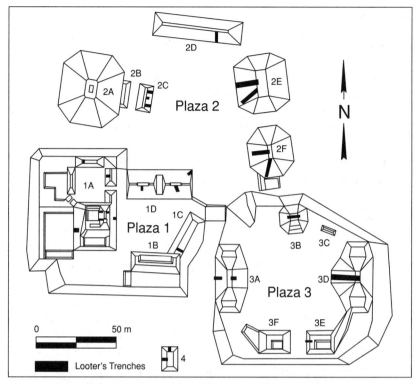

Fig. 6.3. Yalbac (map produced by S. M. Graebner and J. Wakeman).

acropolis (1A). The acropolis is ca. 57 × 52 m and over 20 m in height. It has four sunken plazas on top, and at least 18 structures. One of the looter's trenches (LT 1) on top has exposed two rooms, one with an intact corbel arch and red-plastered walls. Another (LT 2) has exposed a bench that overlooks Plaza 1.

We also surveyed the area around the core. The majority of settlement consists of solitary mounds, though we also noted groups of three to six structures, all constructed with cut stone. Surface ceramics were collected from 78 structures, which predominantly date to ca. A.D. 700–900 but range from ca. A.D. 400 to 1150–1500 (Conlon and Ehret 2002). Over 150 hinterland structures were mapped in an area roughly 5 km². The highest density of structures is located northwest of Yalbac in hilly areas largely on Class II (Seven Mile, Chorro series) and Class III (Piedregal series, Hill phase) soils. The core was built on Class II land (Chorro series), surrounded by Class IV land (Tambos series).

Discussion

In the Belize River Archaeological Settlement Survey (BRASS) area where Fedick (1988) first devised the predictive settlement model, he found the highest residential density in Class II soils, followed by Class I soils (table 6.3). Settlement generally concentrated in the well-drained alluvium adjacent to the river, as well as on the well-drained fertile, limestone-derived soils in the surrounding higher elevations (Ford 1990; Ford and Fedick 1992). During the Late Preclassic period (ca. 400 B.C.–A.D. 250), settlement increased and spread throughout the well-drained upland areas. This pattern more or less continued through the Late Classic period (ca. A.D. 550–850), when settlement spread into areas with poorer soils, or slow-draining marly soils (Ford 1990). Evidence from areas with large tracts of productive land indicates the presence of farming activities, wealth differentiation, and civic-ceremonial centers (Fedick and Ford 1990; Ford 1991a; Ford and Fedick 1992). Evidence from areas with less productive land indicates the presence of diverse economic activities, less wealth, and few, small, or no centers (Lucero 2001). Similar to settlement patterns in the BRASS area, VOPA settlement also largely corresponds to agricultural potential of the soils.

It is clear that the fertile alluvial soils found at Saturday Creek provided its former inhabitants with the means to sustain a relatively dense community for over a millennium. While Class I soils of Saturday Creek have a relatively high settlement density, it is lower than that found in the upper Belize River area (table 6.4). This pattern might partially be explained if the unsettled areas of the settlement were used for particular crops such as cotton and cacao. As figure 6.2 illustrates, there are sections in the mapped area that do not show any settlement. In addition, we were not able to map all the structures in the unplowed area due to dense vegetation; this fact would at least partially account for the differ-

Table 6.3. Residential unit density by soil class in the upper Belize River area

Class	RU/km²	Structure/km²
I	98	157 (average 1.6 structures/RU)
II	208	291 (average 1.4 structures/RU)
III	46	46
IV	3	3
V	0	0

Source: After Fedick 1996a: tables 7.3, 7.4.

Table 6.4. Average structure/residential unit per km^2

Class	VOPA	BRASS
I	97/84	157/98
II alluvial	48/48	_[1]
II non-alluvial	189/157	291/208
III	0[2]	46/46
IV	0	3/3
V	19/11	0

Notes: 1 = not present in the Brass survey transects; 2 = data not available for Old Tom's Milpa, only for Cara Blanca.

ence. No settlement was found on Class V soils in the BRASS area or at Saturday Creek.

The relatively rich Class II soils with only a few limitations found at Old Tom's Milpa provides a reasonable explanation for the location of settlement in the flat-lying area. The large mound on top of the hill could have provided local religious or administrative functions for the farmers living below. Settlement density differs from that found in the BRASS area, perhaps because access to the area was controlled by a landowner. Water would not have been a problem, as there is a creek within walking distance, just over 1 km.

Yalbac's location near water and good land provided the means to sustain large enough populations to build monumental architecture. The core of Yalbac lies on top a natural, and perhaps modified hill on Class II soils surrounded by Class IV soils nearby pockets of Class II and Class III land. Yalbac Creek provided water for daily needs, as well as a probable trade route. Hinterland farmers provided foodstuffs and labor for Yalbac royal and elite families. Our preliminary density figures are not adequate to compare with BRASS data.

Settlement density at Terrence Flowers' Pasture is comparable to that found in the BRASS area. The mounds on Class II soils for the most part were relatively small compared to other areas. It is possible that the area was used for living areas and home gardens, and that milpas were located somewhere else. This fact likely has to do with the area being hilly and with limestone outcrops. In addition, the flat-lying areas are clayey (Class IV). When it is dry, it is rock hard; when it is wet, it becomes a mire. Consequently, this area is not suitable for living or planting. The noticeably larger structure on the west side of the pasture could have provided some local religious and/or political functions for the densely packed community.

Three Sisters is located near water on well-drained alluvium (Class II), with a much lower settlement density than that found in the upper Belize River area. The density is more in line with BRASS alluvial settlement on Class I soils—largely dispersed solitary mounds. It may have been the case that inhabitants in the Three Sisters area grew cash crops such as cacao and cotton, and that occupants of the large structures located on top of the platform owned or controlled surrounding land.

Milpa 1 settlement appears to represent a community of relatively well off farmers based on the distribution of obsidian and polychrome pottery. This is not surprising since they lived on Class II soils abutting Class I alluvium.

The only settlement found in the Cara Blanca area was within the poorly drained Class V lands, which suggests that the restricted settlement in this area had a special purpose, perhaps religious in nature. Openings in the earth, especially pools and caves, were and are considered by the Maya as portals to the underworld or Xibalba (Andrews and Corletta 1995; Thompson 1970). Its location on the edge of the pool is similar to other sacred water bodies (e.g., Chichen Itza, Dzibilchaltun). The concentration of so many pools in one area might indicate that Cara Blanca was a sacred place to the prehispanic Maya, perhaps as a pilgrimage center (e.g., Lake Amatitlan, Guatemala; Borhegyi 1959). The major centers of Yalbac and San Jose are both about 10 km from Cara Blanca, and the minor center of Saturday Creek is just over 10 km distant. The Maya may have collected sacred water for special religious and ceremonial events that take place either at the pool(s) or centers.

As table 6.4 shows, there is some variability in average BRASS and VOPA settlement densities. It is clear that in both cases, the greatest settlement densities are in the best available lands of the uplands (Class II). The model seems to work quite well for predicting the type of land with which dense settlement is associated. The second-highest densities are in the best soils of the alluvial bottom. In the VOPA area, the third-highest densities are in Class II alluvium, just as might be expected. In both areas, the Maya avoided settling lands of lower capability. The one notable exception is Cara Blanca, which suggests that the Maya did not build there with agricultural considerations in mind.

Evaluating the land-based model for settlement requires some accommodation for differences in scale of resolution between the generalized 1:50,000 scale soil maps and the observations made in the field. In a few instances, field observation indicated that ancient settlement and the immediate surrounding vicinity consisted of land that was more level or better drained than the generalized class of land as characterized by the land-class map. In all such cases, in the VOPA area as well as in the BRASS area, where there was a difference between the land class observed on site and that characterized on the 1:50,000 scale map, the settlement was always situated in a better land class than that of the generalized map. This type of discrepancy is to be expected when working with generalized maps, and is fairly easy to compensate for when associations between soil types are well known and when differences in land classification pertain to easily distinguishable characteristics such as slope.

Conclusion

Willey et al. (1965) realized the significance of the relationship between settlement and social structure. The results of the VOPA survey project show that understanding the economic landscape can reveal key aspects about settlement patterns and, consequently, social organization. Obviously, in areas with large tracts of good land, archaeologists find higher settlement densities. There is also evidence for greater wealth differentiation and political power represented through larger centers and more monumental architecture and exotic goods.

In conclusion, the use of a model to predict settlement location based on soil type is quite useful when taking into account available economic resources. However, it is also clear that factors other than economic ones need to be taken into consideration when using this survey strategy, specifically the sacred landscape. Even with plenty of critical resources available, Cara Blanca was only sparsely settled. Did elites at Saturday Creek or the nearby major centers of Yalbac or San Jose control this potential sacred area? To fully appreciate prehistoric sociopolitical organization, archaeologists are going to have to understand how aspects of the varied landscape—economic, social, and sacred—articulated. The use of the predictive model in conjunction with archaeologists appreciating the different aspects of the landscape can provide significant data in our attempt to reveal ancient Maya lifeways.

Acknowledgments

We would like to thank John Morris, Acting Archaeology Commissioner in 1997 and 1998, Allan Moore in 1999, and George Thompson in 2001. We could not have conducted the research in 1997 through 1999 without the support of Robert Vitolo, John and Carolyn Carr of Banana Bank, David Brennan, Berniece Skinner, Robert Vannix, and a NMSU Minigrant. Funding for the 2001 season was provided by a National Science Foundation grant (BCS #0004410). Ceramic analysis in the 2001 season was conducted by James Conlon and Jennifer Ehret, which is gratefully acknowledged. We would also like to thank Warren Walker for generating the GIS map, and James L. Wakeman and Lonnie Mehlin for their surveying assistance in 1997.

7

Cahal Pech

The Middle Formative Period

Paul F. Healy, David Cheetham, Terry G. Powis, Jaime J. Awe

Cahal Pech is a medium-sized Maya center located about 2 km south of the confluence of the Macal and Mopan Rivers (map 1). The central precinct is situated atop a steep hill overlooking the Belize River Valley with a commanding view of the Maya Mountains to the south (fig. 7.1). Excavations indicate that the site flourished during the Classic period (A.D. 250–900), when its sustaining area may have been as large as 10 km² (Awe 1992:60; Ball 1993b). The Classic period central precinct consisted of at least 34 large masonry structures compacted on an imposing acropolis approximately 1.5 hectares in size. This area featured temple pyramids up to 24 m tall, single and multistoried range structures, large public plazas and small elite courtyards, two ballcourts, reservoirs, an entrance ramp or causeway, and seven plain stone monuments (Awe et al. 1990, 1991; Awe and Healy 1994:195; Ball and Taschek 1991; Ferguson et al. 1996; Satterthwaite 1951). All excavated central precinct architecture (10/34 structures, 34 percent) revealed Late Classic construction or refurbishing. This Late Classic period configuration, however, was the outcome of nearly 2,000 years of civic planning (Healy 1999; Healy and Awe 1995a, 1995b, 1996). A similar trajectory of growth, albeit on a smaller scale, is evident at several groups of residential and civic-ceremonial architecture in the Cahal Pech periphery.

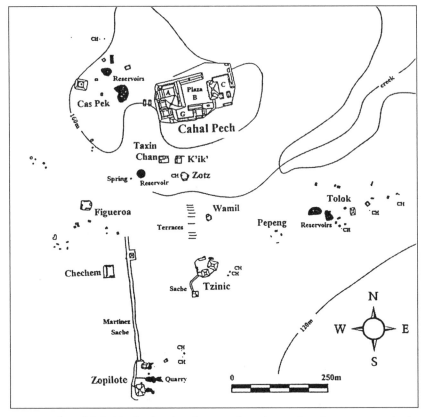

Fig. 7.1. Plan of Cahal Pech, showing the central precinct and settlement groups in the southern periphery.

Architecture and Settlement

Most of the Classic period architecture at Cahal Pech covers earlier (Formative period) construction. The accessibility of these early deposits enabled us to enhance the Formative period archaeological record of the valley, a desirable objective in light of significant advances being made in early Maya research in northern Belize (Hammond 1986; Hammond 1991b; Hammond et al. 1991), the central Petén (Laporte and Valdés 1993), the Mirador Basin of northern Petén (Dahlin 1984; Forsyth 1989, 1993; Hansen 1990, 1991a; Matheny 1986a, 1986b, 1987), and elsewhere.

The stratigraphic excavations of Structure B-4 (Awe 1992:106–143; Cheetham 1995) and a series of large-scale, horizontal excavations and smaller test pits into Plaza B (fig. 7.2) (Cheetham 1996) yielded data that

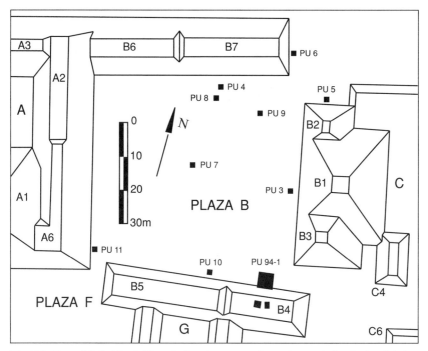

Fig. 7.2. Plan of Cahal Pech Plaza B showing excavation units carried to bedrock (after Cheetham 1996: fig. 1).

enabled the definition a new phase for the valley, called Cunil (ca. 1100–900 B.C.). These excavations also exposed extensive deposits dated to the succeeding early (ca. 900–700 B.C.) and late (ca. 700–350 B.C.) facets of the Middle Formative period (hereafter called EMF and LMF), equivalent to the early and late Jenney Creek phases at Barton Ramie (Gifford 1976).[1] The total exposure of Formative deposits in Plaza B (excavations carried to bedrock) was approximately 55 m².

A series of radiocarbon dates generated on charcoal samples from Plaza B exposures (table 7.1) bracket the sequence of Cunil phase buildings between 1100 and 900 B.C. Structure B-4 provided the most detailed and lengthy stratigraphic sequence at Cahal Pech: 13 building platforms, the first 10 of which were built during the Cunil, EMF, and LMF phases.[2] Prior to any known construction, however, there is some evidence that the paleosol below Structure B-4 was a living surface. This very compact, dark and greasy deposit (20–30 cm thick) yielded abundant chert debitage, but no ceramics aside from minute, trampled sherds on the topmost surface. Cheetham (1995:27) tentatively suggests that this slowly formed deposit is

Table 7.1. Middle Formative radiocarbon dates from Cahal Pech site core and settlement zone

Site	Provenience	Phase	Beta #	Radiocarbon age b.p.	Radiocarbon age b.c.	Calibrated 1 sigma b.c.	Calibrated 2 sigma
Cahal Pech	B-4 12-sub	Cunil	77207	2930 ± 50	980 ± 50	1200–1020	1275 (1120) 980
Cahal Pech	B-4 11-sub	Cunil	56765	2730 ± 140	780 ± 140	1020–795	1270 (845) 525
Cahal Pech	B-4 11-sub	Cunil	77204	2710 ± 120	760 ± 120	980–795	1135 (830) 745 and 700–530
Cahal Pech	B-4 10a-sub	Cunil	77205	2800 ± 50	850 ± 50	1000–890	1045 (925) 825
Cahal Pech	B-4 10c-sub	Cunil	40865	2740 ± 70	790 ± 70	940–820	1030 (885) 795
Cahal Pech	B-4 9-sub	EK	40864	2720 ± 60	770 ± 60	915–815	995 (840) 795
Cahal Pech	B-4 7-sub	LK	40863	2470 ± 90	520 ± 90	785–405	810 (750, 695, 540) 385
Tolok	Str. 14 Level 5	LK	77201	2370 ± 60	420 ± 60	485–465 and 425–385	760–670 and 550 (400) 365
Cas Pek	Str. C Level 11	LK	77203	2230 ± 50	280 ± 50	375–195	390 (335, 290, 230) 165
Tolok	Str. 1 bedrock	LK	77199	2220 ± 100	270 ± 100	390–150	415 (350, 300, 215) 5

Source: After Awe 1992: appendix 2, 405–406; Healy and Awe 1995: tables 1–2.

Notes: All samples are wood charcoal. Dates in parentheses indicate calibration curve intercepts. EK = early facet Kanluk (EMF); LK = late facet Kanluk (LMF).

indicative of a preceramic occupation, but larger-scale excavations are required to determine its true nature.

The first substructural platform in the Structure B-4 sequence (13–sub) is 0.48 m tall as measured from the south, the north side merging with the grade of the natural hill. It was constructed of packed marl and earth intermixed with ashy loam. The small excavation unit revealed a posthole and drain at the edge of the mound summit. The layout of the wattle-and-daub superstructure remains unknown, but the configuration of the platform suggests that the building(s) was round or apsidal. The subsequent platform (12–sub) is 0.84 m tall (south side). It too was constructed of packed marl and is circular in plan with two small, crude steps leading to the summit from the south side. The four postholes evince no obvious pattern, but the shape of the platform (estimated diameter 7.2 m) suggests a circular superstructure. The earliest radiocarbon date (Beta-77207, 2930 ± 50 b.p., calibrated to b.c. 1200–1020 1 sigma) is associated with the fill of this platform (table 7.1). The third Structure B-4 platform (11–sub) involved raising and leveling the area to the immediate south. Although little can be said of the Structure B-4/11–sub superstructure due to a lack of postholes, a 20-cm-high east-west riser separates the south "patio" from the building platform, which is the earliest architecture at Cahal Pech coated with lime plaster.

Structure B-4/10–sub consists of four late Cunil lime-plastered building platforms (a–d) roughly level with an elongated east-west "plaza" bordering the north side of the natural hill. The initial platform (10a-sub) is a flat surface with several postholes, but their irregular spacing prevents description of the superstructure plan. Platform 10b-sub is bilevel, with a 0.5 m recessed square or rectangular interior floor (the preceding 10a-sub platform). The subsequent platform (10c-sub) is the most elaborate Cunil phase residence in the sequence. It was built directly over Structure B-4/10b-sub, although the interior floor was elevated an additional 30 cm. Like its predecessor, 10c-sub is aligned 15 degrees west of magnetic north, but its square or rectangular superstructure was more carefully finished with stripes of red paint on the exterior walls (Awe 1992:120). A second wattle-and-daub domestic structure was located directly north (Cheetham 1995:22). The final platform (10d-sub) consists of two poorly preserved floors, with only one posthole evident.

The close of the Cunil phase marked the end of residential occupancy at Structure B-4. A series of five small temples were built during the EMF and LMF phases, beginning with Structure B-4/9–sub and culminating with Structure B-4/4–sub. Each of these platforms, which range from 0.50 m to just over 3.0 m in height, has north-facing stairs, thickly plastered surfaces, and once supported a wattle-and-daub superstructure.

Traces of three Cunil phase residential units were also discovered below Plaza B (Cheetham 1996). Lacking plaster floors, recessed building interiors, and painted exterior walls, these structures are less elaborate than the late Cunil Structure B-4 buildings. Nonetheless, a significant amount of labor was invested in paving the patios and interior floors of some of these buildings with small, thin slabs and rounded pieces of limestone. With the exception of Structure B-4, much of the community's living surface appears to have been prepared in this manner.

Based on the spacing of the four known residential units below Plaza B, two buildings per unit (as evidenced at Str. B-4) and the known limit of the natural hilltop, Cheetham (1995:20) estimates that eight residential units were dispersed across this area in Cunil times, thus forming a small village of 35–70 people. This estimate only includes the crest of the hill. When peripheral settlements are included the numbers rise to 75–150 persons (Cheetham 1995:29–30), but this range too may be conservative if, as seems likely, additional "core" residences also were constructed on two flat areas or terraces that flanked the east and west sides of the natural hill below extant Plazas A and C (see figs. 7.1, 7.2).

Plaza tests also have documented the evolution and developmental trajectory of early settlement at Cahal Pech. The core of the initial, Cunil phase settlement was located below Plaza B, and possibly Plazas A and C. Aside from the orientation of later Structure B-4 architecture, there does not appear to be any discernible pattern to the aggregate arrangement of Cunil residences below Plaza B. However, by the end of the phase the south side of the area was elevated and leveled such that a single floor surface of tamped marl and cobblestone ran its entire length. There is some evidence that water runoff from higher ground to the north was channeled, and possibly collected, via small haphazard drains cut into this surface (Cheetham 1996:fig. 9). It is possible that the early compact cobblestone surface that characterized much of the site, especially to the north, was laid down to facilitate the collection of water. If so, this is the earliest known example of hydraulic engineering in the Maya lowlands.

During EMF times, the south and east sides of Plaza B were leveled and coated with lime plaster, thus forming the site's first formal ceremonial plaza, an L-shaped configuration. The middle of the natural hill—part of the old cobblestone surface—remained exposed, but there are no traces of EMF residences in this area. Apparently, the residential component of Plaza B had been eliminated or curtailed to make way for temple buildings and ritual space. Cheetham (1996:22) suggests that the area to the west (below Plazas A, D, and E), which was leveled and plastered for the first time toward the end of this phase, may have become the new locus of an emerging elite at Cahal Pech. Although this remains to be demonstrated, during the Classic period this area was a palatial setting occupied by the site's rulers (Awe et al. 1992).

The newly constructed L-shaped plaza was bordered by two successive Structure B-4 temples (9– and 8–sub). Construction of Structures B-1 through B-3 (an E-Group arrangement by Late Formative times) may have originated in this phase, but only Structure B-2 has been probed and its earliest platforms (Str. B-2/11 and 10–sub) date to LMF times (Awe 1992:99–106). The narrow, deep excavation into the center of Structure B-2 reportedly reached sterile level (Awe 1992:102), but subsequent excavation along the building's north side exposed cobblestone surfaces that are earlier and lower in elevation than the recorded LMF platforms (Cheetham 1996:9–11), raising the possibility that earlier Structure B-2 platforms are present and the E-Group arrangement was conceived during EMF times.

During the LMF, the civic-ceremonial architecture inaugurated during the preceding phase was amplified. Construction fill was used to elevate Plaza B above the apex of the natural hill, thus approximating the plaza's current dimensions. This enlarged ritual space was plastered and raised on several occasions, suggesting that the initial effort occurred early in the phase. Slightly variable plaza floor depths (Cheetham 1996:table 1) reveal a north-south grade that facilitated the rapid dispersal or capture of rainfall, an engineering achievement with probable roots in the Cunil phase. To the west, the area below Plaza A was once again elevated and plastered. The depth of this surface relative to Plaza B (about 3 m lower) indicates that by the outset of LMF times a stair, platform, or some other architectural feature separated the east and west sides of Cahal Pech. This physical break may have separated the ceremonial and residential compounds of the site, although evidence for the latter is lacking for this period.

With the enlargement of Plaza B came the rebuilding of ceremonial buildings and possible inauguration of new forms of architecture. Structure B-4 was rebuilt no less than three times during this era, and the east side of the plaza was bordered by Structure B-2 and quite likely Structures B-1 and B-3. Structure B-2 consisted of two successive, low plaster platforms, one of which (Str. B-2/11–sub) supported a perishable superstructure (Awe 1992:104). Based on analogy with known Middle Formative E-Groups (e.g., Laporte and Fialko 1993:fig. 12), we suspect that these surfaces extend to the south, thus forming one long rectangular platform below Structures B-1 to B-3.

Several settlements in the periphery of Cahal Pech were occupied during the Middle Formative period. Ceramic data suggest that at least four (Cas Pek, Tolok, Zubin, and Zopilote) were founded during Cunil times, although Cunil architecture has not been found. Middle Formative settlement is particularly high on knolls with well-drained terrain within 2 km west and south of the central acropolis. Settlement was less dense to the north, with the Yaxox (Ford and Fedick 1992:41), Melhado (Willey and Bullard 1956:42–44) and Ch'um (Powis et al. 1996) settlement groups clustering on an elevated strip of land on the southern bank of the Mopan River.

Habitation in the periphery consists of mound clusters (groups) that vary in size and configuration, including Cas Pek (Lee 1996; Lee and Awe 1995), Tolok (Powis 1996; Powis and Hohmann 1995; Powis et al. 1996), Tzinic, Zopilote (chapter 8), Zotz and Zubin (Iannone 1996). During LMF times, most of these settlements had small reservoirs or associated subterranean chambers (*chultunob*) in addition to small-scale domestic and civic architecture (Powis 1996). However, clear differences in scale, form, function, and complexity are evident. For example, evidence of architectural variability includes round structures at the Tolok and Zotz groups (Aimers et al. 2000) (figs. 7.3 and 7.4). The Tolok examples (Strs. 14 and 15) were centrally located within a patio group (Powis 1996), Structure 15 being the smaller and earlier of the two, measuring 5.5 m in diameter and 0.40 m in height. Structure 14 measures 9.5 m in diameter and 0.55 m in height, making it the largest known LMF round structure in the Maya lowlands. The Zotz group building (Str. 2/2nd) measures 3.6 m in diameter and 1.2 m in height. Both the Tolok and Zotz round structures have tapering upper sides and exposed floor surfaces. Each of these open-air platforms contained a number of special deposits (e.g., burials and caches) and was likely used for family/community–oriented ritual performances (Aimers et al. 2000:83).

The Cas Pek group includes a large platform (13 × 10 m) that revealed complex building techniques, including multiple construction pens for building fill (Lee 1996:81). The Middle Formative occupants of this settlement were heavily invested in shell ornament production, as indicated by abundant marine shell refuse, numerous small chert drills, and finished shell disk beads (Hohmann 2002; Lee 1996; Lee and Awe 1995).

The largest nonresidential cluster of architecture at Cahal Pech is Zopilote, located 750 m south of the site core at the terminus of the Martinez

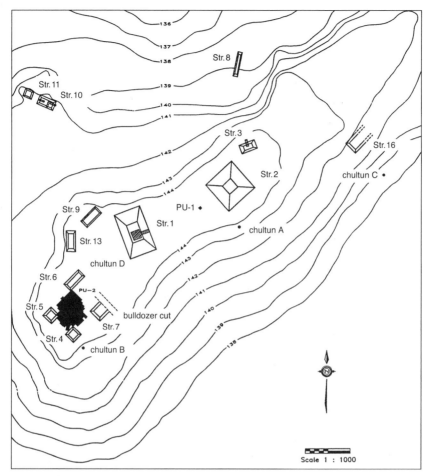

Fig. 7.3. Plan of the Tolok Settlement Group, Cahal Pech (after Powis et al. 1999: fig. 3). Circular platforms 14 and 15 (fig. 7.4) are located between Structures 4 through 7.

causeway (chapter 8). The principal temple of this group (Str. A-1) was 12 m in height in Late Classic times, making it the largest building in the periphery. The construction of large-scale architecture at Zopilote, however, began much earlier. Four Middle Formative temples have been exposed with Structure A-1, ranging in height from 2 m (EMF) to 5.5 m (LMF). These masonry constructions once supported wattle-and-daub superstructures and each was the tallest temple at Cahal Pech (including temples of the site core) during its time. The final LMF building is noteworthy for its relative size and the probable association of a carved stela, the only carved monument known at Cahal Pech (see chapter 8).

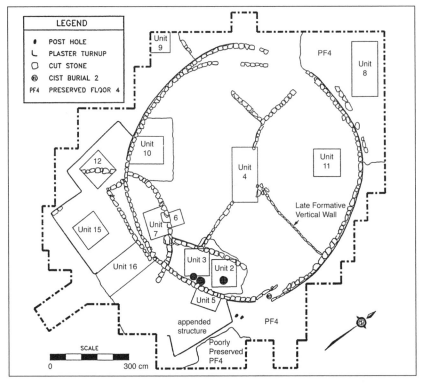

Fig. 7.4. Late Middle Formative circular platforms (Structures 14 and 15) at the Tolok Settlement Group, Cahal Pech (after Powis and Hohmann 1995: fig. 10).

It appears that all major environmental zones of the valley were occupied during the Middle Formative period (Ford and Fedick 1992:40). By the end of this era, settlement at Cahal Pech and the neighboring communities of Baking Pot, Blackman Eddy, Buenavista, Pacbitun, and Xunantunich was dense and complex. At Cahal Pech, approximately 75 percent of all mounds tested yielded evidence of LMF construction or architectural modification (Awe 1992:356). Many were simple house platforms with perishable buildings, but others are truly monumental architecture.

Artifacts

Ceramics

Investigations in the core zone and periphery of Cahal Pech have yielded over 20,000 sherds dating to the Cunil, EMF, and LMF phases. Typologically, ceramics of the EMF and LMF phases correspond to early and late facet Jenney Creek phase ceramics from Barton Ramie (Willey et al. 1965:

325–332; Gifford 1976:68–83), located approximately 16 km to the east. The collection of EMF and LMF pottery from Cahal Pech is represented by the previously defined Jocote and Savana ceramic groups, with lesser amounts of pottery from the Joventud, Pital, and Chunhinta groups.

The unusual, early pottery recovered from architectural fill, cache, and living surface contexts in the lower levels of Structure B-4 and below Plaza B was used to define the Cunil ceramic complex (fig. 7.5) (Awe 1992:226–230; Cheetham and Awe 2002). At Cahal Pech, the complex consists of two wares, eight groups, and fourteen types. Recently, Cunil pottery has been identified at other valley sites, including Pacbitun (T. Powis, personal observations 2000), Xunantunich (Strelow and LeCount 2001), Barton Ramie (D. Cheetham, personal observation 2000), and Floral Park and Blackman Eddy, where it has been used to define the Kanocha phase (see chapter 3). Cunil is one of several closely related pre-Mamom ceramic complexes that formed the region's first stylistic horizon, encompassing the Belize Valley and territories to the west (Lakes Yaxha-Sacnab vicinity through central Petén) and southwest (Pasion River region) (Cheetham 2001; Cheetham et al. 2002). Ceramics of the subsequent EMF phase demonstrate an outgrowth from the preceding Cunil tradition, with such hallmark types as Jocote Orange-brown and Savana Orange having clear precursors in Cunil.

Some Cunil pots carried incised motifs (fig. 7.6), several of which are identical to early "mythico-religious symbols" from other regions of Mesoamerica (Cheetham 1995:26–29, 1998, 2001). The presence of these Olmec style or pan-Mesoamerican symbols on pottery and other media at Cahal Pech (e.g., a carved jadeite flame eyebrow cached in Str. B-4/10–sub) may signal the employment of status-creating strategies by emerging Cahal

Fig. 7.5. Reconstruction of Cunil phase ceramic vessels from Cahal Pech (drawing by Ayax Moreno, courtesy of the New World Archaeological Foundation).

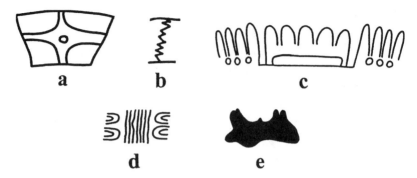

Fig. 7.6. Select motifs from Cunil phase ceramics, Cahal Pech (after Cheetham 1998: fig. 7): (a) kan cross; (b) lightning; (c) avian serpent; (d) music bracket; (e) flaming eyebrow.

Pech elite. Such leaders may have enhanced their prestige via control of exotic products, knowledge, and symbols obtained through long-distance exchange networks (Cheetham 1998).

Ceramic Figurines

Excavations at Cahal Pech have produced 423 figurine fragments (human and animal forms), the largest collection of hand-modeled ceramic figurines from any lowland Maya site (Cheetham 1998, 2002; Healy and Cheetham 1996). Some 358 of these have been assigned to the Cunil, EMF, and LMF phases on the basis of technological, contextual, or stylistic criteria (fig. 7.7). No whole anthropomorphic figurines have been recovered and all fragments are from secondary or tertiary contexts.

Lithics

Far less is known about Formative period lithic technology than Classic and Postclassic period technologies (Potter 1991), and what is known stems largely from Late Formative studies (Dreiss 1988, 1989; Mitchum 1991; Shafer 1991). At Cahal Pech, most Middle Formative obsidian artifacts consist of flakes and blades. The obsidian artifacts from stratigraphic Formative period deposits reveal a flake-to-bladelet sequence of development, with prismatic blades largely replacing flakes by the outset of the LMF at Cahal Pech and other lowland Maya sites (Awe and Healy 1994:197–198, table 1). Thereafter, prismatic blades were the predominant type of obsidian artifact. A similar developmental sequence has been recorded for Chiapas, Mexico (Clark 1987:261–265, 1989:218–222;

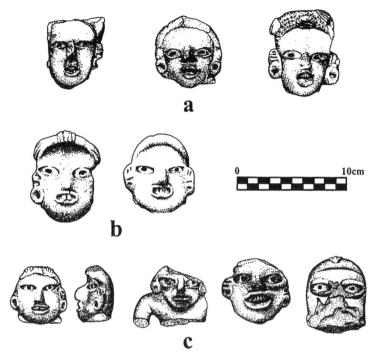

Fig. 7.7. Formative period hand-modeled ceramic figurine heads from Cahal Pech (after Awe 1992: figs. 71–75; Cheetham n.d.: figs. 3–5): (a) Cunil phase; (b) EMF phase; (c) LMF phase.

Clark and Lee 1984:236–238), and Pacific coastal Guatemala (Coe and Flannery 1967:63), where flakes (hard-hammer percussion) occur in Early Formative deposits, followed by blades in the Middle Formative. At Cahal Pech, the shift to a blade/core technology occurred during a time of population increase, heightened construction activity, and increased social inequality.

Trace element analysis of Cahal Pech Formative period obsidian artifacts reveals an early reliance on three major sources located in the Guatemalan Highlands, hundreds of kilometers away (Hohmann and Glascock 1996; and contrary to Awe et al. 1996). Recent analysis of an additional 70 obsidian specimens from Cahal Pech has revealed that the site was receiving obsidian only from the El Chayal (ECH) source during Cunil times, but by the Middle Formative the San Martin Jilotepeque (SMJ) source was dominant (72 percent), with smaller amounts from ECH (24 percent), and especially Ixtepeque (IXT) (4 percent) (Hohmann and Glascock 1996:table 5). Obsidian analyzed from Late Formative contexts at

Cahal Pech reveals a similar pattern of source utilization. The obsidian source supply during the Middle Formative at Cahal Pech matches that for the Maya lowlands in general. During the Classic and Postclassic periods, SMJ obsidian was used less often, while the ECH and IXT sources became significant in lowland obsidian trade (Dreiss 1989; Hammond 1972, 1991; Healy et al. 1984; Nelson 1985).

The non-obsidian-chipped stone subassemblage (almost exclusively chert) from Cahal Pech reveals strong similarities to the few described Middle Formative Maya subassemblages from northern Belize (e.g., Cuello and Colha) and west and central Petén (e.g., Altar de Sacrificios and Tikal) (Iannone and Lee 1996). The eclectic nature of these collections indicates the active exchange of technical skills and knowledge. A specialized chert burin spall technology has been identified in association with the production of Middle Formative shell ornaments (Hohmann 2002).

The dominant category of ground stone artifacts consists of granite manos and metates. These traditional maize-grinding tools occur in both EMF and LMF deposits at Cahal Pech. Worked slate objects, such as tabular, plaquelike pieces, pendants, and other sawed or drilled fragments form the second most common category of ground implements (Healy et al. 1995). Third is a small number of ground limestone tools. The final category embodies polished stone (greenstone, occasionally jadeite) artifacts—beads, pendants, spools, adornos (or mosaic pieces), and polished pebbles or "triangulates." The most striking specimens consist of a small, polished jadeite "flame eyebrow" and fang recovered from a late Cunil phase offering on the floor of Structure B-4/10c-sub. These objects, which originally formed part a larger mosaic, hint of early Maya connections with the Gulf Coast Olmec (Awe 1992:307–308; Cheetham 1998).

Other Materials

Worked marine shell (especially *Strombus* sp.) is abundant in Middle Formative deposits at Cahal Pech. More than 200 small shell disk beads were retrieved from Cunil through LMF deposits in the site core and peripheral settlements, suggesting the active, and possibly large-scale, production of shell jewelry. At Cas Pek, the recovery of complete and broken shell beads, beads in various stages of production, and shell detritus provide clear evidence that the inhabitants of this group were economically specialized in shell bead manufacturing during LMF times, if not earlier (Hohmann 2002; Lee and Awe 1995).

There is also evidence for a small worked bone industry, primarily tools carved from mammal bone, most likely of the whitetail deer. Needles and pins were the most common bone artifacts recovered. In addition to pots and hand-modeled figurines, the fired clay industry included perforated disks, plain disks, and notched sherds made from broken pottery vessels, as well as roller stamps and small beads.

Fauna

Excavations at Cahal Pech have yielded over 17,000 faunal remains from at least seven zoological classes and 31 taxa (table 7.2), making it one of

Table 7.2. Identified fauna from Formative period Cahal Pech, Belize

Vertebrates	Invertebrates
Mammalia	**Pelecypoda**
Didelphis marsupialis	*Nephronaias* sp.
Agouti paca	**Gastropoda**
Dasypus novemcinctus	*Pomacea flagellata*
Mazama americana	*Pachychillus glaphrus*
Rodentia	*Pachychilus indiorum*
Sylvilagus sp.	*Strombidae*
Tayassu sp.	*Prunum* sp.
Canis familiaris	*Oliva* sp.
Odocoileus virginianus	*Scaphoda*
Osteichthyes	*Dentalium* sp.
Sparisoma sp.	**Brachyura**
Scaridae	
Scarus sp.	
Epinephelus sp.	
Lachnolaimus sp.	
Lutjanidae	
Siluriformes	
Serrenidae	
Reptilia	
Chelonia	
Iguanidae	
Crocodylus sp.	
Aves	
Meleagridae	
Crax Rubra	

Sources: After Powis et al. 1999:table 1; Stanchley 1992, 1993, 1995.

the largest faunal assemblages from any lowland Maya center (Stanchly 1992, 1995, 1999). Vertebrate remains from the site core, Cas Pek, and Tolok groups exceed 4,000 specimens (23.7 percent) from fish and, to a lesser extent, small and large-sized terrestrial game like white-tailed deer (*Odocoileus* sp.) and rabbit (*Sylvilagus* sp.). Invertebrate freshwater and marine species number nearly 13,000 specimens (76.3 percent), the vast majority of which are freshwater snails (*Pachychilus* sp.) or riverine clams (*Nephronaias* sp.). Reliance on snails and clams as a protein supplement has been suggested for Classic Maya populations (Healy et al. 1990). Their dietary contribution may have been more significant during Middle Formative times (Healy 1999:89), although isotopic evidence has yet to demonstrate this (see below).

Paleobotany

The identification of Formative period floral remains from soil samples has yielded important new insights into early Maya plant exploitation in the valley (Lawlor et al. 1995; Wiesen and Lentz 1999). Paleobotanical samples, largely composed of charred seeds and carbonized wood, demonstrate that the Formative inhabitants of Cahal Pech relied on a traditional diet of squash (*Curcurbita* sp.), maize (*Zea mays*), and possibly beans (*Phaseolus* sp.) (Lentz 1991; see also Miksicek 1991). In the core zone, maize cupules were recovered from Structure B-4/9–sub, the first EMF building in the B-4 architectural sequence, and Structure B-4/11–sub, a mid–Cunil phase building platform. These are the earliest macrobotanical maize remains known from the Maya lowlands (Lawlor et al. 1995: 157, 160).

Soil analyses also revealed a cottonseed (*Gossypium* sp.) (Wiesen and Lentz 1999:63) from below the initial Cunil phase cobblestone surface in the center of Plaza B (Cheetham 1996:7–8), as well as a tiny (1 mm^2) textile-impressed fragment of plaster, possibly representing twisted cotton fibers, from Structure B-4/9–sub (Lawlor et al. 1995:157, fig. 1). Fragments of coyol palm (*Acrocomia aculeata*) fruit have also been identified from the structural fill of Structure B-4 Cunil platforms (Wiesen and Lentz 1999:table 1). Lentz (1990) hypothesizes that coyol use was important during the Classic period at Copan. The Coyol palm is often found in disturbed lands, such as areas of secondary growth or abandoned agricultural fields. Charred nutshell or calabash fragments were also common in Middle Formative deposits at Cahal Pech (Lawlor et al. 1995:158–160), as were charred pieces of pine (*Pinus* sp.), palo mulato (*Astronium graveo-*

lens), wild fig (*Ficus* sp.) and malady (*Aspidosperma* sp.) wood. The wood species demonstrate that the inhabitants of Cahal Pech exploited a variety of ecological contexts, including the upland pine ridge and lowlands tropical rainforest (Wiesen and Lentz 1999). Some woods were likely employed as fuel, others for timber, and wild fig may have been used for the production of paper. The presence of wood from large deciduous trees suggests that stands of primary forest were still available for exploitation near Cahal Pech during the Middle Formative period (Wiesen and Lentz 1999:65).

Subsistence, Diet, and Health

The discovery of a rich LMF midden at the Tolok settlement group has shed new light on early subsistence in the valley (Powis 1996; Powis et al. 1999; Powis et al. 2000). Plant remains from this deposit indicate a diet consisting, in part, of cultivated plants such as maize, beans, and squash (Lawlor et al. 1995; Powis et al. 1999:374; Wiesen and Lentz 1999). These data support Fedick's (1989:240) earlier prediction that an extensive swidden (slash-and-burn) agriculture system existed in the valley by the Middle Formative period. Products of the coyol palm, ramon, and fig trees also may have contributed to the diet during this time. These plant foods were supplemented by a mixture of terrestrial game (deer and agouti), marine reef fish (parrotfish and grouper), small quantities of freshwater fish (catfish) and abundant freshwater clams and snails (Powis et al. 1999: 374; Powis et al. 2000). Along with earlier plant and animal remains from the site core (Lawlor et al. 1995; Stanchly 1992, 1995; Wiesen and Lentz 1999), the Tolok remains indicate that the inhabitants of Cahal Pech maintained a mixed subsistence pattern from Cunil through LMF times.

The surprising presence of Caribbean reef fishes this far inland indicates that the Cahal Pech Maya or their coastal neighbors were capable of preserving seafood for the 100+ km trip up the Belize River (Powis et al. 1999:374). Classic period salt-making communities have been identified along the Belize coast (McKillop 1995:225; chapter 16), and the Tolok data suggest that salt making was practiced much earlier. Alternatively, the marine fish identified at Tolok may have been smoked or transported alive in canoes partly filled with saltwater (N. Hammond, personal communication 1999).

Chemical analysis of human bone has yielded results that broaden the picture of Middle Formative subsistence at Cahal Pech. Stable isotope analysis of skeletal remains, in particular, has provided new data regarding diet and health (Powis et al. 1999; White 1999). Like several other lowland sites where similar studies have been conducted, the isotopic evidence from Cahal Pech indicates that maize was a staple crop by LMF times. This reliance, however, was less stringent than during the Classic period, probably because the diet was much more diverse. The appearance of distinct social classes by the LMF is suggested by the variable nature of the isotopic data. Unlike wild plant foods, game, and freshwater fish, the distribution of C-4 based foods (like maize and imported marine fish) appears to have been limited (White et al. 1996). For example, despite their probable role in agricultural production, the rural segment of the Cahal Pech population did not enjoy the full range nor quantities of crops consumed by the budding elite (Powis et al. 1999:373).

The Formative period skeletal remains from Cahal Pech (N = 23) reveal a variety of skeletal pathologies, including porotic hyperostosis, a cranial inflammation due to an anemic state. This condition, however, appears to be much more common in Classic period skeletal remains from the site, thus indicating an overall decline in health and nutrition between these periods. Other signs of ill health include mandibular periodontis infection, periostitis in the long bones, minor cases of osteoarthritis and a few cases of trauma related injury (with evidence of healing). Artificial cranial modeling and dental modification (pyrite and jadeite inlays) also have been identified (Song 1996). The occurrence of dental enamel defects such as linear enamel hypoplasias (LEH) reflect episodes of chronic, often low grade, stress. Some of these cases may be due to malnutrition, fever, vitamin deficiencies, and/or localized trauma (Wright 1990). Hypoplastic enamel defects are often associated with children (ages 2–4 years) and linked to stresses at the time of weaning (Saul 1972; Saul and Saul 1991; Song 1995, 1996, 1997; White 1986, and others), but the situation may not be this simple. Goodman and Song (1999) argue that LEH in children may be related to this being a peak period of enamel growth with increased sensitivity to metabolic disorders. Estimates of stature remain tenuous given the small number (N = 3) of Formative skeletons at Cahal Pech sufficiently preserved. All adult skeletal remains amenable to stature estimation reflect the height ranges established for Formative period populations at other lowland sites (Altar de Sacrificios, Cuello, and Tikal). Overall, the skeletal pathologies and dental defects identified from Formative period skeletal remains at Cahal Pech are quite limited and rarely severe, suggesting relatively good health and nutrition when compared to the Classic period (Song 1995, 1996).

Ritual Activity

Several lines of archaeological data from Cahal Pech assist in elucidating Formative period ritual and the role it may have played in fostering social and political change. Awe (1992:339–343) has identified several caches associated with Structure B-4. The earliest, dated to the first half of the Cunil phase, consisted of the lower jaw of a crocodile that probably formed part of a ceremonial mask. A more elaborate cache, deposited in a late Cunil Structure B-4 building (10c-sub) before it was deliberately burnt, contained over 120 objects, including carved jadeite mosaic pieces, obsidian flakes, marine shell objects, a smashed partial vessel, chert flakes, and several complete animal bones (canine and peccary) drilled for use as pendants. These caches, and other lesser examples from succeeding temple platforms, may have served as dedicatory or termination offerings during special commemorative events, perhaps the petitioning of supernaturals for protection or the release of the spirits associated with the buildings (see Garber 1989:47–50).

Formative period burials at Cahal Pech also reveal repetitive ritual activity. The few human remains recovered in Cunil and EMF levels were burnt and may represent evidence of cannibalism or special treatment of deceased ancestral remains. In contrast, LMF burials were all extended, supine, with head to the south. Grave types of this phase include simple and cist burials, but only the latter contained grave goods, likely reflecting status differences. The orientation of these burials marks the commencement of a striking regional burial pattern that persisted in the valley until the end of the Classic period.

The discovery of several LMF burials in round structures at the Tolok and Zotz groups indicates that these open-air platforms functioned as burial shrines. It is clear, however, that they also functioned as important ritual loci (Aimers et al. 2000), as demonstrated by the absence of super-structures, copal residues on floors, and their overall "stage-like" qualities. As noted earlier, these platforms were constructed in at least two locations, the largest example (Str. 14 at Tolok) measuring just over 9 m in diameter.

The presence of EMF and LMF spouted vessel fragments at Cahal Pech, including several large specimens from a LMF midden below Tolok Structure 1 (Powis et al. 1999:367), provide some evidence of ritual feasting, as does the concentration of faunal remains in the vicinity of Cunil phase Structure B-4 residential platforms (see Stanchly 1992). Recent findings from the site of Colha, in northern Belize, have shown that some Middle

Formative spouted vessels contain residues of cacao (*Theobroma cacao*) and that they were used almost exclusively for the ritual drinking of liquid chocolate (Hurst et al. 2002; Powis et al. 2002).

As noted earlier, some Cunil phase pots carry Olmec style or "pan-Mesoamerican" (see Marcus 1989:170) motifs such as kan crosses, flaming eyebrows, V-shaped clefts, and gum brackets. Fragments of these pots were especially frequent in the vicinity of Structure B-4, suggesting that the ideology and external connections behind these symbols may have been manipulated by the residents of this building to initiate a system of social ranking (Cheetham 1998).

The unusually large collection of ceramic figurines from Cahal Pech are most likely ritual objects, but their precise function is elusive. Two of the many possible functions for human effigies include fertility fetishes (Rands and Rands 1965:535–560) and ruler portraits (Grove and Gillespie 1984:28; Hammond 1989). According to Awe (1992:255–286), the modal and contextual analysis of the Cahal Pech specimens support Marcus's (1993:4, 1998) conclusion that anthropomorphic figurines were made and used by women to invoke and communicate with the spirits of deceased ancestors.

From the above lines of evidence we can conclude that there was a high degree of interest in ritual during the Formative period at Cahal Pech and other valley communities. Religion was most likely animistic, with a strong belief that certain inanimate objects (mountains, trees, structures) and wild animals had spirits. The occurrence of caches, ritual objects, special function structures, and iconographic motifs on objects imply that many of the rites and cannons of religion and their associated symbolism were formalized by the Middle Formative period, if not earlier (Awe and Cheetham 1993).

Conclusion

There is now strong evidence that Maya lowland groups made the transition from egalitarian to rank and stratified societies during the lengthy Formative period (Awe 1992; Cheetham 1998; Clark et al. 2000; Clark and Hansen 2001; Clark and Cheetham 2003; Hammond 1992; Healy 1999; Powis 1996; Powis et al. 1999; chapter 3). During this time, several diagnostic traits of complex culture were first established (Awe and Cheetham 1993; Hammond 1986:403; Sharer 1992:131). Recent archaeological investigations at Cahal Pech and other valley sites demonstrate that by Cunil times several prominent hilltops above the valley were settled.

Throughout the Middle Formative period the inhabitants of these communities were involved in hunting, fishing, shellfish gathering, and the farming of crops like maize, beans, and squash. This diverse subsistence regime provided the population with a fairly nutritious diet and a generally good level of health.

By at least late Cunil times, several small settlements had been founded in the periphery of Cahal Pech, likely by relatives of the core population. While these constituted distinct residence groups throughout the Middle Formative period, they were surely tied to the political and religious fortunes of the nearby core zone. By the end of this period the population of Cahal Pech and its hinterland was probably under 1,000 persons, likely constituting a large village or town headed by a chief.

From the founding of Cahal Pech there are indications of growing social and economic complexity. Nondomestic ceremonial structures and formal plazas were constructed by at least the beginning of the EMF, and exotic goods like marine shell, volcanic ash, jadeite, and obsidian were regularly procured from afar. Trade with other villages in the Maya lowlands was also established by this time. Clear evidence of craft production at Cahal Pech is limited to shell ornaments, but it is highly likely that pottery vessels, figurines, and lithics also were made locally. The technical and formal properties of the ceramics and lithics from each Middle Formative phase demonstrate in situ cultural development (cf. Ball and Taschek 2004) and linkage with later material culture of the valley and other lowland zones. The repeated use of termination caches—initially associated with Cunil residences and later with EMF and LMF temple buildings—containing the same kinds of objects provides evidence for enduring, complex ritual practices by the same culture, as does the persistence of a single anthropomorphic figurine style and the recurrent construction of circular platforms and other forms of ceremonial architecture in the same locations. In many ways, the early Maya of Cahal Pech were as conservative as they were progressive.

The degree of religious, artistic, and architectural sophistication that flourished throughout the Middle Formative period could hardly have been imagined by Mayanists only a few decades ago. Events in the Middle Formative period fostered the dramatic political and cultural changes that followed in the Late Formative period when, throughout the Maya lowlands, there appeared the first recognizable Maya kings and the establishment of hereditary dynasties that would rule, in some cases, for centuries to follow (Freidel and Schele 1988a:87–93). Research at Cahal Pech and other early sites make it clear that these spectacular political events were built on a sturdy cultural foundation laid down by Maya peoples during the preceding millennium.

Notes

1. The uncalibrated phase spans are as follows: Cunil (1000–800 b.c.), EMF (800–650 b.c.), and LMF (650–300 b.c.).
2. The stratigraphic ordering of Structure B-4 architecture presented here differs from and supercedes all earlier publications and reports.

Acknowledgments

Funding for the research at Cahal Pech between 1988 and 1996 was derived from a variety of international sources, including the Social Sciences and Humanities Research Council (SSHRC), the Central Research Fund (University of London), Gordon Childe Fund (Institute of Archaeology, University of London), Committee on Research (Trent University), Canadian Commission for UNESCO/CIDA Assistance Program, and the Overseas Research Student Award from the United Kingdom. We wish to thank these agencies for their generous support. In Belize, the investigations were assisted through the cooperation of the Belize Department of Archaeology, a series of archaeological commissioners, department staff, and site caretakers, who collectively ensured that investigations could progress successfully each season. While the sheer numbers prevent us from naming each separately, we humbly acknowledge the hard work and commitment of a large number of American, Belizean, British, Canadian, and Spanish students, staff, and field directors, without whose selfless efforts, dedication, flexibility, and teamwork the objectives of the Belize Valley Archaeological Reconnaissance and Belize Valley Preclassic Maya Projects would not have been possible to achieve. We remain indebted to all of you. Lastly, we wish to thank the editor, James Garber, for his constant goodwill and enduring patience.

8

The Role of "Terminus Groups" in Lowland Maya Site Planning

An Example from Cahal Pech

David Cheetham

Of the many kinds of Maya architecture, the elevated causeway or *sacbe* (Yucatec Maya for "white [sac] road [be]") is perhaps the most striking. These "expensive artifacts" (Kurjack and Garza T. 1981:300), some of which are scores of kilometers in length, required an enormous amount of raw material and labor to complete. Because the Maya lacked draft animals and wheeled vehicles at the most basic level, causeways functioned as traffic corridors for the movement of people and goods (Ashmore 1981:45). Additionally, some causeways may have functioned as water management systems (Scarborough 1993:29–31).

At least three functionally different classes of causeways can be discerned from the archaeological record. The most impressive, and labor intensive, are the lengthy intersite causeways that connect distant urban centers (e.g., Benavides 1981:fig. 10; Graham 1967:fig. 27; Villa Rojas 1934). These enormous undertakings served to mark political territory and facilitate the swift deployment of military personnel (Chase 1992:45, fig. 3.3; Freidel 1992:114; Kurjack and Andrews 1976; Schele and Freidel 1990:498). Core causeways connect large groups of ceremonial and residential architecture within site cores (e.g., Adams 1981:231; Bullard and Willey 1965:301; Coe 1967:20; Fash 1983:283–286; Smith 1950:83–84). Ceremonial processions certainly occurred along core causeways, which may have originated to fulfill this purpose, but their most common function seems to have been the daily movement of large numbers of people and goods in the urban setting. The most poorly understood class is the intrasite causeway. These connect the site core with a prominent cluster of ceremonial (temple) buildings in the periphery, often called "terminus groups" or "causeway termini." Although terminus groups have been interpreted as key administrative, economic, or ceremonial locations controlled by the core elite (Folan 1983:53; see also Ashmore 1989, 1992; Earle 1991a; Folan 1991; Kurjack 1974), the removed location and unfettered access to these architectural complexes suggest that their function, however elite it may have been, was a public affair. Thus, terminus groups should assist in reconstructing the nature of core-periphery (elite-commoner) interaction.

Morphology and Function

Prehistoric Maya centers with terminus groups are fairly common in western Belize and the easternmost part of the Petén (map 2).[1] The general layout of terminus groups in this area (fig. 8.1) is deceptively similar, consisting of a group of peripheral buildings set on a platform attached to the site core or epicenter via a raised causeway. On closer inspection, however, a high degree of variability is evident. All 10 examples in figure 8.1 have different orientations, as measured along the causeway in the general direction of the site core (see table 8.1). Even at closely spaced settlements in the valley (Cahal Pech and Pacbitun) and Dolores area of the Petén (Ixkun, Xaan Arriba, Mopan 3–East, and Ixtonton) common orientation is lacking. These data suggest that causeway orientation was dictated by practical considerations such as topography and the desire to link preexisting buildings to the site core with a causeway, rather than cosmological concerns.

There was no standard length for intrasite causeways. Indeed, the illustrated examples range from a relatively short 150 m (Mopan 3–East Group F) to slightly less than 1 km (Caracol 2 Stelae Group) in length. Moreover, some causeways sharply change direction or gradually turn prior to reaching their terminus (e.g., Pacbitun Mai and Caracol 2 Stelae Groups), while others are connected to a separate causeway emanating from the site core (e.g., Caracol Machete Group). In both cases, a clear sight-line from the site core to the terminus along the causeway was impossible. Along with variability in orientation, the lack of straight-line causeways weakens the likelihood of cosmological interpretations.

As indicated in table 8.1, the central axis of the principal temple buildings (or the most distant one from the causeway entrance in cases of mul-

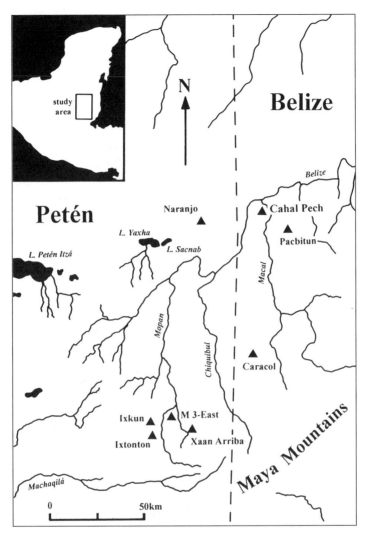

Map 2. The east-central Maya lowlands showing sites with terminus groups discussed in text.

tiple temples) is variable, yet close to the orientation of the associated causeway in most cases. The overriding factor in the orientation of these buildings was the creation of a dramatic impression upon entering the terminus group. This interpretation assumes that temple buildings were inaugurated during or after the construction of the causeway, but the haphazard orientation of causeways in this and other regions reflects the incorporation of preexisting architecture into a redefined site core.

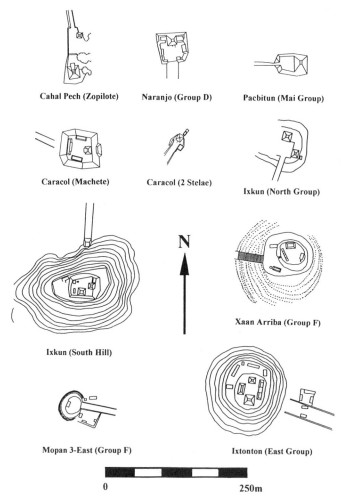

Fig. 8.1. Terminus group site plans (after Cheetham 1995a:fig. 1), Naranjo (after Graham and Von Euw 1975), Pacbitun (after Healy 1990:fig. 3), Caracol (after A. Chase and D. Chase 1987:figs. 52, 49), Ixkun (after Laporte 1996:fig. 13), Xaan Arriba (after Suasnávar 1995:fig. 2), Mopan 3-East (after Gómez 1996:fig. 4), and Ixtonton (after Laporte 1996:fig. 7).

Some terminus groups in the study area include clusters of residential architecture, as at Caracol (Jaeger 1987), but most consist of a raised platform supporting one or more temples and, occasionally, small ancillary buildings. This formation is especially true of terminus groups situated within a kilometer of site cores, indicating that distance was an important determinant in whether or not terminus groups had a residential compo-

Table 8.1. Morphological data of select terminus groups from the east-central Maya lowlands

Site (group)	Distance from site core (m)	Sacbe length (m)	Sacbe width (m)	Sacbe orientation*	Number of temple structures	Temple orientation	Number of ancillary structures	Platform surface area (m²)	Number of stelae monuments
Cahal Pech (Zopilote)	750	281	4–6.5	352°	2	352° (A-1) 278° (A-2)	1	2,275	2
Naranjo (Group D)	250	250	18	180° W	1	172°	6	1,200	3
Pacbitun (Mai)	230	230	7–8	(irregular)	1	270°	0	620	0
Caracol (Machete)	420	420	12–16	293° SW	1	268° (L3)	2	1,600	0
Caracol (2 Stelae)	800	800	12–16	(irregular)	1	209°	2	220	2
Ixkun (North Group)	280	280	11	196°	2	196°, 280°	0	620	0
Ixkun (South Hill)	220	170	19	8°	2	8°, 280°	2	780	0
Xaan Arriba (Group F)	360	260	14–16	275°	1	173°	3	4,900	0
Mopan 3–East (Group F)	150	150	10	99°	1(?)	112°	5	900	0
Ixtonton (East Group)	440	540	22	116°	3	8°, 97°, 188°	4	3,500	0

* As measured from terminus toward site core (magnetic North).

nent. For example, the Mai Group at the site of Pacbitun (fig. 8.1) consists of a solitary west-facing temple located some 230 m east of the site core with no trace of residential architecture. In cases where one or more potential residential or ancillary buildings occur, they are no larger (and in many cases much smaller) than common housemounds. If elite residency was indeed maintained at these locations, elaborate residential constructions should be present. At the very least, domestic artifacts and other elite trash such as polychrome sherds should be frequent in the architectural fill of terminus group buildings and platforms.

Recently, Ashmore (1991) has argued that ancient cosmological precepts guided the location and arrangement of some types of Maya architecture. Examination of intrasite causeway orientation and the morphology of terminus groups, architectural traits particularly amenable to this kind of manipulation, indicate that a cosmological explanation is inappropriate for this kind architectural complex, at least in the east-central area of the Maya lowlands. The only standardized aspects of terminus groups are their location on a natural hill or artificial platform, at least one prominent temple building directly facing the causeway entrance, and distinct separation from the site core. In short, armed with only survey data to guide interpretation we can do little more than exclude a cosmological function and suggest that intrasite terminus groups were indeed key administrative, economic, or ceremonial locations built and controlled by the site core elite, as suggested twenty years ago by Folan (1983:53).

The Zopilote Terminus Group

Zopilote consists of two temples (Strs. A-1 and A-2) and a small "ancillary" building (Str. 4) located 750 m south of the Cahal Pech site core at the terminus of the Martinez causeway (figs. 7.1 and 8.2). Set on a raised, bilevel platform on the south side of an east-west trending ridge, the site offers a commanding view of Cahal Pech and the surrounding countryside. Although ceremonial architecture at Zopilote spans the early Middle Formative through Classic periods (ca. 900 B.C.–A.D. 900),[2] residential architecture was not constructed. The Martinez Causeway, which maintains a course slightly west of magnetic north, extends 280 m north from the platform where a third temple building (Str. 3) is located. From here the causeway continues for another 50 m to the north edge of the ridge where it apparently ends, though it may have continued at ground level (and thus is undetectable) to the northwest side of the site core where an entrance ramp/causeway is located.

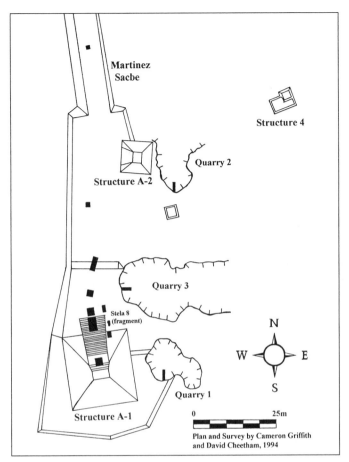

Fig. 8.2. Plan of the Zopilote Terminus Group showing excavation units (black squares) and salient features.

Unfortunately, the Zopilote Group was severely looted in the 1970s or 1980s, with the most extensive damage at Structures A-2, -3, and -4. For this reason, investigations focused on Structure A-1, although the construction sequences of all other buildings were recorded. Structure A-2 is a 4-m-high temple building dating primarily to the Late Classic period. The temple faces west and was rebuilt on at least six occasions. Structure 3 is a small, 2.6-m-high temple located on a small platform appended to the east side of the Martinez Causeway near its northern end (figs. 7.1 and 8.2). The building faces west (toward the causeway) and its stairway is offset to the south. It was constructed in a single episode during the Late Classic to house a vaulted (looted) tomb of finely cut stone. Although salvage efforts

131

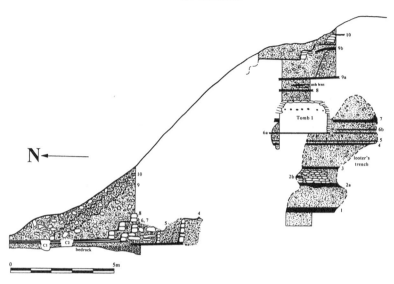

Fig. 8.3. North-south profile of pyramidal Structure A-1, Zopilote Terminus Group, Cahal Pech.

failed to recover cultural material from this tomb, its form, orientation, and location all indicate a high-status burial.

Structure A-1 is the principal building at Zopilote. Composed of 10 superimposed temples reaching 12 m in height at the close of the Classic period (figs. 8.2 and 8.3), it is the largest temple building in the periphery of Cahal Pech. Throughout the Middle Formative period (ca. 900–350 B.C.), Structure A-1 was the only building at Zopilote. The first three temples in the architectural sequence vary in height from 2 m (ca. 900–700 B.C.) to 4 m (ca. 500 B.C.), supported perishable superstructures, and were built on top of bedrock with no additional architectural embellishment of the surrounding terrain (such as a formal, leveled plaza). These buildings are as large, or larger, than contemporary structures in the site core of Cahal Pech (Awe 1992:210–212; Cheetham 1995), indicating that Zopilote was an important locus of ceremonial activity centuries before the initial construction of the Martinez causeway (see below). The final Middle Formative temple platform (Str. A-1/4th), at 5.5 m in height, was certainly the largest temple at Cahal Pech when it was built (ca. 400 B.C.). The first formal platform/plaza at Zopilote was also completed at this time.

Throughout the Late Formative period (350 B.C.–A.D. 350), Structure A-1 continued to be the only building at Zopilote. Architectural phases 5 through 7 were constructed during this time. Although excavations failed to clear large portions of the summits of these buildings, the small exposures suggest that they too supported wattle-and-daub superstructures. During the first two centuries of the Late Formative the first phase of the Martinez causeway was completed and Structure A-1 was again rebuilt. During the latter half, the Martinez causeway was raised and Structure A-1 was rebuilt two more times, reaching a height of 7.75 m (A-1/7th) around A.D. 200–300. At this time the only building surpassing its height at Cahal Pech was Structure A-1 (and possibly B-1) in the site core (Awe 1992:76, 99). Notable features of all the Late Formative Structure A-1 temples at Zopilote are the severely fire-blackened lower stairways and adjacent platform/plaza areas, suggesting the frequent burning of incense on these surfaces. This is a marked contrast with core temples, the surfaces of which show little or no evidence of repetitive incense burning.

Structure A-1 was rebuilt three times during the Classic period. Like earlier temples, the lower stairways and adjacent platforms of these buildings were charred by the frequent burning of incense. Two of these buildings date to the Early Classic, including the penultimate structure (A-1/9th) built at the close of this period (ca. A.D. 580–630). This 8.5-m-tall temple was constructed to house the vaulted tomb (Tomb 1) of an elite individual built within the core of earlier, Formative period architecture. Two burials were located in Tomb 1. The primary burial was of a young adult male in an extended position (head to the south) along the west wall. Several jade dental inserts located in the cranial area indicate that this individual was a high-status member of the Cahal Pech community. The secondary burial consisted of the cranium of a young adult male placed between two partial hemispherical bowls at the feet of the primary burial.

The contents of Tomb 1 included large concentrations of cedar (including round pole remnants) around the burials, indicating that the human remains were placed on a wooden pallet. Other artifacts include a human-effigy jade pendant, two jade beads, a stingray spine, two Spondylus shell ear-flares, a disc-shaped shell adorno, a large perforated freshwater shell, two small stone balls, and a stone bead. In addition, multiple layers of extremely thin, multicolored, and elaborately painted stucco veneer fragments were found in a 18 × 18 cm area below a polychrome plate. The laminated condition of the stucco fragments suggests that they were part of a codex. Similar remains have been found in elite burials at Uaxactun (Kidder 1947:70; Smith 1950:fig. 125) and the "Sun God's Tomb" at

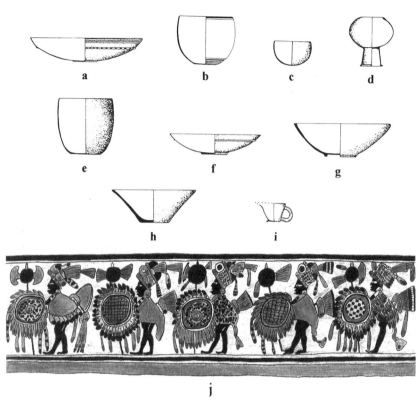

Fig. 8.4. Ceramic vessels from Tomb 1, Structure A-1, Zopilote Terminus Group: (a) Dos Arroyos Orange-polychrome; (b) Saxche Orange-polychrome; (c–d, i) Pucte Brown; (e) Balanza Black; (f) Minanha Red; (g–h) Hewlett Bank-unslipped; (j) roll-out illustration of b.

Altun Ha (Pendergast 1969:24–25). Seven whole pottery vessels accompanied the primary burial, including two polychromes (fig. 8.4). Vessel 2, in particular, is a barrel-shaped vase executed in black, brown, and red/orange on cream (fig. 8.4b, j). Five males with distinct profiles and elaborately adorned feather and animal skin costumes are depicted on the vessel exterior. In each case, the decorative elements comprising the headdress, shield, and spear/axe are individualized. This realistic scene probably portrays a formal military procession of warriors representing their specific high-status positions, lineage, or center affiliation.

During terminal Late Classic times (ca. A.D. 680–880) the tenth and final rebuilding of Structure A-1 was completed. The earlier platform/plaza was also raised and modified, creating a two-level platform, and the Martinez causeway was elevated once again. In addition, the lower por-

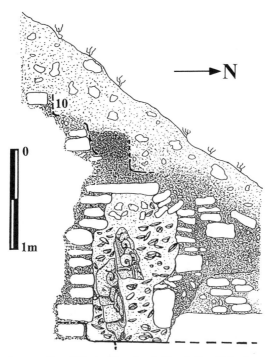

Fig. 8.5. West-face profile of "Stela Chamber" (Tomb 2) within the central staircase of Structure A-1, Zopilote Terminus Group.

tion of a plain stela monument (Stela 8) found along the east side of the Structure A-1 stairway dates to this phase of architecture. It was either purposely broken and moved to this location or fell from the summit of the building. The final Structure A-1 building also included a tomb (Tomb 2) built within the lower section of its stairway (fig. 8.5). This tomb was constructed of roughly hewn limestone blocks, vaulted, and topped with a large capstone. Unusual for its contents, Tomb 2 included a Formative stela monument (Stela 9; fig. 8.6) as the primary "burial." Typical of wraparound sculpture carved in the round (see Clancy 1990:22), Stela 9 depicts a human figure (from head to waist) within the mouth of a highly stylized feline characterized by multiple scrolls and a bifurcated tongue. Hieroglyphic inscriptions are lacking. The monument appears to have been purposely defaced (or ritually terminated) and broken into two large pieces prior to being buried in Tomb 2.

Although the original context of Stela 9 is unknown, it was probably removed from the old platform surface during the construction of A-1 10th and its refurbished platform/plaza. Specifically, Stela 9 may have been pulled from a U-shaped pit dug into very compact bedrock directly in

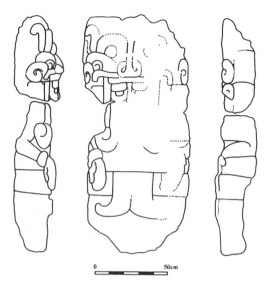

Fig. 8.6. Stela 9 from Tomb 2 at the Zopilote Terminus Group, Cahal Pech (drawing by Nikolai Grube).

front of Structure A-1. This pit (fig. 8.3, feature C1) was capped by the final platform/plaza surface, conforms very closely to the butt-end dimensions of Stela 9, penetrates all earlier platform/plaza surfaces and is located exactly along the central axis of the building. At precisely the time when Tomb 2 was under construction, two unslipped bowls were placed rim to rim in this pit, which is much wider and deeper than required to accommodate them. The timing of this event seems certain since a cache of two identical bowls was placed in a much smaller circular pit below the lower stairway directly in front of Tomb 2. This pit, unlike its counterpart, conforms to the dimensions of the cached vessels and does not unnecessarily penetrate bedrock.

If, as seems likely, the pit in front of Structure A-1 was the original location of Stela 9, this monument would have been erected before or during the construction of the initial platform/plaza and 5.5-m-tall A-1/4th temple (ca. 400 B.C.). Style, iconography, size, and execution all indicate an early date for Stela 9 (Awe and Grube 2001; Awe et al. 1995; Cheetham 1994). In fact, although a few Formative monuments are known from the Maya lowlands (e.g., Hansen 1991a:14, 1991b; Jones and Satterthwaite 1982:fig. 65m–p), Stela 9 most closely resembles monuments from the Pacific Coast region, where zoomorphic carvings framing humans were common during the Middle and Late Formative periods (Norman 1976:figs. 5.25–5.27; Orrego 1990:52–53).

To maintain Stela 9 in an upright position, ensure the stability of the stairway, and enable multiple offerings to be deposited, the interior of the Tomb 2 "stela chamber" was tightly packed with soil. Beginning from the top, the disarticulated remains of two or more infants were found just below the capstone. Associated artifacts included nineteen smashed Late Classic vessels and six whole or fragmented obsidian blades. Below the vessels, and continuing to the base of Stela 9, were some 200 small, un-slipped hemispherical bowls and 225 proximal, medial, and distal adult human phalanges (finger bones). Although only 7.5 percent of the phalanges were found inside intact bowls, the remainder were likely deposited in a similar manner and dislodged from their bowls as the tomb was packed with soil or were later disturbed by rodent burrows or root disturbance. Similar, though much less imposing "finger-bowl" caches are reported from several other Maya sites (Dillon et al. 1985). At Caracol, small bowls containing the bones of human fingers are reported in early Late Classic contexts from several areas of the site, including the Machete terminus group (A. Chase and D. Chase 1996a:72).

If all fingers from each individual contributing phalanges to Tomb 2 were used (3 phalanges per finger, 24 per person), at least nine individuals are represented. However, the number of contributors may be much higher if, for example, a single finger was extracted from each individual (N = 75). With one exception, cut marks are not evident, indicating that the phalanges were extracted postmortem from skeletal remains or decomposed bodies. Finally, 36 human adult mandibular incisors were scattered at the base of Stela 9 along with four obsidian blade fragments, one whole blade, and three freshwater shells. The minimum number of individuals represented by the incisors is nine, suggesting that they were taken from the same skeletal remains as the phalanges.

Zopilote in a Belize Valley Context

By at least the first half of the Late Formative period, Cahal Pech was established as one of several chiefdoms in the valley. Although palace structures were yet to be constructed, the inhabitants could boast of three large plazas, at least five temple buildings, numerous range platforms, and a ballcourt in the Core Zone. Settlement in the periphery was also exten-sive and complex. Excavations at most minor centers, patio groups, and solitary mounds within a 2-km radius have yielded architecture dating to this time.

Four of the five temple buildings in the site core were located in Plaza

B, a large ritual space capable of accommodating 1,000 or more spectators. Its focal point was three contiguous temple buildings, an "E-group" architectural complex located along the east side of the plaza. The central temple of this complex (Str. B-1) was at least 5 m in height, flanked by two smaller temples approximately 3 m tall (Awe 1992:103). To the immediate south stood Structure B-4, a 3.5-m-tall temple building that supported a pole-and-thatch superstructure (Cheetham 1995:20–21). Another temple building, although of indeterminate height, likely stood some 75 m to the west below Structure A-1. This building was 15 m tall by the first or second century A.D. (Awe 1992:76). Despite intensive excavations, no evidence exists that would suggest stelae monuments were erected in Plaza B or any other area of the site core during the Late Formative period, or that elite burials were placed in any of the five temple buildings.

This pattern is repeated throughout the Belize Valley. Although relatively large Late Formative temples are reported at the sites of Blackman Eddy (chapter 4), El Pilar (chapter 15), and Actuncan (J. McGovern, personal communication 1993), palace structures are lacking and elite burials have not been found in the principal temple buildings. The overall picture of the valley during the Late Formative is one of several chiefs overseeing small polities including the immediate periphery of each center. Political power, though certainly inherited, was exercised and demonstrated by means of religious ceremony (see Freidel and Schele 1988b). Although these polities were undoubtedly competitive, at present there is no evidence that any one chiefdom exerted political hegemony over the entire valley until the Early Classic, with the formation of city-states based at sites outside the Belize Valley.

The Late Formative was, nevertheless, a time in which politico-religious leaders were beginning to be depicted in sacred space. During the first half of the Late Formative, a stela monument was erected at the base of the principal temple structure at Actuncan. James McGovern, the investigator, suggests that this monument was erected sometime before A.D. 250 (personal communication 1993). On stylistic grounds, Actuncan Stela 1 can be reliably dated to the early Late Formative. Notable in this regard is its stylistic resemblance to other early Maya (Hansen 1991a) and Zoque (e.g., Norman 1976) stelae. Actuncan Stela 1 depicts an elaborately dressed, striding individual carrying a ceremonial staff against a background of scrolls. Thematically, Stela 1 demonstrates an interface of personal and supernatural power.

The amalgam of personal and supernatural power at a still earlier date is demonstrated by Cahal Pech Stela 9 (fig. 8.6). Although the original context of Stela 9 is not known for certain, at the time of its carving, most likely about 400 B.C., Structure A-1 at Zopilote was the largest temple building at Cahal Pech and thus as likely a location as any other for the placement of a stela monument. On the whole, it would appear that Zopilote's ritual space, which had existed for at least 500 years, was transformed by the probable addition of Stela 9 and the construction of the Martinez causeway at a slightly later date (ca. 350–100 B.C.). This shift in function possibly involved the commemoration of the individual depicted on Stela 9. Ritual procession along the causeway was probably part of this homage, as was the frequent burning of incense at the base of the Structure A-1 temple buildings. Stela 9 itself may have been a receptacle in which incense was burned—a small, hemispherical bowl-like depression carved in its top may have functioned in this manner, although clear evidence of staining is lacking.

The Zopilote terminus group was a sacrosanct ritual space where elite imagery most likely made its initial appearance in conjunction with a temple structure. If the interpretation of original context is correct, Stela 9 remained a prominent feature—perhaps even the focal point—of Zopilote until it was entombed over 1,000 years later. It is also the only known carved monument at Cahal Pech.

Despite several rebuilding episodes, the function of Zopilote does not appear to have changed during the Late Formative and Early Classic periods. In fact, not until about A.D. 600 is a change in function evident, when Structure A-1 was transformed into a funerary temple. Tomb 1, with its elite primary burial, carefully prepared cranium offering (possibly a captive or retainer) and militaristic imagery, suggests that the shift in function involved the burial of an elite person directly involved in and/or administering warfare. This tomb is the most elaborate burial yet encountered at Cahal Pech.

The Classic period was a time when warfare was common throughout the Maya lowlands (see Demarest 1992; Webster 1977, 1993, 1998). The primary objective appears to have been the creation and maintenance of city-states through the acquisition of tribute from subject polities. If we are to trust the boasts of kings, stelae monuments tell us a great deal about these military campaigns and political alliances.

The city of Naranjo, located immediately west of the upper Belize Valley, is the site that likely controlled the valley for much of the Classic period (Ball and Taschek 1991; Houston et al. 1992; chapters 11 and 12). The city-state standing of Naranjo was established by at least A.D. 546

when its king, Ruler 1, became allied with Calakmul, a major Maya center situated some 120 km to the northwest (Martin and Grube 1995; Schele and Freidel 1990:175). Ruler 1's political and military exploits lasted some 70 years and were commemorated at the Group D terminus immediately north of Naranjo's central precinct (see fig. 8.1). According to A. Chase and D. Chase (1987:60, 1996a; Martin and Grube 1995), Naranjo's political power was interrupted in A.D. 631, when it was defeated by Caracol and Calakmul, its old ally. This subjugation lasted until A.D. 693, when Naranjo appears to have reestablished itself as the preeminent polity in the area (Schele and Freidel 1990:189).

Intense rivalry and warfare between Caracol and Naranjo, however, began years before Caracol's victory in A.D. 631. Epigraphic data suggest that Caracol waged war against Naranjo in A.D. 626 and 627 (Schele and Freidel 1990:176–177). That the smaller centers of the valley were involved in the initial conflicts seems certain given the proximity of Naranjo. The only good evidence of Cahal Pech's participation in regional warfare at this time comes from Tomb 1 of Zopilote, which dates to this period of political instability. The composition of Vessel 2, particularly the individuality expressed through costume and identity, suggests an intersite military alliance involving Cahal Pech. In the absence of hieroglyphic texts an alliance with Naranjo cannot be demonstrated. In any case, the individual buried in Tomb 1 was undoubtedly one of the highest ranking elites at Cahal Pech, possibly even its ruler.

The timing of this burial demonstrates the importance of warfare in the political evolution of a medium-sized Maya center. Seemingly, it was in the best interest of Maya city-states such as Naranjo to maintain and even bolster the political leadership of medium-sized centers under their control. By the same token, the nominal leaders of medium-sized centers such as Cahal Pech could seize the opportunity presented by their involvement in regional warfare for self-aggrandizement at the local level. The most effective way to achieve this would be through explicit association with longstanding places of ritual significance. In selecting Zopilote as the place for Tomb 1, the deceased's lineage could capitalize politically on Zopilote's local importance by claiming descent (real or fictitious) from the individual depicted on Stela 9 if, in fact, this monument was standing at Zopilote. At the very least, the selection of the Zopilote terminus group as the location for Tomb 1 provided an impressive, unique venue for homage unmatched by any other location at Cahal Pech during the seventh century A.D.

The presence of a ruling elite is clearly evident in other areas of Cahal

Pech during and after the early seventh-century A.D. Temple buildings in the site core became funerary in nature, several uncarved stelae were erected, and the construction of elaborate palaces began. The latter undertaking, in particular, involved the addition of two residential palace plazas, effectively expanding the west side of the acropolis.

The Tzinic minor ceremonial center (fig. 7.1) also experienced a fluorescence at this time (J. Conlon, personal communication 1995). Around A.D. 700, immediately after Naranjo reasserted itself in the valley, an elite individual was entombed in a 6-m-tall temple (Str. 2) at Tzinic and an uncarved stela was erected at it base. As with Zopilote Structure A-1, the Tzinic locale seems to have been selected for this elite burial by virtue of its longstanding ceremonial importance (Str. 2 having been some 4 m tall by ca. A.D. 200) and highly visible peripheral location.

Discussion

Ashmore (1989:283, 1992:178) suggests that causeways were a medium that both required and proclaimed the wealth and power of its commissioners and the importance of the specific architectural complex at the road's end. Data obtained from several terminus groups in the east-central area of the Maya lowlands strongly support this statement. If the antiquity of the Cahal Pech Zopilote Group and the haphazard orientation of causeways and terminus temples in this area are any indication, key peripheral ceremonial buildings were well established before they were linked to site cores by a causeway. Thus, when viewed from a diachronic perspective, terminus groups represent the fusion of two disparate classes of architecture—distant temple buildings and causeways.

This view profoundly affects how we interpret the function of terminus groups and how they came to be incorporated into Maya site planning. Cosmological concerns do not appear to have played much, if any, role. Instead, the incentive for connecting peripheral ceremonial buildings to the site core seems to have been to create a sense of functional continuity. As such, terminus groups represent an integral part of the corpus of ceremonial architecture enfranchising and embellishing the power of elites residing in site epicenters. They were quite literally an extension of the site core into the immediate peripheral zone of habitation.

Some time ago, Marcus (1983a:204–206) pondered why Maya centers are characterized by "multiple nuclei" of large architectural groups. Although she did not provide an answer, she noted that the evolution of this pattern would remain obscure until adequate chronological control was achieved. In other words, there was (and remains) a need to carefully date the separate parts of large Maya sites in order to begin to understand this pattern of urban growth. Terminus groups may help to explain the disjunctive nature of many Maya urban centers. The "separate but equal" (Marcus 1983a:204) plaza groups characteristic of the multiple nuclei pattern usually have one or more prominent temple buildings that predate associated core causeways and elite residential structures. It is not unreasonable to suggest that, in most cases, one of these "core groups" would have been the initial Formative community, and that the others were the most immediate peripheral sites, perhaps consisting of little more than one or two small temple buildings set on a natural hill or prominent location. By sheer accretion these latter groups would be the first entities to be incorporated into an expanding site core. Proximity to the original community and later construction would obscure the possibility that they were once distinctly separate ceremonial sites.

The site of Uaxactun provides a good example of this sort of growth. From about 1000 to 900 B.C., Plaza E (Ricketson 1937) was the locus of a pre-Mamom village. Plaza A, a mainly Classic period architectural group located about 1 km to the west (Smith 1950), includes a centrally located temple, Structure A-1 (Smith 1937), the foundation of which contains a pure deposit of pre-Mamom pottery (personal observations 1999–2000). As declared by Smith (1937:193), the "importance of Structure A-1 to the ancient Maya may be readily appreciated when its central position, elevation [highest in Group A], and associated stelae are considered." To this assessment we may now add much greater antiquity and physical separation from the initial Uaxactun community.

In short, the disjunctive multiple nuclei pattern of Maya cities may be attributed to growth around small, preexisting ceremonial sites (fig. 8.7). Terminus groups would appear to be such sites, but too far removed from the original community in most cases to be completely obscured and modified by later urban sprawl and, thus, become one of the nuclei.

Temple buildings that would eventually be transformed into the focal point of terminus groups were initially small ceremonial sites of local importance. These sites presented elites with the opportunity to expand the site core and, thus, solidify their base of power. If Webster (1985:385) is correct in stating that Maya elites comprised no more than five percent of the population and were solely consumers, direct control of peripheral areas would have been necessary for their very existence. As consumers, they would require the labor, food, and other items produced by the do-

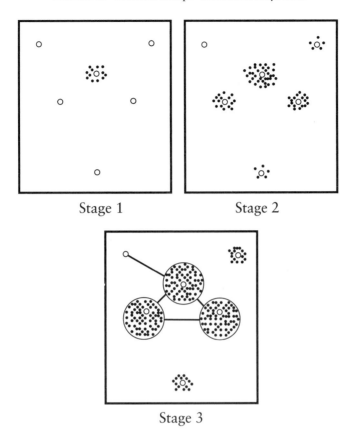

Fig. 8.7. Idealized evolution of a "multiple nuclei" Maya center: Stage 1, initial village and outlying ritual loci; Stage 2, settlement of outlying ceremonial loci; Stage 3, mature multiple nuclei urban center with terminus group and outlying minor centers.

mestic population. In the absence of coercive power, the display of wealth and personal accomplishment at peripheral locations of some historical standing would be a logical step toward achieving this goal.

The Zopilote Group exemplifies this arrangement. Throughout its history, the temples at this location were as large, or larger, than those in the Cahal Pech site core. Architectural, sculptural, and burial data at Zopilote suggest that the function of this terminus group shifted at times when political change is evident in the valley and much of the central Maya lowlands. The changes at Zopilote, moreover, seem to have preceded the functional shift of ritual space in the Cahal Pech site core. In short, it would appear that political statements heralding new forms of social organization at Cahal Pech were first made where the impact was most desirable—

the periphery. Between 350 and 100 B.C., Zopilote was integrated into the Cahal Pech site core with the construction of the Martinez Causeway. The probable association of Stela 9, a very early carved monument with both human and supernatural aspects, with a preexisting temple structure of some importance suggests that chiefly personages were able to directly connect themselves with this ritual space through permanent, visual proclamation of supernatural mediation.

Both religion and human agency have been taken into account when reconstructing Late Formative Maya political structure. In accounting for the absence of palaces and funerary temples during this period, Sharer (1992:134; see also Blanton et al. 1993:172) describes political authority as having "been based on the mediation between gods and men . . . [through] monumental public ritual architecture dedicated to the gods rather than individual rulers." This theocratic interpretation seems highly likely, especially since the ability to marshal the labor necessary to create public architecture would have been contingent upon supernatural mediation in the absence of political structures cross-cutting traditional kin lines. This view may account for the near absence of elaborate Late Formative tombs and residential palaces (Coe and McGinn 1963).[3] However, as chiefly power became more entrenched the depiction of mediators became more common.

By the Late Formative, naturalistic depictions of elites in ritual acts were painted and stuccoed on building walls at some lowland centers (Saturno 2002; Schele and Freidel 1990:figs. 4.3, 4.8, 4.9; Valdés 1987, 1988). Along with the placement near temple buildings of early stelae depicting individuals (Hansen 1991a, 1991b), the painted or stuccoed scenes suggest that the prestige of leadership was gradually attaining the readily visible prominence that supernatural deities maintained upon the stucco facades of temple structures (Freidel 1985; Freidel and Schele 1988a, 1988b). In other words, the chiefly mediator was able to directly associate his image and lineage's interests with religious temple structures. Supernatural and politico-religious power was undoubtedly strengthened through this coupling. This was undoubtedly the preamble to the funerary temples and stelae that were to become a prominent feature of the Maya landscape during the Classic period.

Early in the seventh century A.D., Structure A-1 at Zopilote was transformed into a funerary temple for a paramount Cahal Pech elite, possibly the community's ruler. Tomb 1, in particular its cranium offering and vessel displaying a procession of warriors, suggests that the ruling lineage of

Cahal Pech was directly involved in regional warfare and political alliance. Far from being disruptive, the warfare of the seventh century A.D. provided an opportunity for the nominal leaders of this medium-sized Maya center to further aggrandize themselves in the periphery. Epigraphic data from another terminus group, Group D at Naranjo (Schele and Freidel 1990:186), strengthens the case that the activities occurring at these loci during the Classic period involved the sanction and participation of the highest-status nobles within these communities. The extravagance of the terminus group architectural complex, in short, suggests that rather than the ancestral shrines of related nobility, these locations became the shrines of ruling lineages.

Perhaps the most striking confirmation of an elite ritual role of the Zopilote Group, however, is the stela chamber. Here, an ancient monument was used as a dedicatory offering to the newly constructed Late Classic temple, along with several infants and the fingertips and incisors of at least nine deceased individuals. The severe blackening of the plastered steps above the stela chamber, and the lack of additional burials in this late temple, suggests the importance and continued reaffirmation of its contents and their historical/religious significance throughout the remainder of the Late Classic period.

Why were some large groups of peripheral architecture marked for causeway construction and others not? In cases where peripheral temples had a resident population from early times, proprietary rights may have thwarted linkage with the site core. This would account for the apparent lack of residential buildings at most terminus groups, where such rights were not an impediment. For whatever reason, it seems clear that most terminus groups in the east-central area of the Maya lowlands lacked elite residential architecture.

This scenario may also apply to groups of temple buildings located close to site cores but lacking a causeway connection. The Cahal Pech Tzinic Group, located some 250 m northwest of Zopilote (see fig. 7.1), is a good example. Tzinic consists of two temples, at least one elite tomb, a plain stela monument and five small residential building platforms (J. Conlon, personal communication 1994). If high-status Maya lived at Tzinic, they certainly lived modestly compared to the palatial setting enjoyed by the site core elite. Access to Cahal Pech core palaces was highly restricted (Awe et al. 1991), whereas access to Tzinic was unfettered. Moreover, evidence that the Tzinic "residential" platforms supported perishable buildings is lacking despite considerable excavation. The small, seemingly domestic mounds that are sometimes found at minor ceremonial centers like Tzinic may have been ancillary ritual platforms.

The above observations and interpretations are not necessarily applicable to other areas of the Maya lowlands where terminus groups are present. Although not in the lowlands proper, the site of Copan serves as a good example. Here, the eastern causeway and several "side sacbes" connect a clearly elite residential sector with the main group. A second causeway continues from this point, possibly terminating at a small hilltop ritual site to the west (Fash 1983:282–283). In both cases the terminus is located about 1 km from the center, thus providing an "emic definition of the maximum extent of the site core" (Fash 1983:283, 286). In short, the Copan example demonstrates that intrasite causeways in this area were built to fulfill both elite residential and civic-ceremonial purposes (see also Leventhal 1981:198). Why is the Copan pattern different from that of the central Maya lowlands? As noted by Marcus (1983a:206), Copan has "a single major complex of public architecture that dominates all others." Peripheral temples do not seem to have been a major element of the early building program (indeed, Late Formative settlement data are largely lacking [see Fash 1991:71–72]), which would have curbed the development of multiple nuclei. If this assessment is correct, as the elite population increased during the Classic period and residential space in the site core remained relatively unchanged, lesser elites would have been compelled to establish residency at nondescript peripheral locations. One way to magnify the importance of these "haphazard" (Fash 1991:156) elite residential loci and maintain explicit ties with the core paramounts was the construction of intrasite causeways.

In conclusion, the cultural remains from Zopilote indicate political and ritual ties with the site core of Cahal Pech beginning around 350 B.C. and possibly much earlier. Evidence of these ties include Formative temple buildings as large, or larger, than those of the site core, the probable use of an early stela monument, causeway construction, and Classic period temples that include two of the most elaborate tombs at Cahal Pech. These data suggest that Zopilote—and likely many other terminus groups in the east-central area of the Maya lowlands—was a key, isolated ritual location from very early times that was eventually appropriated by ruling elites for the repeated commemoration of political and religious achievement. The terminal architecture is of the utmost importance, as it represents the motivation for the construction and ultimate destination of the causeway. In viewing this relationship, it must be remembered that these ritual nodes would be accessible without a causeway, and probably were in most cases for many centuries. Clearly, the large-scale investment of labor and resources indicate that the causeway became a necessary, if not vital part of the symbolic whole, facilitating the increasingly elaborate processions to its terminus. Because Zopilote and other intrasite terminus groups were constructed beyond the site core, they made power both visible and "accessible" to the majority of the domestic population. This was perhaps their most important function.

Notes

1. In selecting sites with terminus groups, I was limited by the availability of site plans and a desire to show examples from several distinct topographic zones (river valleys, uplands) in the larger study area. Thus, the clustering of sites evident in figure 8.1 (Mopan River Valley) should not be interpreted as definitive evidence of more terminus groups in that area. A complete list of sites with terminus groups would likely result in a fairly even distribution.

2. All dates and phase spans in this chapter are reported in calibrated years B.C./ A.D. Uncalibrated spans for the Middle Formative phases are 800–650 b.c. (EMF) and 650–300 b.c. (LMF). A small quantity of Cunil phase (1000–800 b.c. calibrated to 1100–900 b.c.) sherds (see chapter 7) were recovered with EMF material below the initial Structure A-1 platform, raising the possibility of a still earlier building (temple?) in the centermost area below A-1.

3. Important exceptions include looted Late Formative vaulted tombs at secondary sites in the Mirador Basin (R. Hansen, personal communication 1999) and an early palace complex at El Mirador (Landeen 1986). To me, these and other data (see Hansen 1991b; Matheny 1986b, 1987) suggest that a state was created in the Mirador Basin by 200 B.C. or shortly thereafter. Nonetheless, I concur with Sharer (1992) that supernatural mediation was the basis of political authority during this early period.

Acknowledgments

Research at Zopilote was conducted as part of the Belize Valley Archaeological Reconnaissance Project (1988–93) directed by Jaime Awe. I am grateful to the many people who provided assistance, advice, and encouragement at different stages of this research: Jim Aimers, Wendy Ashmore, John Clark, Jim Conlon, David Driver, Jocelyn Ferguson, David Glassman, Cameron Griffith, Nikolai Grube, Warren Hill, John Hodgson, Bobby Hohmann, Gyles Iannone, David Lee, Efrain Martinez, Terry

Powis, Jim Puc, Rhan-Ju Song, Karl Taube, and Julian Vinuales. I am especially grateful for the insightful comments and editorial advice of Barbara Stark and an anonymous reviewer on an earlier draft of this chapter, and to Jim Garber for the opportunity to participate in this volume. Finally, I thank the directors of the Peabody Museum at Harvard University and the National Museum of Archaeology and Ethnology in Guatemala City for providing access to collections of early pottery from Uaxactun.

9

Buenavista del Cayo

A Short Outline of Occupational and Cultural History
at an Upper Belize Valley Regal-Ritual Center

Joseph W. Ball and Jennifer T. Taschek

The site of Buenavista del Cayo extends along the uppermost terrace of
the Mopan River slightly more than 400 m back from its present east
bank at an elevation of 104 m within the rolling uplands triangle loosely
defined by the confluence of the Mopan and Macal Rivers (Ball and
Taschek 1991) (map 1). Just under 5 km to its east, across a plateau-
landscape interspersed by deeply cut runoff-ravines, deep, black soils, and
an expanse of marshland, the Cahal Pech regal-residential citadel-center
sits atop the highest knoll of a steeply rising bluff at an elevation of 166 m
(Ball 1993a; Ball and Taschek 2001). A little under 6 km to the south,
Xunantunich crowns an artificially leveled limestone ridge (Main Plaza
elevation, 172 m) and is easily visible from most ground-level as well as
platform-elevated positions at Buenavista and from two or three elevated
locations at Cahal Pech. El Pilar lies just over 13 km to the north-north-
west, and roughly 14 km due west lies the major regal-ritual city, Naranjo.
Another important city-center, Ucanal, is located about 40 km to the
southwest, a distance roughly comparable to that at which the aggressive
Classic-era Vaca Plateau city, Caracol, lay to the south (42 km). Tikal lies
a somewhat greater distance (54 km) to the west-northwest.

Although well known to residents of the area, and in spite of a history of
archaeology in the region beginning in the 1890s, existence of the "Buena
Vista" site continued to be overlooked or ignored by scholars until nearly
1970.[1] Our own work at the site began with its survey, mapping, and

formal registry—in fact, "re-registry"—with the Belize Department of Archaeology in early 1981, following which our active field investigations at the site continued through 1992.

A medium-sized center of the "Level 9" class in Hammond's (1975) nine-level typology of Classic period Belize coastal zone sites, Buenavista physically consists of three, large, conjoined plaza-complexes (East, Central, and West Plazas) of varying but considerable complexities (fig. 9.1). The center proper covers about 18 hectares (roughly 44 acres) and counts among its 12 hectares of contiguous monumental architecture at least 13 carved and uncarved but painted stelae and altars, two ballcourts, an acropolis-palace, two major plaza-groups, and more than 10 additional courtyard groups.[2] Two of its pyramidal platforms stand today still to heights of more than 24 m. Like any other center, Buenavista had its own, unique developmental history, and in this chapter we provide an overview of that history from the Middle Preclassic through the Terminal Classic/ "Early Postclassic"[3] periods. The historical, cultural, and functional relationships of Late Classic Buenavista to the other "major centers" of the upper valley, Cahal Pech and Xunantunich, are discussed in chapter 12.

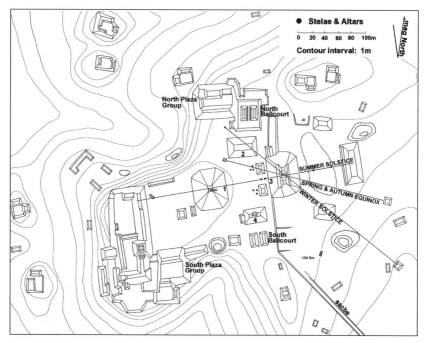

Fig. 9.1. Buenavista. Plan view of site core indicating all referenced groups and structures.

Site History

Middle Preclassic Settlements (ca. 950–650 B.C.)

Our earliest recovered evidence of occupation for the Buenavista locality dates from the early facet of the local (upper valley) Kanluk ceramic phase and was found at four discrete loci in the center proper and eight others across the circumjacent landscape within a 2-km arc. We found no traces whatsoever of the problematic "Cunil"[4] assemblage at Buenavista, and we believe it unlikely to have been present at or in the immediate vicinity of the site. We base this on the consistent, specific occurrence-contexts of documented Cunil occurrences as concentrated deposits on and overlying bedrock beneath overlying, important, later ceremonial platform-structures at Cahal Pech, Xunantunich, and Blackman Eddy (chapters 3 and 7).

All twelve of the recorded Kanluk phase loci lie on or above the third terrace of the Mopan or farther back from the river. While all can be assigned to the Kanluk phase of the Middle Preclassic period (ca. 800–650 B.C.), we are unable to state their relative temporal positions or relationships to each other with any reliability or accuracy. There is no reason, however, to believe that the twelve occupational loci either were fully contemporaneous with each other or spanned the entire length of the three hundred years-long Kanluk ceramic phase. Redundant, limited inventories of mixed domestic artifactual, ceramic, and structural data from multiple loci across Buenavista suggest each identified Kanluk context to have been the site of either a single discrete farmstead or a small agricultural hamlet.[5]

No burials or human remains from this period were encountered, nor did we encounter any evidence of either dressed masonry or plastered masonry architecture. On the other hand, a two-building patio group near the southern edge of the Classic period Guerra de Buenavista settlement yielded solid evidence of the specialized, Kanluk phase manufacture of a small-size, asymmetric or "twisted" chert biface characteristic of Middle through Late Preclassic chipped stone industries throughout much of the southern Maya lowlands (fig. 9.2; Rovner and Lewenstein 1997:fig. 7a–d). Local nodular chert bifaces, rejects, blanks, fragments, and debitage had accumulated in a 55-cm deep deposit on and off the one course high patio of tamped clay supporting the group.

Atop nearby Cahal Pech Hill, 10th through sixth century B.C. occupational evidence is both richer and more concentrated; however, most of it actually occurs as redeposited fill in the cores of sixth-century B.C. and later platform-architecture, a circumstance that has misled some investigators to evaluate the residents and events at Cahal Pech as somewhat more

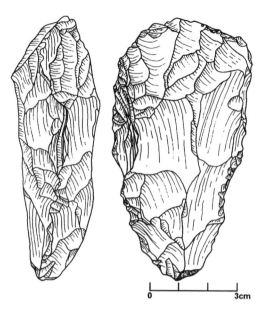

Fig. 9.2. Middle Preclassic (Kanluk phase) twisted biface, Guerra locality.

precocious than actually was the case (e.g., Cheetham 1998). Still, the cultural data from the ridge-top are rich and do indicate a substantial and steadily growing population on the hill and across the upland and bottoms below it from the eighth or ninth century B.C. on (chapter 7).

The Later Preclassic and "Protoclassic" Era (ca. 650/550 B.C.–A.D. 240~420)

Traditional archaeological Maya chronologies (Middle/Late Preclassic divide, ca. 300 B.C.), broad-based Maya ceramic chronologies of the last quarter century (Middle/Late Preclassic divide, ca. 200 B.C.), present radiometric chronologies (Middle/Late Preclassic divide, ca. 400 B.C.), and the appearance of plaster-finished masonry architecture and artifactual distributions suggestive of intersite and intrasite social ranking as dated radiometrically and from associated ceramics (ca. 550–450 B.C.) do not conveniently coincide in the Belize Valley to provide a neat and tidy date for the inception of a distinct zonal "Late Preclassic." Instead, there is a temporally staggered appearance over a period of time extending from about ± 650 B.C. to 400 B.C. of public architecture, architectonic sculpture, iconographically significant imagery, better but differentially executed ceramics, and other "special" artifacts suggesting the existence of social inequalities and the emergence of social ranking during this span (Ball and Taschek 2003).

Without question, the most precocious locus of such events currently documented in a convincing manner by means of convincing data is that of Blackman Eddy in the central valley. There, evidence supporting the existence of intersite-level (i.e., intersettlement or intercommunity) social distinctions and ranking has been demonstrated to have been present by the middle to late seventh century B.C. (chapter 3). Suggestions of comparable situations involving the Barton Ramie, Cahal Pech, Tolok, Nohoch Ek, Buenavista, Actuncan, Arenal, and El Pilar sites do exist but are reliable and convincing only for a period postdating 500~400 B.C. within a broad time frame that now seems to have witnessed a multiplicity of such events both within the valley and elsewhere.

At Buenavista, the earliest evidence of "real" (formal) architecture found occurred in the north-south alley running between the South Plaza-Group and the southeast face of the Palace, a passageway that in the full Late and Terminal Classic provided a focused and possibly important vista of the royal "Ancestor Mountain," Structure A-6, at distant hilltop Xunantunich. It consisted of a red-stained, plastered platform atop a thick plaster flooring. Core inclusions of crisp (i.e., "fresh") trash and an in situ, sealed structural cache (fig. 9.3) fixed the age of the platform within the Umbral ceramic phase (ca. 550–200 B.C.), a date in good agreement with other overall assessments of the earliest likely valid dating for the appearance of true formal architecture elsewhere in the upper valley, as at Cahal Pech, Tolok, Nohoch Ek, and their environs (Aimers et al. 2000).

Data from structural and open space testing indicate the likelihood of significant Preclassic settlement remains and construction in the southwestern sector of the site both beneath and west (riverward) of the Late Classic palace complex. By the late first century B.C., Buenavista was a major architectural center and presumably a significant focus of ceremonial activity for the upper valley.

The apparent ceremonial heart of the early center established the Central Plaza as a spacious sacred space defined by a triad of frontally staired platforms each exceeding 10 m in height (see fig. 9.4). The platforms framed the east, north, and west sides of the plaza, which was open on its south. Formal, ritual access to the Late Preclassic plaza appears to have been via the south ballcourt, which lay a distance of 50 m to its immediate south (see fig. 9.4). The ballcourt itself is a single-phase (thrice refurbished) construction of first-century B.C. date, contemporary with major individual architectural phases of the plaza-platforms. At least in the cases

Fig. 9.3. Terminal Middle/Initial Late Preclassic (Umbral phase) structural cache, Buenavista.

of the west and east platforms (Structures 1 and 3), we found evidence of earlier constructions dating back to the beginnings of the Late Preclassic period or earlier.

Some 140 m to the southwest of the Central Plaza, the South Plaza Group also had grown into a substantial and elaborate residential platform-complex of presumable elevated status by this same time. Thick, hard, well-floated, and frequently refurbished plaster pavements stretch away from the group to its south and west. Slightly farther west, an almost labyrinthine complex of platforms, courtyards, and building-footings and foundations dating to this time were encountered.

Plaster-surfaced masonry platforms of contemporaneous Late Preclassic date have been reported from several other sites in the upper valley including Cahal Pech (Awe 1992; Awe et al. 1990; chapter 7), Nohoch Ek (Coe and Coe 1956), and Actuncan (McGovern 1994) among others. Platforms of considerable size (>10 m) appear to have been present at some of these (e.g., Cahal Pech), and at Actuncan and Cahal Pech at least, the

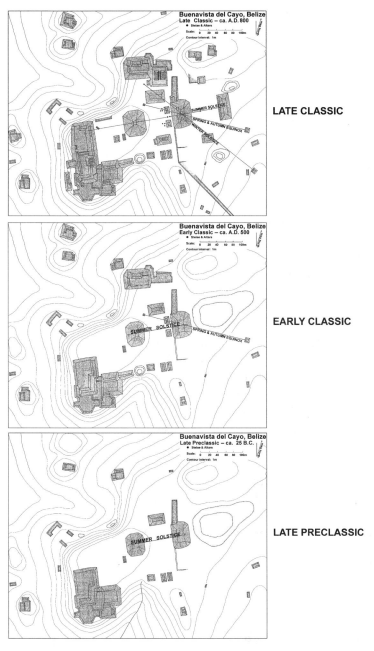

Fig. 9.4. Footprint plans of Late Classic (ca. A.D. 800); Early Classic (ca. A.D. 500); Late Preclassic (ca. 25 B.C.). Buenavista del Cayo center.

Late Preclassic architecture occurred within contexts of considerable configurational complexity (Awe 1992; Awe et al. 1990; McGovern 1994; chapter 7). At both Actuncan and Cahal Pech (Awe and Grube 2001; Ball and Taschek 2003), this extended even to the presence of sculpted stone stelae.

By the first century A.D., the upper Belize Valley was heavily populated and already home to several centers of socioorganizational focus. Beyond that, the data actually still do remain too disparate and uneven to allow for any honest interpretation of their relational significance. Nonetheless, to hazard one observation, the tripartite structure comprising Cahal Pech, Buenavista, and Xunantunich (Actuncan) may owe its initial establishment to this era (chapter 12).

There is little evident change in the overall archaeological-material record from the late Xakal (typological Late Preclassic, ca. 100~50 B.C.– A.D. 150) through the Madrugada (typological Protoclassic) ceramic phases, but those changes that did occur might well have been profound culturally. First, while there is overall a smooth continuity in the material cultural record of the valley, analytically noticeable (Preclassic/Protoclassic) changes did occur, and while some of these likely were no more than "natural" local evolutions in ceramic technology and style (Brady et al. 1998), some may have had considerable local social or political significance (e.g., the limited importation of Petén Gloss Ware black Balanza and polychrome Dos Arroyos group dishes, bowls, and other vessels). In this respect, there is an enormous expansion in the distribution if not the size of the zonal population throughout the upper valley (the diagnostic indicator for this being unslipped cauldrons and other domestic utility pottery of the Chan Pond ceramic group), and there also occur the first clear indications of local, intracommunity status-differentiation in multiple burials both at and in the environs of the Cahal Pech citadel.

Without question, two of the most interesting and important questions concerning the Belize Valley Preclassic that remain are when did it end, and how did it relate to the subsequent rich and lengthy full Classic cultural tradition of the valley. Viewing this volume among other things as a guide for future research, the authors would identify determining both the historical relationships between the "Preclassic" and "Classic" occupations and cultural traditions of the upper Belize Valley and the real chronology of their interface as high priority issues. What we are convinced of based on the data amassed to date is that this interface did not involve a smooth and natural developmental "evolution" from the one tradition into the other.

The Early-Middle Classic Continuum (ca. A.D. 240~420–670~690)[6]

The Ahcabnal ceramic phase (ca. A.D. 240~420–540)[7] heralds and corresponds to the Early Classic period in the upper Belize Valley. Just what transpired to demarcate and establish Ahcabnal is unclear; however, it was marked by dramatic discontinuities in long-established ceramic types, groups, wares, and functional forms in use at both elite and commoner levels and presumably manufactured by the potters and potting communities of the upper valley (Clowery and Ball 2001).

Ahcabnal is associated with marked augmentations in the size and distribution of the resident zonal population and with a proliferation in the numbers of new suburban residential patio groups and plazuelas established both in the immediate environs of Buenavista and across the rural countryside surrounding it and Cahal Pech—a pattern apparently also present downriver to the east in the Baking Pot vicinity (chapter 5).

Within the Buenavista center proper, there were major surges in large-scale, formal architectural activities involving both the public monumental and private residential arenas (see fig. 9.4). On the Central Plaza, Structure 2 (north platform) underwent a major enlargement and elaboration while both Structures 1 and 3 experienced lesser but significant additions and modifications. Several smaller public structures also were added to the center at this time. Significant residential construction occurred on the sites of both the North Plaza Group and South Plaza Group (see fig. 9.4) including the addition to the latter's northeast platform-top corner of a small sweatbath that remained in use throughout the subsequent Middle and Late Classic periods (Ball 1993a:fig. 48).

As noted, Ahcabnal was distinguished by multiple dramatic discontinuities in the local ceramic traditions of the upper valley occurring sometime between ca. A.D. 240 and 420. These disjunctions ranged from replacement of the deep-rooted Tumbac Unslipped Ware Jocote–Chan Pond unslipped domestic utility ceramic tradition by the Uaxactun Unslipped Ware Triunfo-Cayo tradition to complete disappearance of the longstanding "waxy" (thick, adherent, "polished") surface-slipping tradition and its replacement by a new "glossware" (thin, flaky, "glossy") tradition. Other significant events in local ceramic history also occurred at this juncture. The signature Belize Valley Late-Terminal Classic basin and jar blackware group, "Mt. Maloney," first appeared as a domestic utility slipped ware with Ahcabnal and grew steadily in importance through and following it. Black (Balanza group) glossware bowls and dishes and orange-base polychrome bowls first appeared in the upper valley in Terminal Preclassic

(Madrugada phase) contexts (Brady et al. 1998:26–27). Apparent imports initially, by the time of Ahcabnal, high quality blackware and brownware vessels were being produced locally in a limited range of service-forms such as basal-flanged dishes, tripod cylinder-vases, and flat-base cylinder-vases and bowls (e.g., Taschek and Ball 1999:fig. 7c).

Whatever the full extent and significance of these discontinuities and replacements in the overall cultural history of the valley—and in this chapter we will offer no attempt at interpreting or explaining them—what is certain is that they did occur, that they were both profound and consequential, that they did sharply demarcate the local Preclassic from Classic ceramic traditions, and that they heralded the start of a ceramic if not a full cultural tradition that thereafter would persist into the 10th century or later.

The subsequent Gadsden phase (ca. A.D. 540–670) of the Middle Classic period was largely an era of consolidation and developmental elaboration of the Ahcabnal base. Little other than minor, gradual, developmental modifications in the stylistic and formal repertoires of the upper valley ceramic industries can be detected over most of the sixth and seventh centuries. Then, almost simultaneously, a number of earthshaking events took place that dramatically but separately transformed both elite public ceremonial lifeways and the technology and economics of pottery production in the valley.

Effected in major ways were the valley's overall central-place configuration, its individual large centers, monumental architecture, ceremonial caching patterns, ritual paraphernalia, pottery serviceability and longevity, and all those cultural patterns and behavioral activities presumably associated with these. In concert, these events and cultural acquisitions ushered in and demarcated the full Late Classic era in the upper Belize Valley (chapter 12).

Late Classic Florescence to Terminal Classic Decline (A.D. 640~660–950+)

The ritual dedication of the massively remodeled Central Plaza included the deposition of three complementary matched subfloor caches along the upper centerlines of Structures 2, 3, and 4. The most elaborate of these, that of Structure 3, incorporated scattered marine shells; a red-painted, modeled stucco statue of a cross-legged hunchback dwarf (fig. 9.5; Ball 1993a: fig. 39); and, encapsuled in two lip-to-lip ceramic dishes, a cosmographic model made up of riverine and marine sands, obsidian and chert eccentrics, a tennis ball–sized sphere of polished obsidian, vari-

Fig. 9.5. Stucco statuette of hunchbacked dwarf from primary centerline cache, Structure BVc-3.

ous seashells and corals, several bloodstained stingray spines, a complete Yucatán Bobwhite (Colinus nigrogularis), and a capping of ceiba kapok (Ball 1993a:fig. 41).

The emplacement of these caches likely comprised a single, momentous ritual that at one and the same time activated and empowered the Buenavista Central Plaza complex as the sacral heart of the center.

Reflecting the specific personal interests of the authors, much of the postfield analysis of SDSU project data undertaken to date has focused on the zonal ceramic industries and architectural traditions, the contextual relationships of these to each other and other artifact categories, and the sociobehavioral significance of those relationships (e.g., Ball 1993b; Ball and Taschek 2001). Within this context, we found one particularly intriguing development among the ceramic traditions of the late-seventh-century upper valley—and one of considerable possible political historical significance—was the appearance on some decorated finewares of an octopodlike design seemingly associated specifically and exclusively with the Buenavista center. Appearing first on a few, rare, most probably imported Palmar Orange-polychrome vases, what we have termed the "Buenavista Device" by the middle to late eighth century was featured regularly on the signature zonal whiteware (cream) polychromes (fig. 9.6). It continued to

Fig. 9.6. The "Buenavista Device": Late Classic (Late Paloverde ceramic phase) bowl, palace complex, Buenavista del Cayo.

be depicted well into the ninth century, the latest recovered examples possibly dating from the late facet Sacbalam phase (ca. A.D. 850–900+) of the local "Collapse" or immediate post-Collapse era.[8] While we are reluctant to identify this device as the "emblem," "sign," or other symbol of Buenavista or its ruling house, it very plausibly did have precisely some such import or significance.[9]

The broad regional orientation of our data collection and analysis also served to highlight the unique and special qualities of materials recovered from deposits associated with the palace complexes at Buenavista and Cahal Pech as compared to those from all other contexts sampled throughout the valley by both ourselves and others (Ball and Taschek 2001). One finding in this regard that has had an impact on Maya studies well beyond the central western Belize theater has been our archaeological documentation of the existence of (Late) Classic period "palace schools" of decorated ceramic vessels, an idea first voiced by Clemency Coggins (1975) and later developed by others (Ball 1989; 1993b; Ball and Taschek 2001; Reents 1985; Reents-Budet et al. 1994, 2000).

Data supporting the existence and nature of a "Buenavista palace school" have been provided on several previous occasions (Ball 1989; 1993b; Reents-Budet et al. 1994, 2000), and we here wish only to remark the documented existence of a Late Classic "palace school" involving a special-purpose, high-status painted ceramic industry at Buenavista and to

Fig. 9.7. The Buenavista "Palace School": Late Classic (full Paloverde ceramic phase) polychrome vase, palace complex, Buenavista del Cayo.

impart that we have recovered and continue the process of carefully analyzing and documenting the evidence supporting both its onsite production and its dynamism over time.

Sometime early in the eighth century, an exceptionally fine cylinder-vase for kakaw presentation/consumption was commissioned from an artist in service to the royal courts of Naranjo and Ucanal by the great Naranjo king and warlord, K'ul Ahaw K'ak' Tiliw Chan Chaak (see Houston et al. 1992; Martin and Grube 2000:75–77; Taschek and Ball 1992). Executed in tones of red and orange-red on white accented by blue labial and basal banding (Taschek and Ball 1992:490), the vase was given a distinctive and incontrovertibly deliberate cachet by facing the standing personages depicted toward their right rather than left per the usual canons of Late Classic Maya vase painting (Linda Schele, personal communication, October 1994). Without here attempting to explore the possible significance of this deviation or other stylistic and programmatic elements associated with it, we note that it initiated a distinctive local standard faithfully adhered to by the "fineware" (palace/court) pottery-painters of the upper Belize Valley for a century or more to follow (fig. 9.7).

Yet another intriguing event in the ceramic history of the valley that occurred in the mid-seventh century was the reappearance of volcanic ash tempering among some of the zonal redwares. Ash tempering had had a deep and lengthy history in the valley, having been present from the very beginning of the Middle Preclassic on. It remained important through most of the Kanluk ceramic phase, but by late Kanluk increasing quantities of carbonate-tempered pottery were appearing in upper valley assemblages. This trend continued through Umbral (550–200 B.C.) and into Xakal, and by the late aspect of the Xakal ceramic phase (50 B.C.–A.D. 150), ash tempering had disappeared from local potting industries. It is entirely absent from the Madrugada, Ahcabnal, and early Gadsden ceramic phases, finally reappearing as part of the momentous events of the mid-seventh century.

It merits noting that the reappearance of volcanic ash tempering did not coincide with and does not archaeologically mark either the Ahcanal/Gadsden nor the Gadsden/Mills boundaries. This important economic and technological event transpired sometime during the course of the Gadsden ceramic phase transforming zonal redware traditions. The use of volcanic ash-tempering expanded in Mills extending to local buffwares, creamwares, and polychromes, and to more local redwares, but not all. The producers of the important lower valley Garbutt Creek and Vaca Falls [Roaring Creek] and less common Dolphin Head groups (Gifford 1976:226–243), for example, never employed this tempering agent. It thereafter remained important through the Late and Terminal Classic periods surviving even into the local ("Late") Postclassic era. Just what the cessation and reappearance of volcanic ash as a tempering agent reflect historically is not clear. Anything from the depletion of a limited quantity natural resource and the later discovery of another source of such to the closing or opening of specific routes of commercial interaction or any combination of these might have been involved. The history and significance of volcanic ash tempering in the economic history of the valley present interesting and important questions for future research.

The Terminal Classic Aftermath (A.D. 950–1100~1200)

Among the three major Late Classic centers in the upper Belize Valley, only at Buenavista del Cayo did a remnant Late Classic palace population appear to have survived the collapse and its aftermath of the ninth and 10th centuries on into the 11th. Eventually, this small group of "hangers-on" was joined or replaced in the 11th or 12th century by northern peninsula émigrés. The latter represented a minimal presence, however, and by the close of the 12th century, Buenavista as well lay abandoned and void of human occupants.

Sporadic occupations of the larger center and its ruined facilities continued on at least into the regional Terminal Classic (ca. A.D. 900~950–1150+), but we found no hints of even ephemeral occupation thereafter until the 20th-century acquisition of the then-forested locality by the Guerra family of Benque Viejo del Carmen and its conversion into the clear-cut and rapidly overgrazed Buena Vista cattle and sheep ranch of today.

Of more than trivial historical or cultural importance to the history of the lowland Maya during the centuries following the conventional Late Classic "Collapse" at ca. A.D. 800~900, however, was our recovery at three separate loci on the Buenavista site and one at Nohoch Ek of single household-level ceramic and artifactual "signatures" indicating the direct, physical derivation of the materials concerned from the northern coastal plain of Yucatán. In each of these cases, not only the "style" and "appearance" of the objects concerned but their actual paste and temper attributes indicate their exotic, imported status and their approximate zone of origination.[10] The transported articles included ceramic cauldrons essential to nixtamal settlement and preparation of the food base, sacan ("lav" in Belizean Creole), and items associated with the household spinning of twills and twines and their conversion into usable cloth. In the ethnographic present still, long-distance movements by individual families are accompanied most often by the transport, curation, and multigenerational use of "female artifacts," that is, implements and tools stereotypically associated with women or women's roles in present-day "traditional" Maya culture.[11]

The ephemeral, short-term reoccupations of the Buenavista locality until the 20th century are in marked contrast to situations elsewhere in the greater Belize Valley from Tipu on the Macal River (Cohen et al. 1997) to Baking Pot (chapter 5) and other sites (Aimers 2002a; Willey et al. 1965) along the Belize River proper in the lower valley and beyond. We have no easy explanation for this beyond the apparent reality of a severely reduced and thinned population either concentrated into fewer, denser settlements or reliant upon a more mobile subsistence economy than was the case up through the Terminal Classic. Data to test any such hypotheses, however, will have to come from sources other than the archaeological remains of Buenavista.

Conclusion

In this chapter, we have provided an outline of the known cultural history of the Buenavista del Cayo center in a way that we hope will prove useful to other archaeologists working in the greater central-eastern Petén–central-western Belize zone and to Mayanists in general. Several serious misconceptions, incorrect assumptions, and erroneous statements concerning Buenavista and its history have appeared in the literature over the last 10 years or so, and it is our hope that this short but accurate authorized sketch of its history from early Middle Preclassic to Postclassic times will eliminate or at least reduce the frequency of such misstatements in the future. Additionally, it is our intent to make known more widely something of the wealth of data recovered by the SDSU Mopan-Macal Triangle archeological program. We have not attempted to explore those data or their import or to address any of the several intriguing themes introduced. The space made available to us simply did not allow this. Instead, we hope that we have indicated something of the breadth and richness of the cultural historical and sociobehavioral data and information resulting from the project. Considerable quantities of data remain in what likely will be a lengthy process of analysis and presentation by our students, our colleagues, and ourselves and we expect their gradual publication to continue over many future years.

Notes

1. The site finally was reported officially in 1968 by Elias Alfaro, a staff member of the Belize Department of Archaeology, and in 1969 it was formally recorded in the National Register of Archaeological Sites by Commissioner Peter Schmidt. We first visited the site in early 1981 in the company of Alfaro.

2. For comparison, the Rio Bec regional capital center, Becan, covers about 19 hectares (47 acres) of space. The Cahal Pech citadel or core, in contrast, occupies an 11-hectare area (about 27 acres) defined by the modified crest of a high limestone ridge overlooking the Macal Gorge, not at all dissimilar in size, orientation, or spatial situation from the ridge overlooking the Mopan River some 9 km to the southwest that supports the site of Xunantunich.

3. Along with many of our colleagues, we have come to doubt the usefulness and validity of the term and concept "Early Postclassic," or even the existence of such a period. As now is being convincingly established for the more northern regions of the Maya lowlands, it appears far more probable that an extended "Terminal Classic" culture persisted into or through the 11th and even the 12th century in many areas until finally truncated, displaced, or replaced by a disjunctive "full"

(Late) Postclassic tradition. No evidence presented to date from the Belize Valley in any way credibly suggests otherwise.

4. We employ the term *Cunil* for the upper valley manifestation of this assemblage based on its priority in the literature (Awe 1992; Awe et al. 1990). Interested scholars and researchers should be aware, however, that any reliable definition of the assemblage and its content should and must be based on the more recent recognition and documentation of the "Kanocha" assemblage at the lower Belize Valley site of Blackman Eddy (see chapter 3) due to serious persistent and still continuing discrepancies, inconsistencies, and internal self-contradictions in all descriptions of the "Cunil" material offered to date (e.g., Awe 1992; Cheetham and Awe 1996; Cheetham 1998).

5. The recovered inventory includes an abundance of chipped-stone tools and implements of local chert, numerous ground-stone food-processing implements of porphyritic granite, a handful of ceramic figurine fragments, a small number of prismatic obsidian blade segments, and enormous quantities of shell from large-size specimens of edible local riverine snails (*Pachychilus* sp.) and clams (*Nephronaias* sp.).

6. A "final" absolute chronology for the Buenavista-Cahal Pech locality remains a work-in-progress at this writing. Over 80 radiometric determinations and 50 obsidian hydration measurements pertaining to the Late Preclassic through Terminal Classic chronology of the two sites have been obtained to date and are in the process of being evaluated, collated, and rectified among themselves and with the conventional ceramic chronologies applied to the central-western Belize region. The chronometric parameters provided in this chapter reflect as yet unresolved uncertainties in the ongoing reconciliation of these multivariate data.

7. Unresolved ambiguities and inconsistencies involving several major ceramic horizon markers, central Mexican-originating green obsidian, and two sets (totaling eight) of seemingly contradictory radiometric dates make a reliable determination for the start of Ahcabnal realistically impossible at this point. Depending on how one chooses to interpret the presently available data, the phase could conceivably have begun from as early as A.D. 240–260 to as late as A.D. 420 (see Brady et al. 1998). We hope to be able to resolve this very important issue in the not-too-distant future.

8. The "device" also is present on a severely eroded fragment of a shattered limestone lintel from the front room of Structure 4. Dating from the late mid-seventh century, this lintel was one of only five sculpted stone monument fragments (all severely eroded) recovered at Buenavista.

9. There is what could have been a corresponding "Cahal Pech device" consisting of a personified bloodletter/hummingbird design common at that center from early Middle into Terminal Classic contexts, but it lacks the specificity and exclusivity of the "Buenavista Device" and does appear on some Middle and Late Classic cache-vessels and palace wares at the latter site as well as at Cahal Pech.

10. Among the most interesting materials recovered was a true Balantun Black-

on-slate: Balantun Variety (Chichen Slate Ware: Northern Plains paste variant) restricted orifice, bolster rim, strap-handled basin (Smith 1971:16; 174–175; fig. 15); several crumbly, thin-wall, generic "late" unslipped bowls and wide-mouthed jars; two green obsidian blade segments; and an elliptical ceramic spindle whorl decorated with a prefiring-incised raptorial bird design—an artifact type widespread on, but until now known only from the northern plains of Yucatán in Pure and Modified Florescent (Terminal Classic/Early Postclassic) contexts (Taschek 1994:215–216; fig. 57d).

11. This is based on information obtained between 1985 and 1989 from multiple female members of the Guerra, Manzanero, Mena, Rosas, and Salazar families of Benque Viejo and San Ignacio regarding stone manos and metates and pottery cooking vessels brought by their grandmothers from Poptun, Dolores, and other locales in Guatemala when they and their families emigrated to British Honduras late in the 19th century or at the start of the 20th.

Acknowledgments

The investigations reported on in this chapter were supported in part by grants from the U.S. National Science Foundation (Award Nos. BNS-8310677 and BNS-8719157); the United States Agency for International Development; the Belize Ministry of Tourism and Environment; the Foundation for the Advancement of Mesoamerican Studies, Inc.; San Diego State University and the SDSU Foundation; the Acacia Foundation of San Francisco; and multiple private donors. Permission to carry out fieldwork in Belize was graciously extended by the Honorable Glenn D. Godfrey, Minister of Tourism and Environment; by successive Belize commissioners of archaeology, Harriot W. Topsey, Winel Branche (acting commissioner), Allan Moore (acting commissioner), and John Morris (acting commissioner); and by Pablo Guerra and Hector Guerra, on whose lands the Buenavista site is located. We especially wish to acknowledge the late Harriot W. Topsey for encouraging us to pursue investigations at Cahal Pech and Buenavista del Cayo and continuing to support our work at those sites through 1992.

Among the numerous project staff and workers who participated in and contributed to the progress of these investigations, we would especially like to acknowledge the efforts of Field Assistants Eduardo Alfaro, Elias Alfaro Jr., Ubaldamir Alfaro, Eduardo Chi, José Chi, Ventura Cocom, and Gilberto Uck; Field Staff Laura Bernd, Marc Brown, Steve Elder, Cynthia James, Richalene Kelsay, David Major, Barbara Otto, Dominique Rissolo, and Carol Winkler; Project Foreman Armando Bautista; Lab Supervisor

JoAnne Gilmer; and Lab Assistants Sara Clowery, Bruce Lumsden, Amin Salazar, and Chad Tritt.

Our overall appreciation and understanding of Buenavista and Cahal Pech also have benefited from discussions regarding particular aspects of their archaeology with colleagues Jaime Awe, Ron Bishop, Geoff Braswell, Dorie Budet, John Clark, Arthur Demarest, Jim Garber, Steve Houston, Gyles Iannone, Takeshi Inomata, Kevin Johnston, David Stuart, and David Webster. We thank them each for their input, suggestions, and critiques, as we do the two anonymous reviewers of this volume.

All illustrations used in this chapter were produced by Jennifer Taschek. We, of course, assume full responsibility for any errors of fact or interpretation or other shortcomings from which the chapter may suffer.

10

Xunantunich in a Belize Valley Context

Richard M. Leventhal and Wendy Ashmore

We begin this chapter with what can best be termed "a call to theoretical arms" for researchers working in or near the Belize River Valley and, indeed, for investigators throughout the Maya lowlands. In many respects, we have a unique interpretive opportunity due both to the amount of research that has been and continues to be conducted within the environs of the valley, and to the amount of data presently available that can and should be used to examine and test models of political, social, and economic development in the Maya lowlands.

Building on a decade of their own research in this area, Joseph Ball and Jennifer Taschek reopened an important theoretical discussion of how the occupation of the Belize Valley was ordered and integrated, and, to a lesser extent, how it developed through time (Ball and Taschek 1991; Willey et al. 1965). We use their model as reference for our work at Xunantunich, and for understanding the ancient occupation in the valley as a whole.

Ball and Taschek set forth their model in a 1991 article in *Ancient Mesoamerica* titled "Late Classic Lowland Maya Political Organization and Central Place Analysis: New Insights from the Upper Belize Valley." In this article, they argue convincingly for a broad regional approach that allows them to identify a primary polity centered upon Naranjo that, they argue, controlled the valley. We agree generally with this large-scale interpretive picture.

A second major part of Ball and Taschek's model is their functional analysis of the sites located in the valley that constituted part of Naranjo's polity. It is this second part of the model with which we, at Xunantunich, disagree. They identify a series of communities in the upper valley and then argue that the site of Buenavista del Cayo was the principal local "urban center," having administrative and other functions for serving and integrating the populace at large. Ball and Taschek also discuss Xunantunich and Cahal Pech, both of which, they argue, are restricted access, elite residential citadels that functioned as subsidiaries to Buenavista del Cayo during the Late Classic.

We disagree along two lines. The first and probably the most important is that the Ball and Taschek model is almost entirely synchronic in its chronological viewpoint. Many of the differences and contrasts between the sites must actually be identified as diachronic shifts. The most obvious statement of this is that we would argue that Buenavista del Cayo and Xunantunich are more sequential than contemporaneous. Ball (1993a) has argued that Buenavista del Cayo dates primarily to the early and middle parts of the Late Classic (A.D. 500/550–650/700). In contrast, we did not find substantial evidence of occupation at Xunantunich earlier than A.D. 600–670 (LeCount 1996; LeCount et al. 2002). We have encountered many Middle Preclassic ceramics redeposited in fill but have recovered little in situ evidence of occupation or intact construction for this time period. Dates for Xunantunich then extend from this early A.D. 600/670 time period to at least A.D. 900, with continuity into the Terminal Classic period.

We believe that this broader, diachronic view significantly enriches our understanding of the ancient world of the Belize River Valley. Maintaining this chronological perspective, we then turn to our second major point of disagreement with Ball and Taschek, which focuses on their functional identifications for sites such as Xunantunich and Cahal Pech. Xunantunich cannot be identified as simply a "castle on the hill"; rather, we believe that it is the administrative and ritual center that succeeds Buenavista del Cayo as the paramount site for this western part of the valley.

Our developmental model for the valley includes Xunantunich only at the beginning and end of the Maya occupation in the region. Collectively, research in the middle and upper Belize Valley region outlines a sequence of occupation beginning about 1000 B.C. (Awe, personal communication 1992; Ford and Fedick 1992; Willey et al. 1965; chapters 3 and 7). In this Middle Preclassic time frame, as in much of its later history, the Belize Valley was characterized by relative decentralization of organizational structure and authority. At Xunantunich, we find evidence for what might best be described as a small Middle Preclassic village. By the early centuries A.D., however, in Late Preclassic and Early Classic times in the valley, population grew dramatically in both agriculturally productive valley bottomlands and adjacent fertile uplands. The beginnings of political central-ization were also evident at this time. The most tangible such evidence was monumental civic architecture and sculptured stelae, bearing hieroglyphic texts, portraits of local rulers, or both. Although monumental architecture has been found in a number of locations in the Belize Valley region, only four area sites have yielded early stelae thus far: Blackman Eddy (chapter 4), Pacbitun (Healy 1990a; chapter 13), Actuncan (McGovern 1992; Wil-ley et al. 1965), and Cahal Pech (Awe 1992; Awe and Grube 2001). This Late Preclassic and Early Classic time period witnessed the emergence of cities like Tikal, Rio Azul, Naranjo, and Caracol as political giants in the lowland Maya world. This early trend in the Belize Valley toward growth and eventual centralization around a large site is truncated, however. During the Early Classic, a series of small to medium-sized centers define small competing polities in the valley. It is possible the contemporary Belize valley stelae were already marking the borderlands of larger poli-ties—linking Pacbitun with Caracol's domain, for example, or Actuncan with Naranjo.

At the beginning of the Late Classic, Buenavista del Cayo expands sig-nificantly and this may mark Naranjo's first or continued attempt at con-trolling the valley and more clearly demarcates the "tension zone" be-tween its own polity and that of Caracol (A. Chase and D. Chase 1987). It was during the reign of Smoking Squirrel of Naranjo that the subordinate center, Buenavista del Cayo, apparently peaked in development as an ad-ministrative center for the upper Belize Valley (Ball and Taschek 1991; Houston et al. 1992; Taschek and Ball 1992; chapters 9 and 12). After the mid-eighth-century death of that ruler, however, texts at Naranjo faded quickly to silence, and at Buenavista, new construction apparently ceased. Archaeological evidence suggests Xunantunich was in existence at that time, but not in the form we see today.

In A.D. 780, however, a new growth spurt apparently took place at Naranjo. By this time, Caracol's rulers had failed to erect stelae for virtu-ally a century (since 9.12.0.0.0., A.D. 672, with one known exception in 692; A. Chase and D. Chase 1987; Culbert 1988, 1991), and Tikal's dynasty was increasingly in disarray (Jones 1977, 1991). Perhaps seizing the opportunity provided by the decline of competitors or overlords, Na-ranjo's dynasty erected four monuments in 780 alone, and dedicated a profusion of others over the next 40 years.

Naranjo's known epigraphic record ceased abruptly in A.D. 820 (9.19.10.0.0; Martin and Grube 2000), contemporary with the probable date of the earliest sculptured stela at Xunantunich, Stela 8. Xunantunich's three sculptured stelae are often linked stylistically to those of Naranjo, and one of its eroded monuments bears what is probably an explicit reference to the latter site (i.e., an emblem glyph at position C2 on Stela 8). What is more, the setting of Xunantunich's sculptured stelae has close counterparts at Naranjo, not only in the setting of stylistically similar monuments, but indeed, in the layout of the civic core as a whole (Ashmore 1998). Finally, centralized power in this part of the valley seems to shift from Buenavista del Cayo to Xunantunich at the end of the Late Classic and beginning of the Terminal Classic.

We now turn to our archaeological work at Xunantunich to present some data to back up our model of Xunantunich as a Late and Terminal Classic "full service" valley center. Located atop a ridge overlooking the Mopan river in west-central Belize (map 1), Xunantunich is a Maya civic-ceremonial center of Late and Terminal Classic times. That much has been known for more than 50 years (Thompson 1940; Willey et al. 1965). In the 1980s, archaeologists began to look more closely at several portions of the Belize Valley and adjacent areas, and have collectively outlined the broad sweep of ancient developments in the region as a whole (e.g., Awe 1992; Ball and Taschek 1991; Ford and Fedick 1992; Graham et al. 1985; Laporte and Torres 1987). By the early 1990s, then, Xunantunich could be recognized as the latest in a succession of local political and ritual capitals, collectively the seats of competing or sequential local paramounts in this part of the upper Belize Valley, through the end of the Classic period.

We begin consideration of the organization of Xunantunich by examining our new map (fig. 10.1) and, in particular, a series of entry and exit points, connecting the central part of Xunantunich with the valley to the east and southwest. A major sacbe has been defined that runs north from Group D (Braswell 1998). The sacbe is a 14-m-wide, plastered roadway with small raised parapets on both sides. It was initially defined at the northern edge of Group D. This entry point into Group D is marked by a stela. Sacbe 1 continues from Group D to the north and then turns to the west, entering the main plaza between Structures A-4 and A-6, a point similarly marked by a stela. After extensive excavation of this sacbe by Angela Keller, we believe that this roadway provides a processional avenue between Groups A and D. This sacbe creates a physical connection between these two groups, and thereby, implicitly, a political link between the noble or royal lineage resident in each.

An entrance/exit area can also be identified on the western side of Group A almost directly opposite the Sacbe 1 entrance. This western entry

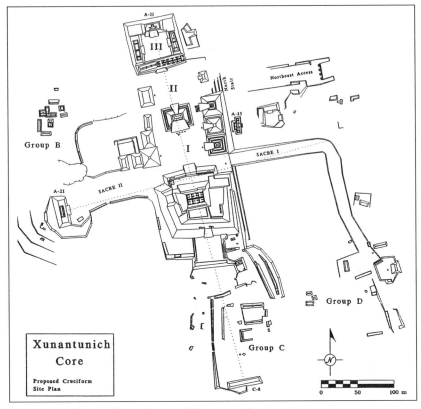

Fig. 10.1. Final map of central area of Xunantunich.

is associated with Structure A-21, on the southwest edge of the main group. Although preliminary examination of this area has proven inconclusive, we are fairly confident of the existence of a primary set of east-west entrance points into Plaza A-I and the central part of ancient Xunantunich.

We offer a couple of comments at this point in relation to the entrance points and sacbe just described for Xunantunich. It is not unusual to find stelae marking the entrance points of *sacbeob* into a central section of ancient Maya cities. Copan is a good example with Stela H, at the western terminus of the Sepulturas causeway (Fash 1991). What is most interesting is another similarity with Copan. Both Copan and Xunantunich are primarily north-south oriented centers with primary access points along sacbes to the east and west creating a broad-scale quadripartite orientation for both sites. The neighboring and possibly controlling site of Naranjo has a similar north-south quadripartite layout.

To conclude this discussion of the internal organization of Xunantunich, we need to add a diachronic perspective, as we begin to see this site change during and after the collapse, a period of political and social instability (Thompson 1940). We have tentatively marked the initial construction of the city at about A.D. 600/670 (LeCount et al. 2002). Extensive excavations in Group A involved clearing, trenching and/or tunneling into several key buildings including Structures A-1, A-6 (the Castillo), A-11, A-12, and A-20. In addition, Group D was excavated in detail by Jennifer Braswell (1998). Tunnels into the Castillo on the south side of the building revealed the first major building phase dated ceramically to A.D. 600/670. This early building was found immediately on top of fill consisting of Middle Preclassic material probably scraped up from the abandoned Middle Preclassic village mentioned above. However, even with this extensive excavation program, we did not recover enough information in this central group to know the full range of constructions pertaining to this early time period.

With construction of Structure A-1 and the marking of the two central entry points, Plaza A-I became the most important public space at Xunantunich. In fact, we believe we can demonstrate that this public space and access to it changed dramatically as Xunantunich weathered the period of the Classic collapse (and continued until about A.D. 1000). We hypothesize that the area of the Castillo north to Plaza A-III was originally a single open plaza with a ballcourt (Ballcourt 2; Structures A-17 and A-22) located on the west side of this open space. Structure A-1, built near the end of the Late Classic, abruptly bisected the formerly continuous space, and thereby began to focus access and activity within the new Plaza A-I. Ballcourt 2 was not destroyed or covered over with the construction of Structure A-1 (Jamison 1996). Rather, it remained in place as ritual space. In addition, we see emphasis upon this plaza defined even more clearly with construction of a low wall that connects the southeast corner of Structure A-1 and the west side retaining wall of Structure A-3. This wall would hinder movement between Plazas A-I and A-II. Such demarcation of public space is also evident to the south of the Castillo where, during the end of the Late Classic, we have documented construction of a series of enclosed courtyards, which limited access to the Castillo and the northern plazas. Clearing and trenching excavations along with the analysis of remains in this southern area indicate that the focus shifted away from this area during the Terminal Classic as the site contracted inward toward Plaza A-I. We see this constriction of Xunantunich as the result of social, political, and economic tension during the period of instability brought about by the wider collapse. Tensions and instability continue into the post-Collapse period.

We would like to add one final note about the excavations of Structure A-1. Only one main construction phase was identified in the massive excavation trench through this building. Within this single Late Classic building phase, we see a highly structured and organized construction system for the substructure. Small construction bins were identified and are roughly rectangular in shape and no more than 1.0–1.5 m on a side. These bins hold defined layers of fill or fill of all one color or texture. Pink fill, black fill, gray/brown fill, small cobbles, large cobbles, limestone rubble were not simply mixed together. Each was deliberately placed in a separate and clearly bounded location. Previous discussions of such fill techniques have argued for different families or groups being responsible for the construction and fill of certain bins or areas. However, this highly defined and differentiated layering and color separation leads us to consider the deposits as "symbolic fill," which not only constituted the building but also placed this important building into the symbolic framework of the ancient Maya worldview. Specifically, we view the construction technique evident in A-1 as related not simply to labor systems, but also to identification of the laborers and their kin as constituents of the very substance and essence of the building. Thereby they became an inextricable part of the city as a whole.

Finally, we turn briefly to Structure A-6, the Castillo. There are two things we want to note from our research. First, the shifting focus and contraction of the site toward Structure A-1 is also evident in the Castillo. The final multiple phases of construction have been defined. The earlier building, A-6–2nd, had three doorways facing each cardinal direction. With the final construction phase, A-6–1st, the focus shifted to two directions—north and south only, with greater emphasis on the north. With the final shift away from the southern areas during the Castillo's use, the northern Plaza A-I focus dominated.

A second point about the Castillo concerns discovery of a new section of a monumental plaster frieze on the west side of the building (MacKie 1961, 1985). This frieze is another portion of the one well known on the east side of the building, initially excavated in the 1950s (Satterthwaite 1951). The frieze adorns the exterior of the A-6–2nd vault, and originally ran around all four sides of the building. With construction of A-6–1st, the ancient Maya covered the east, west and south side of A-6–2nd and its frieze, keeping the north side open at all times to Plaza A-I. The north and south sides have eroded away, leaving fragments on the east and west. The preservation of the newly documented western section of the frieze proceeded with great help from the Getty Conservation Institute and Mexico's Instituto Nacional de Antropología e Historia.

As with most monuments in the Maya lowlands, this frieze was a political statement placing the ruling lineage and its ancestors into the context of power in the Maya view of the world. The most important element on the frieze, as preserved on the west side, is a partially eroded but full-sized seated figure, sculpted in the round (fig. 11.1b). The figure appears to be a portrait of a Xunantunich ruler. We speculate that three full-sized portraits were originally located on each side of the building. This human representation is broadly similar to the stone-carved ancestors or lords on Copan Structure 10L-22A (Fash 1991). The style of rendering in the Xunantunich frieze is quite similar to that of frieze sculpture recently revealed from the same time period at Ek Balam.

Virginia Fields (chapter 11) has examined and begun the interpretation of the iconography on both the east and west sides of this building. She argues that this frieze reveals the Xunantunich rulers reenacting the creation of the world, presenting themselves as the center or *axis mundi* of this world and therefore of the Xunantunich community. Although at present we lack surviving evidence, we speculate that a similar frieze likely adorned Structure A-6–1st as well as A-6–3rd. As mentioned above, the construction of the later building (A-6–1st) created a north-south focus but the primary orientation was to the north. Rulers and nobles could step out of A-6–1st onto the roof of A-6–2nd, with the original lineage frieze partially exposed below them and the hypothesized frieze from the last building above them. The Late Classic and Terminal Classic rulers at Xunantunich thereby created a powerful symbol (the Castillo) of their power linked to the past (lineage), the present (themselves), and the future (continuity of the lineage). From Structure A-6, they could also look out upon the populace assembled before them on civic and ceremonial occasions, a populace represented directly by the gathering of individuals, and embodied symbolically in the mass of Structure A-1.

As discussed above, a sacbe connects Group A with an important outlying architectural cluster, Group D (Braswell 1998). Group D consists of a series of platforms associated and clustered around Structure D-6, the largest pyramid of the group (6 m). Two plain stelae have been found in this group; one defines the connection of the sacbe, and the other is located along the central axis of Structure D-6. Group D is an elite residential group with presumed lineage or other kin-based ties to the ruling family of Group A.

Structure D-6 marks the central ritual building associated with this elite family. Structure D-7, located just to the north, was constructed at the end of the Late Classic and was still occupied in the Terminal Classic. D-7 is a range structure and an elite residential building that faces to the north, unlike D-6's orientation to the west. As evidenced by the sacbe, we believe that D-7 marked a shift in focus to the north and perhaps to the ruling family, rather than facing solely to the west as a local, semi-independent family.

Information about the hinterlands is consistent with that from the site core and adds a dimension concerning political, ritual, and economic integration of their respective residents. Settlement study in the Xunantunich area involves both systematic and opportunistic investigations in several distinct and complementary areas (Ashmore et al. 2000; Connell 2000; Robin 1999; Yaeger 2000a, 2000b).

Our systematic survey examined settlement within three transects across the landscape, a sample designed for ready comparability with that of Anabel Ford's Belize River Area Settlement Survey (BRASS) (Ford 1985; Ford and Fedick 1992) as well as the broad surveys of other local projects (Yaeger 2000a). All three XAP transects were 400 m wide, to maximize capture of settlement units. Transect T/A1, cut across the area between the Mopan and Macal rivers, linking Xunantunich with the small but imposing site of Dos Chombitos, about 8 km to the southeast. Within this corridor, three distinct clusters of structures were discerned, which seem to relate to greater Xunantunich as well as hamlet-like communities, centered respectively on Dos Chombitos and, midway along T/A1, the Chan site (Robin 1999).

The same region-wide developmental dynamics described above similarly characterize the rural settlement along T/A1. Occupation was fairly widespread as early as Middle Preclassic times, but reached peak distribution and maximal community growth in the Late Classic. It is during the latter period within which Maya farmers created the abundant hill slope and cross-channel terracing observed today. In Terminal Classic times, settlement contracted markedly, nucleating more tightly around Chan and Dos Chombitos. On present evidence of architectural form and preliminary artifact study, the former seems to have been a hamlet-like settlement throughout its occupation; its largest, focal patio groups appear to be principally residential in function. Dos Chombitos, on the other hand, seems to have had a ritual arena at its core, marked by an uncarved stela and a pyramid some 12 m high, bounding the north side of a large public plaza.

The other two formal transects ran, respectively, north from Xunantunich along the Mopan (T/A2) to the site of Callar Creek, and north from Dos Chombitos along the Macal (T/A3), to the ridge between Tipu and Chaa Creek. T/A2 intercepted the western edge of the imposing site of Actuncan, providing a broader settlement context for that precocious and important site (McGovern 1992). Similarly, T/A3 crossed the Negroman/Tipu settlement documented a decade earlier by Elizabeth Graham and her colleagues (Graham et al. 1985), and enriches both sets of investigations. Preliminary analysis of T/A2 and T/A3 data suggests settlement distributions distinct from that on T/A1, due in part to topographic and edaphic contrasts, and apparently in part to differential political and economic pulls. The T/A2 terminus site of Callar Creek is almost directly opposite Buenavista del Cayo, across the Mopan River. Its form suggests civic functions, perhaps linking Buenavista del Cayo and communities to the south and west.

A fourth settlement sample centers on Chaa Creek and adjacent hillslopes and plains. Samuel Connell (2000) studied this important zone, whose imposing masonry architecture and plain stelae imply a locally prominent political and economic standing for its leading families. Connell has inferred their control of both terrain adjoining the Macal and a plain extending west from the Chaa Creek hills. The latter offers not only the most expansive stretch of flat arable land in the area, one of the few local tracts farmed commercially today, but also the easiest passage between the Macal and Mopan.

At the far western end of the possible portage described above are remains of a hamletlike settlement on a tract known today as San Lorenzo, and nearest the Mopan, a series of irregularly arranged cobble mounds, which do not appear to be domestic features. These mounds are scattered along the lowest terraces on both sides of this stretch of the Mopan, and their location seems the best clue to this ancient function, as likely part of a transshipment station. They seem to date to Late Classic times, when all sites in the implied portage system were actively occupied.

At San Lorenzo, Jason Yaeger (2000a, 2000b) pursued intensive excavation of individual patio groups and mounds of San Lorenzo. He examined localized community organization and integration in Late and Terminal Classic times. In San Lorenzo, as elsewhere, occupation peaked in the Late Classic, but continued on a reduced scale into the Terminal Classic. Differential distribution of ritual paraphernalia and vessels for feasting suggest to him diminished integration both within the San Lorenzo community and in relation to neighbors. Cynthia Robin (1999) documented parallel phenomena within the Chan community, on a smaller scale of population density, and at a different rank within the peasant populace.

In all, the Xunantunich settlement study documented an actively evolving system that peaked in scale and complexity in the Late Classic. In Terminal Classic times, populations contracted into smaller communities, and new construction tended to be relatively expedient in material and effort.

Conclusion

To summarize the picture that emerges from this work and these excavations is one of a burgeoning center at Xunantunich, the nexus of both sacred and secular activity. The center is supported by a sizable population in its immediate periphery that was formally connected to the surrounding settlement in the valley. We also see Xunantunich as a center that began to contract into itself during the time of the social and political unrest of the collapse and Terminal Classic.

As we discuss at the beginning of this chapter, there is a great need for a diachronic context within which to examine and interpret occupation in the Belize River Valley. In such a context, Xunantunich emerges as a major force as Buenavista del Cayo and earlier local centers declined. Indeed, Xunantunich appears suddenly and spectacularly during the middle of the Late Classic period. There is, however, no tight cluster of occupation and settlement around this large, new elite center. Rather, local settlement remains rural, with small, secondary centers as primary focal points for the surrounding population. With the onset of the wider collapse, and with political, social, and economic chaos attendant on that collapse, settlement around Xunantunich began to cluster more closely around these traditional nodes of stability.

We estimate that the rulers at Xunantunich maintained their power for at least 100 years after the wider Classic period collapse (LeCount et al. 2002). Their authority appears less and less secure with time. Its more tenuous nature is seen in architectural shifts at the civic center, and in settlement contraction in its hinterland. We have yet to understand fully the reasons for Xunantunich's ultimate abandonment (but see Ashmore et al. 2000). Ongoing study of its extended hold on local authority will, we trust, continue to yield insights about ancient Maya society in the Belize River Valley and beyond.

Acknowledgments

The Xunantunich Archaeological Project was developed in 1991 at the invitation of the Department of Archaeology, Government of Belize, then under direction of Acting Archaeological Commissioner John Morris. We would like to thank Mr. Morris, Alan Moore, and others in the Department of Archaeology, for their support and encouragement. We would also like to thank the USAID, the National Science Foundation, the University of California, Los Angeles, the University of Pennsylvania (Department of Anthropology and Research Foundation), the Getty Conservation Institute, and consultant Carlos Rudy Larios V. We would also like to thank Rudy and Margaret Juan; our labor force, including our foreman, Florentine Penados; the people of San Jose de Succotz; and our archaeological colleagues working in the region.

11

The Royal Charter at Xunantunich

Virginia M. Fields

Architectural sculpture in the form of monumental, polychromed, modeled stucco masks appears abruptly in the Maya lowlands during the Late Preclassic period at such sites as Cerros, El Mirador, Tikal, Uaxactun, and Lamanai (Freidel and Schele 1988a). This great public art created a symbolic landscape within which religious and political ceremonies took place and political doctrines underlying the concept of kingship and the cosmos were expressed.

The tradition of architectural sculpture continued throughout the Classic period, both in the southern and northern lowlands, blossoming into myriad local styles. The so-called Palace of the Stuccoes in northern Yucatán, for example, which was built near the close of the seventh century, is adorned with a stucco frieze that encircles the upper facade. The frieze comprises a unique composition of anthropomorphized birds and animals, whose metaphorical meaning perhaps concerns sacrifice, death, and the Maya underworld (Miller 1991).

Also at this time, the Puuc area of the Yucatán is home to a tradition of mosaic stone sculpture, in which pieces of carved and shaped stones were assembled into geometric motifs and patterns as well as masks representing supernaturals and other beings and objects. These were tenoned into the facades of monumental public buildings (Sharp 1981).

Architectural decoration in the southern lowlands during the Late Classic, however, more typically focused on themes of rulership, such as royal portraiture and insignia, dynastic narratives, and the relationships between the natural and supernatural worlds embodied in the ruler's experience. At Palenque, brilliantly painted stucco reliefs in a palette made up of mostly reds, blues, and yellows, adorned the piers of buildings, functioning like stelae in other Maya cities (Schele 1985). Relief sculpture portraying the actions of kings and queens was also placed on basal platforms, entablatures, and roof combs. At Palenque, large stone armatures were constructed, to which modeled stucco was attached, and oversized figures, shaped fully in the round, were inserted into roof comb niches (Robertson 1977).

Yet another localized tradition of modeled stucco architectural sculpture occurred at Xunantunich in the waning years of the Late Classic period. This tradition is expressed in a dual register composition that combines the great facade masks reminiscent of the Late Preclassic with the narrative style of Late Classic architectural relief sculpture as seen at Palenque.

Xunantunich sits on a hilltop in the west-central area of Belize, in the western end of the Belize River Valley, overlooking the Mopan River. In Ball and Taschek's (1991) model of political organization in the upper Belize River Valley, they proposed the existence of a large polity, centered at Naranjo, which controlled a series of communities in the valley. The principle, local administrative center in the upper Belize Valley during the early and middle parts of the Late Classic (between A.D. 500 and 700) was apparently Buenavista del Cayo, whose ties with Naranjo are documented by the hieroglyphic inscription on the Buenavista vase (Houston et al. 1992). Xunantunich apparently succeeded Buenavista as the primary administrative urban center in the western Belize Valley around A.D. 700 (Leventhal et al. 1993; chapters 10 and 12).

The largest and most imposing building at Xunantunich is Structure A-6, which rises more than 40 m above Plaza A-1. Plaza A-1 is the most important public space at Xunantunich, and Structure A-6 undoubtedly served as the primary ritual building for the city (Leventhal 1992; chapter 10). A large staircase on the north side of the structure led down to Plaza A-1, while a staircase on the south side of the Castillo led to a recently discovered architectural group, thereby placing Structure A-6, also known as El Castillo, in the middle of the central area of Xunantunich (Leventhal 1992; chapter 10).

The lower two-thirds of the building comprises a series of terraces built onto the pyramidal structure, while the upper section of the building reveals evidence of two building phases. The earlier building phase, know as A-6–2d, dating to around A.D. 800, consisted of a superstructure that faced all four directions with three doorways on each side. A plaster frieze encircled the upper portion of the building on all four sides. Investigations of the west side of Structure A-6–2d by Julia Sanchez during the 1993 field season revealed that the frieze, located above the doorways, was made of roughly shaped stone that was then covered with plaster. Traces of red paint were found on fragments of plaster from the fallen door lintel at the south end of the west side (Sanchez 1993).

The portion of the frieze on the eastern side of A-6–2d was excavated in the 1950s by Linton Satterthwaite and others, and it has been almost completely reconstructed several times over the course of the past forty years. The east, west, and south sides of A-6–2d and the frieze were covered by the ancient Maya with the construction of A-6–1st, while the north side, facing toward Plaza A-1, was left open. Access to the southern group was also retained, but over time, focus shifted to the northern access.

The north and south (front and back) sides of the frieze were destroyed with the gradual deterioration of the building from the time of its apparent abandonment around the 11th century A.D. The western side of the frieze was excavated during the 1993 and 1994 field seasons, revealing an entirely distinct iconographic program from that found on the eastern side of A-6–2d. Unfortunately, the western side is also partially eroded, leaving approximately one and two-thirds sides of a formerly four-sided sculptural frieze, making interpretation of the entire composition difficult.

The following is a brief description of the surviving fragments of the Structure A-6–2d frieze. By setting the frieze in the context of Late Classic period lowland Maya sculptural themes, it is possible to suggest a role for the frieze in relating the divine right of kings of Xunantunich.

The frieze on the eastern side of Structure A-6–2d comprises two horizontal registers in which the components of the composition, as well as the two registers, are separated by framing bands of plaited cloth or twisted cords and elements representing celestial phenomena (fig. 11.1a). The twisted or plaited cloth or twisted cords suggests the location Na Ho Chan, a supernatural location in the sky where creation of the universe was initiated (Freidel et al. 1993). This place is evoked in a black background vessel, which shows the birth of a god at Na Ho Chan Witz Xaman (First-Five-Sky-Mountain-North) (Freidel et al. 1993:fig. 2.31). The young deity, framed in twisted cords, is flanked by two aged gods who play a role in the divine acts of creation.

Three monumental masks, situated above three doorways, dominate the lower register of the frieze. The central mask, excavated during the

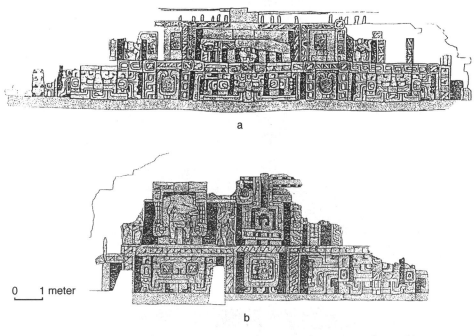

Fig. 11.1. Architectural friezes on Xunantunich Str. A6-2d: (a) eastern frieze; (b) western frieze. Drawings by Delia A. Cosentino.

1994 field season, presents a long-lipped supernatural with a crossed-band motif in its forehead, reminiscent of the depiction of Chak Xib Chak (fig. 11.2) on the Cosmic Plate, which also carries a reference to Na Ho Chan in its inscription. It also recalls the portrayal of K'inich K'an Joy Chitam II in the guise of Chak Xib Chak on a carved limestone panel from Palenque (fig. 11.3). The watery associations of Chak in combination with the celestial associations evoked by the lunar signs, skybands, skybearers, and Venus/star signs in the upper register of the frieze further imply the celestial location Na Ho Chan. Chak is also recognized as playing an important role in the acts of creation (Taube 1986).

The two masks framing the composition in the lower register are more readily identifiable as Pax gods, characterized by the crossed bands in their jawless mouths and the streams of "goo" issuing from their mouths. The phonetic reading of Pax in the inscriptions is *te,'* tree, and these masks may evoke the concept of the World Tree, the central axis of the Maya cosmos. The World Tree is the path of communication between the natural and

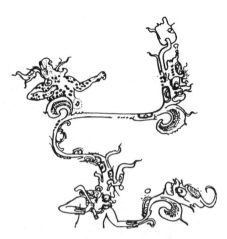

Fig. 11.2. Chak Xib Chak on the Cosmic Plate (after Schele and Miller 1986: pl. 122b). Drawing by Linda Schele. © David Schele, courtesy Foundation for the Advancement of Mesoamerican Studies, Inc.

Fig. 11.3. Limestone panel from Palenque (after Schele and Miller 1986: fig. VII.3). Drawing by Linda Schele. © David Schele, courtesy Foundation for the Advancement of Mesoamerican Studies, Inc.

supernatural worlds as it is defined at the center of the cosmos, and the king personifies the World Tree.

The remains of a serpent-headed throne, surrounded by a skyband, appear above the central mask in the eastern frieze. The placing of three throne stones, one a jaguar, one a serpent, and one a water lily, during the acts of creation centered the cosmos and allowed the sky to be lifted from the primordial sea (Freidel et al. 1993:66–67; Looper 1995).

The frieze on the western side of Structure A-6-2d also comprises two horizontal registers, whose elements are separated by similar framing bands of different types of plaited or twisted cords or cloth, and beadlike elements (fig. 11.1b). Formerly, the lower register consisted of three monumental masks, located over three doorways. Unfortunately, the upper courses of the west wall of Structure A-6-2d collapsed toward the south, causing the frieze in that area to also collapse (Sanchez 1993). Two masks remain, separated by a day sign cartouche containing a profile depiction of an axe-eyed creature wearing a headdress of God K, whose name has been identified as K'awil (Stuart 1987). Given the pattern on the eastern side, the mask at the southern end of the west wall probably matched the axe-eyed mask at the northern end.

The upper register is set back about half a meter, and its upper region is eroded. From north to south, the register contains a now-headless figure, who once faced north, and who may also be a skybearer; the remains of a three-dimensional seated figure, framed by a skyband and feathery or leaflike elements, which terminate in elaborate knots; a dancing figure, whose hands rest on, or clutch, ropes or cords that drop from the skyband overhead and whose head is turned to the south; a cross-sectioned shell, framed in a cartouche that is open at the top and resting on a thronelike base; and finally, three vertical columns, two of which resemble plaited cloth or rope and one that resembles columns of hieroglyphs, although none are legible (except one resembling an oversized *k'in*). The remains of another serpent-headed throne rest on one of the plaited columns.

The frame around the three-dimensional seated figure recalls the feathery thrones seen on a red background vase in a scene that strongly resonates with themes of death and warfare (Freidel et al. 1993:pl. 39). A similar scaffold frame, decorated with feathers and shrunken heads, enclosing a scene of decapitation and sacrifice, occurs at Tonina (Yadeun 1992). Because of the severe erosion to the upper area of the Xunantunich figure, however, it is difficult to determine if corresponding death and warfare iconography appeared here. The figure may also represent an ancestor or subsidiary lord, as seen on Copan Structure 22A (Fash 1992: fig. 11).

Adjacent to the enthroned figure is a dancing figure, whose proportions are those of the skybearers who appear on both eastern and western facades, but who appears to be spewing "goo" like a Pax god. This figure clutches cords that descend from the skyband in a scene corresponding to those found in both carved monuments (such as Caracol Str. 3; see Taube 1994:figs. 3a–d, where this association was first defined) and painted books (such as the Paris Codex, p. 22; see Freidel et al. 1993:fig. 2:32). These cords are identified as the sky umbilicus, or the cords of the sky, *xtab ka'anil* (Freidel et al. 1993; Taube 1994). These cords represent the vector of sustenance between the sky and the earth that was manifested at the birth of the Maize God.

The role of the cross-sectioned shell, which rests on a thronelike base and is framed by an open-ended cartouche, is less clear in this composition of mythico-historic significance. In combination with the cartouche located below the shell, a possible reference to ancestors may be stated. Here, a beautifully modeled profile head, marked with axe eyes and mouth barbel, wears a headdress of the god K'awil. Rulers who wear the smoking axe of K'awil primarily do so after death, such as K'inich Janaab' Pakal I on the Palenque sarcophagus lid. Cranial torches denote ancestors, and there may be such an expression here. K'awil is also associated with the ritual and sacrificial actions that represent the reciprocal relationship that exists between people and the gods.

These emblems may also represent ancestral names or toponyms. On the carved frieze at Tonina, for example, figures sit on day sign cartouches in which their names and/or titles may be related (Yadeun 1992). A representation similar to the Xunantunich example is the image engraved on a

Fig. 11.4. Vessel from Seibal Burial 14 (after Sabloff 1975: fig. 392).

vessel from Burial 14 at Seibal (fig. 11.4) (Sabloff 1975:fig. 392). Here, a jawless K'awil-like profile head is represented as a witz-monster, a personified mountain with a cleft forehead; the head is framed by skyband elements, implying a celestial location for this personified mountain.

The presence of the remains of a serpent-headed throne in the center of the composition mirroring that on the eastern facade suggests a parallel function for Structure A-6–2d to Copan Structure 22A, identified by Fash (1991:131–134, 1992) as a *popol nah*, or community house. Ten *pop*, or mat, signs are built onto the entablature of this four-sided building, signifying its identification as a *popol nah*, which was designed for meetings of community councils. Eight human figures were also depicted on the entablature, each seated cross-legged over a hieroglyph, which Fash (1991:131) suggested were place names of communities in the Copan realm.

In his analysis of Quirigua Stelae A and C, Looper (1994) suggested that the serpent headed throne is associated with women and ancestor communication. The ruler who commissioned the Structure A-6–2d frieze was undoubtedly portrayed sitting on this central throne.

The mask on the northern end of the lower register of the western facade is characterized by axe eyes, associating it with the number six, or the word *wak* in Maya. An identical mask most likely was found at the southern end of the western frieze. As the Pax gods on the eastern facade are read as *te,'* tree, so too is *wak* related to the concept of the World Tree, which is named *wakah kan* or *chan* ("Raised-up Sky"). The notion of a four-sided house whose corner posts are world trees constitutes the fundamental metaphor for the Maya cosmos (Taube 1994), a concept compatible with the four-sided Structure A-6–2d. The World Tree (and the ruler as World Tree) is the axis of communication between humans and the gods or ancestors.

The central mask on the western facade has characteristics of the sun god with its square eyes, tau tooth, and mouth barbels. The mask lacks its lower jaw; the patron of the month Pax happens to be the sun god without a lower jaw.

An intriguing iconographic and epigraphic parallel to the composition of the Xunantunich frieze is found on the paired Quirigua Stelae A and C, whose north faces are shown in figure 11.5. Elements at Xunantunich that correspond to Stela A include cords dropping from the skyband above, clutched in the right hand of the king, who is dressed as the world tree in the form of the axe-eyed god of the number six (*wak*); he is also adorned with jaguar characteristics and is dancing. On Stela C, the king, dressed

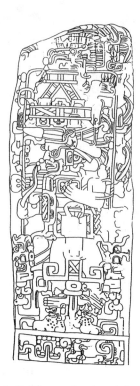
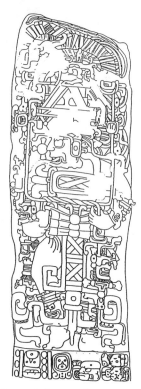

Fig. 11.5. Quirigua stelae A and C, north faces (drawings by Matthew Looper).

as the tree in the form of the Pax god again clutches cords dropping from a skyband. These are *hotun*-ending monuments that were dedicated at 9.17.5.0.0, which also commemorate the act of creation: the hieroglyphic inscription on Stela C opens with the date 13.0.0.0.0 4 Ahaw 8 Kumk'u, the date when creation began, and the text continues on to relate the placing of the three throne stones, which are the symbolic prototypes for the hearthstones used in Maya homes for over three millennia (Freidel et al. 1993:67). The three throne stones centered the cosmos as the hearthstones center the home.

The south faces of these two monuments (fig. 11.6) reveal the king holding a jaguar throne stone on Stela C and a snake-headed throne stone on Stela A, replicating the actions of the gods who set the equivalent throne stones at creation. By depicting himself in this manner, the king portrays himself as the architect of the *k'atun* and as the driving force behind the events of creation (Looper 1995).

Fig. 11.6. Quirigua stelae A and C, south faces (drawings by Matthew Looper).

A corresponding message is conveyed by the architectural frieze at Xunantunich, which by its form and content, reveals the ruler as recapitulating creation and reiterating his role as the *axis mundi* of his community. For the ancient Maya, creation was at the heart of what they represented in their art and architecture (Freidel et al. 1993:60). The epic of creation as related on such Classic Maya monuments as the Tablets of the Cross, Foliated Cross, and Sun at Palenque, as well as at Xunantunich, parallel the 16th-century Quiché Maya creation epic, the *Popol Vuh,* in the manner in which the story of creation is incorporated into the political charter of a Maya city.

Acknowledgments

I would like to thank Richard Leventhal for inviting me to take part in the Xunantunich Archaeological Project. I greatly appreciate the gracious hospitality extended to me during my stay in Xunantunich in 1994, where I benefited from discussions, iconographic and archaeological, with members of the staff and crew. I would also like to express my thanks to colleagues who provided me with many insights into the interpretation of the frieze, especially Karl Taube, Linda Schele, and Stephen Houston.

12

Buenavista del Cayo, Cahal Pech, and Xunantunich

Three Centers, Three Histories, *One Central Place*

Jennifer T. Taschek and Joseph W. Ball

Although each of the known major Late Classic centers of the Mopan-Macal triangle (Buenavista, Cahal Pech, and Xunantunich) did have its own individual and unique history, the sociopolitical dynamics of the Late Classic period joined them together into a single upper valley system. This chapter considers their separate Late Classic site histories and how these merged into a single central-place system (fig. 12.1).

Dramatizing the far-too-often forgotten reality that changes in archaeological categories are not organically related and rarely tend to coincide, a series of striking events occurred over the later decades of the Gadsden ceramic phase (ca. A.D. 540–670) that heralded the dawn of a century of cultural florescence and prosperity in the upper valley manifest most spectacularly in the monumental architectural building programs carried out at Buenavista, Cahal Pech, and Xunantunich.

Late Classic Florescence to Terminal Classic Decline in the Belize Valley (A.D. 640~660–950+)

The Seventh Century at Buenavista del Cayo

The upper Belize Valley cultural florescence of the middle seventh through early ninth century was ushered in by a spectacular reconfiguration of the Central Plaza at Buenavista that included the ritual deactivation of the south ballcourt (see Ball and Taschek 2001:182–183) and the contempo-

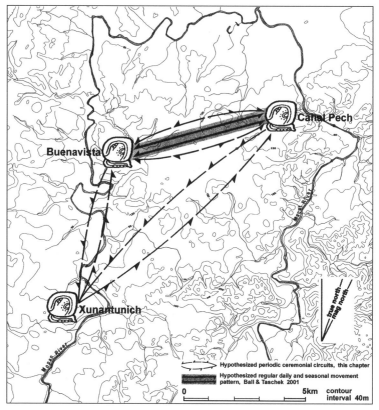

Fig. 12.1. Three centers, three hearthstones: The upper Belize Valley Late Classic "Jade Hearth."

raneous construction of Structure 4 (South Plaza Unit) and the north ballcourt (see figs. 9.1, 9.4). Major programs of enlargement and elaboration also transformed Structures 1, 2, and 3, the North Plaza Group, South Plaza Group, Palace, and East Plaza. Most if not all of the center's known stelae and altars were emplaced at this time, and a new tradition in offerings for structural caching was introduced involving the inclusion of sets of chert and/or obsidian eccentrics at focal points in structural cores, beneath or at the base of stelae and altars, or as accompaniments to some human burials (Otto 1995; Taschek and Ball 1992, 1999).

The Seventh Century at Xunantunich

Spectacular as was the mid-7th-century remodeling of the Central Plaza at Buenavista, it pales in comparison to another great architectural undertak-

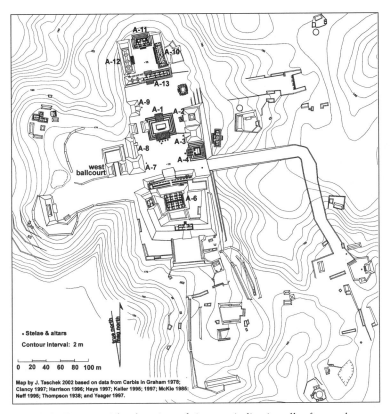

Fig. 12.2. Xunantunich: plan view of site core indicating all referenced structures.

ing of the era: the grand-scale raising of the center at Xunantunich (fig. 12.2). Based on our own analysis and interpretation of the Xunantunich data,[1] we place the inauguration of large-scale, monumental ceremonial construction at the site during this same era and, in fact, see it as part of the same episode.[2] So inextricably interwoven was this relationship, in fact, that we strongly suspect the "early" Plaza A Ballcourt at Xunantunich— eventually partly buried by Structure A-1a—to have been the spiritual and physical replacement for the South Ballcourt at the Buenavista site, and the construction of the former to explain the contemporaneous deactivation of the latter. These constituted not two coincident but unrelated or even related events, but one.

The first construction phase of A-6, "El Castillo," the awe-inspiring Late Classic "Ancestor-Mountain" and shrine that today still dominates the upper valley from Cahal Pech to Las Ruinas (Arenal) was begun at this time as part of a monumental reshaping of the Xunantunich ridge

193

into a secluded but spectacular and highly visible holy place sacred to the deified deceased and ancestral deities of the ruling house of the upper Belize Valley and all those subject to them or residing in their realm. By the start of the eighth century, Structure A-6–3rd, the Plaza A Ballcourt, the open-fronted (north) palace-group (Structures A-10, A-11, A-12), and at least some of the Plaza A—flanking east side (A-2, A-3, A-4) and west side (A-7, A-8, A-9)—pyramidal platforms had been completed (see fig. 12.2). It is the latter that together with Structure A-6 give the center its distinct and special place in the tripart central place system of the upper Belize Valley and identify what this was, for they are dedicated funerary monuments, the interment places of select members of the valley's Late Classic elite.

Neither A-1 nor A-13 (the palace-fronting audiencia) existed at this time, and we know virtually nothing of the absolute or relative chronologies of the east-side and west-side funerary platforms. The center's Core Zone would have presented a very different aspect from that familiar to us today: a relatively simple north-side palace-group facing south through and beyond a plaza ballcourt flanked by an unknown number of ancestral burial monuments toward the newly raised sacred Ancestor Mountain, A-6–3rd, itself possibly or not a funerary monument, but without question a symbolic shrine to the deified ancestors of the valley's ruling elites. This was, indeed, a holy place.

We presume a progression of constructions and/or entombments along the east and west edges of Plaza A over the late seventh through eighth or early ninth centuries, but this continues to await verification. What we do know is that probing at the start of the 20th century documented the presence of Late Classic interments accompanied by chert and obsidian eccentrics and other furnishings, including jadeite ornaments, within at least some of these platforms.

The Seventh to Ninth Centuries at Cahal Pech

Cahal Pech also saw significant renovations and additions during this period. Structures 3, 4, and 5, the east-side funerary monuments on the Main Plaza, were enlarged substantially, and the East Ballcourt was constructed immediately behind Structure 5 (fig. 12.3). Across the Main Plaza to the west, the on-site Cahal Pech "Ancestor Mountain" (Structure 9, from the top of which Structure A-6 at Xunantunich is easily visible to the southwest) was enlarged to its full Late Classic height. At its east base, a linear series of platforms (two or three; this was not determined) were built

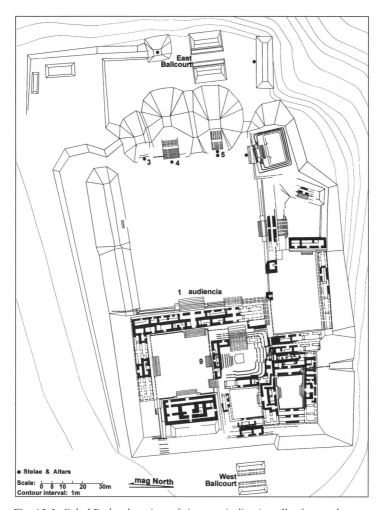

Fig. 12.3. Cahal Pech: plan view of site core indicating all referenced structures.

defining an open-access Main Plaza area (to the east) from a controlled access West Plaza, very soon thereafter further segregated by construction of the first phase of the monumental Cahal Pech audiencia (Structure 1), a screenlike partition between the overtly public space of the Main Plaza and the controlled access zone of the West Plaza.

Evidence of contemporaneous enlargements, additions, and new constructions also were recovered from the general East Plaza, the south side of the Main Plaza, and the regal residential complex comprising the southwest corner of the Cahal Pech citadel-center. All of these underwent yet further enlargements and embellishments throughout the eighth century during both the Mills (ca. A.D. 670–750) and Paloverde (ca. A.D.750–820) ceramic phases. Compared to either Buenavista or Xunantunich, significant architectural renovations and new construction were both more continuous and more elaborative at Cahal Pech, although never quite so spectacular as at either of the other two centers.

The Eighth to Tenth Centuries at Buenavista del Cayo

The mid-7th-century boom at Buenavista initiated a century and a half of cultural florescence and architectural growth for the center. Building programs took place across the site throughout the Late Classic period. These were neither continuous through time nor simultaneous in their occurrence, but took place as seemingly sporadic spurts of activity involving one building or group or another over the length of the late seventh and eighth centuries. Growth and prosperity continued through the eighth century, but sometime just shortly preceding or following the turn of the ninth, it experienced a sudden and dramatic interruption, the cause(s) of which remain to be determined.

Coincident with the realized late-eighth-century architectural expansion at Buenavista were a number of impressive projects started but never completed. These varied enormously in their archaeological "visibility" and detectability, and our own program likely did not identify them all. As one sees it today, the southwest corner of the Buenavista site reflects the composite building efforts of the fourth or fifth through eighth centuries plus the ninth-century ambitions of the then-ruling lords of the center. Most of these ambitions were to remain unrealized, but over the very late eighth to early ninth centuries, truly prodigious enlargements of the Buenavista Palace to the north were undertaken, including the inception of a grand audiencia or reception hall similar to those already present by then at Cahal Pech (Structure 1) and Xunantunich (Structure A-13).

Like the center's single sacbe (see fig. 9.1), also begun at this time to run for a few hundred meters southeastward from the corner junction of the Central and East Plazas only to peter out in an empty field, these projects were started but then abruptly stopped and abandoned in varying stages of incompletion. We do not know why. Habitational use of one or two of the south palace buildings did continue through the ninth and well into the tenth century or even later based on good ceramic, artifactual, and radiometric data and their depositional stratigraphy. These late occupants were not intruding squatters but genuine hangers-on, and their limited but definite presence indicates a hard to explain persistence of the original populace for some decades or more after the high-status residents of Cahal Pech and Xunantunich appear to have vanished from those centers.

The Eighth and Ninth Centuries at Xunantunich

Xunantunich continued to grow in size and complexity from the late seventh into the ninth century. Over this time, Structure A-6, the great Ancestor Mountain shrine, was renovated and added to on several occasions. The most substantial of these, the Structure A-6–2nd addition, dates to the very late or early ninth century. A final outer skin or shell, today largely removed through collapse or excavation, was added sometime well before A.D. 900 and was largely responsible for the preservation of the stucco friezes on the east and west faces of A-6–2nd.

Toward the end of the eighth century or early in the ninth, the Xunantunich site was transformed radically by the additions of Structure A-1 in the middle of Plaza A, and A-13, a parallel-chambered audiencia with a central portal passageway that closed and screened the open south side of the existing palace-group (see fig. 12.2). The construction of A-1 involved the partial burial and incorporation of the existing Late Classic ballcourt, and it was likely in conjunction with this that a new, second court was added to the west of Structure A-7. As to the audiencia, it was built rapidly at what seems to have been the same time that what would have been a far more ambitious building of the same type was abandoned unfinished at Buenavista. That at Xunantunich was completed, that at Buenavista not. We find ourselves compelled to ask, did the one replace the other?

By the first quarter of the ninth century, Xunantunich had achieved most of its present configuration. Based on the architectural programs of the late eighth–early ninth century, it also may have taken on a number of nonceremonial social and political roles earlier evidenced only at Cahal Pech and Buenavista. If so, we believe it probable that this had more to do with its defensible topography than with any local shifts in power, prestige, wealth, political authority, or ideological importance; however, we recognize that this remains an unanswered question, one open to a variety of possible answers or resolutions (chapter 10).

The Ninth and Tenth Centuries at Cahal Pech and Xunantunich

The latest identified architectural undertaking at Cahal Pech was the construction of the diminutive West Ballcourt, most probably sometime in the early ninth century (fig. 12.3; Ball and Taschek 2001:184–185, fig. 6.8). From that time on, the failure of Cahal Pech as a viable center and court appears to have been rapid but not sudden, the process rather than event taking place within a single generation (see Ball 1993a:47–48).

Events at Xunantunich remain far less clear as to their sequence and chronology, but there too it would appear that failure was a real and escalating process by the middle to late ninth century. Failure as a "center" seems to have occurred well before A.D. 900, although an ever shrinking population likely persisted into the 10th century, and sporadic visits and even brief, small-scale occupations of the site continued up through its 20th-century designation as an archaeological reserve.

Buenavista del Cayo, Cahal Pech, and Xunantunich

To simply state that the relationships that existed between Buenavista, Cahal Pech, and Xunantunich were complex and likely changed in nature and intensity over time is to assert the obvious and simplistic.[3] What exactly were those relationships, how did they develop, and how did they change through time are the real and important questions that need to be confronted head on. From the very start of our own investigations, we attempted to address these issues in meaningful but realistic ways (Ball and Taschek 1991), and have continued to do so.

Cahal Pech and Buenavista del Cayo: Complementary "Seats of Power"

We have elsewhere recently explored the relationships of Buenavista and Cahal Pech in depth, and have argued that the Late into Terminal Classic archaeological data currently available from the two sites indicate the concurrent use of the palace compounds at each by the same physical population in a manner tantamount to a complex "Summer Palace" (dry season/Cahal Pech)—"Winter Palace" (rainy season/Buenavista) arrangement (Ball and Taschek 2001). In our reconstruction, we identify the hilltop Cahal Pech citadel as serving primarily a high elite if not regal residential and private ritual function throughout much of each year, with Buenavista providing both a theater for many important communal administrative, economic, and public ceremonial services and activities as well as a warm and cozy rainy season residential alternative.[4]

In addition to royal residence, some activities, such as royal audiences or tribunals and local governance, may have taken place at both centers based on the shared presence at both of architectural facilities appropriate to such activities and depositional evidence at each suggesting their occurrence. We would note that the late eighth- to early ninth-century examples of these facilities at Cahal Pech are decidedly larger and grander than their counterparts at Buenavista, but functionally equivalent facilities were present at both centers.

Other activities—such as more personal (familial) and private royal rituals, including funerary ceremonies and bloodletting on the one hand (fig. 12.4) and more community-significant rituals and economic management on the other—appear to have occurred as the primary or exclusive functions of one center or the other. In brief, from at least the late seventh century on, Cahal Pech served as the principal royal home, stage for royal audiences and displays, and focus of private royal ritual for the lords of the upper Belize Valley. During this same time, Buenavista functioned as a public center and theater for community organization, economic activity, and regal sociopolitical ceremony. Complex architectural, artifactual, ceramic, and contextual records document the systemic integrity and complementarity of the two centers and strongly support the contention that their respective palaces served one and the same single royal court governing the same, single realm encompassing the upper Belize Valley drainage of the lower Mopan and Macal Rivers.

We have not been able to determine how far back in time the organic connection between Buenavista and Cahal Pech might have extended; however, we have not identified any evidence supporting its existence predating the late middle seventh century. It is entirely possible that the two originally were independent, which is not necessarily to say competitive, centers. An initial Preclassic pattern of multiple, small, independent centers including among others Blackman Eddy, Cahal Pech, Buenavista, Actuncan, and Arenal is certainly a possibility not ruled against by the known data. What we are certain of is that by the late seventh century the roles of the two centers as constituent elements of a single functional system had been established.

Also undetermined is exactly how the ties linking the two centers might originally have come about. While acknowledging that we simply may have failed to recognize earlier evidence of a deep-rooted (Preclassic) connection first to become tangibly visible in a series of late-seventh-century activities overtly and clearly affirming it, it is equally possible that any

Fig. 12.4. Late Classic (Paloverde ceramic phase) polychrome bloodletting bowl from Cahal Pech.

one or another of several new-sprung mechanisms or events ranging from marriage or political alliance to the acquisitive takeover of one center by the other could have been involved in their affiliation. We were unable to determine this from the data available to us, but we presently believe it to be the more likely case. What we do know is that each of the two centers underwent major programs of spatial reconfiguration and architectural elaboration during the late seventh century, and the characters of these do suggest a close functional interlinking of their occupants and cultural roles at and after that time (Ball and Taschek 2001).

Having stated the foregoing provisos, we call attention to one intriguing set of data from the "greater" Cahal Pech zone that, in concert with the contemporaneous overbuilding of that site's two principal "Ancestor Mountains" (Structures 4 and 9) and the construction of its first ceremonial ballcourt, does seem to suggest a major disjunction in the socioceremonial and dynastic histories of that center such as might reflect the influence or imposition of some intrusive external agent or force. The relevant data involve the elaborate, ceremonial chamber-burial of a broken-off stela shaft carved in the Greater Isthmian style of the Late Preclassic era (Stela 9; fig. 12.5). Formally entombed with great pomp and ceremony in a vaulted chamber beneath the front stairs of a 12-m-high pyramidal platform located in a plaza-group some 700 m south of the Cahal Pech citadel, Stela 9 is believed by its excavators and other researchers to have been

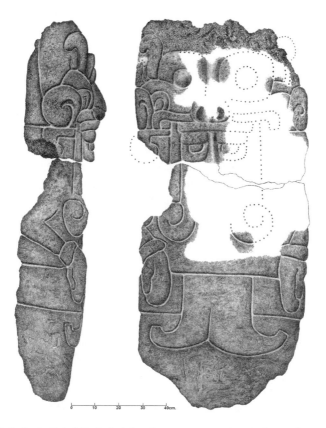

Fig. 12.5. Stela 9, Cahal Pech (height of monument, 1.6 m) (after a photograph and drawings by Nikolai Grube, 1994).

relocated from an original Preclassic place of erection somewhere within the site-core proper. Although concrete evidence for this is lacking, several lines of circumstantial evidence suggest that it might have stood originally at the north or east foot of Structure 9 or the west base of Structure 4. The enormity and importance of this event and this monument are reflected clearly in the associated ritual deposits. These included the disarticulated remains of at least two (possibly three) infants and one fetus or stillborn infant, more than 200 miniature unslipped "cache" (offering) bowls holding 225 human phalanges, and 45 human mandibular incisors and other skeletal fragments.

The teeth and other fragmentary skeletal remains were strewn about the base of the reerected stela, and the offering bowls and phalanges were set spiraling up around it in the matrix of loose soil used to infill the chamber.

The infant bodies were placed just above the stela immediately beneath the roofing capstones. The sealed chamber was covered over by the front stairs of a 12-m-high Late Classic funerary platform supporting a second, utilized vaulted tomb.

In light of all that we have learned over the last 20 years concerning ancient Maya ritual, ancestor veneration, kingship, and ceremony, there would seem to be only a limited number of ways to "read" this context. One straightforward, simple assessment is that it reflects a late mid-seventh-century disruption and deposing of a deep-rooted resident tradition of genealogical descent, identification, and ancestral veneration at Cahal Pech, and its displacement by a decidedly distinct and yet not entirely unsympathetic or destructive agency. The histories of numerous "feudal," "segmentary," and other manners of early or archaic states are filled with examples of such unions, and the authors believe some such similar scenario involving the "House" of Cahal Pech and that of Buenavista may be recorded in the Stela 9 context. At the very least, the possibility of this clearly warrants further consideration and investigation.

Xunantunich, Buenavista, and Cahal Pech: A Special Relationship

The relationship of Xunantunich to both Buenavista and Cahal Pech was immensely different from the foregoing in our opinion. We are convinced that the Xunantunich site-core—Plaza A and its principal structures, excluding A-1, A-13, the West Ballcourt, and some others—was conceived of and established as a "holy place" and sacred space for the upper valley elites as one important aspect of the political, social, and ritual reorganization of the valley coinciding with and likely resulting from the decisive military defeat of Naranjo by Caracol in the second quarter of the seventh century (see Martin and Grube 2000:72–73). Structure A-6, "El Castillo," was intended to be and was an awe-inspiring "Ancestor Mountain" shrine and possible pilgrimage objective or even monastic retreat visible throughout the length and breadth of the upper valley as it still is today. Visible to the south of and approached from the modest north end palace-group (Structures A-10, A-11, and A-12) through the initial Late Classic Plaza A Ballcourt, we believe the great monument likely to have been shrine, temple, pilgrimage destination, and retreat for meditation all rolled into one as well as a prominent declaration of the regal status and divinity of the valley's ruling elites.

Even discounting the misleading absence of the long-fallen and disintegrated painted and modeled stucco friezes and facade decorations that once adorned the fronts of Structures A-10, A-11, and A-12, the Xunantunich palace is striking in its sparseness and simplicity, especially when compared with the intricate, sprawling, and extensively added to and reconfigured complexes at other centers in the area like those at Cahal Pech, Buenavista, El Pilar, and Pacbitun. The palace likely owes its plainness and simplicity to two factors. One was its relatively short-use history as compared to those at Cahal Pech or El Pilar, for example. Equally important in our opinion, however, is the probability that for most of its history, the Xunantunich palace served only as an occasional, temporary residence for royal visitors who inhabited it only for short, periodic visits to the site for ancestral rituals, funerary rites, pilgrimages, or other ceremonial purposes. The palaces at El Pilar or Cahal Pech were, in contrast, sites of permanent, year-round, long-term residence. They thus grew and were remodeled heavily as necessary over the centuries of their use. While it too did undergo some minor alterations and renovations over time, the Xunantunich palace always remained simple and basic. It was adequate for its purpose.[5] What are probably high-status burial crypts, each marked by its own materially or stylistically distinctive stela, dating to the Late into Terminal Classic era line the east and west edges of Plaza A. The saga likely recorded by these would indeed be worth knowing.

Xunantunich did eventually supersede Buenavista as the apparent node of upper valley sociopolitical administrative as well as elite ancestral and funereal rites and ceremonies. This occurred at the turn of the eighth to ninth centuries, and is reflected architecturally in the contemporaneous abandonments of major construction programs at Buenavista (e.g., the southeast sacbe and north palace audiencia) and contemporaneous implementation and completion of others at Xunantunich (Structures A-1; A-13; and A-18–19 [the West Ballcourt]).

Early in the ninth century, the screening barrier represented by the east-west running audiencia (Structure A-13) was added closing the previously open south end of the palace compound. The addition of this building signaled important changes in the roles of both the palace and the Xunantunich center. Rather than functioning primarily if not exclusively as a private royal retreat and site of honorific ancestor-rites and funerary activities as we believe they did before A.D. 800, the palace and center at this time became alternative locations for many administrative and other public ceremonial activities previously most likely sited at the main valley organizational center, Buenavista del Cayo. While the reasons for this transfer of functions remain unclear, they more than likely reflect the unsettled and violent political climate that characterized the early ninth century throughout most of the southern Maya lowlands. The controllable access ridgetop situation of Xunantunich provided a safety and defensibility not present at the valley floor, riverside Buenavista location.

The retrenchment or renascence was short-lived, however, and by the second half of the ninth century, Xunantunich also appears to have failed or been failing as an active organizational center. In the end, as already stated, the last identified remnants of the upper valley's Late Classic elites appear to have made their home in the south end buildings and courtyard of the Buenavista palace. If nothing else, these were warm, secluded, and protected from prying attention either from the nearby Mopan River or most elsewhere in the valley. Like Xunantunich, Cahal Pech had lain deserted and empty of all but a few, rare transients for a good century or more by the time of their final passing.

Conclusion

In this chapter, we have presented and discussed our views of the upper valley's three major Late Classic centers—Buenavista, Cahal Pech, and Xunantunich—as components of a single, dynamic, functional system having readily identifiable and sensible social, political, ideological, and ceremonial roles and relationships. Too many others have for far too long continued to declare the isolation or independence of these three sites asserting their relationships to have involved at most a temporal (historical) sequentiality or a spatial proximity with consequently presumable economic and sociopolitical "interactions." We dispute such simplistic "models" and label them anthropologically and historically naive. We offer our own alternative as a viable, data-grounded hypothesis for future researchers to test with honest and objective vigor.

Notes

1. We were not part of the 1992–1997 UCLA Xunantunich Archaeological Project and do not pretend to control its data to any degree. However, we have studied the numerous reports, papers, and dissertations resulting from that project carefully, and we believe that we have fully and correctly digested and understood its publicized findings. In synthesizing them for our own use, we have been more concerned with discovering and understanding any possible relationships of Xunantunich, Buenavista, and Cahal Pech to each other than with arguing the unique-

ness or highlighting the individuality and unique history of any one center. To pay lip service to the obvious fact that none of these centers existed in a cultural histori-cal vacuum but then go on to treat each as developing and failing as an isolate is neither a viable nor an acceptable approach to elucidating their history and nature. We believe their relationships to have been systemic, and we have considered them in that light. We will further expand and elaborate on these relationships from this perspective in the future. The synthesis presented in this chapter draws on the following sources: Braswell 1998; Gann 1918, 1925; Harrison 1996; Jamison 1996; Jamison and Wolff 1994; LeCount 1996, 1999, 2002; McGovern 1994; McKie 1985; Robin and Yaeger 1996; Thompson 1942; Yaeger 1997. Also see chapter 10, this volume.

2. Lisa J. LeCount recently has provided a newly updated construction chronol-ogy for Late Classic Xunantunich and its principal monuments (LeCount et al. 2002). Although differing slightly in some minor details, her appraisal essentially corresponds to the schema presented here.

3. Too little data are available for Actuncan to allow a realistic or valid evalua-tion of its historical or cultural relationships to the other centers in our opinion. This is a major and important deficiency, and one that without question demands to be addressed in the future. Actuncan lies only a little over 4 km from Buenavista upriver on the opposite bank of the Mopan.

4. Perhaps needless to say, the data suggesting and arguments supporting our reconstruction are both rich and complex and not readily susceptible even to out-lining in this brief treatment. Interested readers are directed to our recent explora-tion of these data, "The Buenavista-Cahal Pech Royal Court: Multi-palace Court Mobility and Usage in a Petty Lowland Maya Kingdom" (Ball and Taschek 2001).

5. Trash, refuse, and kitchen facilities found concentrated in an area just to the east of A-12 suggest that food preparation for the palace residents took place there and possibly elsewhere outside the compound. Almost no other evidence of daily life or activities of any kind was recovered during the investigations by the UCLA Xunantunich Project. To a large extent, this very likely was due to and helps con-firm the periodic, short-term habitational usage of the Xunantunich palace.

Although it was built atop the remains of a Middle Preclassic village dating to 700 B.C. or earlier, the Xunantunich palace was a fairly late addition to the site. It was built in two, separate, single construction episodes with a number of sec-ondary, minor refurbishments and modifications. The original palace consisted only of the west, north, and east structures that faced onto a courtyard open to the south and provided both direct access to and an unobstructed view of the great, symbolic "Ancestor Mountain," Structure A-6, and the main plaza ballcourt later partially buried beneath Structure A-1. Since in the eighth century the access and view-blocking mass of the audiencia (Str. A-13) did not exist, the views of "El Castillo" and the ballcourt would have been especially good from the com-fortably breezy upper-story rooms atop Structure A-11, a frontally staired two-story building at the north end of the compound believed by its investigators to have functioned as the residence of the actually reigning king or queen and their immediate retainers.

Acknowledgments

The investigations reported on in this chapter were supported in part by grants from the U.S. National Science Foundation (Award Nos. BNS-8310677 and BNS-8719157); the United States Agency for International Development; the Belize Ministry of Tourism and Environment; the Foundation for the Advancement of Mesoamerican Studies, Inc.; San Diego State University and the SDSU Foundation; the Acacia Foundation of San Francisco; and multiple private donors. Permission to carry out fieldwork in Belize was graciously extended by the Honorable Glenn D. Godfrey, Minister of Tourism and Environment; by successive Belize commissioners of archaeology, Harriot W. Topsey, Winel Branche (acting commissioner), Allan Moore (acting commissioner), and John Morris (acting commissioner); and by Pablo Guerra and Hector Guerra, on whose lands the Buenavista site is located. We especially wish to acknowledge the late Harriot W. Topsey for encouraging us to pursue investigations at Cahal Pech and Buenavista del Cayo and continuing to support our work at those sites through 1992.

Among the numerous project staff and workers who participated in and contributed to the progress of these investigations, we would especially like to acknowledge the efforts of Field Assistants Eduardo Alfaro, Elias Alfaro Jr., Ubaldamir Alfaro, Eduardo Chi, José Chi, Ventura Cocom, and Gilberto Uck; Field Staff Laura Bernd, Marc Brown, Steve Elder, Cynthia James, Richalene Kelsay, David Major, Barbara Otto, Dominique Rissolo, and Carol Winkler; Project Foreman Armando Bautista; Lab Supervisor JoAnne Gilmer; and Lab Assistants Sara Clowery, Bruce Lumsden, Amin Salazar, and Chad Tritt.

Our overall appreciation and understanding of Buenavista and Cahal Pech also have benefited from discussions regarding particular aspects of their archaeology with colleagues Jaime Awe, Ron Bishop, Geoff Braswell, Dorie Budet, John Clark, Arthur Demarest, Jim Garber, Steve Houston, Gyles Iannone, Takeshi Inomata, Kevin Johnston, David Stuart, and David Webster. We thank them each for their input, suggestions, and critiques, as we do the two anonymous reviewers of this volume.

All illustrations used in this chapter were produced by Jennifer Taschek. We, of course, assume full responsibility for any errors of fact or interpretation or other shortcomings from which the chapter may suffer.

13

The Ancient Maya Center of Pacbitun

Paul F. Healy, Bobbi Hohmann, and Terry G. Powis

Pacbitun is situated on the southern rim of the upper Belize River Valley at the juncture of two contrasting environments (tropical rain forest and pine ridge). To the north lie lowland broadleaf forests, rolling hills, and rich agricultural soils. To the south are pine-covered uplands and the infertile sandy soils of the Maya Mountains (map 1). The region is interspersed with a number of springs and creeks.

Archaeological investigations were initiated by Trent University at Pacbitun in 1980 with preliminary survey and mapping. This initial field season was followed with extensive excavations in the site core and investigation of the surrounding area. Our investigations have revealed a nearly 2,000-year site history with abandonment of the center about A.D. 900. During this time Pacbitun evolved from a small Preclassic farming community to a substantial hilltop acropolis city.

Chronology

The chronological history of Pacbitun is based on the analysis of site ceramics, with regional comparisons made to the established cultural sequence of the nearby Belize River Valley (Awe 1992; Gifford 1976; Willey et al. 1965), and a suite of 22 radiocarbon dates. From these, a six-period cultural chronology has been established. Refinements of the earliest portion of the sequence continue based on recent explorations of Formative deposits (Healy 1999; Healy and Awe 1996). The chronological sequence is as follows:

A.D. 700–900	Terminal Classic period	Tzib phase
A.D. 550–700	Late Classic period	Coc phase
A.D. 300–550	Early Classic period	Tzul phase
100 B.C.–A.D. 300	Terminal Preclassic period	Ku phase
300–100 B.C.	Late Preclassic period	Puc phase
900–300 B.C.	Middle Preclassic period	Mai phase

While evidence for a terminal Early Preclassic period habitation dating as far back as cal. 1100 b.c. (chapter 7) now exists at neighboring Cahal Pech and some associated Cunil phase (Early Preclassic) sherds have been found at Pacbitun in mixed deposits, none of these have occurred (so far) in a pure, stratified context (Awe 1992; Cheetham and Awe 1996). Site habitation ends at the close of the ninth century. At least one post-abandonment burial has been identified from the site.

Architecture and Site Plan

Pacbitun is a compact acropolis center. The Core Zone is marked by five primary plazas (A–E), surrounded by a variety of masonry structures atop a modified natural limestone hilltop (fig. 13.1). The majority of the farming population occupied hundreds of housemounds, possibly as much as 4 km away. The largest open area of the Core Zone, Plaza D, measures about 5,525 m² while the smallest, Plaza C, is only about 900 m². The south side of Plaza B is marked by a set of three enclosed courtyard groups each surrounded on four sides by multichambered range structures. Most likely, this was the Classic period elite residence compound. One range building, Structure (Str.) 23, has been excavated. The north side of Plaza B is girded by an enormous range building, Structure 8, some 100 m long and about 8 m tall (maxima). On the east, Plaza B is bordered by a major temple-pyramid, Structure 2, straddling Plazas A and B.

Plaza A, about 6 m above Plazas B–E, is the highest level ground at Pacbitun. This plaza appears to be the ritual and ceremonial center of Pacbitun. Two of the most elevated edifices at the site (Strs. 1 and 2), a pair of stepped pyramids with (once vaulted) superstructures, face one another across the plaza. From atop Structure 1, one can view the entire Core Zone, associated rural settlement, and valley ceremonial centers approximately 10 km away. Plaza A also is the locus of most of the 20 known Pacbitun monuments, including a stela and altar complex situated in the center of the plaza. Structure 1 is made to appear even more massive by two smaller flanking temple pyramids, Structures 4 and 5. This configuration forms an E-Group complex. The north and south sides

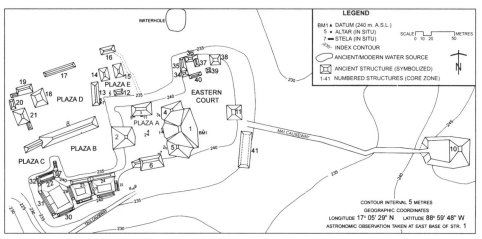

Fig. 13.1. Plan of Pacbitun Core Zone.

of Plaza A are framed by two large ranges (Strs. 3 and 6), with associated stelae.

Plaza E, to the north of and below Plaza A, is marked by the presence of a ballcourt, one of the earliest documented for the Maya lowlands. The investigations in Plazas B–D have unearthed evidence for a small Middle Preclassic village of perishable buildings located directly below what would become Plaza B in the Classic, with traces of similar Formative habitation underlying Plazas C and D as well (Hohmann and Powis 1996, 1999).

Also in the Core Zone is a pair of causeways (*sacbeob*). The Mai causeway extends 230 m east from Structure 1 and the Eastern Court to a large Terminus Complex, complete with elevated platform and temple-pyramid (Str. 10). The Tzul causeway is 1,000 m long and extends from the south side of Plaza A to a second Terminus Complex to the southwest of the Core Zone.

E-Group Evolution

Plaza A at Pacbitun is characterized by an E-Group Complex. E-Groups have been identified at numerous ceremonial centers in the valley, including Baking Pot, Barton Ramie, Blackman Eddy, Cahal Pech, and El Pilar (Aimers 1993; Ruppert 1940). The Pacbitun E-Group architecture consists of a standard trio of temple-pyramids aligned along the eastern edge of the plaza, directly opposite a lone temple-pyramid (fig. 13.1). Excavations revealed that habitation here began in the Middle Preclassic (520 B.C. ± 100,

Beta-25378). Structures 1 and 2 were first, but winglike stepped platforms (initially without superstructures) were soon constructed adjacent to Structure 1.

Central trenches dug into the front of all four Plaza A temple-pyramids have provided a detailed construction sequence. While the three eastern structures were initially separate and distinct platforms, by the middle of the Ku phase the central edifice, Structure 1, had engulfed Structures 4 and 5 to create one massive construction. At this time Structures 4 and 5 were less than 3 m tall, while Structure 1 was at least 3 m high, and possibly twice that height. At the end of Pacbitun's history, we know that Structure 1 remained the tallest edifice at Pacbitun, estimated at 16.5 m (with a 4-m-tall vaulted temple), while Structure 2 stood 11.2 m; Structure 4, 12.2 m tall; and Structure 5, about 10.9 m in height.

Aimers (1993) has examined the proposed function and operation of Maya E-Group Complexes at sites in the Belize Valley and beyond. Based on field testing he has raised questions about the validity of the solar hypothesis (Blom 1924) and suggested instead that a system of cosmic geomancy may have been responsible for the distinctive and repeated orientation of these buildings.

Palace Complex

Three quadrangular courtyards (Courts 1–3) form the southwest corner of the Core Zone. They are elevated above (and overlook on the south face) the Tzul Causeway (fig. 13.2). Excavations of Structure 23 have revealed that construction of this "palace" was initiated at the Late Preclassic Ku phase / Early Classic Tzul phase transition. It underwent six major reconstructions until the Terminal Classic Tzib phase (Bill 1987). In the last century of use, the addition of a new central spine wall, running the length of Structure 23, prevented pedestrian traffic from moving easily between the north side of the structure facing Plaza B, and the south side facing the interior of Court 2 (Healy 1990a:253). Benches were located in the lateral chambers on the north side at this time. By contrast, the south side lacked raised benches and the rooms overlooked a small, private courtyard. The seclusion was enhanced by the bordering ranges (Strs. 27–29), probably comparable in size and form to Structure 23. Even pedestrian passageways at the plaza level between the plaza and the courtyards were reduced, and possibly closed off, at this time.

During the Late-to-Terminal Classic, a small (3 × 3 m) extension was added to the exterior west end of Structure 23. This would have effectively blocked access to, and even a view of, the inner quadrangle court from

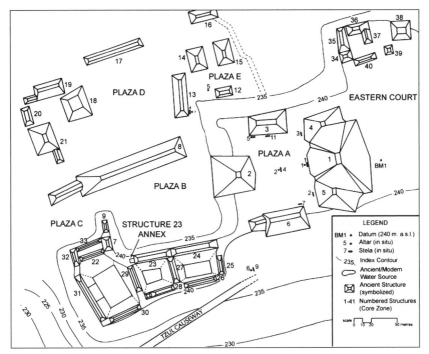

Fig. 13.2. Plan of the elite residential court zone at Pacbitun, especially Structure 23 and the slate workshop.

Plaza B. The auxiliary building, Structure 23-annex, appears to have been a specialized slate workshop and storage facility connected to the elite residence (Healy et al. 1995:343). There is growing evidence for attached elite specialists, with workshops, existing at a number of Classic Maya sites (Aoyama 1995; Inomata 2001). By the end of its existence, Structure 23 had multiple functions: (1) an elite residence (south side), a function that likely began in a modest manner at the end of the Late Preclassic; (2) administrative-public functions, connected to rooms facing Plaza B (north side); and (3) craft production, involving slate (west end), probably connected with elite kin-groups in Court 2.

Ballcourt

An open-ended masonry ballcourt was constructed during the Late Preclassic Ku phase (100 B.C.–A.D. 300). It is one of the earliest ballcourts known from the Maya lowlands (Healy 1992:237; Scarborough and Wilcox 1991; Smith 1961). Strs. 14 and 15, about 17.5 m long, created a playing alley measuring 4.8 m wide. Investigations revealed four major stages of modification. The presence of a ballcourt of such antiquity indicates precociousness for the center in ritual, and probably political, matters during a time of considerable social change in the central Maya lowlands (Healy 1992:238).

Several other early Maya ballcourts are also known from the eastern lowlands, such as Cerros (Scarborough et al. 1982) Colha (Eaton and Kunstler 1980) and possibly Blackman Eddy (chapter 4), all in Belize. Even at this early date, there is a considerable degree of uniformity in the architectural form across the Maya subarea (Scarborough 1991:137). This reinforces the idea, already evident from regularities in Late Preclassic Maya pottery, that lowland centers like Pacbitun were actively communicating with one another and establishing cultural and religious traditions in the Late Preclassic period that would be crystallized in the Classic period (Hammond 1985).

Excavations at Pacbitun revealed an evolution of ballcourt architecture, spanning about 1,000 years (Healy 1992:233–237). The court was remodeled, rebuilt, and likely repainted (red), many times. Some of these changes, such as those undertaken in the Early Classic Tzul phase (A.D. 300–550), were relatively minor (i.e., superficial replastering efforts). In other cases, as during the Late Classic Coc phase (A.D. 550–700), the reno-

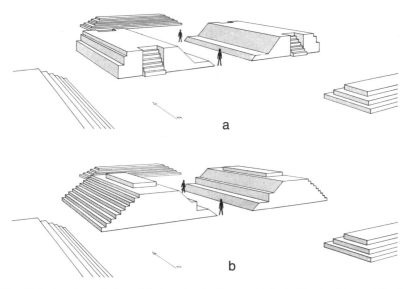

Fig. 13.3. Artist's rendering of the Pacbitun ballcourt: (a) Early Classic; (b) Late Classic.

vations were quite striking, including the addition of a new playing wall with an entirely different surface angle (fig. 13.3).

Secular and Ritual Activity

Excavations at Pacbitun have provided new insights into both political and religious practices at the site. Several sets of cultural activity help define local customs and place the role of Pacbitun into a broader lowland Maya context.

Monuments

The lowland Maya were erecting stelae (possibly with painted decoration) as early as the Late Preclassic to honor and aggrandize site rulers and their dynasties (Hammond 1982). Altars, typically paired with stelae, are abundant throughout the Classic period (A.D. 300–900) in the Maya lowlands (Clancy 1985), and both types of monuments have been found at Pacbitun.

Investigations revealed the remains of at least 20 fragmentary stone monuments, including 13 stelae and 7 altars. All were made of limestone, with one exception (probably slate) and in general were poorly preserved. The presence of these monuments suggests that Pacbitun had a well-established elite class and indicates that the site played a prominent role in the eastern region of the central lowlands.

Only three monuments at Pacbitun retain any trace of carving (Stela 6, Altar 3, Altar 4). The two carved altars are small fragments. Of the monuments that could be securely dated four were raised during the last half of the Classic (either the Coc or Tzib phases, A.D. 550–900), while three belong to the Early Classic (Tzul phase, A.D. 300–550).

One monument (Stela 6) did retain part of a Long Count date (Healy 1990b). The shattered irregularly shaped, 2 m tall, limestone stela was found lying face up in Plaza A. Despite a fragmented (but articulated) condition, the low relief composition of the stela can be partially reconstructed (fig. 13.4). The scene is dominated by a seated personage with an outstretched arm. The individual, elaborately attired with ear flares and other globular jewelry, wears an ornate headdress, part of which is decorated with a crested bird. A vertical, eroded, and indecipherable glyph column occurs on the upper left corner. Another text, which begins with an Initial Series Introducing Glyph and a bar-and-dot Long Count date, is situated just behind the seated central figure. Although the entire

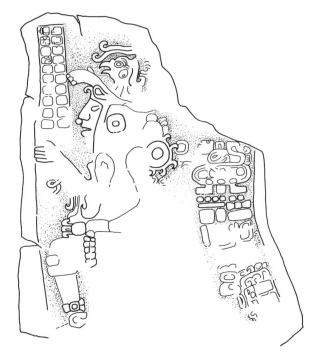

Fig. 13.4. Stela 6 at Pacbitun (reconstruction), dated to ca. A.D. 475.

inscription is not preserved, the initial calendrical units read 9.2.5.[?].[?] (Healy 1990b:110). This indicates that Stela 6 was carved to commemorate an event dating to the Early Classic about A.D. 475 (GMT Correlation). Pacbitun Stela 6, Blackman Eddy Stela 1, and a stela from Zopilote are three of the earliest stelae in the Maya lowlands.

Burials

Investigations in the Core Zone of Pacbitun have produced 21 burials in the following grave types: tomb (1), crypt (11), cist (5), and simple (4). All but two of these were found in temple-pyramid constructions in the Core Zone. The burials have been dated to the Middle Preclassic (1), Late Preclassic (1), Early Classic (1), Late Classic (10), and Terminal Classic (7) periods. One additional burial was post-abandonment. Grave offerings are typical for those in the Maya lowlands, though with a greater representation of slate artifacts (Healy et al. 1995; Welsh 1988). Pottery was the most common funerary offering (132 vessels).

Earlier burials at Pacbitun tended to be simpler, while later burials were often more elaborate. For example, a Middle Formative cist burial (BU C-1), found below Plaza C, contained only a mano fragment and three simple vessels, while one Terminal Classic grave (BU 2–1), from Structure 2, contained a large, finely flaked chert bipoint, numerous pieces of greenstone, 27 vessels, and an assortment of ceramic musical instruments (Arendt et al. 1996:130–132; Healy 1988). The most elaborate grave at Pacbitun (BU 1–9) was a 3-m-long Late Classic vaulted tomb from deep within Structure 1 (chapter 14).

From these 21 graves, 27 individuals have been identified: 11 males, 11 females, and five of unknown sex. Three individuals were children. There were numerous multiple graves at Pacbitun, with most containing an adult male and female buried together. There was also a striking degree of uniformity in burial practices in the Core Zone. Except for three urn burials and two flexed (one Preclassic and one post-abandonment), all other individuals were found in an extended position, mostly supine, with legs crossed and heads oriented to the south (Healy 1990a:255). This is a pattern that has been previously identified at other sites in the valley (Welsh 1988:225, table 112; Willey et al. 1965). The occurrence of multiple burials at Pacbitun is reminiscent of interment practices found farther to the south, especially in the Caracol region (D. Chase and A. Chase 1996; Healy et al. 1998).

Four possible sacrificial burials have been identified from the Core Zone. BU 2–5 and 2–6 are simple urn graves, containing the skeletal remains of children who were likely sacrificed and buried along the primary axis of Structure 2 in dedicatory ceremonies associated with architectural renewal. In addition to these an adult, of unknown sex, was found interred (BU 5–2) directly beneath Stela 2, at the base of Structure 5, much like a sub-stela cache. Similarly, a trio of individuals was found buried (BU 1–3) directly below Stela 1.

Caches

There are 20 caches known from Pacbitun. Twelve are of the Terminal Classic period (A.D. 700–900). Most of these offerings were associated with architectural features or, in two cases, were located beneath stelae; the majority (16/20) were pottery caches. There were three caches with purposely buried fragments of monuments.

Ritual offerings began in the Mai (900–300 B.C.) phase and continued to the Tzib (A.D. 700–900) phase. The offerings suggest a trend of increasing numbers of caches, growing ritual complexity and expanded wealth until the Late Classic period with some signs of degradation of caching practices in the final Tzib phase. Jade offerings, for example, occur in Tzul and Coc phase caches, but are absent from any Tzib phase caches. Some examples demonstrate the range and variation of practices through time.

Cache B-1 (Early Middle Preclassic). A darkened posthole for a perishable early Mai phase pole-and-thatch-roofed structure contained a simple offering of marine (probably *Strombus gigas*) disk beads (N = 51). These may have once been strung together, as part of a necklace or bracelet, or perhaps were contained loose in a pouch made of perishable material and placed in the posthole before the support post was laid. Some Maya today place subsurface offerings in new homes in order to appease deities (Vogt 1969:462).

Cache 15–1 (Early Classic). This Tzul phase offering was found in association with two ceramic vessels placed lip to lip, nested in plaza fill on the primary axis of Structure 15, one of the ballcourt range structures. The vessels were tightly packed with nearly 200 freshwater snail (*Pachychilus indiorum*) shells (unaltered), presumably as a food offering to the supernatural (Healy et al. 1990). Additionally, the cache contained the following: polished celt; jadeite bead; large, finely chipped green obsidian bipoint; large, stemmed, plano-convex chert point; stingray (Rajiformes) spine, fitting valves of a small thorny oyster (*Spondylus americanus*), and six, small (< 3 cm) flat, notched, lozenge-shaped objects (possibly abstract human forms) made of slate (2); white shell (2); and orange/pink shell (2). The chert point was almost certainly imported from Colha in northern Belize, the greenstone probably from the Motagua Valley in southern Guatemala, while the green obsidian came from central Mexico (Bishop et al. 1993:53; Hammond et al. 1977; Shafer 1991:fig. 5; Shafer and Hester 1983; Spence 1996).

Cache 1–4 (Terminal Classic). A massive pottery horde, associated with the ultimate (Tzib phase) building phase, was placed in a roughly prepared chamber (1.4 × 1.2 m) on the centerline of Structure 1. Over 90 Belize Red vessels had been placed in a specially prepared chamber under the final stair. The vessels (primarily dishes) were tightly stacked and nested inside the specially prepared cist. Most had been crushed from centuries of ground pressure.

During the Middle Preclassic, Cache B-1 consisted of a small number of simple beads, manufactured locally, but made of an exotic raw material (marine shell) (Hohmann 2002). The Early Classic offering, Cache 15–1, was certainly grander, containing both local products (slate, *jute*) and exotic remains (jade, green obsidian, marine shell, honey brown chert), some of which were manufactured elsewhere and imported in their finished form. This demonstrates the increased wealth of Pacbitun at this time and the heightened complexity of ceremonial behavior that emerged between A.D. 300–550. The Terminal Classic offering, Cache 1–4, is the largest identified at Pacbitun, impressive in its size and quantity of offerings but composed entirely of locally made, and likely mass-produced, wares. While the cache was elaborate, even ostentatious in a sense, it probably reflected a less costly investment of local goods. In fact, the workmanship of most of the items cached during the Terminal Classic declined sharply from the Early Classic, though the total number of offerings was often considerable. In the rare instances where Terminal Classic caches contained goods other than ceramic vessels, these were invariably inferior in quality, sometimes in a poor condition, and often of a humble nature (Healy 1990a:255–256).

Settlement and Subsistence

Settlement Pattern and Population Projections

In an effort to understand the spatial distribution of the population and the demographic history of Pacbitun, survey and mapping was undertaken in the Periphery Zone. Four separate transect zones (300 m wide by 1,000+ m long) were mapped from the site epicenter outward (Richie 1990; Sunahara 1994). In addition to the transects, a subsequent settlement survey was conducted in quadrants in the intervening areas (Campbell-Trithart 1990).

Mapping of the Periphery Zone identified numerous rural structures (N = 211) in the four transects, and an additional number (N = 185) in four quadrants, for a total of 396 structures (table 13.1). Test excavations of a sample of these (25.1 percent of transect structures; 11.4 percent of quadrant structures) revealed ceramic, lithic, faunal, and architectural evidence that indicates that the vast majority of the mounded structures were residential in function. Possible part-time use of some domestic structures for small-scale craft production was suggested by the recovery of slate and shell debitage.

Sixty-eight structures were found in the two eastern transects (113 structures/km²) and 143 structures were identified in the two western transects (238 structures/km²). The average density in the four transect zones was 175.8 structures/km² (table 13.1). The higher density on the

Table 13.1. Settlement of the periphery zone of Pacbitun

Survey units	Number of structures	(Percentage of total)	Number of structures excavated	(Percentage of structures excavated)	Str./km2
NE transect	31	(14.7)	8	(25.8)	103.3
SE transect	37	(17.5)	10	(27.0)	123.3
NW transect	72	(34.1)	17	(23.6)	240.0
SW transect	71	(33.7)	18	(25.3)	236.7
Total	211		53	Average	175.8
NE quadrant	53	(28.7)	6	(11.3)	212.0
SE quadrant	43	(23.2)	5	(11.6)	172.0
NW quadrant	46	(24.9)	5	(10.9)	184.0
SW quadrant	43	(23.2)	5	(11.6)	172.0
Total	185		21	Average	185.0

Sources: After Campbell-Trithart 1990; Healy 1990a; Richie 1990; Sunahara 1994.

western side can be attributed to more gently rolling terrain and pockets of land with greater soil depth and fertility than normally occurs on the east. The water supply (springs and creeks) was also somewhat better to the west.

While excavations revealed indications of rural housemound use as early as the Late Preclassic, there is no doubt that settlement in the Periphery Zone was heaviest during the Terminal Classic. All structures tested in the four transects exhibited occupation during the Tzib (A.D. 700–900) phase (Richie 1990:199; Sunahara 1994:128).

Investigations in the quadrant areas provided an opportunity to compare information with the transect surveys by conducting a nearly 100 percent pedestrian survey in cleared fields. The survey of the quadrant areas, largely located between the transects, produced an average combined settlement density of 185.0 structures/km^2 (Campbell-Trithart 1990:307), which is slightly higher than earlier estimates of mound density generated by the transect method (table 13.1). This is likely due to the quadrant survey being closer to the Core Zone. Using these site density estimates, demographic calculations for average family size based on ethnoarchaeology (Kolb 1985), and conservatively estimating the overall site size to be 9 km^2, Pacbitun likely had a sustaining population of at least 4,000 (50 percent occupancy rate), and possibly as many as 8,000 (100 percent occupancy) inhabitants at about A.D. 700–900.

Zooarchaeological Data

The residents of Pacbitun used animals for both subsistence and ceremonial purposes (Baker 1988; Emery 1987, 1991:48; Stanchly 1999). The range and variety of fauna are similar to those identified at other lowland Maya sites (Carr 1986; Hamblin 1984; Pohl 1976; Wing and Steadman 1980). The majority of vertebrate species identified in the assemblage were likely hunted in an opportunistic manner (table 13.2).

Table 13.2. List of Identified Taxa from Pacbitun, Belize

Order/class family	Genus/species	Common name
Mammals (Mammalia)		
Artiodactyla		
Cervidae	*Odocoileus virginianus*	White-tailed deer
	Mazama americana	Brocket deer
Tayassuidae	*Tayassu pecari*	White-lipped peccary
	Tayassu tajacu	Collared peccary
	Tayassu sp.	Peccary
Perissodactyla		
Tapiridae	*Tapirus bairdii*	Baird's tapir
Sirenia		
Trichechidae	*Trichechus manatus*	Manatee
Primata		
Cebidae	*Alouatta villosa*	Howler monkey
Carnivora		
Candidae	*Canis familiaris*	Domestic dog
Felidae		Cats
Lagomorpha		
Leporidae	*Sylvilagus brasiliensis*	Forest rabbit
	Sylvilagus floridanus	Eastern cottontail
	Sylvilagus sp.	Rabbit
Rodentia		
Dasyproctidae	*Agouti paca*	Paca
	Dasyprocta punctata	Agouti
Erethizontidae	*Coendu mexicana*	Porcupine
Cricetidae	*Oryzomys* sp.	New World rat
	Ototylomis phyllotis	Big-eared climbing rat
Heteroyidae	*Liomys salvini*	Salvin's pocket mouse
Geomyidae	*Heterogeomys hispidus*	Hispid's pocket gopher
Edentata		
Dasypodidae	*Dasypus novemcinctus*	Nine-banded armadillo

continued

(Table 13.2 continued)

Order/class family	Genus/species	Common name
Marsupialia		
Didelphidae	*Didelphis marsupialis*	Opossum
	Marmosa sp.	Mouse opossum
Birds (Aves)		
Galliformes		
Phasiandidae	*Meleagris ocellata*	Ocellated turkey
	Meleagris gallopavo	Common turkey
Cracidae	*Crax rubra*	Great curassow
Passeriformes		Perching birds
Reptiles (Reptilia)		
Testudinata		
Dermatemydidae	*Dermatemys mawi*	Central American river turtle
Kinosternidae	*Kinosternon sp.*	Musk turtle
	Staurotypus triporcatus	Loggerhead turtle
Emydidae		Pond turtles
Cheloniidae	*Chelonia* sp.	Green turtle
Crocodylia		
Crocodylidae	*Crocodylus acutus*	American crocodile
	Crocodylus moreleti	Morlet's crocodile
Serpentes		Snakes
Amphibians (Amphibia)		
Anura		Frogs and toad
Fish (Osteichthyes)		
Ictaluridae	*Ictalurus* sp.	Catfish
Rays (Chondrichthyes)		
Rajiformes		
Dasyatidae		Stingray
Myliobatidae		Eagleray
Crustaceans (Crustacea)		
Brachyura		
Gecarcinidae	*Callinectes sapidus*	Blue crab
	Cardisoma guanhumi	Blue land crab
	Menippe mercenaria	Stonecrab

Sources: After Baker 1988; Emery 1987, 1991; Healy 1990a; Stanchly 1999.

Analysis of ecozone utilization suggests that most hunting was done primarily in uncut forests (Emery 1991:50). Animals like the great currassow, monkeys and the white-lipped peccary, prefer the virgin forest as do most of the large felines. Hunting by *milperos,* was also very likely

(Pohl 1977), but the faunal data from Pacbitun suggests that hunting trips into primary forests may have been of somewhat greater importance (Emery 1991:50). Many other species identified were most likely hunted in *huaymil,* or regrowth forests. This was probably the second most important ecozone for faunal exploitation. Collared peccary, agouti, and armadillo, occasionally, are found here. A third ecozone of importance was the cut forest (including residential areas and agricultural lands). These forests would have attracted brocket and white-tailed deer as well as collared peccary, turkeys, snakes, and sundry rodents. Pacbitun is farther from a riverine ecozone, but some elements of the assemblage, like river turtles and freshwater gastropods, suggest that frequent trips were likely being made to smaller, nearby creeks for both water and edible species (Emery 1991:51; Healy et al. 1990). Remains of crocodiles and iguanas are further evidence of exploitation of riverine resources.

Finally, there are some rare, exotic species including remains of stingrays and marine molluscs. These, and other species, were used for ritual purposes (Pohl 1983). For example, five carefully cut and ground bone tubes found in a royal burial (BU 1–9) were made from an assortment of artiodactyl remains (peccary, brocket deer, and white-tailed deer) and may have functioned as panpipes. Musical instruments have been found closely associated with funerary rites at Pacbitun (Healy 1988). Finally, in addition to ritual items, some animal bone was carved into utilitarian artifacts (a possible bone weaving shuttle, needles, and beads) (Emery 1991:48–52; chapter 14).

Intensive Agriculture

Hillslopes surrounding Pacbitun bear traces of ancient Maya terracing. Elsewhere, Healy et al. (1980, 1983) have argued that such forms of agrotechnology represent an intensification of farming. It remains unclear whether such systems were the consequence of gradual, accretional evolution, or more rapid, centrally directed development (A. Chase and D. Chase 1998a; D. Chase et al. 1990). Mapping of several terraced fields and excavation of terrace plots have been conducted. These indicate that almost all terrace systems were built and utilized in the Late-Terminal Classic period.

Isotopic Evidence for Diet

Research by White et al. (1993) of a sample of human skeletal remains from Pacbitun (N = 21) has provided some additional insights to diet and the impact of intensive agriculture on site abandonment. Using stable carbon and nitrogen isotopes of human bone collagen, it was possible to provide a diachronic reconstruction of diet. Not surprisingly, the research showed that corn (*Zea mays*) was the major food staple for the Classic period (White et al. 1993:348). Among adults, males consumed about 10 percent more C4 foods such as maize. Differential access to food resources has been documented at other Maya sites (Cohen 1989; Reed 1992). Children (N = 3) were consuming far fewer C4 foods than either males or females. This pattern differs from evidence at Copan and Lamanai. Two of these children were recovered from contexts that suggest they were sacrificial offerings.

Individuals buried in more elaborate graves, such a crypts, enjoyed the greatest consumption of C4 foods (70 percent of their diet composed of maize). Those individuals buried in simpler graves (pits or urns), consumed a noticeably smaller quantity of C4 foods (as little as 51 percent). An examination of elite burials from the Core Zone vs. low-status burials from mounds in the site periphery revealed that the aristocracy at Pacbitun had better access to maize. An elite female found in a crypt (BU 2–1) in the Core Zone of the site had lower levels of C4 foods than contemporary elite males but higher levels than contemporary low-status males in the Periphery Zone. Collectively, these data suggest that privileged status at Pacbitun included access to greater quantities of maize. In sum, access to food resources, specifically maize, seems to have varied at Pacbitun by age, sex, and social level.

Looking at temporal trends, White and colleagues (1993:366–367) found that while maize increased in consumption during the Early and Late Classic (Tzul and Coc phases), there was a decline of about 10 percent in the Terminal Classic Tzib phase. Settlement studies show a population rise from the Preclassic through the Classic. There appear to be attempts to increase maize production in the final period through labor-intensive construction of agricultural terraces in the hilly, less desirable, farming zones around the site. This suggests that all available relatively level lands were already in use by this time. Attempts at agricultural intensification, therefore, may be interpreted as a deliberate, planned response to rising population pressures and an indication of an increased demand for a storable staple like maize in the absence of other available farmlands. The strategy was not totally successful, as isotopic studies reveal maize consumption overall likely declined for most of the population in the Terminal Classic.

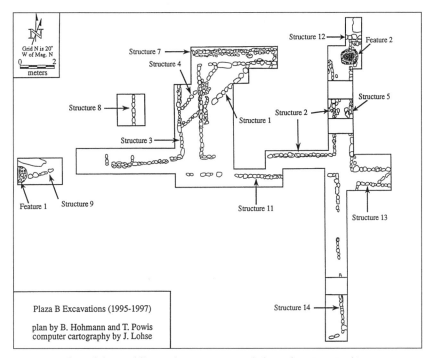

Fig. 13.5. Plan of the Middle Preclassic structures below Plaza B at Pacbitun.

Recent Research at Pacbitun

Hohmann and colleagues (Hohmann 2002; Hohmann and Powis 1999:8, 19; Hohmann et al. 1999:21–23) identify over a dozen Mai phase (900–300 B.C.) structures that were buried below Late/Terminal Preclassic and Classic deposits forming the fill of Plazas B, C, and D (fig. 13.5). All of the Middle Preclassic structures identified thus far are quadrangular in shape, marked by tamped marl floors with multicourse stone foundations. Some show traces of perishable wood-and-thatch-roofed buildings. There are no indications of round Middle Preclassic structures, as have been noted at several other early Belize Valley sites (Aimers et al. 2000; Powis 1996; chapter 3).

Charcoal from Preclassic structures came from several types of large tree species including pine (*Pinus* sp.), turtle bone (*Pithecellobium* sp.), and ramon (*Brosimum alicastrum*) (Wiesen and Lentz 1999:table 1). Many of the Formative structures are parallel to one another with small alleys or walkways located between them. The buildings often terminate and corner in an orderly fashion.

Over 6,000 Preclassic artifacts consisting primarily of ceramic, shell, and lithic remains, were recovered along with an assortment of faunal, botanical, and radiocarbon samples. Of particular interest is a sizable collection of shell disk beads, chert drills (likely used in the bead manufacture), and a variety of hand-modeled ceramic figurines.

Four radiocarbon dates were obtained; these fell between 620–450 B.C. (cal. b.c. 905–375, 2 sigma, 95 percent probability). These determinations securely set the date for initial habitation of Pacbitun, and enable a division of the Mai phase into early and late facets. Early Mai (900–600 B.C.) phase structures were simpler in form and somewhat smaller in size than late Mai (600–300 B.C.) phase buildings. The latter were not only larger structures, but better made as well and situated atop higher platforms with taller (at least 3 course) cut limestone foundation walls. Some of these early structures, such as Plaza B Sub-Structure 2, were quite substantial (8.3 × 4.6 m) suggesting that early residents were investing more time and energy in their constructions (Hohmann and Powis 1999:14).

Pottery included types from the Belize Valley Middle Preclassic ceramic groups such as Savana and Jocote (Gifford 1976; Hohmann and Powis 1996, 1999). Lithic artifacts were made of slate, chert, chalcedony, granite, jade and obsidian, the latter derived from three sources (El Chayal, Ixtepeque, and San Martin Jilotepeque) in the Guatemalan highlands (Awe and Healy 1994; Awe et al. 1996; Hohmann and Glascock 1996). Slate artifacts and debitage are abundant from the Middle Preclassic period onward at Pacbitun (Healy et al. 1995; Hohmann and Powis 1996:117). Large quantities of debitage from both freshwater and marine shells, but especially from the Fighting Conch (*Strombus gigas*), were found. The amounts of shell scrap, along with the recovery of hundreds of small, flat disk beads, bead fragments, preforms, or irregularly shaped and drilled "spacers," as well as dozens of small, chert burin drills, suggest that Pacbitun was an early craft production site for a type of simple shell jewelry (Hohmann 2002).

Preclassic subsistence at Pacbitun was based on maize (*Zea mays*) production. Paleobotanical evidence for maize exists in the form of preserved corn kernel cupules along with secondary evidence like granite manos and metates (Wiesen and Lentz 1999:table 1, 64). Flotation of soil samples also produced the remains of edible fruit from the coyol palm (*Acrocomia aculeata*). Preclassic period hunting of tropical forest game, such as deer, tapir, peccary, agouti, rabbit, and armadillo, was important, as was gathering (turtles and shellfish) (table 13.2).

The Middle Preclassic deposits have produced over 150,000 *jute* (*Pachy-*

chilus sp.) specimens, the vast majority of which had their spires clipped in order to facilitate extraction of the animal. Other shellfish included both freshwater clams (*Nephronaias* sp.) and snails (*Pomacea flagellata*). The altered snail shells are found in such an overwhelming abundance that it can hardly be disputed that *jute*, and probably the other freshwater shellfish, were basic foodstuffs and their collection a significant element of subsistence practices (cf. Healy et al. 1990; Moholy-Nagy 1978).

This evidence, as well as carbon and nitrogen isotope data from Preclassic skeletal samples from nearby Cahal Pech, suggests that while maize was widely grown, and important, the Preclassic occupants lived on a more diverse diet than in the Classic. They also appear to have had, in general, a fairly good state of health (Powis et al. 1999; Song 1996). This pattern seems born out by osteological data from Preclassic human remains at Cuello as well (Saul and Saul 1991).

Ultimately, the late Middle Preclassic structures were abandoned and a middenlike deposit (up to 114 cm thick in places), loaded with organic remains and shell, was laid over the entire area to level the area for the construction of Plaza B. This dark midden layer has been dated to 400–300 B.C., a time when major site planning and construction was begun.

Summary

Pacbitun reflects a pattern of gradual evolution that appears typical of many other mid-sized Maya sites in the valley. Centers like Pacbitun were settled fairly early and became significant civic-ceremonial foci by the Early Classic. At the time Pacbitun was established, this part of the valley was still partly covered by mature, primary, broadleaf forest. The inhabitants lived in a unique ecological mosaic, ranged over a wide area in order to exploit necessary resources, and established long-distance trade networks to acquire exotic goods (obsidian, jade, and marine shells) by about 500 B.C. (Awe and Healy 1994; Fedick 1996).

It remains unclear, at present, to which major center Pacbitun was politically linked during the Classic though Xunantunich (about 15 km away) is a likely candidate, especially in the Late Classic when the latter flourished (LeCount 1999; LeCount et al. 2002; Leventhal and Ashmore 1997; chapter 10). The sprawling metropolis of Caracol (about 30 km away) is also a possibility (chapter 20; A. Chase and D. Chase 1996b), though most Pacbitun material culture (especially pottery) is more closely tied to the valley. Certain Pacbitun burial patterns (extended position, head to the south) reflect valley practices, while other customs (e.g., multiple burials) are more reminiscent of Caracol (D. Chase and A. Chase 1996; Healy et al. 1998).

The slate industry at Pacbitun was especially prominent throughout the site's long history. Slate outcrops occur along nearby creeks, and the distinctive, malleable stone was likely quarried here and then worked into specific artifacts at the site. Slate debitage is common across the site core, and a wide range of slate artifacts have been documented (Healy et al. 1995). While conjectural, it is reasonable to suggest that some of the numerous slate objects found at sites elsewhere in the Maya lowlands were manufactured at Pacbitun. At least one specialized Late Terminal Classic slate workshop has been identified.

The characteristic hilly terrain likely led to the Classic period development or adoption of hillslope terrace agriculture. Traces of this labor-intensive agrotechnology have been found as much as 4 km away. The terrace plots are reminiscent of those previously documented from the valley to the north (Fedick 1994) and Caledonia and Caracol to the south (A. Chase and D. Chase 1998a; Healy et al. 1980, 1983). In the end, despite its long cultural history and record of adaptability, Pacbitun collapsed and was abandoned like so many other lowland Maya centers, with no significant evidence for habitation beyond A.D. 900.

Acknowledgments

Investigations conducted at Pacbitun were licensed by the government of Belize through the Belize Department of Archaeology, the cooperation of which is gratefully acknowledged. Research at Pacbitun would not have been possible without the permission, interest, and support of Alfonso Tzul, the property owner, his family, and the local workmen from San Antonio and San Ignacio who helped in numerous ways with our field investigations. We are grateful to all of them for their years of friendship, generosity, and kindness. Funding for the Pacbitun research was provided by grants from the Social Sciences and Humanities Research Council (SSHRC) of Canada (#s 410-85-1157, 410-88-1161, and 410-94-0506) to the senior author. Additional support was provided by the Trent University Committee on Research and the Ahau Foundation. Over the past decade, a number of colleagues have provided assistance to the authors on the Pacbitun research, especially (in alphabetical order): Jim Aimers, Carmen Arendt, Wendy Ashmore, Jaime Awe, Joe Ball, Cassandra Bill, Arlen and Diane Chase, David Cheetham, Anabel Ford, Jim Garber, Peter Harrison, Tom Hester, Gyles Iannone, Richard Leventhal, and Lori Wright. We thank

Polydora Baker, Kitty Emery, and Norbert Stanchly for faunal analyses; Scott Fedick and David Lentz for paleobotanical analysis; Michael Glascock for trace element analysis of obsidian; Hermann Helmuth and Rhan-Ju Song for osteological analysis; and Fred Longstaffe, Henry Schwarcz, and Christine White for isotopic analysis. Settlement information is based primarily on unpublished Trent University theses written by Melissa Campbell-Trithart, Clarence Richie, and Kay Sunahara. Maps, plans, artifact illustrations and photographs were prepared by Melissa Campbell-Trithart, Ruth Dickau, Rick Fisher, Rita Granda, and the authors. To all of these colleagues, we express our sincere appreciation for their help. We alone are responsible for the interpretations included herein.

14

Defining Royal Maya Burials

A Case from Pacbitun

Paul F. Healy, Jaime J. Awe, and Hermann Helmuth

Excavations undertaken of Structure 1 at Pacbitun, an ancient Maya center located on the southern rim of the Belize Valley, revealed a well-preserved elite grave of a tall, adult male. The vaulted masonry tomb, labeled Burial (BU) 1–9, was impressive in its size, the labor involved in its construction, and the richness and diversity of its burial offerings, which included jade, pyrite, slate, marine shell, bone, cinnabar, and pottery. In this chapter, we discuss the ancient Maya "cult of the dead" and examine known royal burial customs from several Classic period sites. We identify five major attributes for the characterization of Maya regal burials and, finally, conclude that BU 1–9 housed the remains of a Late Classic period ruler of Pacbitun.

Structure 1

Structure 1 was the single most imposing example of Pre-Columbian masonry architecture at Pacbitun. In its final stage, the front (west) face of Structure 1 measured almost 18 m wide, with a Terminal Classic central stair nearly 12 m wide. Atop the plastered summit was a one-room masonry building (once vaulted) with a single, central doorway in both the front and rear walls of the superstructure. Including an estimated height (4 m) for the vaulted building, Structure 1 at completion would have been over 16 m tall. This was the most elevated structure at Pacbitun, and the size was enhanced further by the building location atop Plaza A, the central and highest plaza at the site (see chapter 13 for a discussion of the investigations in the site core).

The considerable architectural bulk of Structure 1 was doubled by the construction of a pair of flanking temple-pyramids, Structures 4 and 5. From excavations of all three structures, it is apparent that each began as a separate structure but were joined by the Late Preclassic period into one massive architectural unit that dominated the entire east end of Plaza A. This type of triple-structure, or E-Group architectural configuration, with abundant elite burials positioned on the central axis, is replicated at other Belize Valley sites (Aimers 1993; Awe et al. 1991; Ruppert 1940).

Excavations of Structure 1 included a 4-m-wide bisecting trench that cut into the west face of the pyramid, from the summit to the plaza floor. This trench penetrated as deeply as 8 m into the interior heart of the structure, exposing a series of earlier, encased buildings. Indeed, at least five major architectural phases, and many other minor subphases of modification, have now been identified. From these tests we know that Structure 1 was initiated during the transition between the Middle to Late Preclassic (ca. 500 B.C.) and was largely abandoned, along with the rest of the site, by the start of the 10th century A.D.

Interestingly, Structure 1 was not only the single tallest and most imposing architectural unit at Pacbitun but also produced the largest number of elaborate graves and caches (nine of each). The pattern of elite burials in Structure 1, virtually all on the central axis, provides another example of the use of ancestors to delineate an *axis mundi* (McAnany 1995).

The Excavation and Contents of Burial 1–9

BU 1–9 occurred during the first portion of Phase 4 (of the five major architectural phases). From the collective experience of excavation of eight different structures in the Core Zone, we believe that this was a period of major architectural renewal at the site, and particularly for Structure 1. In fact, the interment of the individual found in BU 1–9 probably was, in several ways, the single most significant event in the evolution of Structure 1 and, judging from the magnitude of associated activities, possibly in the entire history of the site.

During architectural Phase 4 of Structure 1 (now estimated to have occurred about A.D. 550–700, the Coc phase at Pacbitun), an important person died and was laid to rest in the only known large, vaulted tomb at the site. The tomb locale had to be specially prepared with a 5-m-deep shaft, directly along the centerline of Structure 1, through a series of earlier pyramidal forms. This ancient excavation must have been an undertaking of enormous proportions that (unfortunately for us) also disturbed a substantial part of the central, axial stair of Structure 1 in the process.

After clearing through the ancient, backfilled shaft (5 m deep and at least 3 m², filled with loose dirt, rocks, sherds, stucco, and damaged architectural rubble), we encountered a thick (8–10 cm) bed of thousands of chert flakes spread across the entire excavation area. These flakes, in turn, covered 16 large (1+ m long, uniformly 50 cm wide), trimmed, slate slabs that served as the roofing and cover for the hollow chamber of BU 1-9. The slabs were removed to provide access to the hollow tomb. This condition was a rarity at Pacbitun; most burials had been backfilled with earth and rock, presumably for structural consolidation and stability.

While there were a total of 20 burials unearthed in the Core Zone of Pacbitun, most (11) were of the crypt type (Welsh 1988). BU 1-9 was the only true masonry tomb encountered. The tomb was large (nearly 3 m in length, a long axis north-south, and 1 m wide), with well-preserved walls of cut stone standing 12 courses high (about 130 cm). It was roughly oval in shape, tapering gently at the north and south ends, and was capped by a shallow corbel vault, with six slate roofing slabs sealing the tomb. The remaining slate slabs were wedged atop these, sometimes three deep (fig. 14.1).

Because the BU 1-9 cavity was not in-filled, the tomb produced one of the most well preserved examples of Pacbitun burial practices. It also

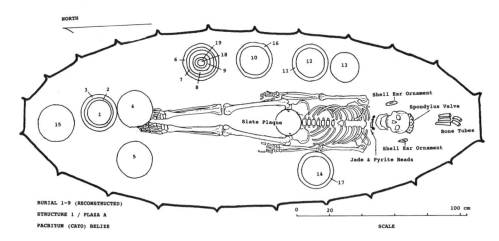

Fig. 14.1. Stylized plan of Pacbitun BU 1-9 (tomb) interior.

proved to be one of the richest graves in terms of material culture recovered from a burial context, and had well-preserved osteological remains of the deceased. The floor of the burial chamber was covered by about 7–10 cm of fine dirt that had presumably filtered through the roof and side walls. Encircling the fully extended body were the remains of 19 painted vessels, many complete, about one quarter polychromes, the remainder monochrome, mostly black or brown-black tone. The ceramics represented a variety of different forms; 10 bowls, 4 dishes, 2 vases, 2 pitchers, and 1 jar, with some stacked or nested inside others.[1]

The ceramic forms and style of decoration help fix the date of the burial to the early part of the Coc phase of the Late Classic period (figs. 14.2 and 14.3). Other mortuary furnishings were polished jade and iron pyrite beads (3 jade, 1 pyrite tube), a matching pair of circular shell earflares, five hollowed bone tubes (possibly panpipes, fig. 14.4), a drilled, circular, slate disk, presumably the backing to a polished pyrite mosaic plaque, or mirror (pyrite polygons had corroded away). Of particular interest was a large marine (*Spondylus americanus*) valve with an eroded painted symbol on the inside surface (fig. 14.3b). The *Spondylus* shell was positioned at the back of the head, like a skullcap.[2] BU 1–9 was also one of only four elaborate burials at Pacbitun to display residues of red ochre, or cinna-

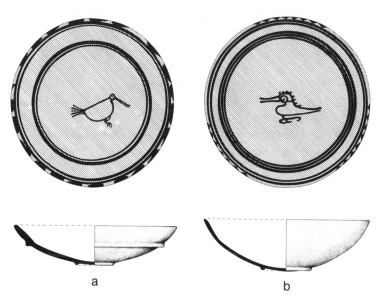

Fig. 14.2. Ceramic vessels from Pacbitun BU 1-9: (a) Black-on-Red dish, vessel no. 4 (diameter 28.7 cm); (b) Black-on-Red dish, vessel no. 11 (diameter 28.4 cm).

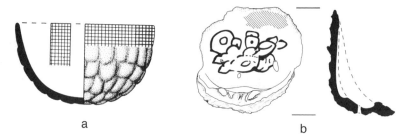

Fig. 14.3. Artifacts from Pacbitun BU-1-9: (a) small, tan bowl, vessel no. 9 (diameter 10.3 cm); (b) drawing of *Spondylus* valve, found beneath cranium, with eroded hieroglyphic symbol on inside (length 12.2 cm).

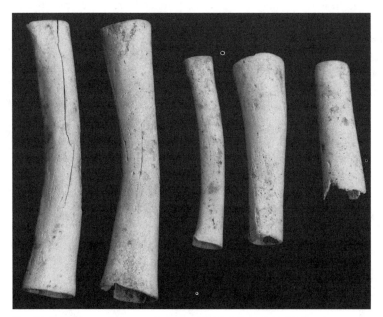

Fig. 14.4. Hollow, cut bone tubes from BU 1-9 (length 7–15.5 cm).

bar. In the case of BU 1–9, the pigment had been liberally sprinkled over the entire body but was especially evident on the head and chest areas.

The skeletal remains belonged to an adult male, about 45 ± 5 years old. He was a relatively tall individual (ca. 170 cm) compared to the average Maya of the Classic period.[3] He had been carefully laid on his back (supine), his body fully extended, head to the south and face up.[4]

Following the sealing of BU 1–9 with tight-fitting slate slabs and a thick bed of chert flakes, the huge, gaping shaft to the tomb had been back-filled and a new facade erected over Structure 1. Included in this building renewal was a special stair block, situated directly over the location of BU 1–9. This unusual architectural feature contained Pacbitun BU 1–1 and 1–2 and several caches. We also suspect that Stela 1 (the largest at the site) and Altar 1, both uncarved monuments, were positioned in front of the renewed Structure 1 stair at this time. The positioning of these monuments was accompanied by the sacrifice of at least three individuals (BU 1–3), whose remains were laid beneath the stela butt on the central axis of Structure 1.

Discussion

Maya burial practices have been examined by several investigators (Hall 1989; Ricketson 1925; Ruz 1965, 1968; Welsh 1988). Coe (1956, 1975) has suggested that the ancient Maya were heavily focused on the tomb, in a kind of "cult of the dead," or ancestor worship. Adams (1977:98) has argued that this ancestor worship had generated a type of "royal cult" with the Maya elite perceived as semidivine. The archaeological correlates for this "royal cult" consisted of three major components: the grave, the temple built over it, and the associated monument typically raised in front of it (Moholy-Nagy 1985:155).

Studies of royal tombs at Altar de Sacrificios (Smith 1972), Altun Ha (Pendergast 1969), Calakmul (Carrasco Vargas et al. 1999), Copan (Bell et al. 1999; Sharer 1999; Sharer et al. 1999; Stuart 1997), Palenque (Ruz Lhuillier 1973), Rio Azul (Hall 1989), and Tikal (Coe 1990; Shook and Kidder 1961; Trik 1963), suggest a high degree of uniformity for certain mortuary customs. Were there particular offerings, grave goods, or accoutrements that Maya rulers, the most elevated of all elite, felt compelled to take with them in their journey to the afterlife? If so, how early were such conventions developed?

Hall (1989:275) suggests that "a system of royal mortuary symbolism" probably began by the Late Preclassic. BU 125 at Tikal (ca. A.D. 173 ± 45) is one of the earliest lowland Maya elite burials with many of the hallmarks of royalty already present. Recent research at Copan has identified two Early Classic royal burials (Hunal and Magarita tombs) from deep within the earliest acropolis architecture, one of which likely belongs to Yak K'uk' Mol, founder (ca. A.D. 426) of the site dynasty (Bell et al. 1999; Sharer 1999).

Arlen Chase (1992:37) suggests that "Rulers can be identified primarily by the markers associated with their interments in conjunction with the special locations of such interments . . . [and] no one (single) marker identifies a ruler; a combination of markers must exist for the appropriate identification to be made . . . (including) codex remains, cinnabar, mirrors, stone vessels, jadeite jewelry . . . ceremonial bars, certain rare shells, textual materials, and perhaps stingray spines."

Haviland and Moholy-Nagy (1992:53–54) are largely in agreement with this list and state that the tombs of Maya kings included large quantities of fine pottery, jade jewelry, *Spondylus* shell, stingray spines, pyrite mosaic mirrors, stone vessels, and cinnabar, plus jaguar pelts, placement of masses of chert and obsidian debitage over tombs, and human sacrificial victims. They also put an emphasis on grave size, quality of grave construction, quantity and quality of objects in it, and impressiveness of the structure built over such tombs.

Coe (1988) has explored the iconography of royal Maya burials. He suggests that certain classes of objects were *essential accompaniments* to elite Classic Maya burials. Jade (for its value as a Maya symbol of life), ritual bloodletters (especially stingray spines, or sharpened obsidian blades), codices, enema ritual paraphernalia, dogs and other animals, musical instruments, and copal incense are singled out. He also identified mirrors and beds of chert (or obsidian) flakes as particularly important. Mirrors (or plaques) he described as items of "supreme importance" and the "embodiment of Maya rulership" arguing that "they (mirrors) seem confined to the highest-status tombs" (Coe 1988:227–228; see also Schele and Miller 1983).

In regard to the act of covering Maya graves with flint chips, Coe (1988:232) states that only the "greatest Maya tombs were sealed with a layer of flint chips and flakes," and that the "flint (or obsidian) capping of major tombs . . . would be a recognition that the tomb itself was actually *within* the Underworld, or Xibalba." Hall (1989:308), in his study of traits manifested in the elite tombs of Rio Azul and other Maya sites, offers an alternative interpretation of the debitage layers. He sees them as representative of "physical residues or indications of lightning . . . that struck the ground to form a cave (the tomb shaft)." He also asserts that placement of the debitage layers above tombs was a practice reserved only for the most important Maya (Hall 1989:191).

Finally, Welsh (1988:table 99) has identified specific burials of rulers at Tikal (8) and Palenque (1). Our comparison of the burial features and grave goods from these known (and/or widely accepted) regal tombs reveals that they, again, share many attributes that can be grouped as follows:

(1) burial in tombs (as opposed to crypts or cists): (a) often tombs of large size; (b) tombs built of, or covered by, special material (vaulting, slate slabs, painted capstones, beds of chert/obsidian);

(2) typically (tombs) situated in the most imposing site architecture (temple-pyramids are most usual);

(3) opulence in grave goods (especially marked by nonlocal or specialized materials): (a) use of cinnabar; (b) multiple ceramic vessels, often polychromes; (c) jade jewelry; (d) bloodletters (stingray spines, sharpened obsidian blades); (e) marine shells (particularly *Spondylus* valves and/or "skull valve"); (f) slate-backed pyrite mosaic "mirrors" (plaques);

(4) co-occurrence of human sacrifice;

(5) erection of an associated monument (stela, altar).

Conclusion

While it is impossible to link BU 1–9 unequivocally with the uncarved Stela 1 erected in front of Structure 1 (and its associated human sacrifices), this elaborate Pacbitun tomb included many of the key markers of Maya rulers that seem to have been held in common by the Maya and can be archae-ologically identified. On the basis of the location of BU 1–9, deep inside Structure 1, the largest temple-pyramid at site, the type of burial (over-sized, vaulted, masonry tomb), and the type of grave goods (considering both quantity and quality), there is an obvious indication of an elite inter-ment.

However, the additional occurrence of a painted *Spondylus* valve, the slate-backed "mirror," abundant use of cinnabar, and sealing of this grave with slate slabs and masses of chert flakes, indicate that the tall, adult male individual in BU 1–9 was an important Pacbitun lord, and quite likely a Late Classic–period site ruler. As Hall (1989:262) has argued, there is growing evidence to suggest "a pattern of elite mortuary behavior" with particular "traits in various combinations, [which] occur for the most part in tombs containing Maya rulers or other individuals of the highest stand-ing in Classic Maya society." These powerful individuals continued to in-fluence Classic Maya society well beyond their mortal lifespans. The pres-ence of their bodily remains housed in some of the most impressive and centrally located architecture at Maya centers likely became foci for numerous later elaborate rituals and commemorations. These entombed ancestors functioned to link new rulers to familial bloodlines and the inheritance of political power, status, and wealth (McAnany 1995). In this sense, Pacbitun BU 1–9 clearly reinforces the notion of a widely held Classic Maya "royal cult" and kingship.

Notes

1. This diversity of vessel classes raises the question of whether special "food service sets" may be represented. Similar kinds of ceramic vessel sets have been noted from royal burials at Dos Pilas (Reents-Budet 1994:82).

2. Moholy-Nagy (1985:149) argues that *Spondylus* was valued by the Maya almost as much as jade and was a "prerogative of the elite. . . . [T]heir appearance in burials may be taken as indication of an elevated social status of the deceased." At least six of the burials of identified rulers at Tikal (BU-10, Curl Nose; BU-23, Shield Skull; BU-48, Stormy Sky; BU-116, Ruler A/Ah Cacau; BU-160, Jaguar Paw Skull; and BU-196, Ruler B/Yaxkin) have *Spondylus* valves, including the special skull-covering valve (cf. Moholy-Nagy 1985:154, figs. 10.6 and 10.7). At Rio Azul, such "skull shells" were associated with very elaborate Early Classic burials (Tombs 19 and 23) (Hall 1989:81, 138).

3. Haviland and Moholy-Nagy (1992:fig. 4.1) indicate the average stature of occupants of small houses at Tikal was 156.5 cm, 159 cm for occupants of intermediate-sized houses, and 164 cm for the ruling elite. Danforth (1999:table 5.1) cites a mean stature estimate of 158.3 cm for Late Classic Maya males (N = 82). At 170 cm, the individual from Pacbitun BU 1–9 was very tall, even among the Maya aristocracy.

4. It should be noted that there was considerable uniformity in burial practices in the Core Zone of Pacbitun in regard to body position (extended, supine) and head orientation (south). The overwhelming majority of Core Zone burials had the same body position and head orientation (south). This is a Belize Valley burial pattern first noted by Willey (et al. 1965), and appears to commence by at least the Middle Preclassic periods (Awe 1992:336–339).

Acknowledgments

We wish to acknowledge the financial support of the Social Sciences and Humanities Research Council of Canada (SSHRC Grant #410-85-1157 and #410-88-1161 to the senior author) and Trent University (Committee on Research and Department of Anthropology). Special thanks are also extended to the Belize Department of Archaeology (the late Commissioner Harriot Topsey) for authorizing the license for research at Pacbitun (Permits 70/4/84, 70/5/86, and 70/5/87), and to the Pacbitun site property owners, especially Alphonso Tzul and the late Gumercindo Mai. The research would have been impossible without the assistance of these individuals and institutions, and the general cooperation of the citizens of San Antonio (Cayo) and San Ignacio. Helpful comments were received from Jim Garber, Grant Hall, and anonymous reviewers. A shorter version of this chapter was presented at the 59th Annual Meeting of the Society for American Archaeology in Anaheim, California (1994).

15

Integration among Communities, Center, and Regions

The Case from El Pilar

Anabel Ford

Complex societies and early civilizations depended on a hierarchical structure to organize and integrate constituent populations and mobilize resources. Archaeologically, this is manifest in the arrangement of individual settlements, variability in local communities, and composition of
regional centers. The organization of residential production and consumption provides a foundation for interpreting the nature of settlements,
diversity among communities provides insight into the complexity of local centralization, while the functions of and interactions among centers
provide clues to regional dynamics. Local organizational centers coordinated communities and component households on the one hand, and
managed regional relations on the other. Further, the degree to which
power is consolidated and the level at which it is expressed—the community, the center, the region—is directly linked to the basis of support in
the hierarchy. For early civilizations, the basis of support was derived
from agriculture. Since agriculture is a fundamental component of the
economy, it is critical to understand the manner in which the subsistence
base was manipulated to support development of hierarchies in early
complex civilizations. Archaeological examples of complex societies provide an excellent testing ground for identifying household, community,
and regional mechanisms of organization and integration because, ultimately, wealth in these societies must be tied to the production potential
of land and control of labor. This chapter examines issues of organiza-

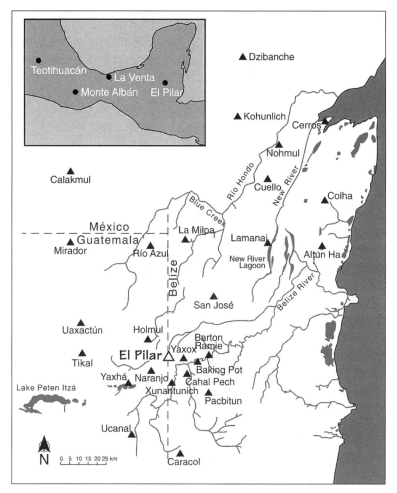

Map 3. The central Maya lowlands with Maya centers indicated.

tion and integration of the ancient Maya in the Belize River area and the significance of the major Maya center of El Pilar within that area (map 3 and fig. 15.1).

Background

While tropical forests offer distinct environmental conditions that undoubtedly impacted evolutionary events, the organizational solutions achieved by the ancient Maya have obvious parallels with other complex

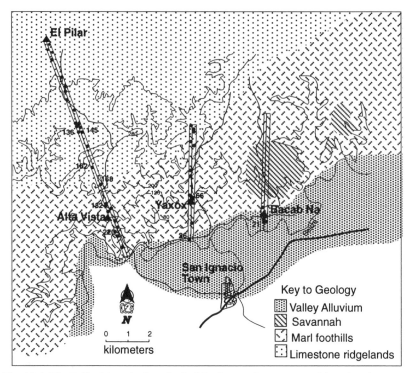

Fig. 15.1. The Belize River Archaeological Settlement Survey area with regional transect surveys, test excavations, and full-scale excavations indicated.

agrarian civilizations. Land resource distribution is an essential factor. The land resources of the Maya lowlands are distributed over the region in a mosaic pattern, rather than in contiguous stretches that concentrate resources and population for direct control. The discontinuous nature of these agricultural resources acted as a dispersive force on settlement and presented unique organizational and managerial problems that frustrate hierarchical controls. Given that the Maya civilization flourished for centuries, it is clear that the elite bureaucracy developed a successful and effective management system. This fact raises the critical problem of how the organizational hierarchy of complex societies facilitated social integration, despite significant variations in resource distribution.

Through the course of the long-term archaeological program of the Belize River Archaeological Settlement Survey (BRASS), we can broadly characterize the chronology of settlement and community patterns in the area (Fedick 1988, 1989; Fedick and Ford 1990; Ford 1990; Ford 1991a, 1991b; Ford and Fedick 1992). The research area naturally divides into three major resource zones based on local geographic characteristics and agricultural potential. Survey transects traversing these geographic zones from the Belize River north provide that basis of the settlement sample for interpreting patterns of land use of the area (fig. 15.1).

The survey phase (1983–1989) of the research identified settlement distributions and compositions that correlated with the quality of agricultural land resources. Settlement patterns across space and over time and residential unit distinctions in the Late Classic period evince variation by these resource zones: settlement densities are high in the primary agricultural resource zones of the valley and ridgelands and low in the secondary zones of the foothills (Fedick 1989). In addition, a range of residential unit sizes are associated with social and economic distinctions. Larger residential units have more exotics and wealth items and are concentrated in the ridgelands (Ford 1990).

The survey was followed by an intensive excavation phase (1990–1992) in which residential units representative of distinctions in the three major land resource zones were examined. Seven residential units were selected in a two-step process from the data of the survey phase. All tested residential units were grouped by labor investment, a proxy for size, and landform, indicative of production. The data set of residential units were, then, ranked by composition of artifact assemblage (ceramics, stone tools, debitage, obsidian, etc), and the median was selected as the representative of each group.

Differences among the residential units of the resource zones were illuminated through the intensive excavation of these representative sites. This provided insight into the nature of households as well as community production and consumption activities in the area (Hintzman 2000; Lucero 1994, 2001; Olson 1994; Steinberg 1992).

The results of the completed intensive residential unit excavations begin to distinguish the settlement relations among the three major resource zones of the Belize River area: the moderately settled valley, the sparsely settled foothills, and the densely settled ridgelands (fig. 15.1). Settlement concentrations were found in the best agricultural zones of the valley and ridgelands. The poorest zones, the foothills, were characterized by scattered low settlement density. The relative homogeneity of residential units in the valley and foothills allows for a characterization of residential production and consumption. Excavations at residential units in the third and most important resource zone, the ridgelands, however, reveal far more diversity than that encountered in the other two zones. The data of the excavations from the ridgelands suggest that there is considerably more variation in size, composition, construction techniques, and artifact assemblages among the ridgeland residential units than other zones.

The importance of the ridgelands in the Belize River area is demonstrated by a long settlement prehistory, high settlement densities, concentration of large elite residences, and the prominent presence of the major civic-ceremonial center of El Pilar. El Pilar is a major center of the Maya area, with 50 hectares of monuments in the core area (fig. 15.2). The core area is connected by a unique causeway system that crosses the modern political boundary of Belize and Guatemala. The construction sequence of the monuments is only now emerging from excavations of target sectors. The earliest construction phases date to the Middle Preclassic, around 700 B.C. and suggest a significant investment in public architecture at this time. Building and remodeling continues unabated through the Classic period and major works were still undertaken in the Terminal Classic period from A.D. 900–1000. The core monumental area is surrounded by a dense and complex settlement of more than 200 structures per square kilometer.

These outstanding qualities of ridgeland communities distinguish them from communities in other zones and relate the importance of this zone to

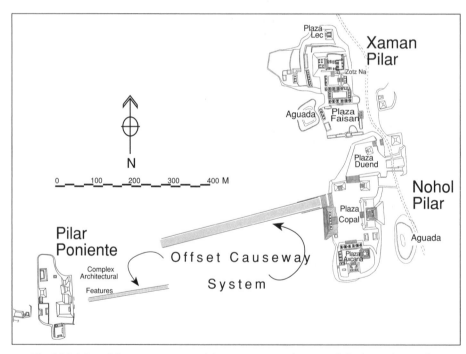

Fig. 15.2. Map of the greater extent of the major regional center of El Pilar (Belize)/ Pilar Poniente (Guatemala).

the subsistence economy in the region. Here, I provide a review of the BRASS project's database as it addresses issues of household activities, community organization, and local centralization, particularly in the Late Classic period of the Maya lowlands. The results provide vital information on household variation and community patterns in the Belize River area as well as insight into the integration of the area from the El Pilar ridgelands with implications for understanding patterning in the region as a whole.

Resources and Settlement of the Ancient Maya in the Belize River Area

The ancient Maya were an agricultural society and their viability depended largely on the success of their farming populace. Broadly speaking, there are four basic land resources that together create the continuum of variation in the central Maya lowlands (Fedick 1994, 1995; Fedick and Ford 1990) and form the composite resource mosaic that both the ancient and contemporary populations of the region could utilize:

(1) well-drained uplands—primary agricultural resources;

(2) slow-drained lowlands—secondary agricultural resources;

(3) riverine-associated swamps—secondary agricultural resources;

(4) closed depression swamps—nonagricultural resources.

It is the relative proportions of these four basic lowland resources that contribute to the subsistence potential of local areas, and it is the distribution of the primary agricultural resources that was the foundation of the ancient Maya regional economic landscape. The mosaic of this overall landscape is reflected in settlement patterns and residential unit activities of the Maya. Densely settled areas were the most intensely utilized and the lightly settled areas were the most extensively used. This is also reflected in the residential constructions.

Field research on local resources, settlement, and residential patterns in the Belize River area has been aimed at addressing organization and integration in the Maya area. Settlement survey data have aided in identifying patterns that were associated with the major resource zones—the valley, foothills, and ridgelands (Fedick 1989). Test excavations were conducted at a 12.5 percent sample of residential units (N = 48) in the survey transects (fig. 15.1). Intensive excavations focused at 9 residential units representing median small, medium, and large units within each major resource zone (see fig. 15.1). In addition, the residential unit identified with the highest obsidian density in the test excavations was the subject of intensive activity area excavations. We now have a general impression of the overall landscape.

The Community of the Valley

The valley is characterized by a uniform but small proportion of primary agricultural resources (6 percent) restricted along the river, an average settlement density of 98 structures/km^2, a high proportion of single-structure, medium-sized residential units and few large residential units (Ford and Fedick 1992). Intensive excavations included a medium and a small residential unit in the valley zone, revealing general similarities in terms of construction techniques and artifact assemblages (Ford 1991a). Houses had a long occupation history from the Middle Preclassic to the Terminal Classic. They were modest in size, consistent with the survey assessment, and were built in unpretentious proportions—neither small and insignificant nor large and imposing—covering about 200 m^2. Successive constructions and remodelings over time used earth and clay fill, faced and natural stone foundation walls, and plaster floors. The constructions were always enlargements, but the efforts were well within the range of a household enterprise.

Household assemblages of the Late Classic period valley sites are robust, typically including the full range of requisite household goods and a presence of luxury items. Residential units were continually occupied, and a premium was placed on the land between them. The overall impression of valley residential units and the valley community is one of homogeneity made up of a relatively affluent permanent farming populace with little ability to invest beyond their immediate household level.

The Community of the Foothills

The foothills are characterized by a high proportion of secondary agricultural resources (61 percent, fig. 15.1) situated along the flanks of the ridges above the valley, with average settlement densities ranging from 3 to 46 structures/km^2, a predominance of small single-structure residential units, and minimal elite presence. Intensive excavations took place at a medium and a small residential unit of the zone. Constructions were no earlier than the Late Preclassic and abandoned before the Terminal Classic period. While these residential units were similar to each other in construction techniques and activities represented, they were in sharp contrast to the units of the valley. Construction consisted solely of rubble fill foundations with brief construction sequences composed of carefully sorted and packed fist-sized cobbles that filled in the uneven marl-bedrock surfaces and formed the foundations of perishable superstructures covering ca. 25 to 140 m². There was little or no evidence of formal floors and walls. These are ephemeral residential units accessing the more extensive secondary farmlands of this zone where the nearest neighbor may not be closer than 2 km.

Artifact assemblages were skewed at foothill residential units. The production of lithics (chert) was high and included a relatively significant proportion of production byproducts (Ford and Olson 1989; Michaels 1993). There is also evidence to suggest some level of ceramic production (Lucero 1994). Household items, such as grinding stones, were underrepresented. The overall impression of foothill residential units as well as the foothill community is one of a relatively marginalized mobile populace, utilizing the more extensive secondary agricultural resources of the area. The widely spread residences of this zone are similar in that they show evidence of sporadic and intermittent use, little remodeling, and few basic domestic artifacts. In addition to agricultural pursuits, the evidence suggests that residences of the foothill zone were independently investing in the production of household goods to supplement basic subsistence activities (Ford and Olson 1989).

The Community of the Ridgelands

The ridgelands are characterized by the highest proportion of primary agricultural resources occurring in small and large patches comprising some 74 percent of the western ridgelands that make up 34 percent of the Belize River area. The average settlement density in the ridgelands range from 46 to 208 structures/km²; many are multistructure units. Furthermore, the ridgelands have the greatest number of elite residences and the presence of the most imposing of monumental public architecture. Intensive excavations were undertaken at large, medium, and small example residential units, as well as a large residential unit with high obsidian density.

Unlike the residential units of the valley and foothills, where a general similarity was encountered in the community, the ridgeland units are composed of a diverse and variable group in terms of length of occupation, construction techniques, and activities represented. Residential unit constructions ranged from small single-structure rubble foundations to major platforms supporting corbelled-arch rooms. Rubble construction characterized the small single-structure residential unit that resembled the foothill units in form and composition, with extremely brief construction se-

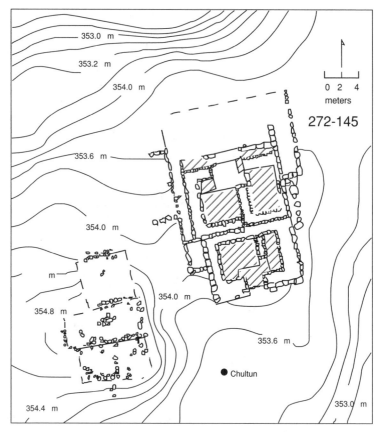

Fig. 15.3. A large ridgeland residential unit excavated in 1992 by the BRASS project.

quences, without formal floors, little use of foundation walls, no clear evidence of remodelings, and an area less than 12 m². Formal faced stone walls, substantial foundation platforms, and finely prepared plaster floors characterize the multistructure medium and large residential units that covered 400 to 1600 m² in area (fig. 15.3). No general pattern in construction techniques could be determined from the excavation sample. Rather a wide range was employed, depending upon the situation.

Artifact assemblages were equally variable in the ridgelands. The small residential unit had few associated artifacts and range was very limited. Ceramics suggest a combination of uses in the area, but the architectural components were largely Late Classic in date. The medium residential unit, occupied through the Classic period consists of finely cut limestone block walls and well-plastered rooms with a complex floor plan. Despite this clear effort in construction, artifacts densities were low and general household inventories absent. The large residential unit, built from the Late Preclassic through the Terminal Classic period, had both residential and public architecture. This residential unit had considerable quantities of all major artifact types, including a wide variety of luxury items rarely encountered in other zones (Ford 1991a). While it is clear that the nature of the artifact assemblages from each residential area relates directly to local activities, no standard assemblage composition emerges from these ridgeland excavations. Rather, the overall impression is one of considerable complexity. This is hardly surprising as the ridgelands represent the concentration of occupation in the area.

An additional ridgeland residential unit, located in the densely settled ridgeland community we named Laton near the excavations of the example large residential unit, was investigated because of the high densities of obsidian encountered in the testing phase. This large three-structure residential unit covered ca. 1,050 m² in area. Intensive excavations at the obsidian residential unit concentrated on the defined open areas of the plaza, terrace, and platform spaces to identify the nature and scope of obsidian production activities (Olson 1994). Tremendous quantities of obsidian blade production byproducts were recovered in all excavated areas. In one small terrace deposit of blade debitage (Area A), we recovered over 13,000 pieces of obsidian: a density of 1.7 million obsidian pieces/m³ (Hintzman 2000). The material of this deposit represents rejected blade production of obsidian from highland sources (Olson 1994). Another deposit behind a structure (Area B) contained 33 complete, but exhausted, prismatic blade cores. Both these unusual deposits suggest provisional discard areas stashed for future use. Further, in the general open areas of the residential unit there are no areas with less than 3,000 obsidian pieces/m³. The technologies used to reduce the obsidian cores and the conservation strategies employed to extract more obsidian blades through careful rejuvenation methods (Hintzman 2000) further substantiates the value of the raw material of obsidian.

While obsidian production is present in other areas of the Maya region (Clark 1988, 1989; Mallory 1984), this obsidian production assemblage is entirely unique. No such collections have been reported for any other lowland Maya site, including Tikal (Moholy-Nagy, personal communication 1993). The excavations clearly defined the surprising scope and magnitude of the obsidian production enterprises at this large residential unit. Despite extensive excavations throughout the monumental centers of the Maya lowlands and the importance placed on obsidian, this is the first identified production site of any magnitude in the Maya region. The only contexts with densities of obsidian debitage equivalent to the residential unit at Laton across the Maya area are only known at centers: building dedications, substela caches, and tombs.

The evidence of obsidian production at this elite residence in a peripheral community of the Belize River area underscores the complexities of obsidian procurement, production, and distribution in the Maya area. While it is clear that obsidian was procured by this elite residential unit for production and distribution, it is equally clear that it was not directly controlled by major centers, such as El Pilar or Tikal (Olson 1994). In the Belize River area, as with the entire Maya lowland region, obsidian products, that is, prismatic blades, are ubiquitous. They are recovered, albeit in different densities, from the smallest house to the largest center (Rice 1984). This suggests that obsidian production was treated within a different sphere of the society where products were distributed to constituents as a reward, probably for participation in the subsistence economy, validating the local authority. The byproducts were carefully curated, and fit into a prestige scheme in the elite ceremonial realm, reinforcing the hierarchical structure of the political economy (Olson 1994).

Summarizing the ridgeland community is not straightforward. The general picture of ridgeland residential units as well as the ridgeland community at large is one of economic heterogeneity and diversity, especially in comparison to the relative homogeneity of the foothills and valley zones. This is not entirely unexpected as the residential units of the ridgelands comprise 85 percent of the Belize River area's settlement. The data broadly characterize the disparate complexion of the zone. This concentration and diversity in ridgeland settlement represent a contrast between the haves and the have-nots, between administrative and peasant households, between established homes and temporary field houses. Unlike the comparative uniformity of activities encountered at residential units in the valley and foothills, the ridgelands supported diverse occupations that not only focused on intensive subsistence production, but also on multiple service and production specialties coordinated and supported by the elite political economy of the area.

The Ridgelands of the Belize River Area

The key to community organization and the source of local integration in the Belize River area is among the settlements of the ridgelands. Valley residents were afforded increased or preferred access to lands by restrictions on settlement expansion in that zone. How was settlement restricted in the valley over time and in the Late Classic, in particular, to enable residents there to take advantage of the rich alluvial soils? Foothill residents were involved in several types of independent manufacturing activities besides the extensive subsistence opportunities of the zone, characteristic of marginalized agriculturists. Such specialists would have relied on exchange to meet aspects of daily needs. What were the mechanisms whereby products of foothill specialists circulated to settlements of the other zones? Obsidian production appears to be highly controlled and attached to elite residential units in the ridgelands. How were luxury items, such as obsidian prismatic blades, controlled and distributed as a privilege? The elite hierarchy was the source of land control, the facilitators of local exchange, and the managers and controllers of wealth goods.

Integration of settlement in the Belize River area depended on the elite hierarchy. That hierarchy was centered in the ridgelands at the regional center of El Pilar. The ridgeland escarpment where El Pilar is prominently situated, extends from Guatemala's Petén into Belize, 10 km north of the Belize River Valley. The location of El Pilar in the Belize River area and in the central lowlands indicates its prominent position as a major regional center of power (map 3 and fig. 15.4). El Pilar ranks equally in architectural complexity to regional Maya centers (Adams and Jones 1981); it is the largest center in the Belize River area, more than three times the size of

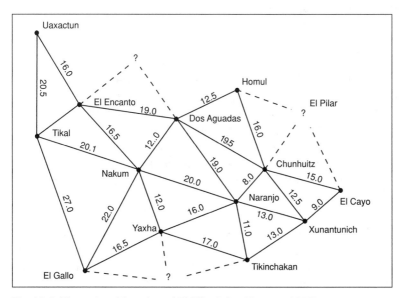

Fig. 15.4. The regional location of El Pilar (after Flannery 1972).

other well-known centers, such as Baking Pot or Xunantunich, and equal to Tikal's nearest neighbors, Yaxha and Uaxactun.

The center of El Pilar was the seat of major local power with clear regional ties with the Maya lowlands. The layout speaks to its complexity (Wernecke 1994). It is divided into at least three primary sectors: Xaman (North) Pilar, Nohol (South) Pilar, and Pilar Poniente (West). The western section has not been thoroughly explored, yet our rapid assessments of 1998 and 2001 indicate that more monuments are in the vicinity. The eastern and western sections are connected by an offset causeway system extending between two large public plaza areas (fig. 15.2). Survey and excavations have been concentrated in the eastern side of El Pilar in Belize. The western section, Pilar Poniente, is across the border in the Republic of Guatemala.

Based on mapping programs at El Pilar that began in 1984, and were expanded in 1986 and then annually since 1993, more than 30 public and private monumental plazas have been identified that cover more than 50 ha of public works. The monuments of El Pilar include many large temples and platforms reaching 17 to 21 m in height, range-structures character-ized by well-preserved standing room vaults, two ballcourts, a major acropolis with a labyrinth of palaces, and a system of causeways accessing the main open public plaza, Plaza Copal. This is the plaza that is linked to Pilar Poniente, another public sector to the west in Guatemala (fig. 15.2). The architectural preservation of the center is remarkable, despite the loot-ers' trenches that have penetrated the upper portions of some of the major structures.

In 1993, a detailed study of the center of El Pilar began, establishing the foundation for a long-term program of interdisciplinary eco-archaeo-logical research (Ford 1998). The archaeological plan is segmented into mapping, excavation, and structure consolidation and sequenced so that each aspect informs the next, with long-term conservation clearly in mind. Major work to date has concentrated on Nohol Pilar and the public area around Plaza Copal, where we have begun the task of understanding the construction history in this sector of the site (Wernecke 1994). From the research, we have developed an understanding of the complexity of the northern acropolis zone. Excavations of the buildings of Plaza Jobo from 1996 to 2001 demonstrate successive remodelings and additions that transformed more isolated constructions into labyrinths of rooms over the course of the Classic period (Ford et al. 1997). The result was the evolution of more restricted spaces.

We have also taken time to assess structure orientation, building styles, and the degree of preservation in the major plazas of the center. Based on small-scale exposures, limited examinations of stairways, and concentrated probe for corners, we have established conservation priorities for El Pilar (www.marc.uscb.edu/elpilar/fieldreports/index_fieldreports.html).

Realizing the contemporary need for development in the riverside villages, the program has been involved in promoting the site as a new adventure tour destination where the community participation is an essential aspect of site development (Ford 1998, www.marc.ucsb.edu/elpilar/10years_achievement/adaptive_management/adaptive_management.html). We have partnered with the community based organization, Amigos de El Pilar, and the Department of Archaeology of Belize in the excavations and consolidations of an example Maya house at El Pilar as well as the renaissance of the forest garden around it. Further, we have opened large areas of the center's monuments, created trails, and assisted in the construction of a caretaker's house that encourages access for local and international visitors.

The map of El Pilar provides a general impression of the center's size, and clues to its complexity (Ford et al. 1995; Wernecke 1994). It is clear that the center required considerable public investment derived from a labor pool representative of the settlements of the general area. The local El Pilar community must have been the immediate support for the center, and the density and diversity of settlement in the proximate area speak to the importance of the center (fig. 15.5). Settlement density within 1 km of El Pilar is extraordinarily high at 292 structures/km² (Ford 1990:179). The initiation of the El Pilar Settlement survey supports this assessment.

The four residential units that have been tested in that area, as part of the survey phase, reflect a broad range of sizes, compositions, and assemblage diversities. Full-scale excavations of one large residential unit compound at El Pilar (272–25), where five houses surround a patio, demonstrate the complexity of the permanent residences at the center. Excavations in the 2002 field season in collaboration with K. Kamp and J. Whitaker of Grinnell College, indicated a long occupation for this small site, suggesting a size hierarchy in the Preclassic that was maintained through to the Late Classic.

In addition, there is a major biface reduction locus (LDF chert site) situated adjacent to El Pilar's Plaza Faisan, representing a concentration of chert tool production that must have been coordinated with the functions of the center (Ford and Olson 1989). The data combine to suggest that the community and center of El Pilar figured significantly in the regional economic and political life of the ancient Maya from the Middle Preclassic onward, with major construction initiated no later than 700–600 B.C. and

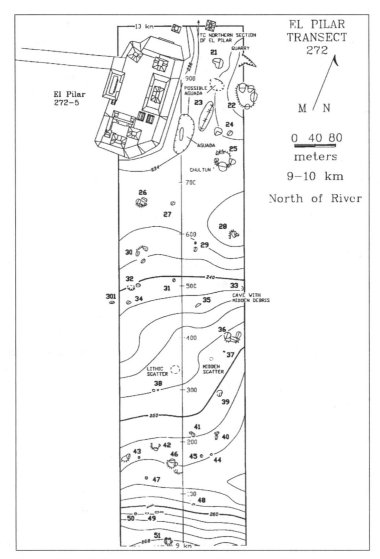

Fig. 15.5. The El Pilar transect just south of the center of El Pilar.

continuing over the course of the next 17 centuries up to A.D. 1000.

Examination of the construction sequences revealed in looters' trench profiles, building excavations of Plaza Copal, and architectural exposures throughout El Pilar has provided an overview of the occupation sequence. Major work has focused on tunnel excavations in the temple Xikna, or EP 7 (Ford et al. 1995: Orrego 1995). The Plaza Copal construction chronology indicates a long, uninterrupted prehistory beginning no later than 500

B.C., in the Middle Preclassic, and continuing through the Terminal Classic period to around A.D. 1000, postdating Tikal's abandonment (Ford and Fedick 1992; Orrego 1995). In addition, many areas of the center have yielded evidence of Terminal Classic construction (Ford and Fedick 1992). Finally, there is indication that the center was used into the Postclassic with the presence of distinctive trade wares that date after A.D. 1000, not only in Plaza Copal but also the northern acropolis area.

The concentrated study of Plaza Copal has revealed a complex sequence of building shifts that help us to understand the evolution of construction and major regional centers in the Maya lowlands. The thrust of the excavations have been at EP 7, or the winged temple Xikna, the easternmost temple in Plaza Copal. The initial excavations also examined other buildings around Plaza Copal.

At least nine major construction episodes have been recognized for the EP 7 temple (Orrego 1995). The earliest constructions date to the Middle Preclassic, and within that period at least three major remodelings were undertaken. The early construction phases are completely unrelated to the later temple of EP 7 (episodes 7, 8, 9). These constructions face the east, buried deep inside the later temple versions. The first two plaza floors are associated with building episodes 8 and 9. In its last Middle Preclassic incarnation, there is a clay platform built of materials from the eastern aguada, or reservoir, representing two public works in one. This is also the first evidence of Plaza Copal to the west of the clay structure.

Later, this Middle Preclassic construction was completely enveloped within the first constructions of the temple. This shifted the activity orientation of the building to face west onto Plaza Copal (related to episodes 5 and 6). All subsequent constructions were designed to increase the size of that temple over a long span of time, from the Late Preclassic to the Terminal Classic periods. Six major temple constructions of Plaza Copal were identified in the EP 7 tunnel excavation. Each of these building episodes related to a plaza floor as revealed in the profile. There is an indication that the last remodeling at the very top of the temple, was arrested before completion, perhaps because of collapse-related problems.

These initial forays into the architectural dimensions of El Pilar clearly illuminate its importance over time both locally and regionally. The size and extent of the monuments along with the long temporal sequence indicate that it drew on a considerable area for its development and maintenance. Early on it must have managed independently, but by the Late Classic period it was certainly part of a major Maya regional hierarchy. The integration within the regional Maya network experienced changes over time, and by the Terminal Classic period El Pilar's local economy was able to support its local efforts when other areas of the lowlands were disintegrating. Even with the extension of control exhibited at El Pilar, there are signs of problems. The final construction efforts at Xikna temple EP 7 were left incomplete and the important obsidian byproducts curated at Laton were never used.

Interpretation

Recent research has contributed significantly to our general understanding of processes motivating the development of social complexity, providing a foundation for investigations of the managerial basis and support of hierarchical organizations. Management, integration, and power in complex societies are consolidated in the integration of households at the community level, organization of communities at the local level, and interaction among centers at the regional level. For the ancient Maya of the central lowlands, management, integration, and power have been largely reckoned as the basis of local distribution of centers and regional relationships among centers. Recent research has demonstrated that broad regional settlement patterns are directly related to the distribution of primary agricultural resources (Ford 1990, 1991a; cf. Boserup 1965; Cohen 1977), diffusing the hierarchy and acting as a force against the centralization process so fundamental to complex societies. Ultimately, the level of organizational control over primary agricultural resources and agricultural production is the key to the power structure of complex societies (Earle 1991b).

Three important variables contribute support to the hierarchical structure and underwrite power in complex societies: the quality of the subsistence base, the distribution of subsistence resources, and the level of critical resource control. The subsistence base and production potential of a region provide the foundation for growth and development. Resource intensification requires the availability of labor (Webster 1990), and limitations in the availability of land can impact the evolutionary trajectory. While resource potential is fundamental to production, distribution of subsistence resources plays a major role in social integration. Geographic constraints such as swamps or mountains, for example, may act as impediments to effective interaction at the local level and coherent integration at the regional level. Finally, the level of resource control sanctions power in the hierarchical structure, be it at the community, local, or regional level (Friedman and Rowlands 1977; Sanders and Webster 1978:265–295; Webb 1975:180–184; Wright 1984:45). If risk management involved capital investments beyond those of a household or community (Johnson and Earle

1987:16, 209), the costs and benefits may be subsidized by the elite in order to consolidate their power (D'Altroy and Earle 1985:190; Service 1975:8; Webb 1987:164; Webster 1985:34C)). The more critical the resource and the greater the risks to households, the more secure the elite hierarchical power structure.

As with all complex societies, the problems that the ancient Maya had to resolve in maintaining their complex hierarchy involved regional interactions, local integration, and community organization. Regional patterns of settlement differentiation and wealth distinctions are evident in the Maya lowlands (Adams and Jones 1981) with differences related to the organization and control of land and labor (Fedick and Ford 1990). The largest and most elaborate public centers in the region are found in association with high settlement densities (Ashmore 1981; Puleston 1973; Rice 1976), concentration of elite residences, and high proportions of primary subsistence resources (Ford 1990, 1991b). Areas in the region were hierarchically integrated through local centers, which were in turn organized through resident elite within communities (Ford 1986:82–94).

The ancient Maya hierarchy focused on control of the primary subsistence resource of the region: the well-drained ridgelands. Production from the ridgeland zones must have been coordinated by the elite hierarchy at successive levels from the individual communities to integrated centers, and the mobilization of resources formed the basis of local interdependence. Although there was potential for self-sufficiency and assertion of independence at the community level because of the decentralized distribution of the well-drained ridgelands, as well as the other resources and landforms, the effectiveness of successive hierarchical controls had to have depended on the degree to which interdependence was, or at least perceived to be, a requisite. Examination of household variability and community patterns, as presented here, is one way to address these problems. To better understand the relationship between individual communities and the central hierarchy of complex societies, such as the ancient Maya, we need more data on community-level production and consumption activities as well as local-level relationships among communities. In this manner, we will begin to identify the potential links between communities and the central hierarchy.

Acknowledgments

Research of the BRASS/El Pilar program has been supported, in part, by a number of funding agencies including NSF, Wenner Gren, University Research Expedition Program, Fulbright, Fulbright-Hays, and private donations. Special gratitude must be extended to Belize's Department of Archaeology for their strong support of the El Pilar Archaeological Reserve as well as the vision of the El Pilar Program. Without the collaboration of the Amigos de El Pilar, the dreams for one El Pilar could not be realized. And I extend my warmest thanks to the Santa Familia Monastery for their support and provisions while we have been working in the field.

16

The Classic Maya Trading Port of Moho Cay

Heather McKillop

Trade within the southern lowlands and beyond was part of the economy of the Maya in the Belize River Valley. They acquired marine shells, manatee bones, and stingray spines from the sea, as well as obsidian, jade, and other trade goods from farther away. The island site of Moho Cay was strategically located in the mouth of the Belize River to facilitate the upriver transportation of goods from the sea and from coastal trade routes. In addition, Moho Cay has a long record of settlement from Late Preclassic through Postclassic times. Artifacts from burials and other features recovered from archaeological excavations tie the island into complex trading relationships with the Maya in the Belize Valley and elsewhere.

Ancient Maya trading ports such as Moho Cay existed by virtue of their ability to provide services related to trade and their location on a transportation route. Trading ports provided transshipment services between seafaring and riverine vessels, food and accommodation for traders, a place to trade, and/or storage facilities for trade goods (Andrews 1990; D. Chase 1981; Freidel 1978; Guderjan and Garber 1995; Hammond 1976; McKillop 1987, 1989, 1996a; Sabloff and Rathje 1975). Moho Cay was located on a riverine transportation route along which ritual and dietary resources from the sea were transported upriver. The island also was situated at the juncture of the Belize River and Caribbean transportation avenues, so that goods carried along the coast by seafaring canoe traders may have been transshipped at Moho Cay into smaller river-going boats for travel upriver. Even with the strong currents on the Belize River during the rainy season, small canoes easily navigate upriver close to shore beyond the force of the downstream current. The continued use of the Belize River and Caribbean transportation routes depended in part on upriver demand for marine goods from the vicinity of Moho Cay and from goods carried in boats along the Caribbean coast from farther away. The long occupation of the upper Belize River Valley from Preclassic through Postclassic times and an ongoing demand for marine and exotic resources argues for enduring trade and communication between Moho Cay and the upper Belize River Valley. By way of contrast, when inland cities in southern Belize were abandoned at the end of the Late Classic, there was no longer an inland demand for salt produced at the Punta Ycacos Salt Works on the coast, the salt works were abandoned, and coastal-inland trade ceased (McKillop 2002).

Complex political and economic relations, including marriage and other alliances, often develop between trading ports and their trading partners to facilitate and maintain trade (McKillop 2002; Sabloff and Rathje 1975). Inland trade of ritual paraphernalia, such as stingray spines for bloodletting and conch shells used as trumpets, was backed by ideological views of the importance of the sea in ritual (A. Chase and D. Chase 1989; Maxwell 2000; McKillop 1996a; Miller 1977). Incorporation of coastal Maya at trading ports into the royal lineages at inland cities by marriage and reciprocal exchanges was evidenced by inland trade goods at Wild Cane Cay and other coastal communities in southern Belize (McKillop 2002). Inland demand for marine resources, particularly those important for rituals, also may have helped to solidify the continued use of coastal transportation routes along the Caribbean (McKillop 1996a).

Ancient and Modern Landscape of Moho Cay

Surface survey and excavation indicated that the prehistoric site on Moho Cay was localized on the dry, grass-covered northern point of the island and once included a large offshore area of undetermined size beyond the northern point (fig. 16.1). The site extended at least 20 m into the shallow offshore area. The larger southern part of the island, composed of mangrove swamp and inundated by seawater at high tide, was devoid of any surface indications of prehistoric use. Excavations confirmed the restricted area of the ancient site. An attempt to delineate the offshore distribution of artifacts was unprofitable due to poor visibility caused by flooding and silting of the Belize River. The site on Moho Cay was destroyed in the process of dredging a harbor for a marina prior to the second archaeological field season—before environmental impact assessments of proposed developments were required in Belize (McKillop 1998).

During one of his visits to Moho Cay in the early part of the 19th cen-

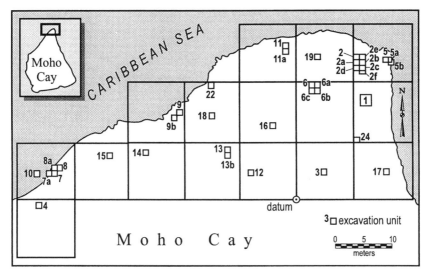

Fig. 16.1. Map of northern point of Moho Cay showing excavation units within 10- × 10-m grids. The insert shows the location of the northern point on Moho Cay.

tury, Gann (1925:18) characterized it as "a small, flat island consisting chiefly of mangrove swamp, but with a little solid sandy patch towards the northeast end. . . . The sea around it is shallow, and the banks of the mainland all around are flat and covered with dense mangrove swamp; in fact, a more desolate and inhospitable prospect it would be impossible to imagine." Colin Gibson (personal communication 1979) characterized the soils on the northern part of Moho Cay where the ancient site was located as likely composed of river-deposited silts and clays, whereas those on the southern mangrove portion away from the site were black peat from mangroves. Chemical and physical analyses of soil samples from the Moho Cay excavations by John Lambert (1980) indicate poor agricultural potential of the island's soils, reinforcing the earlier interpretation by the British Land Use Survey Team that the soils on the Belizean cays were infertile (Wright et al. 1959).

The physical appearance of ancient Moho Cay was different and more favorable for human settlement than it was in historic or modern times. As with other near shore Belizean cays, Moho Cay may have been built up by mangroves on a high part of the limestone platform that forms the sea floor. The cay may have been attached to the adjacent mainland and separated during violent storms or hurricanes (Colin Gibson, personal communication 1979). Moho Cay was inundated by rising sea levels that submerged the archaeological deposits. Submerged coastal Maya sites have been reported along the coasts of Belize and the Yucatán Peninsula of Mexico, notably at Cerros (Freidel 1978), Marco Gonzalez on Ambergris Cay (Graham and Pendergast 1989), Kakalche and Colson Point in central Belize (Graham 1994), and the Port Honduras–Paynes Creek National Park area of southern Belize (McKillop 1995, 2002). In southern Belize, the inundation of Late Classic coastal and offshore island communities by rising seas has been radiocarbon dated by the depths of archaeological deposits below sea level (McKillop 2002). While regional variation along the coasts of Belize and the Yucatán is expected owing to differences in local coastal geomorphology (especially the depth of the inshore Belize barrier reef platform), the general pattern of coastal inundation for southern Belize corresponds to that reported by geologists and geographers for the Western Atlantic from the early Holocene to the present (McKillop 2002). With lower sea level during the ancient occupation of Moho Cay, the soils would not have been inundated or saline. They may have supported economically valuable vegetation, such as the native palms and other trees crops identified in submerged archaeological deposits dating to the Late Classic in the Port Honduras region (McKillop 1994, 1996b).

Previous Research at Moho Cay

Historically, Moho Cay variously has been interpreted as a fishing or manatee hunting station, a temporary campsite, and as a trading station, but its size and significance were masked by sea-level rise and the transformation of the landscape from ancient times. Excavations at other coastal sites in Belize as well as knowledge of the effects of sea-level rise on the coastal landscape indicate instead that many coastal sites were permanent settlements and some, like Moho Cay, also were trading ports (McKillop 2002). An early record of the prehistoric site on Moho Cay is by A. W. Franks (1876) who visited the island in the 1870s and reported finding a plano-convex point. Thomas Gann frequented the island during the early 20th century and made brief published (Gann 1911:78, 1925:19) and unpublished (1917) references to excavations on the island as well as offshore dredging. The latter brought up quantities of manatee bone, "small spear and javelin heads of nearly black flint," and potsherds, while his excavations on the island yielded "abundance of chips of the same dark flint, manatee bones, and rings (perforated potsherd disks) . . . together with numerous potsherds" (Gann 1911:78). He later reported that excavation yielded "tons" of manatee bone, "flint spear heads," and "thousands" of pottery net sinkers. He interpreted Moho Cay as an ancient Maya fishing station. The British Land Use Survey Team noted the presence of a site from Gann's report and recorded Moho Cay and other island sites along the coast of Belize as seasonal fishing spots, typically resembling no more than picnic centers (Wright et al. 1959:110, 256). A. Hamilton Anderson, the first Archaeological Commissioner of Belize, recognized the probability of ancient settlement on the offshore cays, noting in particular that Moho Cay was "apparently a Maya fishing site" (Craig 1966:19). The geographer Alan Craig (1966) interpreted the surface remains at Moho Cay as indicating the site was occupied for a long time by people interested in hunting manatee. He reported that wave action had exposed cultural material along a more than 125-m stretch of bank on the north shore and that the material was nowhere more than 1.5 m above sea level. Craig (1966:20) reported localized deposits of "highly humanized" soil and a continuous occurrence of pottery sherds, chert cores, flakes, and stone artifacts including jade celts and large (25 cm) projectile points. In June 1978, Norman Hammond visited an extensive surface collection of material surface collected from the island and offshore area at St. John's College on the adjacent mainland. Brief reports on the ceramics resulted (Ball 1982, 1984). Hammond (1976) had previously suggested that Moho Cay was a transshipment center, along with other locales strategically located at the juncture of possible coastal water routes and riverine or land routes. Apart from these reports, the existence of the site on Moho Cay was well known and had attracted visitors, surface collectors, looters, and individuals dredging offshore for sand. The 1979 excavations yielded evidence of Late Classic settlement and trade from burials and middens (McKillop 1980).

Excavations

In order to test different parts of the island site, a 10 × 10-m grid was staked out on the island's northern point (fig. 16.1). A location was selected for excavation in each 10 × 10-m grid based on the presence of artifacts on the ground surface or eroding from the bank along the shore. The initial 1 × 1-m excavation units were enlarged when burials and middens were encountered during excavation.

Thirteen features were recognized, including eight burials, three containing two individuals each. The burials were found in soil layer B, a brown clay-silt (Munsell 10YR 4/2), underlying soil layer A, a black silty soil (Munsell 10YR 2/1) that contained middens. The base of the cultural deposits was marked by black mangrove mud devoid of cultural remains at 55 cm deep in Unit 15, at 65 cm deep in Unit 11, and 25 cm deep in Units 20 and 23. Units 20 and 23, not pictured on the site map, were located at the southern edge of the site and contained prehistoric deposits disturbed by historic refuse. The base of cultural deposits was not reached in other excavations due to the difficulty of excavating below the water table. Several post molds and traces of house floors, the latter indicated by red soil layers, were discovered, although no other structural remains were encountered. The association of post molds and floors with burials indicates that bodies were interred either on the floor of buildings prior to their renovation or else pits were dug into floors for interments. The burial fill consisted of household midden deposits that contained pottery sherds, chert, obsidian, and faunal remains.

The Moho Cay burials and other features in soil layer B were cross-dated on the basis of associated ceramics to the early part of the Late Classic, corresponding to Tepeu 1 at Uaxactun (Smith 1955) or Tiger Run at Barton Ramie and other settlements in the upper Belize River Valley (Gifford 1976). The Moho Cay burial ceramics also resemble pottery from the Mac phase at Altun Ha, defined as transitional between the Early and Late Classic periods (Pendergast 1979:table 5). The polychrome pottery from Moho Cay resembled common southern lowland polychromes, particularly Saxche and Palmar polychromes from Seibal (Sabloff 1975) and Altar de Sacrificios (Adams 1971), reinforcing interpretation of the island in trade and communication beyond the immediate environs. Whole and fragmentary vessels and sherds examined in a large collection of artifacts collected by the priests at nearby St. John's College from the shallow offshore area include pottery dating from Late Preclassic, such as Sierra Red, Protoclassic, such as mammiform tetrapod pots, to Late Postclassic times (see Ball 1982; McKillop 1980).

Burials

The area exposed in Units 2–2f revealed a number of human interments with associated grave goods. The Feature 4 burial in Unit 2a consisted of the fragmentary human skeletal remains of two individuals interred with a biconvex-bodied jar with a low-collar rim, three obsidian blades, two stingray spines, and a partially perforated potsherd disk (fig. 16.2). The Feature 9 burial in Unit 2b included fragmentary human bones and two jade earplugs (fig. 16.3). The Feature 3 burial in Units 2c, 2d, and 2f consisted of fragmentary human skeletal remains, a plano-convex stemmed chert point with a round blade, and partial vessels (fig. 16.4). The point was discolored black from its immersion in waterlogged saline soil. A similar

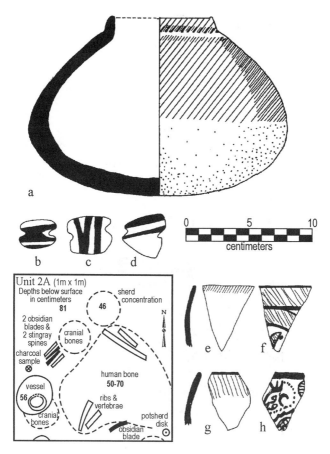

Fig. 16.2. Feature 4 burial in Unit 2a.

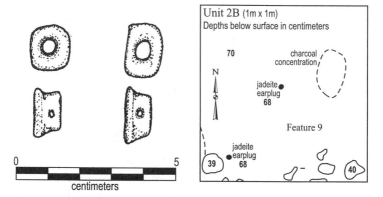

Fig. 16.3. Feature 9 burial in Unit 2b.

263

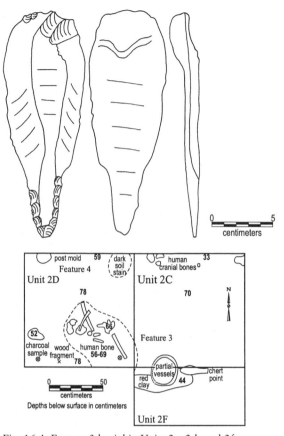

Fig. 16.4. Feature 3 burial in Units 2c, 2d, and 2f.

point, also discolored black, was excavated from Wild Cane Cay (McKillop 1987). For both artifacts, it is the point, which is retouched for use, while the blade has the bulb of percussion and would not have been an effective tool without further working.

Units 5, 5a, and 5b contained the Feature 1 burial consisting of the interment of an adult individual in a flexed position on the right side, head to northwest, accompanied by an infant interment near the adult's feet (McKillop 1980:fig. 7). No ceramic vessels were found in association with these interments. Burial fill artifacts included a potsherd disk (McKillop 1980:fig. 58d), two obsidian blades, 16 side-notched potsherds, and a three-hole, tripod candelero (McKillop 1980:fig. 53a), of early Late Classic ceramic style, providing a terminus post quem age for the burial.

Unit 7a excavations exposed the Feature 2 burial, including the skeletal remains of an adult. The burial was first noticed by a cranium eroding

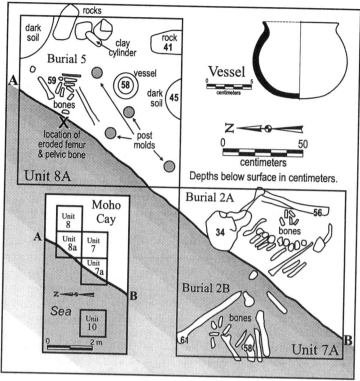

Fig. 16.5. Feature 5 burial in Unit 8a.

from the bank. Excavations at low tide recovered the skull, articulated with the vertebral column, hip bones, and left arm bones of an adult in a flexed position, facing east, head to north (fig. 16.5). The burial was in soil layer B and contained early Late Classic pottery sherds in the fill, including three side-notched potsherds from polychrome, round-side dishes. Disarticulated human skeletal remains were excavated in the adjacent offshore area. No grave goods recovered, although they may have been eroded into the sea and lost.

Excavation of Unit 8a revealed the Feature 5 burial, which consisted of disarticulated human bones, a large clay cylinder (McKillop 1980:pl. 8), and a small bowl with incurving sides and incurving neck (fig. 16.5). Small circular dark stains were sectioned and interpreted as post molds. Since a human femur eroding from the bank indicated the presence of a burial, some material may have eroded into the sea before the burial excavation. A partially articulated human skeleton was exposed and excavated nearby in the offshore area, at low tide, in an area designated as Unit 10, but the extent of the burial was not determined due to the rising tide.

The Feature 6 burial in Units 11 and 11a consisted of a nested concentration of partial pottery vessels, a *Turbinella angulata* gastropod, and fragmentary human cranial material. Many of the fragmentary vessels were from either bichrome or polychrome round-sided bowls with interior painted decoration. The feature was in soil layer B and was below a red soil layer interpreted as the remains of a house floor (McKillop 1980:fig. 12), as seen, for example in other coastal settings at Wild Cane Cay and Frenchman's Cay farther south. Another floor only marked by a localized area of red soil was encountered under the feature 3 burial and near the feature 1 burial. Because of the limited extent of the floor it was clear burial 3 was interred on the floor or below it.

In Unit 16, a human interment with no associated grave goods was noted above and, distinct from, a concentration of partial pottery vessels. The Feature 8 burial in Unit 22 consisted of a bichrome, round-side dish found overturned on a weathered, upright, partial vessel (fig. 16.6). Only fragmentary human skeletal material was recovered. Similar dishes were found offshore, including two found placed lip to lip (fig. 16.6).

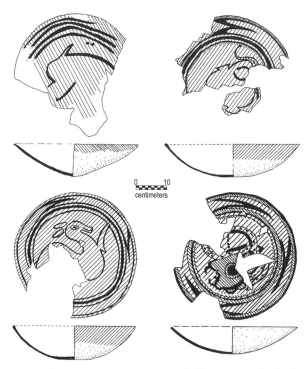

Fig. 16.6. Feature 8 burial in unit 22 included a bichrome, round-side dish, similar to others found offshore.

Manatee Bone Midden

Excavations in Units 6–6c partially exposed a midden, referred to as Feature 7, composed of manatee bones, mollusks, complete and fragmentary chert and obsidian artifacts, and ceramics (fig. 16.7; see McKillop 1980: fig. 9; 1984). Manatee bones were exposed from 10 to 80 cm depth but were concentrated between 20 and 50 cm depth. Many of the bones were broken. Butchering marks were not observed. There was no apparent pattern to the breakage, except that the ribs often were in pieces. This occurrence is certainly due to deliberate breakage as the ribs are thick, solid, and dense. The vertebrae, by way of contrast, are more friable and breakage of the spines could have occurred naturally. While no carved manatee bones were recovered from the midden, several figurine and miniature boats carved from manatee ribs were recorded in Belize City surface collections (McKillop 1984, 1985). The mollusks intermixed with the manatee bones consisted mainly of several large gastropod species, namely *Melongena*

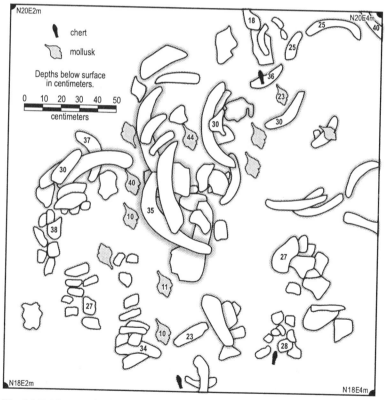

Fig. 16.7. Manatee bone midden in Units 6-6c.

melongena, Strombus pugilis, and *Strombus gigas.* Both whole and fragmentary examples were present. Other mollusk species were noted, as was a small sample of fish and shark vertebrae that were not identified to species (see McKillop 1984).

A higher concentration and greater diversity of complete and fragmentary chert tools were associated with this midden than with other midden (or burial) deposits at Moho Cay. Tools include a variety of scrapers, chopper-pounders, broken macro-blades, broken standard bifaces, broken stemmed points (including plano-convex and bifacially flaked examples), as well as utilized flakes and debitage. The "orange-peel flake" from manufacture of an adze indicates at least some finishing of tools was carried out on the island. Pottery sherds from Feature 7 provide an early Late Classic period age for the midden. Utilitarian and fine ware sherds, side-notched potsherd "net sinkers," perforated potsherd disk "spindle whorls," and solid clay cylinder vessel supports were recovered. The cylinders resemble those identified from the Punta Ycacos salt works in southern Belize as vessel supports used to hold clay pots over fires to boil brine to make salt cakes (McKillop 2002).

The Moho Cay Settlement

During the Late Classic, Moho Cay consisted of a sizable community of houses made from pole and thatch with dirt floors. Dead relatives were buried under the house floors, as indicated by the common recovery of burials at the site associated with structural remains and household debris used as structural fill. An extensive area of the prehistoric settlement has been eroded along the northern shore, resulting in abundant human and manatee bones, as well as pottery and stone tools, in the shallow area beyond the island's northern point (McKillop 1980:pl. 5). Many of the complete pottery vessels and chert, ground stone, and obsidian artifacts now at St. John's College and in other Belize City surface collections, reportedly came from that offshore area (McKillop 1980). The distribution of burials along the north shore, combined with the above evidence, suggest that the offshore area was also a settlement area with houses containing burials.

The presence of the Feature 7 midden consisting primarily of manatee bones but also mollusks corroborates the use of the island as a settlement. Moreover, the abundance of utilitarian pottery and stone tool fragments from excavated fill and middens points to debris from a substantial and permanent settlement. Historic activity had disturbed much of the site, especially in the area of excavation Units 3, 9, 9b, 12, 13, 13b, 14, 15, 20, and 23. These units included an area of concentrated historic activity on the island in which no prehistoric features were recorded, although prehistoric pottery sherds were recovered from the deposits.

In addition to the evidence for permanent settlement, the island was used as a trading port, as indicated by a diverse array of nonlocal goods from within the Maya lowlands and beyond, some of which were transported to the island as complete objects and others as preforms for subsequent finishing elsewhere. Some of the chert preforms were transported to Moho Cay for use on the island: The "orange-peel" flake and other chert debitage from the manatee bone midden are evidence of finishing and use of chert tools at the Moho Cay community. But other chert preforms, notably a large collection of macroblades and unifacial stemmed points, may have been shipped from the chert bearing zone at or around Colha to Moho Cay for transshipment elsewhere and finishing into a desired tool at the destination. While some chert tools were traded farther south along the coast, others were transported up the Belize River, notably large unifacial stemmed chert points (Willey et al. 1965).

Moho Cay and the Belize Valley

The inventory of nonlocal goods and resources from excavations indicates the Moho Cay Maya figured prominently in both coastal and riverine trade during the Late Classic period. The presence of pottery from Late Preclassic to Postclassic times in surface collections from the site demonstrates that use of the island coincided with much of the time of settlement upriver. The recovery of both utilitarian and luxury goods and resources from a variety of distant and nearby locations indicates these island Maya had a variety of trading partners.

Inland trade of marine resources and ritual paraphernalia from the sea was a focus of activity at Moho Cay. Other researchers have found that the closest coast is the typical origin for marine mollusks at inland sites (Cobos 1989). The Moho Cay Maya exploited the sea for fish, stingrays, manatee, and mollusks, and used them for food, as indicated by the remains from the manatee bone midden excavation. Seashells, stingray spines, and manatee bones also were used or modified for ritual and utilitarian uses. Sea traders could add marine resources to their inventories during their brief stays at Moho Cay, as indicated by stingray spines from Burial 4. Conch tools made from the lips of *Strombus gigas* shells (McKillop 1984; O'Day and Keegan 2001:figs. 3–6), small carved shell disks, carved manatee rib boat models and figurines (McKillop 1984, 1985), and pumice floats were noted in surface collections. The placement of stingray spines and un-utilized obsidian blades in burial 4 at Moho Cay shows the ritual equivalence of these goods and nicely demonstrates the ritual and economic integration of the coastal-inland and coastal Caribbean trade routes.

Trade within the southern lowlands has received less attention than long-distance trade of obsidian and other goods from beyond the lowlands, but this intra-lowland trade was quite common and important to the Maya economy in the southern lowlands (Graham 1987b, 1994; McKillop 2002). Marine resources were desired by the inland Maya for ritual (Maxwell 2000) and dietary needs (McKillop 1984, 1985). Northern Belize chert, including preform chert blades and finished tools, granite metates from the Maya Mountains, and pottery similar to upper Belize ceramics, tie Moho Cay to communication and exchange networks of intermediate distance within the southern Maya lowlands. Ceramics, obsidian, granite, and marine resources provide material evidence of trade and communication between the Maya on Moho Cay and their contemporaries up the Belize River and elsewhere.

Although the origins of Moho Cay ceramics remain to be elucidated by chemical or petrographic study of their pastes, there are stylistic similarities with both northern Belize (reinforced by the presence of Colha chert) and the upper Belize Valley (reinforced by the presence of granite metates). Unfortunately, much of the pottery is discolored gray from immersion in salt water, so that the polychrome colors in Petén glossy ware vessels, for example, appear as various shades of gray, a phenomenon also noted for pottery from waterlogged contexts at Wild Cane Cay (McKillop 1987). Round-sided polychrome bowls and dishes resemble Dos Arroyos Orange Polychrome, including the unspecified "K" variety with black bands bracketing chevrons and an interior line decoration, described by Gifford (1976) for Barton Ramie and the Belize Valley. Similar vessels also are reported from Altun Ha, San Esteban, and San Jose. A nearly complete round-sided bichrome bowl was recovered from the Feature 8 burial and similar vessels were surface collected offshore (fig. 16.6). An incomplete, round-sided bichrome dish was recovered from the Feature 3 burial. Many round-sided bichrome and polychrome bowl or dish sherds were included in the Feature 6 concentration of partial vessels—probably a burial. The biconvex-bodied jar with a low collar rim from the Feature 4 burial at Moho Cay most closely resembles early Late Classic vessels from Altun Ha, not far north of the island (Pendergast 1979).

Two similar vessels were recovered from a feature in the coral rock foundation of a structure at Frenchman's Cay (Magnoni 1999).

Obsidian, jade and other greenstone, and basalt metates recovered from Moho Cay provide the evidence that Moho Cay participated in long-distance trade. The dominance of El Chayal obsidian—the main source utilized by the contemporary Maya in the upper Belize Valley—points to coastal transportation from the Maya highland El Chayal outcrop during the early part of the Late Classic (Healy et al. 1984). The obsidian blades from burial 4 were chemically assigned to the El Chayal source. Although El Chayal obsidian may have been transported to upper Belize Valley communities by inland routes, its presence at Moho Cay argues instead for its transport from the southern Maya highlands, down the Motagua River, and north along the Caribbean via Moho Cay during the Late Classic (Healy et al. 1984). The use of this coastal transportation route is reinforced by the recovery of the jade earplugs from burial 9. The Motagua River Valley is the closest source of jade and other greenstones. In addition, basalt for metates originated in the volcanic highlands beyond the southern Maya lowlands.

Conclusion

Moho Cay was a trading port situated at the juncture of the Belize River and coastal Caribbean transportation routes. The Moho Cay Maya extracted marine resources such as stingrays, manatee, conch and other mollusks, and fish that were desired and acquired by the Maya in the upper Belize River Valley. Apart from the lack of documented use of Moho Cay before the Late Preclassic, use of the island from Late Preclassic through Postclassic times corresponds with settlement inland. As the Caribbean is the nearest coast, stingray spines, manatee bone, conch and seashells, as well as seafood, were likely obtained from the Caribbean via Moho Cay.

The excavation of Late Classic burials with associated grave offerings provides a picture of Moho Cay as a settlement and trading port facilitating trade of marine and exotic goods and resources up the Belize River. The Late Classic Moho Cay Maya provided both marine resources and goods from more distant origins, such as El Chayal and Ixtepeque obsidian from the Maya highlands, jade and other greenstones from the Motagua River Valley, and basalt from volcanic regions of Mesoamerica. It is not only the source location of trade goods that might be of interest for communities in the upper Belize River Valley, but also the complex trade relations that developed and were fostered through trading partners, marriage and other alliances, and gift exchanges in order to facilitate the procurement of ritual and subsistence items. Although distant by river from the upper Belize River Valley communities, actual transportation distance was modest, especially when Moho Cay was a key to their procurement of marine resources, and by association, goods transported along the Caribbean coast to this trading port.

Acknowledgments

Excavations were carried out in 1979 under permit 79–2 from the Belizean Department of Archaeology to Paul F. Healy, with encouragement from Archaeological Commissioner Elizabeth Graham and, subsequently, from incoming Commissioner Harriot Topsey. Funding was generously provided by the Dean of Arts and Sciences and Department of Anthropology at Trent University and was carried out with the assistance of Trent University field school students from Belize and Canada. Students included Martin Betcherman, Winnel Branche, Mark Campbell, Alan Creighton-Kelly, Julie Cormack, David Cross, Emory King Jr., Alexis Kostick, Bill Loughlin, Mary Paquin, Briony Penn, Angela Rollins, Bob Rose, Carole Tait, and Bernie Walsh, with Susan McLeod-O'Reilly as my field assistant. With sadness, I acknowledge that the late Winnel Branche was a field school student at Moho Cay, her first archaeological excavations. I appreciate the assistance of St. John's College in providing a laboratory and many other kinds of logistical assistance and friendship, especially Frs. Buhler, Maher, Dieckmann, and Simms, and Br. Croy. Among many others, several Belizeans deserve special thanks, notably the Bedran family of San Ignacio for loan of their boat, Emory King Sr., Emory King Jr., Jaime Awe, Alan Moore, Francis Norris, Leo Castillo Sr., and Joe Wesby. Most of all, I appreciate the encouragement, advice, and insights of Paul F. Healy, my master's thesis advisor.

17

Problems in the Definition and Interpretation of "Minor Centers" in Maya Archaeology with Reference to the Upper Belize Valley

Gyles Iannone

As part of their early settlement research in the Belize Valley, Gordon Willey and his colleagues were among the first to acknowledge the existence of "minor centers." Given their size and complexity, these sites were thought to have served a variety of political, economic, religious, and social functions. Research in the upper Belize River region has figured prominently in the definition and interpretation of "minor centers." Sites of this size and complexity are both ubiquitous in terms of their distribution across the landscape, and with respect to their presence within the literature on ancient Maya settlement. However, these centers remain underexplored, and the significance of their morphological and developmental variability has yet to be fully elucidated. The principal goals of this chapter will be to (1) underscore the existence of a highly variable "middle level of settlement" of which minor centers are a key constituent and (2) highlight a number of methodological and theoretical issues that must be addressed before we can hope to fully comprehend the implications of middle-level settlement variability.

Toward the Recognition of a Middle Settlement Level

In 1954, following his Viru Valley research, Gordon Willey shifted his attention to the Maya subarea and initiated a settlement-oriented project in

273

the upper Belize River region, at the site of Barton Ramie (Willey 1956a, 1956b; Willey et al. 1955; Willey et al. 1965). This undertaking constitutes a significant point in the history of Maya archaeology, and settlement archaeology in general. The stated goals of Willey's Belize Valley archaeological survey were

(1) "the discovery, mapping, and excavation of habitation sites";

(2) the exploration of "the relationship of aboriginal occupation to natural environments; the nature and function of buildings composing habitation communities; and the form, size, and spacing of these communities with reference to each other and to ceremonial centers";

(3) to address "larger questions of land utilization, agricultural potential, population densities, urbanism, the districting or zoning of ancient settlement, and the interdependence or independence of communities or community assemblages" (Willey et al. 1965:15).

The Barton Ramie site, given its abundance of small housemounds and excellent surface visibility, offered Willey and his colleagues the perfect opportunity to redress the large center bias that had prevailed in Maya archaeology to that point, and, in doing so, introduce settlement archaeology to the Maya lowlands (chapter 2). The project was perceived as a means through which an understanding of the entire settlement continuum could be produced. As Willey et al. (1965:7) stated, the "first inquiries about 'ordinary dwellings,' 'houses of the people,' or 'house mounds,' [as opposed to special temple or palace mounds] marks a beginning interest in the larger question of *total settlement pattern*" (author's emphasis).

During their work at Barton Ramie, Willey and his colleagues encountered an architectural assemblage that they postulated to have been "some kind of special precinct or politico-religious center for the Barton Ramie site" (Willey et al. 1955:24; see also Willey 1956a, 1956b). This settlement cluster, later to be labeled BR-180-181-182 (Willey et al. 1965:249), was initially termed a "small 'ceremonial center'" (Willey et al. 1955:24). Willey and his colleagues described this small ceremonial center: "This 'center' consists of a pyramid twelve meters in height and two long, low mounds of a type sometimes called 'palace' mounds. These three structures are arranged around a small raised courtyard." Willey and his colleagues also noted the presence of two other "small ceremonial centers" in the Barton Ramie area, Floral Park (fig. 18.1) and Spanish Lookout. The authors concluded that these "ceremonial centers within these communities of housemounds represent certain religious and political offices and services that were carried out for the benefit of the immediate local community" (Willey et al. 1955:25). They thus considered these architectural assemblages to have been both formally and, to a certain extent, functionally different from the surrounding housemounds *and* the larger centers.

Settlement Archaeology and the Typological Problem

Following initial recognition of the middle settlement level, Willey (1956a, 1956b; Willey and Bullard 1965) attempted to formulate a model for ancient Maya settlement that would include the small ceremonial centers, which by this time had been renamed "minor ceremonial mounds" (Willey 1956a:778). This approach was amplified by Bullard (1960) following his reconnaissance of the northeastern Petén region of Guatemala. Bullard divided the settlement hierarchy into three levels, including "House Ruins," "Minor Ceremonial Centers," and "Major Ceremonial Centers."

Within the survey area, Bullard (1960:367) recognized that house ruins often formed "clusters." He noted further that in some instances one housemound was "somewhat larger than the others," and that small shrines were also present in some cases. However, he concluded that "such architecturally distinguishable buildings are by no means a consistent trait" (Bullard 1960:357). In final analysis, Bullard deduced that the *majority* of house ruins, given their "abundance" and small size, were undoubtedly "the residences of the common people."

Within the Bullard study (1960:359–360), the term *minor ceremonial center* was employed to describe those intermediary architectural clusters previously called small ceremonial centers during the Barton Ramie investigations (Willey et al. 1955:24). According to Bullard (1960:359), the "ruins designated as Minor Ceremonial Centers form a class apart: appreciably larger than the House Ruins, and appreciably smaller than the Major Ceremonial Centers."

In considering the entire settlement population, Bullard (1960:367) observed that the "frequency with which Minor Centers are encountered is clearly in direct proportion to the abundance and density of house ruins in the neighborhood." He noted further that the "clusters" of house ruins formed "subdivisions of zones," the latter term employed to describe the area containing a series of house clusters and an associated minor ceremonial center. Bullard (1960:368) also observed that the minor ceremonial centers were not necessarily located in the center of the zones, but rather were regularly situated in "prominent" locations, often hilltops. He concluded that "zones of settlement were significant community units, the

Minor Center having served as the religious and civic center for the community."

Finally, Bullard (1960:360–362) grouped the larger Maya centers (e.g., Tikal, Uaxactun, Xunantunich) under the category of "Major Ceremonial Centers." He indicated that these sites "vary greatly in size but all are substantially larger than the Minor Centers and contain larger, more elaborate buildings" (Bullard 1960:360). In Bullard's (1960:368–369) view, major ceremonial centers were the "nuclei" for what he termed "districts." Districts comprised a number of zones, each with their minor ceremonial centers. As with these latter settlement units, major ceremonial centers were often located in prominent locales, such as hilltops (Bullard 1960: 369). Bullard felt that major ceremonial centers served the needs of all the surrounding zones in its district. Although Bullard conceded that major ceremonial centers were likely the nuclei of religious and administrative activity for the districts, he also felt it "probable that many of the Maya leaders lived scattered among the rest of the populations perhaps as a sort of rural nobility." One can assume from this statement that he considered "minor centers" to have been the residences for this "rural nobility."

In summary, Bullard's work constituted the first *sophisticated* effort to classify and interpret the entire range of settlement remains within the Maya subarea. His construct was, however, based on surface reconnaissance; excavation data played only a limited role in its formulation. Still, Bullard's tripartite model was accepted by generations of scholars as a realistic archetype for ancient Maya settlement.

Some researchers, having recognized a greater range of settlement variability, have attempted to bring into use more detailed typologies for ancient Maya settlement. Some of these formulations have been more qualitative than others. In 1975, as part of his Corozal Project in northern Belize, Norman Hammond (1975) introduced a nine-tiered construct. He argued that although Bullard's formulation "remained the accepted model, . . . [I]t is not precise enough to be used with the more sophisticated analyses of interactions between sites in an overall network which are now being carried out with the aid of locational theory and recent advances in epigraphy" (Hammond 1975:40). He concluded that Mayanists "need[ed] to look more closely . . . [at] . . . the relative size and complexity of sites as recorded archaeologically in order to appreciate the distinctions." In the typology he devised, Hammond (1975:41–43) divided Bullard's house ruin component into four categories, "single isolated house-platform" (Level 1), "house-compound or plazuela" (Level 2), "informal cluster"

(Level 3), and "formal cluster" (Level 4). Hammond (1975:42) continued to employ the term *minor ceremonial center* (Level 6) "as Bullard described it," in his discussions of what he considered to be "the small-scale version of a major center." According to Hammond, minor ceremonial centers" possess[ed] . . . 2 or 3 defined plazas, each containing at least one major structure, and with evidence of differentiation in plaza function, with one forming the focus of religious activity and one or two others having elite residences and/or administrative buildings." In addition, he suggested the presence of another apparently intermediary site type, the "minimal ceremonial center" (Level 5; Hammond 1975:41; see also Ford 1981:57; Thomas 1981:108). These sites were distinguished from minor ceremonial centers by the number of defined plazas. Still, although the minimal ceremonial center was smaller in size and less formal in plan than the minor ceremonial center, Hammond still attributed "religious," "political," and "economic" functions to them. Above the level of minor ceremonial center, Hammond (1975:42–43) divided Bullard's major ceremonial center into three categories, "small major ceremonial center" (Level 7), "medium major ceremonial center" (Level 8), and "regional ceremonial center" (Level 9). These sites were differentiated from each other based on size and degree of elaboration, and distinguished from the minor ceremonial centers based on size and the presence of features such as ballcourts and stelae.

Willey (1981:403) doubts whether the basic settlement data studied by Bullard and Hammond differed very much, and argues that the divergences in their typologies reflects the fact that the Bullard typology is a result of the "lumping" of settlement units, whereas the Hammond construct is the outcome of "splitting" them. Even though Hammond's typology more accurately reflects the diversity inherent in the overall settlement continuum, there remains a problem in that the construct is difficult to apply in contexts other than the one in which it was formulated. Specifically, although this typology may work well with the sample generated by Hammond in Corozal, a phenomenon that obviously reflects the fact that the settlement sample itself was employed to formulate the typology, difficulties arise when one attempts to classify sites from other parts of the Maya subarea. This problem is especially true for the minor ceremonial centers and minimal ceremonial centers. Given the variability within this segment of the settlement continuum, the rigorous, monothetic typology offered by Hammond is too confining to be employed effectively in the majority of cases. Sanders (1981:359), in a brief discussion of Hammond's construct, has concluded that "[i]n reviewing his data my feeling is what he actually has is an endless gradation of minor and major centers with no very clear-cut hierarchical ranking."

Ashmore (1981) has offered a qualitative typology similar to the one presented by Hammond (other qualitative constructs include Ball and Taschek 1991:157; Borhegyi 1956; Sanders 1960; Thomas 1981; Tourtellot 1970; Willey and Leventhal 1979). However, this typology restricts itself primarily to the lower level of settlement, with only passing attention paid to the middle settlement level. With reference to this latter settlement level, Ashmore (1981:56) concludes that "[h]ere is where I think the behavioral and physical phenomena are so complex that it becomes less profitable to deal with centers as settlement 'elements' or as discrete, ranked types, than to treat them as expressions of more continuously distributed dimensions of complexity."

Given that the overall settlement variability appears to rule out the use of rigid, monothetic classification schemes, such as the one proposed by Hammond, a return to a more malleable, polythetic construct appears warranted. This direction is underscored by the fact that we are dealing with a settlement *continuum* as opposed to a population of discrete settlement types (D. Chase et al. 1990:500; Culbert 1991b:328; Haviland 1970:190). Ashmore (1981:41) has pointed out that "the crux of the typology problem is that, partly because of the ambiguity of the form-function correspondences, we still lack adequate detailed analyses justifying identification of particular feature 'types' with particular, discrete activities or sets of activities." It is tempting, given this scenario, to restore the original Bullard formulation. Unfortunately, not only is this construct too unrestricted to permit detailed, analytical assessment of the variability within the settlement continuum, its functional connotations and terminology also make it untenable. A compromise appears the most fitting solution, wherein the variation of the settlement continuum is divided into a loose hierarchy of settlement levels or types (e.g., Bullard 1960), each level in turn being subdivided into a number of recognizable, polythetic subtypes (e.g., Ashmore 1981; Hammond 1975).

Middle-Level Settlements: Toward a Practical Typology

I propose that Mayanists adopt a very loose, tripartite site typology, with the following settlement types: lower-level settlement, middle-level settlement, and upper-level settlement (see Iannone 1996). In this scheme, it is recognized that one is artificially partitioning a highly variable continuum. At the junction of each partition a "gray" area will exist, where the ability to assign a particular settlement unit to one or another settlement level becomes increasingly subjective. However, such problems accurately reflect the reality of dividing a continuum, and in the end attest to the validity of employing a less rigid typological scheme. The flexibility of classification does mean that highly variable settlement units will be amalgamated together within the broad categories. This also reflects the variability inherent in the settlement continuum. In the end, if we view the classification as a means to an end (i.e., as a step leading toward analysis of the variability both between *and* within the settlement levels), as opposed to an end onto itself, the variability within the broad types does not constitute a problem.

Each of these broad types is further divided into a number of loosely defined (polythetic) subtypes (e.g., "patio groups," "plazuela groups," "minimal centers," "minor centers," "major centers"), in order to provide a more detailed understanding of what settlement forms are typical of each settlement level. In doing so, I hope to show that Mayanists need not limit their use of these *subtypes,* as many seem to serve our purposes just fine. Rather, I wish to stress that, given the overall variability in the middle level of the settlement continuum, it becomes increasingly difficult, and impractical, to pigeonhole these particular settlement units into idealized (monothetic) types (e.g., Hammond 1975). Having, I hope, justified the use of such a classification strategy, I now wish to outline what I perceive to constitute the three settlement levels.

Lower-Level Settlement

In this model, the term *lower-level settlement* is employed in discussing the smallest and least complex architectural units and assemblages within the overall settlement continuum. Lower-level settlement begins with the most basic unit of analysis—Bullard's (1960) solitary "housemound," Hammond's (1975:41) Level 1 "single isolated house-platform," or Ashmore's (1981:47) "minimal residential unit"—and ends with Bullard's (1960) "housemound cluster," Hammond's (1975:41) Level 4 "formal cluster," and Ashmore's (1981:51) "group-focused patio cluster." The constituents of this settlement level are highly variable. However, the majority of this variability is attributable to expanded numbers of individual settlement units, and/or increasing degrees of formal arrangement. The remaining variability reflects the uneven distribution of some architectural features that exhibit slightly greater size and/or apparently functioned in a nonresidential fashion (e.g., shrines; see Ashmore 1981:51; Hammond 1975:21). These occurrences may reflect numerous "developmental" factors (Ashmore 1981:54; McAnany 1995:95, 99), although it should be stressed that, for a variety of socioeconomic or sociopolitical reasons, certain groups do not enter the developmental trajectory at its beginning, but rather exhibit these features from the outset of their occupation. In any event, it is the presence of these traits that leads one into the gray area between lower-level settlement and middle-level settlement. These features (e.g., more elaborate residences, shrines) clearly indicate increasing socioeconomic and sociopolitical inequality both within and between groups. Following the "developmental" model, an increase in such features is expected over time, and a whole range of architectural inventories becomes possible at this point in the settlement continuum. Some archaeologists may find it more appealing to assign certain of these more complex settlement units to the middle-level settlement category. Others may feel more comfortable retaining these within the lower level of settlement. Given the abundance of developmental trajectories available to any social group, and the resulting potential variability in settlement makeup, there can be no right or wrong classification at this juncture.

Middle-Level Settlement

Above the previously discussed gray area, consisting as it does of a multitude of settlement assemblages with recognizably larger architecture and/or special function structures, one reaches a series of sites that have always been difficult to classify. As Ashmore (1981:54) has noted, at this level "there is some question as to the nature of formally identifiable units," although "most Mayanists can agree on what specific sites are or are *not* 'major centers'" (Ashmore 1981:55). This "middle-level settlement" begins somewhere in the gray area, though admittedly a solid line cannot be drawn to suggest an actual starting point. In reality, many of the settlement units in the gray area, given a developmental model, would eventually develop into true middle-level settlement units (e.g., McAnany 1995:95). Other sites of this level may have entered the developmental trajectory in the middle, for a variety of socioeconomic and sociopolitical reasons, and thus appeared as middle-level settlements from their initial construction.

Bona fide middle-level settlement begins with what Hammond (1975: 41) has called "minimal ceremonial center[s]" (see also Ford 1981:57; Thomas 1981:108). In his definition, Hammond stressed that although such sites replicate many of the features present in lower-level settlement, they differ in that the presence of at least one large nonresidential structure suggests that these sites had a degree of "religious," "political," and "economic control." Such settlement units would once again differ very little from some of the gray-area sites previously discussed and may simply indicate further strides along the developmental trajectory or, again, a special series of social relationships that permitted initial construction as a middle-level settlement site.

Following this progression, one reaches the first genuine "minor centers" as originally discussed by Bullard (1960; see also Ford 1981:57; Hammond 1975:42; Thomas 1981:108). Such sites are readily separable from lower-level settlement by their greater size (i.e., spatial extent and structure volume) and complexity of overall site plan. An increase in the number of apparently nonresidential structures also attests to significant differences between these sites and those of the lower level. Hammond (1975:42) has noted that at this point on the continuum sites begin to show clear differentiation between plaza or courtyard function. Whereas one courtyard may primarily serve a residential function, others may be the focus for religious and/or administrative activities. With this separation, these smaller sites are beginning to exhibit a characteristic of upper-level sites (Ashmore 1992). The presence of other distinctive architectural configurations within these middle-level settlement units, such as eastern ancestor shrines, and restricted access plazas, also attests to the "replication" of upper-level traits. Similarities aside, it is still readily apparent that the greatest variability in site plan and architectural components occurs at this level.

With the appearance of the aforementioned characteristics, one reaches the gray area between middle-level settlement and upper-level settlement. Bullard (1960:360) has stated, and many others have assumed, that few other affinities occur between middle-level sites and those of the upper level. He notes that many characteristics of upper-level settlement, such as stelae, altars, ballcourts, and vaulted buildings (and one may add causeways) are generally lacking within "minor centers" (Bullard 1960:360; Willey and Bullard 1965:368). In his discussions, Hammond (1975:42) concedes that, in the case of stone monuments, some minor centers may contain these features if they are "within the ambit of major centers." However, a review of the literature indicates that features such as ballcourts, causeways, stelae, and altars, although not commonplace among middle-level settlements, do occur (Iannone 1996). These occurrences attest to the existence of a gray area between the middle and upper levels of settlement. Whether the presence of such features suggests a long, relatively *autonomous* developmental trajectory, a comparatively short developmental sequence marked by *dependency* on more firmly entrenched sociopolitical and/or socioeconomic entities, or some variety of *semiautonomous* interaction needs to be considered on a site-to-site basis (see also Hayden 1994:202–203). In sum, although middle-level settlement units are the least susceptible to discrete classification, these architectural assemblages are still seen to comprise a loose but distinguishable set of settlement units lying, in size and complexity, somewhere between the lower- and upper-level settlement.

Upper-Level Settlement

With upper-level settlement, one moves into the realm of Bullard's (1960) "major centers." To echo Ashmore (1981:51), most Mayanists would agree as to what does or does not constitute a "major center." Whether one employs classifications such as "small major ceremonial center," "medium major ceremonial center," and "regional ceremonial center" (Hammond 1975:42–43), or more complex schemes such as "regal-ritual city," "regal-ritual center," and "regal-ritual residence" (Ball and Taschek 1991), it is still understood that one is dealing with variations on a theme (Ashmore 1992). The general characteristics of upper-level settlement units are increased size (spatial and volumetric), increased complexity of plan (i.e., further separation of residential, public/administrative, and religious sectors), increased number of nonresidential structures, increased presence of ballcourts, stelae, altars, *sacbeob* (causeways), and vaulted buildings. What differentiates upper-level settlements, with reference to surface features, are degrees of quality and quantity. As Ball and Taschek (1991:157) have argued, "[W]hat distinguished Tikal from other centers was the greater incidence of certain activities and their occurrence on a grander scale than was true elsewhere." The point being, although many sites exhibit special features, such as the twin pyramid complexes at Tikal and Yaxha (Ashmore 1981:58, 1992), all upper-level settlements, with few exceptions (e.g., Lubaantun), share a core list of traits (Ashmore 1981:57–58; 1992). The differences in quality and quantity suggest differences in power, and hence ranking of upper-level settlements is a possible (e.g., Ball and Taschek 1991; Marcus 1976), although by no means a simple undertaking (Ashmore 1981:55). As with the rest of the settlement continuum, there are potentially numerous, highly variable developmental trajectories manifest in sites of this level. However, no matter how small or large, upper-level settlement units share more characteristics with each other than they do with middle-level settlements.

Problems in the Interpretation of Middle-Level Settlements

The previous discussion, although lengthy, was aimed at demonstrating how "minor centers" comprise part of a middle level of settlement exhibiting a wide range of site sizes, plans, and feature inventories (see also Puleston 1983:25). Willey and Bullard's early research in the upper Belize River region can be seen as the first substantive effort to deal with this diversity. Since that time, research in this part of the Maya subarea has continued to play a leading role in the investigation of middle-level settlements (map 1). To date, investigations have been undertaken at BR-180-181-182 (Barton Ramie; see Willey et al. 1965), Spanish Lookout (Willey et al. 1965), Bedran (chapter 5), Callar Creek (by Jennifer Ehret), and San Lorenzo (Yaeger 2000a), all located on the lower alluvial river terraces. Explorations have also been conducted at Floral Park (chapter 18), Ontario Village (chapter 18), and Bacab Na (Ford 1990:169), situated on the higher river terraces. Finally, excavations and/or surveys have been undertaken at the foothill sites of Dos Chambitos (by Jennifer Ehret), Yaxox (Ford 1990:169), Alta Vista (Ford 1990:169), Zubin (Iannone 1996), Zinic (by James Conlon), Zopilote (chapter 8), X-ual-canil (aka Cayo Y; by Gyles Iannone), Nohoch Ek (Coe and Coe 1956; see also Ball and Taschek 1991), and in the vicinity of Chaa Creek (Connell 2000).

As a result of the expansion of research, both in the upper Belize River region and elsewhere, we are beginning to formulate a more accurate picture of middle-level settlement distributions. Driver and Garber (chapter 18) note that, in the middle Belize River region, one of the locations for sites of this size and complexity is at positions "equidistant" between upper-level settlements. Additionally, it appears that middle-level settlements are spaced roughly 2 km from each other, or a similar distance from larger, upper-level settlements. This spacing is consistent with that recognized elsewhere in the Maya lowlands. For example, Hammond (1975:42) has noted that "minor centers" are generally situated 1.75 to 2 km from the site core of Nohmul. As indicated in the preceding section, middle-level settlements can be found in a variety of different environmental settings, including the alluvial valleys, uplands, and foothills. Bullard's (1960:368) earlier assertion that sites of this size and complexity are frequently found in prominent locations, often hilltops, has also been confirmed by recent investigations. Specifically, these centers appear to be particularly prevalent in the foothills zone, where they are commonly found on the crests of hills (Iannone 1996; Willey and Bullard 1965:29). The recent attention that has been paid to sites of this size and complexity suggests that we will soon be able to formulate models to account for their variability. However, before we can hope to fully comprehend the significance of this diversity a number of methodological and theoretical issues must be addressed.

First, regardless of the numerous projects that have emphasized middle-level settlement investigations in places like the upper Belize River region, the majority of research in the Maya subarea has continued to focus on the antipodes of the settlement continuum—the larger, upper-level settlements and the smaller and less complex lower-level settlements (Gonlin 1994; Iannone 1996; King and Potter 1994; McAnany 1995:91). As a result, we have unwittingly structured our field investigations in such a way that we have reified a false urban/rural dichotomy. For this reason, the notion of "rural complexity" has rarely played a significant role in our considerations of ancient Maya sociopolitical and socioeconomic organization. Specifically, in our analyses we have not adequately accounted for either the variability exhibited by middle-level settlement site plans, or the syncretic character of their feature inventories (i.e., the mixing of urban and rural characteristics). These factors must be worked into our interpretations of ancient Maya society.

Second, when we have focused our attention on middle-level settlements we have often emphasized site size, surface configuration, and proximity to larger, and more complex, upper-level settlements (Gonlin 1994; Iannone 1996; King and Potter 1994; see also comments in Schwartz and Falconer 1994:2). For the most part, this emphasis reflects the fact that excavations in middle-level settlements have been limited in scope. This lack of detailed excavations has resulted in an under appreciation of the developmental sequences of such sites, and the broader implications thereof (Iannone 1996; King and Potter 1994). Researchers who have strived to develop an understanding of the development of specific middle-level settlements underscore the variability in site growth exhibited by these centers (e.g., Hendon 1992; Iannone 1996). Clearly, the formulation of a more comprehensive understanding of the growth of such sites is required before the significance of middle-level settlements can be effectively explored (Bawden 1982:181).

Given the variability in middle-level settlement site plans and developmental sequences, we must also be more open to the notion that the inhabitants of such sites may have played a series of diverse roles within sociopolitical and socioeconomic interaction (Haviland 1981:117; Iannone 1996; Puleston 1983:25; Rice and Puleston 1981:155). The variability exhibited by these centers has led most Mayanists to suggest that they served a multifunctional purpose with respect to the broader sociopolitical and socioeconomic hierarchy (i.e., every "minor center" functioned as the locus for variety of residential, economic, political, religious, and social functions). Nevertheless, we must remain open to the fact that a plethora of specialized functions may be signified by the variable character of middle-level settlement morphologies, feature inventories, and artifact assemblages. These diverse functions may include residential (non-elite, subelite, and elite), market, administrative (e.g., water management, agricultural management, and border or "control point" management; see chapters 5 and 18), feasting, and ritual activities (chapter 8). In sum, middle-level settlement variability suggests that, although specific sites may have been entrenched within a structure of hierarchical relationships, the settlement level as a whole is best viewed as having a heterarchical quality. This follows the definition by Crumley (1995:3), in which heterarchy refers to "the relation of elements to one another when they are unranked or when they possess the potential for being ranked in a number of different ways." Different middle-level settlements may have been the loci for different activities. Considered alongside the potential for divergences in developmental trajectories, the inhabitants of such sites may have had a shifting, or heterarchical relationship with both those above and below them.

Conclusion

King and Potter (1994:84) state that "[b]y not expecting social, economic, or political complexity from small sites, we disregard possible important sources of information on the lowland Maya world." Gonlin (1994:195) echoes this sentiment in concluding that "if we do not fully understand rural complexity, we cannot convincingly speak of complexity in general for the ancient Maya." As both of these statements suggest, there is a growing realization that middle-level settlement research must form a major component of our settlement studies. Current research within the upper Belize River region, and elsewhere, has pointed toward the vast range of site plans, feature inventories, artifact assemblages, and developmental sequences that are manifest within the middle level of the ancient Maya settlement continuum. This variability suggests that middle-level settlements, and their inhabitants, played diverse roles within past sociopolitical and socioeconomic interaction.

Acknowledgments

During the writing of this chapter, and the doctoral dissertation upon which it is based, I have benefited from discussions with a number of individuals. These include Wendy Ashmore, Jaime Awe, Warwick Bray, Arlen Chase, James Conlon, Samuel Connell, Jennifer Ehret, James Garber, Elizabeth Graham, Paul Healy, Richard Leventhal, and Jason Yaeger. The editor, James Garber, and anonymous reviewers provided useful comments on an earlier version of this chapter. Finally, I would like to thank the Department of Archaeology in Belize for their support of middle-level settlement research over the years.

18

The Emergence of Minor Centers in the Zones between Seats of Power

W. David Driver and James F. Garber

Since the beginning of settlement research in the Maya area, researchers have focused on the identification of patterns in the forms and distribution of the rural built environment of the ancient Maya, and the recognition of the underlying implications these patterns have for sociopolitical organization. Predicated by initial housemound investigations conducted in the early 20th century (Ricketson and Ricketson 1937; Thompson 1931; Tozzer 1913; Wauchope 1934), the Peabody Museum efforts in the Belize River Valley and neighboring northeastern Petén were the first intensive investigations of settlement distribution and implied social organization (Bullard 1960; Willey and Bullard 1965; Willey et al. 1965). The results of this work suggested a basic hierarchy of settlement classification that has been influential in subsequent Maya settlement research (e.g., Ashmore 1981; Haviland 1981; Kurjack 1974; Puleston 1983).

Settlement Patterns in the Belize River Valley

Initial Investigations

Willey et al. (1965) conducted surveys along the Belize River and its tributaries from Cocos Bank to the Guatemalan border (map 1). While a number of sites along the upper and middle sections of the valley were recorded during this survey, the greatest wealth of information came from intensive investigations of two areas in the central portion of the survey area. Focusing on recently cleared agricultural land, Willey and his colleagues conducted a systematic survey and testing program of almost 3 km² at Barton Ramie and Spanish Lookout, as well as some survey and mapping at the site of Baking Pot (chapter 2).

Bullard conducted a settlement survey of the neighboring northeastern Petén area (1960). This survey focused on the distribution of sites in a large region of northeastern Guatemala, extending from the edge of the Belize Valley survey area westward to Tikal. Due to the nature of the terrain and vegetation, the survey was generally restricted to established trails. The resulting study covered a total of 260 linear km, or approximately 6.25 km² (Rice and Puleston 1981:130) and identified a wide range of sites.

Based on the results of these investigations, Bullard and Willey developed a three-tiered hierarchy of site types consisting of "house-mound groups," "minor ceremonial centers," and "major ceremonial centers" (Bullard 1960:357; Willey et al. 1965:561). The form and distribution of these site types suggested a complementary three-tiered system of sociopolitical organization consisting of "clusters," "zones," and "districts" (Bullard 1960:367; Willey et al. 1965:579).

The lowest level, the cluster or hamlet, was composed of a spatially discrete (ca. 200–300 m²) collection of five to 12 single housemounds, patio groups, and/or small plazuelas. The distribution of the clusters was based primarily on the relief of local terrain and the locations of accessible water (bajos and aguadas). They often included one group that contained a small pyramidal shrine, and was slightly larger and more formal than the rest. These specialized structures, along with the general size of the clusters, suggested the clusters represented some form of kinship group (Bullard 1960:367). Similar settlement distributions have been recorded ethnographically from modern Maya groups (Fash 1983; Vogt 1976, 1983).

The secondary level was designated as a zone, and consisted of several settlement clusters. Located among the clusters of each zone was a larger and more elaborate group, termed a minor ceremonial center. These centers are described as "appreciably larger than the House Ruins, and appreciably smaller than the Major Ceremonial Centers" (Bullard 1960:359). They are described as having one or more small temples with several lower buildings arranged around one to three adjacent plazas. None of these minor centers contained stelae, altars, or ballcourts. Each appeared to be associated with between 50 and 100 housemounds. Seen as loci of low order political power, they appear to have functioned to administer and control the individual clusters of farmsteads within their reach and serve "as the religious and civic center for the community" (Bullard 1960:368).

In the uppermost tier of the hierarchy, the district, major centers oversaw several zones. They contained all the trappings of Maya architectural sophistication, including multiple plaza groupings surrounded by large temples and multiroomed palaces, stelae, altars, and ballcourts. It appeared to Bullard (1960:369) that these sites were located without respect to housemound settlement, nor to locations of water or land, but instead were placed on prominent high ground. Regarding this differential locational strategy, Bullard (1960:369) notes that "the more intimate relationship which was observed between the minor centers and the house ruins is an important indication of differences in function between the two classes of ceremonial centers." The major centers identified as district heads were Benque Viejo (Xunantunich), Cahal Pech, and Baking Pot. In contrast, all public architecture located downriver, appeared to be limited to minor centers.

Recent Investigations

As a consequence of a resurgence of investigation in the region, a much more complex picture of the sociopolitical relationships has begun to emerge for those sites located in the western portion of the Peabody Museum's original survey zone (chapter 12). Yet little remained known about the areas farther downriver (Hammond 1974). In 1990, the Belize Valley Archaeological Project was begun in the middle portion of the valley (chapters 3 and 4).[1] Although focused primarily on excavations at the newly discovered center of Blackman Eddy, the project also conducted reconnaissance and testing of settlements located on the south side of the river from Floral Park to Roaring Creek. The project identified, mapped, and/or tested a number of sites in this area and, as a result, has begun to redefine previous notions of the sociopolitical organization in the middle Belize River Valley.

Based on the locations of these new sites, Garber et al. (1993) presented a model for the distribution of major and minor centers. The model proposed that major centers adjacent to the Belize River (including those along its two branches, the Macal and the Mopan) were located at a consistent interval of 9.9 km. While there were exceptions, the intersite distance remained relatively constant for five of the seven major centers (map 4). The major centers included in this pattern were Xunantunich, Cahal Pech, Baking Pot, Blackman Eddy, and Camelote. The sites that did not fit the pattern included Buenavista and Actuncan.

This model clearly differs from the central place-oriented descriptions normally employed for interpreting Maya settlement distributions (e.g.,

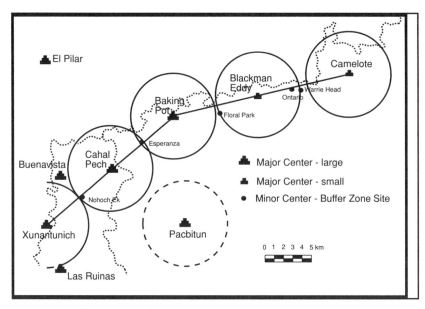

Map 4. The Belize Valley with 9.9-km "districts."

Hammond 1974; Marcus 1993). Undoubtedly, the linear nature of the pattern is influenced by the riverine nature of the topography. However, this description of spatial organization is similar to that reported by Harrison (1981) for southern Quintana Roo. Harrison identified a consistent 26-km distance between a series of major centers. Similar distances have been recognized in various regions (Flannery 1972; Hammond 1974). Marcus (1983b:464) suggests these figures represent average walking distances for full (26–28 km) and half (13–16 km) days, and correspond to effective regions of control in preindustrial state societies. Hammond's evaluation of nearest neighbor analysis recognizes a dense packing of sites/polities in the northeastern Petén region, including the sites of the upper Belize Valley. For the 15 sites in Hammond's study area, mean first-neighbor distance was shown to be 10.4 km (Hammond 1974:325).

Recent work in the upper valley region has pointed toward a high level of complexity in the sociopolitical relationships of that area, especially by the Late Classic period (Ball and Taschek 1991; Ford and Fedick 1992; chapter 12). While the linear model may provide insight into how the system developed, such complexity makes its application difficult for the area west of the Macal/Mopan confluence. In contrast, the nature of both terrain and settlement located downriver suggests that the linear model retains some explanatory value.

The Distribution of Minor Centers

In addition to the equidistant spacing of the major centers, the spatial model proposed by Garber et al. (1993) noted that consistent patterns were evident in the distribution of smaller centers as well (map 4). Minor centers located in the proposed 9.9-km-diameter zones can be categorized into three locational subgroups, designated Types 1–3. Both Harrison (1981) and Puleston (1983) have reported similar patterns. In addition to the regularity of spacing for major centers noted above, Harrison (1981:274–276, fig. 10.2) found minor centers to be located between them at regular intervals of 13 km (Marcus 1983b:462–464, fig. 2). Of the 12 minor centers located in the outskirts of Tikal, Puleston (1983:25–26) was able to identify three distinct groupings. These were located at consistent distances from the site's core at approximately 3–3.5 km, 5 km, and 10 km. While Puleston reported this trend with a cautionary disclaimer, the repeated occurrence of such patterns in the Petén, central Belize, and southern Quintana Roo, suggest that it represents a significant pattern and may reflect functional differentiation among minor centers.

Type 1 Sites

Returning to the Belize Valley, the first category of minor centers, the Type 1 sites, are located within 2 km of a major center. They usually contain one or two temple structures and few or no residential components. Such groups may have served an integrative role by extending the site core into the rural support zone (chapter 8). Excavation at the minor center of Zopilote, a Type 1 site located at the terminus of a sacbe connected to Cahal Pech, have revealed ancestor-related ritual. Similar termini groups are well documented at the site of Caracol (A. Chase and D. Chase 1987). Type 1 minor centers not linked to major center cores by a causeway may have served similar, although not as formalized, functions as well. The minor center of MB is dominated by a single large temple mound (similar to that at Zopilote), and may have served as a Type 1 site for Blackman Eddy (map 1).

Type 2 Sites

Type 2 sites are located beyond the 2-km range and are distributed outward from the major center. This distribution appears to be based on the locations of critical resources such as water and arable land, and may fit the role of the minor center as proposed by Bullard (1960) and Willey et al.

(1965), in which minor centers functioned as a part of the hierarchal political system controlled by a major center. Bullard and Willey may be correct in their characterization of the occupants of these minor centers as dispersed "elites" in the rural zone. For example, work by Conlon and Powis (chapter 5) suggests close ties between the occupants of the minor center of Bedran and the elite of Baking Pot. Other Type 2 sites in the middle valley area include the minor centers at Spanish Lookout (Baking Pot), Barton Ramie (Blackman Eddy), and Teakettle (Camelote).

Type 3 Sites

Type 3 sites are located at points equidistant between two major centers. The consistency of this site location suggests that these centers may have played roles related to the marking and maintenance of these boundary or border areas. There are five examples of such Type 3 sites currently identified in the valley. These include Esperanza (between Cahal Pech and Baking Pot), Floral Park (between Baking Pot and Blackman Eddy), Nohoch Ek (between Xunantunich and Cahal Pech), and Ontario and Warrie Head (both located between Blackman Eddy and Camelote) (map 4).

Type 3 Minor Centers

The consistent and precise location of these minor centers implied that their function might have been to maintain or monitor the transitional territory between the districts of two major centers. Such areas, as intersite buffer zones between districts, should be expected to demonstrate lower densities of settlement similar to that seen between Tikal and Uaxactun (Puleston 1974). In contrast to our assumptions, investigations have now shown that four of the five Type 3 sites are located in areas containing significant numbers of housemounds, while only one (Ontario) is in an area of limited population. This suggests that there may be at least two functional types of minor centers included in this site category. Investigations at Nohoch Ek have documented a number of housemounds and patio groups, in addition to the main plaza group. At Warrie Head, Willey at al. (1965:310–312) recorded three large patio groups and noted "about a dozen smaller rectangular platforms" in the immediate vicinity. During the mapping and test excavations conducted by the Belize Valley Archaeological Project at Esperanza and Floral Park, large numbers of mounds were noted in areas adjacent to the main groups. Although no formal settlement studies have been conducted at these four sites, the intuitive assessments show little evidence of the expected settlement drop-off. However, one Type 3 site does appear to be in a relatively empty buffer zone. A systematic survey at the site of Ontario, a small minor center located between Blackman Eddy and Camelote, documented an extremely light density of associated settlement.

Floral Park

Floral Park is located midway between the major ceremonial centers of Baking Pot and Blackman Eddy (fig. 18.1). The main group was first mapped by Willey et al. (1965). Although no excavations or formal settlement survey were conducted during that study, they noted the presence of a number of housemounds in the nearby floodplain. Kirke (1980) identified a number of "linear indentations" near the site and suggested that they represent the remains of an ancient irrigation system. The presence of similar features at the site of Bedran has been the subject of archaeological investigation (chapter 5). They note that the Bedran ditch system was very productive and that this agricultural system accounts for the material and social status of the Bedran elite. No doubt a similar situation existed at Floral Park. Access to an agricultural surplus gave the ruling family of Floral Park an opportunity to construct sizable public architecture between the Baking Pot and Blackman Eddy districts. Unlike the ruling family at Bedran, the ruling family at Floral Park does not appear to have been integrated into the elite system of either Baking Pot or Blackman Eddy. The material culture recovered from the plazuela at Floral Park can be characterized as ordinary and mundane as opposed to the elite material wealth that was conspicuous at Bedran.

The Floral Park site core is located on an artificially raised limestone outcrop that rises approximately 25 m above the alluvial plain, which continues to the Belize River to the north. The core comprises a single plaza group defined by two large, conical-shaped mounds located on the east and south sides of the platform (fig. 18.1). Structure A1 stands approximately 6.5 m above the larger northern section of the plaza and Structure A2 rises 5.4 m above the southern section. Two residential groups lie nearby. Group 1 is located to the northeast of the site core. Farther to the northeast is Group 2, a complex plazuela group composed of four structures enclosing a central plaza and would have been the residential compound of the ruling family. Numerous other small structures are located to the north, east, and west of the site core in addition to three symmetrical depressions, averaging 2.5 m in depth, which may have functioned as water reservoirs.

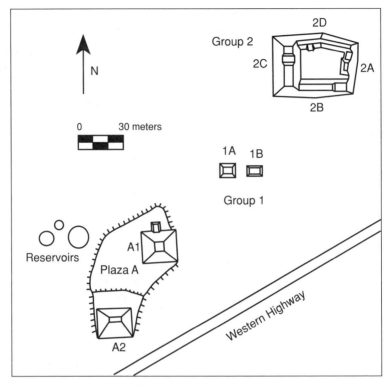

Fig. 18.1. Site plan of Floral Park.

Excavations in the site core were conducted on Structure A1 in 1994 on the summit and northern and western sides of the mound (Glassman et al. 1995). Structure A1 has at least two construction phases. While the majority of construction dates to the Late Classic period, there was also evidence of some Preclassic occupation in the main group. Excavations were also conducted on the north and east structures of Group 2, a plazuela located approximately 200 m to the northeast of the site core (Glassman et al. 1995). The excavations revealed three construction phases, minor caches, and poorly preserved human remains.

Esperanza

Formal investigations were initiated at Esperanza in 2000. The site is located midway between the major ceremonial centers of Cahal Pech and Baking Pot (map 4), in a hilly zone at the base of the Maya Mountains, overlooking the floodplain of the Belize River. The site center consists of a

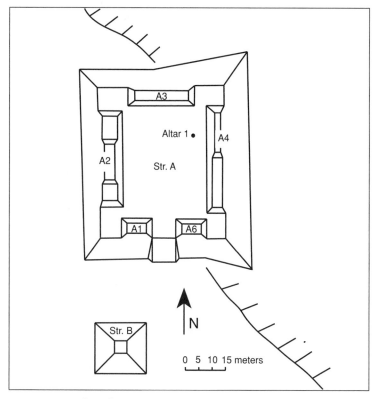

Fig. 18.2. Site plan of Esperanza.

plazuela group constructed on a massive rectangular platform and a single temple mound to the south (fig. 18.2). The rectangular platform of the plazuela group is quite large measuring 58 m north-south by 50 m east-west. It is constructed on the edge of a limestone terrace. On the steeper, eastern edge, the platform rises 8.5 m above the surrounding terrain. On the western edge it reaches a height of 6.3 m. Access to the platform summit was from a broad outset staircase on its south. On the summit of the platform is a series of long low mounds arranged in a quadrangle. A large well-shaped altar was recovered at the base of the eastern mound. Analysis of the ceramic materials from test excavations indicate that the entire platform of the plazuela group was constructed during the Late Classic period.

The single temple mound, Structure B, is located to the south of the plazuela platform and had been severely looted. A trench had been dug into the center of the structure from the northeast, deeply penetrating the center of the structure. This trench was cleaned out, recorded, and expanded to retrieve sealed ceramic samples. This structure had four construction episodes, all dating to the Late Classic. The site and the surrounding area have been cleared for pasture. Although the area has not been systematically surveyed, numerous housemounds are visible from the plazuela in all directions and it is clear that the surrounding hilly zone was densely populated. Agricultural terraces are likely present in the area immediately surrounding the site as well.

Nohoch Ek

Nohoch Ek is situated on a limestone knoll midway between the major ceremonial centers of Xunantunich and Cahal Pech (map 4). Excavations were conducted at the site in 1949 by Coe and Coe (1956) and Ball and Taschek in 1985. It is composed of six range structure mounds arranged around a rectangular plaza (fig. 18.3). To the west of the plaza is a small, low platform supporting three low mounds.

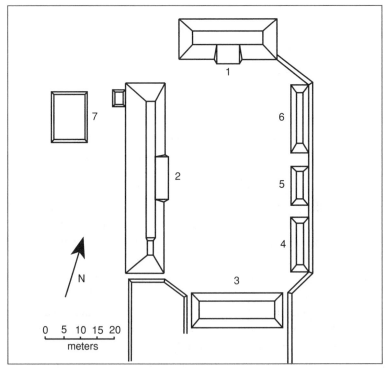

Fig. 18.3. Site plan of Nohoch Ek.

Coe and Coe's work consisted primarily of trenching and limited lateral excavations in the structural platforms that make up the plaza. The investigations by Ball and Taschek focused primarily on lateral excavations of structures and nonstructural living surfaces as a means of examining the Late through Terminal Classic sociocultural role of the Nohoch Ek inhabitants. After a detailed analysis of the excavations, features, ceramics, and other artifacts, they conclude that Nohoch Ek was not a ceremonial, ritual, or civic center that was part of a hierarchy in a system of primary or secondary centers. Instead, the data indicated that it was a substantial residential plaza with associated groups and clusters that were integrated into a complex system of terraced fields present in the immediate area of the plaza core.

In their description of Nohoch Ek, Coe and Coe (1956:370) note that it is located between the modern towns of El Cayo (San Ignacio) and Socotz. Both Cahal Pech (on the outskirts of San Ignacio) and Xunantunich (adjacent to Socotz) were known at the time and thus Coe and Coe were aware of its intermediate position between the two major centers. Earlier, Satterthwaite (1951:22) had speculated on the relationship between Nohoch Ek and the two nearby centers by stating that it was unlikely that a site of this size could have existed independent of Benque Viejo (Xunantunich) or Cahal Pech.

Despite the acknowledgment of Nohoch Ek's position midway between Cahal Pech and Benque Viejo (Xunantunich), Coe and Coe do not consider the notion that it may have been in a buffer zone that was allied to neither. Subsequent excavation and analysis by Ball and Taschek strongly suggest that the architectural construction at Nohoch Ek was well within the means of the ruling family of the site and are emphatic in their assessment of this site that it was not a ritual or ceremonial center. Their analysis indicated that it functioned as a residential group for farmers and that it exhibited relatively substantial architecture, including a specialized structure that may have functioned as a feasting hall. Thus, it is clear that this site was not a ceremonial center administered by a detached population of elites. Although some rural sites closer to ceremonial centers, such as Bedran, may have housed rural elites, this does not appear to be the case for the majority of Type 3 sites.

Ontario

The site of Ontario is a medium-sized plazuela group located in the valley floodplain 300 m southeast of the Belize River (map 4). Recorded by the

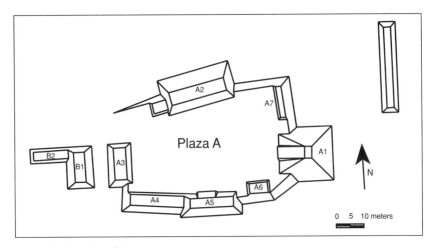

Fig. 18.4. Site plan of Ontario.

Belize Department of Archaeology in 1969, the site lies just off the southern side of the Western Highway at the eastern limits of the small modern community of Ontario Village, approximately 13 km (8 miles) west of Belmopan. Ontario is most likely the site described earlier by Willey and his colleagues (Willey et al. 1965:312).

The first excavations at the site were conducted by the Belize Valley Archaeological Project during its 1993 and 1994 field seasons. The work included survey and mapping of the site core and the surrounding settlement zone, and the excavation of several structures. The site core consists of Plaza A, the primary structural group and what appears to have been a smaller, less formal patio group, Plaza B. The raised platform of the main group ranges from 1 to 3 m in height, and measures 60 × 45 m, covering approximately 2,700 m² (fig. 18.4). The plaza is dominated by Structure A1, a square pyramidal structure located at the group's east end. The summit of the mound rises 5.5 m above the plaza floor. Surprisingly, the west end of the plazuela is defined by a small ballcourt, Structures A3 and B1.

Occupation of the site was demonstrated to have been quite short, probably less than 250 years, with all construction occurring during the Late Classic, and site abandonment at the end of the Terminal Classic. No evidence of earlier occupation was identified in any area of the site. In the main plaza, the architectural sequences indicate three construction episodes, two major and one minor. Interestingly, during the initial phase of construction, the site was laid out much as it looked in its final form, with all major structures in place.

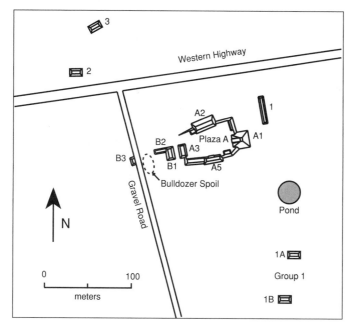

Fig. 18.5. Site plan of Ontario Settlement Zone.

A survey of the surrounding area was conducted in a single 200 m wide transect extending 200 m north and 150 m south of the main group, and covering a total of 7.0 hectares. This work was greatly facilitated by recent clearing with vegetation limited to low grasses and scrub regrowth.

The survey showed an extremely light population density, with only four additional structures identified (fig. 18.5). Located 130 m southeast of the site core, the two mounds of Group 1 lie 46 m apart, with no evidence of any additional associated structures. Both of the mounds measure 12 × 6 m, and are 1.5 m in height. Excavations revealed that each consisted of two major construction episodes, both of which were dated to the Late Classic. In addition, two isolated mounds, Structures 2 and 3, are located approximately 150 m to the northwest of the site core. Although in the same general area, and located only 57 m apart, the mounds do not appear to be associated with each other, or with any identifiable patio space. Based on the surface appearance of the mounds, they both appear to be small substructural residential platforms.

Although the area was relatively clear, the possibility of a "hidden house mound" problem at Ontario is very real (Ashmore 1981:50, 61).

Ethnographic and archaeological studies have demonstrated that the number, complexity, and height of structures within house compounds is directly related to length of occupation and group status (Haviland 1988; McAnany 1995; Sutro and Downing 1988). Consequently, the limited occupation history at Ontario could result in the existence of structures too small to leave surface signatures (thin plaster or packed earth floorings, very low platforms, etc.) Excavations in "vacant terrain" at Tikal identified a significant number of structures that left no surface evidence (Becker 1971:131).

Although the survey transect at Ontario was admittedly small (7.0 hectares), the lack of surrounding population appears to differ sharply from that seen around similarly sized sites in the valley. Unfortunately, there are no comparable settlement studies of other suggested Type 3 sites. However, visual assessments have noted significant numbers of housemounds surrounding the sites of Esperanza, Floral Park, Nohoch Ek, and Warrie Head. Further, in comparing the settlement directly associated with the minor center at Barton Ramie, the "Texas" subdivision (Willey et al. 1965, fig. 4) contains a total of 38 mounds within a 75,000-m² area, or 5.1 per hectare. The density of nonplaza structures (5) within the similarly sized survey area at Ontario is 0.7 per hectare, or seven times less dense. Even at Spanish Lookout, where Willey et al. (1965:294–295) identified 77 mounds in 450,000 m², the density is 1.7 per hectare, still almost two and a half times the density present at Ontario.[2]

Such a difference in settlement density is in contrast to the continuous ribbon strip populations noted by Willey et al. (1965:310, 573) for the surveyed valley areas west of Blackman Eddy. Similar breaks in settlement have been used to suggest boundary zones between polities (Bullard 1960; Puleston 1974, 1983; Sanders 1981). Subsequently, it suggests that there does appear to be a relatively empty population zone between the Blackman Eddy and Camelote districts, at least in the area around the site of Ontario.

The final construction, Structure A1–1st, was associated with a major rebuilding episode during which the entire plaza platform was raised and all major structures except for the ballcourt were significantly modified. At the initiation of this final phase, a high-status burial was placed in the fill and may represent the occasion for its construction. The burial consisted of an adult male, laid in extended position, face up, with his head to the south. The individual had been placed directly atop the tred of the uppermost step of the previous building phase. Grave goods included a perforated and notched flower-shaped shell disk placed at the individual's neck, a grater bowl, a molded ceramic jar lid, several chert blades and celts at the midsection, a limestone barkbeater and small green obsidian eccentric at the feet. The amount and type of items associated with this burial significantly exceed those recovered from other middle Belize Valley sites (e.g., Floral Park) and thus suggest a high-status individual. The inclusion of an artifact of green obsidian is especially rare, appearing in less than 0.09 percent of Late Classic contexts excavated in Belize (Dreiss 1989).

The use of special shrine buildings and associated high(er) status burials has been used by a number of authors as evidence of ancestor veneration and lineage organization for the ancient Maya (Bullard 1960; Freidel and Schele 1989; Hendon 1991; Leventhal 1983; McAnany 1995, 1998). Particularly instructive are the recent attempts to incorporate concepts of the social construction of "place" through the use of special mortuary structures and rituals, and their association to ideologies for the creation of legitimizing occupational histories (Hendon 1991; Knapp and Ashmore 1999; McAnany 1995, 1998; Stone 1992). Therefore, the establishment of the Ontario plazuela group, with its eastern shrine and mortuary presence, might have provided the legitimacy necessary for establishing control over the area, even without the long term occupational history so often seen at sites of similar size.

Obviously, the appearance of a ballcourt at a site of such small size is extremely unusual. Indeed, the lack of a ballcourt was utilized by Bullard (1960:360) as one of the primary criteria in differentiating minor centers from major centers. Ballcourts are considered to have been powerful locations in Mesoamerican ideological and ritual life (Ashmore 1991; Fox 1996; Freidel et al. 1993; Gillespie 1991; Miller and Houston 1987; Scarborough 1991; Schele and Miller 1986). Based on both iconographic studies and links with stories in the Popol Vuh, ballcourts are suggested to have been the focus of definitive rites of warfare, sacrifice, and cosmology. More specifically, a study of Mixtec codices has documented how the ballgame was used in that region to prepare for war and for the maintenance of alliances (Koontz 1994).

Similar functions were suggested by Fox's (1996) study of Maya ballcourts at several relatively small sites in the Cuyumapa Drainage of Honduras. Based on ethnohistoric and archaeological studies, he suggests that ballgame events were complex rituals that included processionals, dancing, mock combat, gifting and feasting in addition to the actual ballgame. Fox (1996) proposed that these complex ballgame rituals were critical in the establishment and negotiation of political power and social identities. Furthermore, he notes that the Cuyumapa Drainage appears to have been a politically decentralized region, with a number of competing centers. As a result of this competitive atmosphere, he argues that the construction of ballcourts and the sponsoring of associated ritual feasts at some of these sites was employed as a strategy for increasing prestige, for the "assertion of centrality by . . . otherwise marginal site[s]" (Fox 1996:494).

In summary, investigations at the minor center of Ontario indicate that the site could have served specialized functions related to boundary maintenance. The site was established during the Late Classic period in a relatively empty buffer zone located between the centers of Blackman Eddy and Camelote. The group contained a large eastern shrine, a feature associated with ancestor-related concepts and ritual that may have provided the prestige and legitimation necessary for its intermediary role. Further, the site was built with a ballcourt, a feature normally found in much larger sites. The ballgame and associated rituals are often affiliated with prestige, alliance maintenance, and warfare and would have provided the appropriate social contexts for marking of the proposed district boundaries.

Conclusion

The initial studies of Maya settlement in western Belize and northeast Petén provided a basic model for understanding Maya settlement and sociopolitical organization in the region (Bullard 1960; Willey et al. 1965). More recent investigations by the Belize Valley Archaeological Project have enabled this model to be further refined. Patterned distributions of the major centers located along the river indicate that some "districts" were located at consistent intervals of 9.9 km. Furthermore, smaller sites or minor centers were consistently located at points approximately equidistant between these larger centers. Traditionally, minor ceremonial centers have been perceived as a rural manifestation of a detached population of elites that serve the ritual needs of a rural population. Recent studies of minor centers have shown that there is considerable variability in the roles of these sites (Iannone 1996; chapter 17). In the Belize Valley, five minor centers are each positioned midway between major ceremonial centers. This pattern is consistent all the way from Camelote on the east to Xunantunich on the west (map 4). The consistency of this pattern suggests that it is not random and that because of their intermediate position, each enjoyed a certain amount of autonomy. In the case of four Type 3 sites, Esperanza, Floral Park, Nohoch Ek, and Warrie Head, they were inhabited not by detached elites of a centrally controlled hierarchy, but rather by rural families expressing agricultural success through precocious rural architecture.

The florescence at these locations is a Late Classic phenomenon. Only Floral Park and Nohoch Ek appear to have occupation predating the Late Classic. At both sites, this pre–Late Classic occupation is minimal and the bulk of the architectural construction is of the Late Classic period. Construction at Esperanza and Ontario dates exclusively to the Late Classic. Dates for the constructions at Warrie Head are currently unknown.

While the concept of empty buffer zones or "no man's land" between settlement concentrations has been noted in various theoretical models (Puleston 1974; Sanders 1981; Willey 1956b), other than at Ontario, these empty buffers are not present at the midpoints between the major centers of the Belize Valley. In fact, the opposite seems to be the case. The midpoints between Cahal Pech–Xunantunich, Cahal Pech–Baking Pot, and Baking Pot–Blackman Eddy contained fairly dense settlements of successful farmers that expressed their prosperity through the construction of relatively substantial architecture. The presence of these Type 3 sites adds to our understanding of the variety in the sociopolitical functions of what have been traditionally referred to as minor centers.

Notes

1. To help differentiate the research efforts described herein, the term "middle Belize River Valley" will be used to separate the current study area from those to the west. Although relatively arbitrary, it covers the topographically similar zone extending from where the floodplain begins to level out and widen just west of Baking Pot and continues east to the Cocos Bank/Roaring Creek area. This usage differs only slightly from previous valley descriptions (cf. Ball and Taschek 1991; Ford 1990; Hammond 1974).

2. Note that the densities for Spanish Lookout and Ontario are quite similar to those Puleston (1974:308) encountered in his settlement survey at Tikal. He identified 1.97 structures per hectare ($197/km^2$) in residential areas, and 0.88 structures per hectare ($88/km^2$) in the intersite areas (as defined by earthworks, etc.). Obviously, the differences between Puleston's extensive data set (the Tikal/Central Petén region), survey methods, and sophisticated calculations (e.g., factoring out of bajo areas) and those from the much more limited estimates from the middle Belize Valley result in the data not being directly comparable. However, while the comparison between the Ontario and Tikal settlement densities is largely intuitive, the densities appeared close enough to be noted.

Acknowledgments

Much of the data from which this chapter was constructed have been presented in numerous interim reports by members of the Belize Valley Archaeological Project. We would like to thank the following for their contributions at many levels: M. Kathryn (Kat) Brown, James M. Conlon, Owen Ford, David M. Glassman, Christopher J. Hartman, Diamond Kaphandy, Jennifer K. McWilliams, F. Kent Reilly, Kevin L. Schubert, Lauren A. Sullivan, and Stephen (Waldo) Troell.

19

The Terminal Classic to Postclassic Transition in the Belize River Valley

James Aimers

Both the Terminal Classic and the Postclassic in the Belize Valley have been characterized as times when squatters and small, village-level groups lived in and around abandoned Classic period centers (Adams 1973; Andrews V and Sabloff 1986; Freidel 1986a; Hammond 1974; Walker 1990; Webb 1973). However, information about the Terminal Classic and Postclassic in the Belize Valley is limited compared to more advanced research on this era elsewhere in the Maya area (Andrews V and Sabloff 1986; P. Rice 1986). To date, only a handful of articles have been published on the Belize Valley that directly focus on the end of the Classic period (Bullard 1973; LeCount 1999; Schmidt 1976/77; Willey 1973). Some information comes from the site of Tipu on the Macal River, but Tipu is better known for its Late Postclassic and Historic period components (Graham 1987a; Graham et al. 1985, 1989; Jones 1989; Jones et al. 1986; Simmons 1995).

Current information suggests a "patchwork" quality to occupation in the Terminal Classic (Michaels 1989:161), with great variation in ceramics and architecture on a site-by-site basis. Terminal Classic ceramics are often found in contexts that suggest the reuse of collapsed or deteriorating architecture from the Late Classic or earlier (Culbert 1973). However, the Terminal Classic in at least some areas of the Belize Valley was a time of relatively robust activity. Excavations at the peripheral Zotz group at Cahal Pech uncovered sherds of Terminal Classic Miseria Appliquéd and Early Postclassic Maskall Unslipped (Aimers 2002b; Gifford 1976:fig. 201). Excavations in 1996 and 1997 in the site core of Baking Pot revealed substantial renovations of Late Classic architecture associated with Terminal Classic ceramic types such as Cayo Unslipped jars with piecrust rims (Gifford 1976:fig. 180g). Similar Terminal Classic diagnostics were uncovered in excavations in the site core of Cahal Pech (Jaime Awe, personal communication 2000, 2002), a site previously thought to have been almost deserted by A.D. 800. A cursory examination of sherds from Ontario Village, Floral Park, and Blackman Eddy revealed substantial quantities of Daylight Orange: Darknight Variety and some sherds of Miseria Appliquéd and Pabellon modeled-carved (Sabloff 1975:figs. 384–385), all considered markers of the Terminal Classic. Finally, excavations by the Western Belize Regional Cave Project have demonstrated that Terminal Classic ceramics are common in caves in western Belize (Jaime Awe, personal communication 2000).

The Postclassic in the Belize Valley is generally considered a period of even greater decline than the Terminal Classic, and remains of this period are rare. Willey (1973:101) suggested that the Early Postclassic "squatters" of Barton Ramie produced "crude and slovenly" ceramics and no new buildings. Nevertheless, many of the Postclassic ceramic types (particularly Augustine Red) are of fine quality and perhaps more than half of Barton Ramie's Classic period population level was maintained into the Postclassic (Culbert 1988:84). Excavations in both the site core and on the periphery of Baking Pot revealed Early Postclassic Augustine Group ceramics in substantial quantities (Aimers 2002b:fig. 11.7), and lesser quantities of Middle and Late Postclassic types such as Palmul incised and Paxcaman Red (Carolyn Audet, personal communication 1998; personal observation). Caves in the Belize Valley have produced Middle Postclassic ceramics reminiscent of those from Lamanai (e.g., at Yaxteel Ahau, Jaime Awe, personal communication 2000), Mayapan, and Tulum (Schmidt 1976/77). Joseph Ball (personal communication 2000) has reported a Late Postclassic "Chen Mul Modeled Mayapan-style effigy-censer depicting a cotton armor-clad warrior" from the front of the central pyramid-platform at Cahal Pech. Overall, however, Postclassic ceramics are rare in the site cores of Belize Valley sites other than Tipu.

Interpretations of the Postclassic New Town phase stress that status differences were less marked than in the Classic period. Correspondingly, elite architecture and paraphernalia characteristic of Late Classic times were produced in diminished quantities, if at all. Tainter (1988) and others characterize this not so much as a "collapse" but as an adaptive societal response to conditions that made the high costs of maintaining an elite undesirable or impossible. Reasons put forth for this change usually in-

clude agricultural-demographic factors, endemic warfare, or some combination of environmental and social factors like these (Culbert 1988;
Sabloff 1973; Sabloff and Willey 1967).

Archaeologists have long noted that the "collapse" occurs at about
the same time that external influences in the southern lowlands intensify
(Sabloff and Rathje 1975). Earlier theories stressed invasion by "Mexicanized Maya," Putun, Chontal, or Itza Maya from the Gulf Coast and
Yucatán (Thompson 1970), while more recent ones have tended to suggest
the influence of changing trade routes and relationships involving these
people (Sabloff and Rathje 1975; Willey and Shimkin 1973). The articulation of trade, warfare, population movement, and population reduction is
a complex but important question for Belize Valley archaeologists investigating the era.

Archaeological data may not provide a clear-cut explanation for the
collapse, and the causes of Terminal Classic-to-Early Postclassic changes
probably varied from region to region (and possibly site to site) in the
Maya area. Whatever the causes, archaeological data in the Belize Valley
and adjacent regions of the Petén indicate reduced populations and a leveling of status with "a continuing peasant population in the outlying communities after the cessation of activities in the ceremonial centers" (Willey
et al. 1965:578).

Stylistic Change in the Terminal Classic–Early Postclassic

Change in the Terminal Classic and Early Postclassic can be approached in
terms of new forms that suggest new activities, but most of the changes in
Terminal Classic–Early Postclassic transition are stylistic rather than functional. Definitions of style are numerous and contested, but style can be
seen as "a form of non-verbal communication through doing something
in a certain way that communicates information about relative identity"
(Wiessner 1990:108). Style is frequently seen as a form of nonverbal behavior, a communicative component of ceramic form that is inseparably
intertwined with function and technology (Sackett 1977; Wobst 1977).
Because of its communicative quality, the use of style in archaeology beyond chronology has primarily been to extrapolate information regarding boundaries and interaction, and the relative identity of individuals or
groups. Given the evidence for increased interregional interaction after the
Classic throughout Mesoamerica, style is relevant to the questions archaeologists have about the Terminal Classic and Postclassic. Although archaeologists in the Belize Valley and elsewhere frequently point out the limita-

tions of stylistic ceramic typologies (especially type-variety) in the reconstruction of culture history and process (A. Chase 1994), style remains central in archaeological assessments of interregional interaction, and is likely to remain so.

The issues are complex because "the connections between material culture and social identity are not always direct" (Masson 1997:229) and although sources of stylistic change may be external, they do not always correlate with population replacement. In approaching these issues, Bill (1997:397) has distinguished between features of material culture that represent identity (sociocultural affiliations) and those that reflect identification (sociopolitical connections). Style may also change for reasons that appear to be little more than matters of fashion or taste. Technology may take on a new appearance but continue to be used in traditional ways, and new forms, even in times of great change, often mask old ideas (Bricker 1981:177–179). Many recent treatments of style stress its contextual nature: style is used consciously to express identity when it is advantageous to do so, or expressed unconsciously when there are no disadvantages (Shennan 1989).

Finally, "as social systems evolve in complexity, so do the determinants of style" (Wiessner 1990:108). Thus, social and historical data are useful in understanding the nature of stylistic differentiation, yet these are precisely the data we lack. For example, the association of specific styles with ethnic groups requires the existence of ethnicity itself, a social category the ancient Maya may not have recognized and that may emerge only in state-level societies or in situations of intergroup stress (Burmeister 2000; Gellner 1983; Hegmon 1998).

Although the association of style with groups of people is problematic, a thorough investigation of this issue is important because the Belize Valley is located between the Petén region and the northern Maya area and shows stylistic connections to both areas in the Terminal Classic–Early Postclassic. Several scholars have noted that "foreign" or "Mexican" symbolism in the Maya area may have denoted socially advantageous external ties, whether real or fictive (Freidel 1979; Stone 1989). The stylistic imitation of more powerful groups has been recognized in various places (Costin and Hagstrum 1995), especially when this provides some advantage. Alternatively, frontier groups may resist the adoption of new artifact types and innovations in situations where resistance has some advantage, or where groups are in competition, as in times of war. Furthermore, people in different factions of the same social or ethnic group may adopt either of these strategies. Thus, the Belize Valley can be approached as a zone of interaction in which individuals used material culture in different ways in pursuit of different goals.

New Forms and Functions in Ceramics, Architecture, and Lithics

A number of new forms, including grater bowls, griddles, C-shaped structures, plaza-central platforms, and side-notched points, are the clearest indicators that the Belize Valley Maya were in closer contact with regions to the north and west after the Classic than they had been previously. Grater bowls occur first in the Terminal Classic at Barton Ramie (Gifford 1976:282) and Xunantunich (Thompson 1940:fig. 46h), but they are more common in Postclassic Augustine Red and Paxcaman Red (fig. 19.1). They are thought to have originated in the Preclassic in central Mexico (e.g., in the Tehuacan Valley) (Chadwick 1971). Griddles are another form that appears earliest in central Mexico and imply changes in diet and cooking. Feinman et al. (1984:335–336) suggest that the introduction of griddles in the Valley of Oaxaca is linked to changes in both diet and work: "They probably went from eating corn in bowls, as mush or cereal, to making tortillas. . . . This is the kind of thing you would expect if people were going out to the field and bringing their lunches. . . . [I]f agriculture were becoming more intensive and [people] no longer had time to go home for lunch."

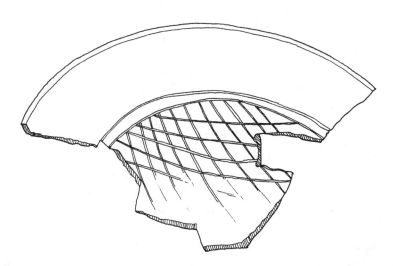

Fig. 19.1. Paxcaman Red grater bowl, Tipu Lot T-142 (vessel diameter ca. 25 cm). Slip is brick red (10R to 2.5YR 4/6-8). Drawing by James Aimers.

Intensive agriculture may not be the best explanation for the adoption of the griddle in the Terminal Classic to Early Postclassic Belize Valley. Instead, farmers may have traveled farther to suitable agricultural land, and desired food that is more portable. A more dramatic explanation is ethnic change: people from central Mexico or areas that were strongly influenced by central Mexico (such as the Gulf Coast) may have moved into the Belize Valley, bringing their cooking traditions with them.

Architecture

Part of the problem in using ceramics to assess boundaries and interaction among groups is the portability of pots. Architecture, in contrast, is not portable, and both domestic and ritual architectural styles have been shown to be good indicators of sociopolitical identity (Low 1995). Because architecture is a context for activity, it has a profound psychological impact (certainly more than dishes) and people often expend considerable energy building in styles that convey their identity, especially in new locations (Wren and Schmidt 1991).

If ceramics are any indication, we can expect that the Postclassic architecture of the Belize Valley to be similar to that of Petén, that is, small, poorly made, and difficult to detect (D. Rice 1986:304–305). Willey (1973: 103) found some evidence of Postclassic construction during excavation of housemounds at Barton Ramie (BR-35 and BR-123), but evidence is rare.

A diagnostic Terminal Classic architectural form is the C-shaped structure (Bey et al. 1997). C-shaped structures in the Petén Lakes District (D. Rice 1986:325, fig. 9.5), Seibal, and Uxmal "may be related to the southward expansion of northern influence" (Bey et al. 1997:15). C-shaped structures appear at Seibal in the Tepejilote phase (A.D. 650–830) and especially during the Bayal phase (A.D. 830–930), while Ixlu has C-shaped buildings by the Terminal Classic (D. Rice 1986:17). C-shaped bench structures occur also at Lamanai and Cozumel (Freidel 1983:15). D. Rice (1986:334) has observed that at "Barton Ramie, Structures BR-19 and BR-145 are both 'plazuela' type mounds which might qualify as C-shaped structures" (Willey et al. 1965:164–165). To date we have no additional evidence for these structures in the Belize Valley, but this may change as more excavation of nonmonumental architecture is undertaken.

Another diagnostic Terminal Classic architectural form is the plaza-central platform. Tourtellot et al. (1992:91–92) suggest that radial plaza-central platforms were dance platforms, and he considers them a Chontal trait at Seibal. Ricketson (1931:4) noted such a platform (Mound N) at

Baking Pot, and the heavily disturbed remains of Mound N were recorded by the author in 1997 and 1998. A ceramic sheet midden at this location contained some of the few Postclassic ceramics uncovered in the site core, including an Augustine Red grater bowl fragment and the only piece of Hubelna Unslipped griddle found at Baking Pot. This unusual platform is similar to forms known from both ceremonial and residential contexts at Mayapan (Proskouriakoff 1962:136) Smith (1962:221–222). Mound N is not on the central axis of the plaza but rather on axis with range Structure F, making the parallel with Mayapan stronger. The assemblage resembles Postclassic range structure/central platform assemblage found throughout the lowlands and often considered a central Mexican or Gulf Coast influence (Leventhal 1983; Smith 1962).

Lithics

Other artifacts that emerge in the Terminal Classic and Early Postclassic include small side-notched points (Aimers 2002b:fig. 11.8). Hammond (1982:70) has suggested that they were brought to northern Belize by the "southward migrating Itza," and they may indicate changes in hunting, possibly in forest that reclaimed abandoned land. Ethnohistoric accounts suggest that these small points were also used in warfare, and the larger side-notched points of the Middle Postclassic at Tipu were "probably designed for use with atlatls or spears" (Graham 1991:324; Masson 1997: 304). The large number (over 100) of fist-sized granite "grooved stones" found at Baking Pot in surface levels may also have been bola-like weapons or mace-heads (Aimers 2002b:fig. 11.8). Lithics could represent evidence for conflict in the Terminal Classic–Early Postclassic of the Belize Valley and cultural changes linked in some way to central Mexico.

Stylistic Change

While new artifact forms are rare, substantial stylistic changes occur in the ceramics of the Belize Valley in the Terminal Classic and Early Postclassic. It is worth emphasizing, however, that stylistically the upper Belize Valley is a united ceramic region from the Preclassic into the Postclassic, showing strong links to the Petén. Even the much-noted change in ceramic style in the Early Postclassic is shared between the Petén and the Belize Valley: the presence or absence and proportions of types among sites varies significantly but not the stylistic attributes of these types.

Of particular importance is the establishment of reliable Terminal Classic diagnostic ceramics by LeCount (1996) and others. A second issue is

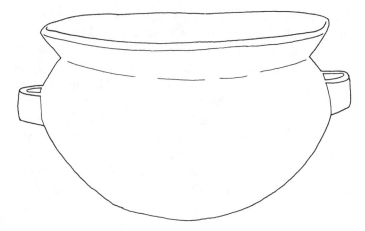

Fig. 19.2. Augustine Red collared Jar, Tipu Lot T-245. Slip is orange-red (10YR 6/2-3). Vessel diameter ca. 32 cm. Drawing by James Aimers.

the level of "continuity and disjunction" in the ceramics of the Late Classic–Terminal Classic–Early Postclassic. Virtually everyone who has written about the New Town ceramics suggests that they represent a significant break with the styles of the past (Bullard 1973:241; Willey et al. 1965: 384–390). Changes include the appearance of scroll and trumpet feet, collared jars (fig. 19.2), a reduction in polychrome vessels, and a (possibly linked) appearance of incising reminiscent of Cehpech ceramics of the Yucatán Peninsula. The magnitude of this ceramic disjunction is debatable and worthy of closer consideration.

Late Classic–Terminal Classic Continuity and Disjunction

After the Classic, scholars have noted the appearance of ceramic motifs and techniques variously called "Mexicanizing," "Putun," "Chontal," or "Itza," implying that there is increased interaction with the Gulf Coast and the Yucatán Peninsula (Fox 1980; Rice 1983). Incising instead of the painted decoration characteristic of the Classic is common in the application of these motifs, which include scrolls, interlocking scrolls, serpentine, and mat motifs, among others (Rice 1983). Pabellon Modeled-Carved is the best-known example of the application of this new iconography. The widespread distribution of these motifs throughout Mesoamerica in the Postclassic led Robertson (1970) to consider them an "International Style" (Nicholson 1981; Smith and Heath-Smith 1980).

These motifs and techniques are interesting for their implications regarding interregional interaction, but stylistic borrowing by the Maya did not begin with the Terminal Classic. Two Teotihuacan-style Early Classic vessels found in Early Classic levels at Baking Pot (Pucte Brown and Lucha Incised) are typical, and examples can be drawn even from the earliest pottery of the valley (e.g., Kanocha and Cunil) (chapters 3 and 7). For the Terminal Classic, Daylight Orange: Darknight Variety (Gifford 1976:fig. 199) is perhaps the best example of a pottery type that confounds attempts at neat stylistic (and chronological) categorization. Originally considered an Early Postclassic type, stratigraphic assessment has more recently placed this type in the Terminal Classic Vaca Falls Group. The most common Daylight: Darknight form is a flared dish that is morphologically consistent among sites and almost identical to the forms of Late Classic types such as Roaring Creek Red and Belize Red. The slip is a vibrant waxy orange, similar to Preclassic slips, with decorative black fireclouding. In the Belize Valley (but not in the Petén), the paste adds to the confusion by appearing to be transitional between the bright orange, medium-to-fine paste of Early Postclassic Augustine Orange (which tends to have few inclusions) and the coarser, darker red-brown of many Classic types. If asked to categorize Daylight Orange: Darknight Variety in the absence of context, I would guess it to be an Early Postclassic (Augustine-like) type. Yet Daylight Orange: Darknight Variety is not found in secure Early Postclassic contexts where they are available (e.g., at Macanche and Tipu). Daylight Orange: Darknight Variety appears to be an example of stylistic hybridization by the potters of the Belize Valley, who applied a slip and surface treatment reminiscent of Preclassic styles to an elaboration of a Classic period form and a hybrid paste.

For the most part, the ceramics now associated with the Terminal Classic can also be considered elaborations of Classic types. LeCount (1996) has pointed out that in the Terminal Classic, Mount Maloney Black bowl lips become flatter (more horizontal), and Cayo unslipped jar rims become more elaborate, with extremely everted or piecrust lips. McRae Impressed ashware bowls presage the Postclassic styles (e.g., Topoxte Red) in the presence of notched basal flanges and tau-shaped feet. The ring bases of the Classic and earlier become more pronounced in the Terminal Classic and beyond.

The two most notable additions to the Terminal Classic repertoire are Modeled Carved vases and Miseria Appliquéd censers (typically in the form of spiked bowls). Tourtellot et al. (1992:91–92) have suggested that spiked censers at Seibal were a Chontal trait, and Modeled-Carved is typically considered an imitation of Fine Orange. Beyond these new types, the main argument for Late Classic to Terminal Classic disjunction has been settlement discontinuity: the absence of Terminal Classic ceramics at many sites.

Concomitant with an increase in incised types in the Terminal Classic is a reduction in polychromes. Forsyth (2000) has noted that the incised wares seem to be inspired by the northwest Maya area, and thus in the Terminal Classic, we see a reversal of ceramic influence: the Petén sites seem to be receiving influence from the northwest rather than the opposite.

Terminal Classic to Early Postclassic Continuity and Disjunction

Early Postclassic ceramics are rarer than those of the Terminal Classic, suggesting a decline in population in the Belize Valley at this time. Stylistic discontinuity between the Terminal Classic and Postclassic is also greater than between the Late and Terminal Classic, suggesting more significant changes in both ceramic production and consumption.

One of the problems in assessing Terminal Classic to Early Postclassic (dis)continuity is the lack of good stratigraphic separation between ceramics assigned to these phases. In the Baking Pot site core, the elaborate unslipped jar rim forms and other diagnostics of the Terminal Classic were found mixed with Early Postclassic types. The Terminal Classic and Early Postclassic interdigitate elsewhere as well, for example at Tayasal in the Petén (A. Chase 1986) and at Lamanai (Pendergast 1986:227). Unfortunately, well-stratified Terminal Classic to Postclassic sequences are rare in the Belize Valley, and these are needed for assessments of the period.

Censers are another aspect of the discontinuity between the Terminal Classic and Early Postclassic at Tipu. No censer material has been found in Early Postclassic contexts, while censers of various types are found up to the Terminal Classic, and in the Middle and Late Postclassic. This may reflect sampling error at Tipu, but at Macanche (Rice 1987:table 7), a site that has a similar assemblage, only four of 173 censer fragments were uncovered from Early Postclassic versus Late Postclassic contexts.

The salient diagnostic of the Postclassic in the Belize Valley and Petén is the scroll or slipper support on tripod dishes (fig. 19.3). In the Belize Valley, the scroll foot is found on Augustine Red tripod dishes in the Early Postclassic and later on Paxcaman Red and Topoxte Red. Notably, the scroll foot is less common as one moves north (e.g., only a handful have been noted at Lamanai). Although the scroll foot is commonly considered a new introduction in the Early Postclassic, I believe that this form is a

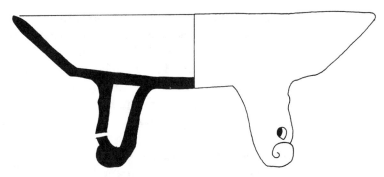

Fig. 19.3. Augustine Red tripod dish with scroll feet, Tipu Lot T-143. Slip is orange-red (10YR 6/2-3). Vessel diameter ca. 28 cm. Drawing by James Aimers.

simplification of zoomorphic effigy feet that can be traced to the Preclassic in the Petén and the Belize Valley (Aimers 2002b).

Another change in the Early Postclassic is a reduction in vessel size, especially dishes and jars, possibly linked to smaller family/corporate groups (Bill 1997:16; Rice 1987:100). At Tipu, there are some indications that Augustine Red tripod dishes change through time, with the feet becoming narrower and the height of the vessel sides decreasing. P. Rice has used such changes in part to separate a Middle Postclassic (Neblina) complex (A.D. 1150–1300) from earlier complexes: "That the changes are primarily dietary rather than strictly social is suggested by modifications in food production technology in the Postclassic period that are specifically correlated with these smaller plates: these include the appearance of molcajetes or 'chile-grinding' bowls, net or line sinkers for fishing, and the disappearance of large chipped stone 'standard bifaces' from Postclassic lithic assemblages" (1987:100). The smaller and lighter New Town pottery may also suggest increased mobility in the Postclassic (Fry 1989:106).

Jars in the Early Postclassic exhibit vertical or almost vertical collared rims, a stylistic change from flared rims that would appear to have little functional significance. Striation on jars is replaced by handles after the Terminal Classic throughout the Valley, a change that may be, as at Altar de Sacrificios "functionally and culturally significant" (Adams 1971:141). Handles are present in Preclassic Belize Valley pottery, and some Postclassic types are similar to Preclassic types (e.g., Postclassic Vitzil Orange-Red Ware is virtually indistinguishable from Preclassic Mars Orange Ware). The readoption of handles in the Postclassic may be part of a larger pattern of ceramic atavism also seen in the surface treatment of Daylight Orange: Darknight Variety.

There is continuity between the Terminal Classic and Early Postclassic ceramics as well. Ash continues to be used as temper, although the Tipu sample suggests that ash declines in the Early Postclassic and rebounds somewhat in the Middle Postclassic and Late Postclassic. As noted earlier, ring bases become taller and more flared through time, as in the "chalice" forms characteristic of Lamanai (Graham 1987a). Some ceramic types (e.g., Achote Black) may have been produced without interruption through the Late Classic into the Postclassic.

The most dramatic changes in the Terminal Classic–Early Postclassic transition lie not in ceramics but in settlement. Current indications are that the majority of known sites in the Belize Valley were not in use in the Early Postclassic, or they had minimal occupations, as at Baking Pot. However, as excavations continue beyond monumental site cores in the valley, there is little doubt that we will become increasingly aware of Postclassic occupation, as it is predominantly on the periphery of site cores and along rivers.

Interpretations

The artifacts of the Belize Valley do not resolve the "smoldering scholarly debate" regarding "intrusion versus . . . in situ evolution" in the Terminal Classic and Early Postclassic (Fox 1987:3). For the most part, the artifacts of the Belize Valley in the Terminal Classic and Early Postclassic are hybrids, a result of neither incremental development nor radical change. Hybrids can be seen as either continuous or disjunctive, but by definition, they synthesize elements of different origins. This is one of the reasons that it is more useful to think of the Terminal Classic–Early Postclassic "collapse" as a transition. It is a process, not an event.

The length and accomplishments of the Classic period are indications of a relatively inward looking, integrated, and stable society. Relatively, of course, since we know trade was widespread and warfare common. Dispersed over the territory now occupied by five countries, the Maya had trade opportunities with various regions, but largely among people who would have identified themselves as Maya despite their linguistic and regional differences. Similarly, warfare seems to have been largely a local affair. The Terminal Classic evidence suggests to me a less stable period of increased interregional contact and decreased cohesion within regions, and some actual immigration of peoples from the north and west.

Evidence for conflict in the Belize Valley continues to accumulate, including an almost life-sized bound captive monument recently excavated near Saturday Creek (Jaime Awe, personal communication 2000). Modeled- (or molded-) carved vessels frequently represent the presentation of a bound captive to an elaborately attired person (Ball 1997:173; Miller 1976:233). Artifacts that may be weapons and the frequency of defensible site locations in the Terminal Classic suggest that conflict and warfare may be a factor in the abandonment of others.

More clearly, however, sites that survived into the Postclassic often had locations advantageous for canoe trade, and were often associated with desirable resources. Jones (1989:140) states that "the wealth and importance of Tipu, clearly, rested upon its success as a producer of fine quality cacao." Barton Ramie, Baking Pot and other Belize Valley sites are also suitable for cacao production (Muhs et al. 1985). Still, so little data is available on the period that anything beyond this is speculative.

The earlier fall of another inward-looking society, Teotihuacan, may have created new opportunities for aggressive "Mexicanized" Maya from the Gulf Coast, who gradually pushed south and east, with varying effects. To one side of the Belize Valley, in northern Belize, we see evidence of large-scale destruction and death, as well as what might be called colonial architecture (D. Chase and A. Chase 1982) in contrast to continuity and even florescence at Lamanai. To the west there is a similar range, from the possibility of an invading foreign elite at Seibal (most recently thought to be from Ucanal) (Schele and Mathews 1998) to the continuity of ceramics at Macanche and Tayasal. The impact of movements from the Maya highlands is another factor to be considered, but this is currently poorly understood (Hammond 1978). The evidence suggests that the impact of interregional contact may have to be assessed on a site-by-site basis.

No site in the Belize Valley has provided dramatic evidence like that of Seibal or Nohmul, but stylistically the artifacts of the Belize Valley frontier do change. In some cases, they do this relatively gradually (Daylight: Darknight) but from the distance that archaeology forces upon us we can see that the change is great compared to earlier periods. Grater bowls and griddles suggest changes in cuisine that can be reasonably related to the physical presence of "foreign" people in the valley. Ceramic styles related to northern Belize and Yucatán less convincingly indicate foreign presence but at least suggest that the Belize Valley Maya were familiar with exotic styles and adopted them eagerly.

There is no question that many sites are abandoned in the Terminal Classic. Massive migrations to Yucatán (forced or voluntary) seem unlikely, and there is no evidence yet of wholesale slaughter or disease, but where exactly the people go is a problem that artifacts in the Belize Valley may not answer. An overstressed environment, disease, and warfare (all of which may be linked) may have reduced the Belize Valley population, and many people may have moved to the north for greater opportunities in and around the emerging power centers there.

As research accumulates, we are finding that despite a decline, there were still substantial Terminal Classic populations in Belize, but the traditional collapse chronology of 100 years (between A.D. 800 and 900) taxes the resolution of the archaeological record compared to longer periods. Furthermore, the collapse period may have lasted up to three hundred years based on stelae and abandonment. A period of 10 or 15 generations in which influences are adopted gradually at some sites and not at all at others is feasible. The adoption or nonadoption of "foreign" traits at different loci may indicate that some sites were occupied by people with affiliations to the north and northwest, while the population of other sites may have remained more locally derived and identified.

Gifford's statement that "the relative decline in [New Town] ceramics is one of the sharpest ever witnessed anywhere" (Sharer and Chase 1976: 288) can only be considered hyperbole by anyone who has handled sherds from the Augustine Red and Paxcaman Red groups, which rival all but the finest Classic wares. Their forms and motifs suggest that the Maya of the Belize Valley, like their neighbors to the north and west had been drawn into (or were on the fringes of) an increasingly cosmopolitan culture. The ceramic styles of the Postclassic in the Belize Valley show a renewed emphasis on religious rather than political themes (Freidel 1983:297; Rice 1983) and art in general seems more portable and less restricted in distribution, as does religious paraphernalia (Thompson 1970:164).

The ceramics of the Belize Valley change with those of the Petén, while similarities with northern Belize are present but less pronounced, as are imports. Ethnohistoric accounts for Tipu correlate with archaeological evidence that suggests the Maya of Tipu were linked to the Itza Maya of the Petén Lakes District, especially Tayasal (Chase and Rice 1985:148). This affiliation may have been a factor in the survival of Tipu. Scholes and Thompson (1977) have noted that 73 of 92 names recorded in a mid-17th-century census at Tipu were Yucatec. Archaeologically, "Tulum-like incision has shown up on one or two sherds from core [at Tipu]—that is, an incised technique that is characteristic of sites such as Lamanai and Tulum but not characteristic of sites in the Petén. A sherd from a Middle Postclassic diagnostic 'chalice' form, first identified at Lamanai, has also been recovered from the Dozier [H12–12] core. If the ceramic sample so far is any indication of the total Postclassic ceramic inventory, then traditions of the Petén, Belize, and the northern lowlands are represented at Tipu" (Graham 1984:3). The Late Postclassic pottery of the Maya is the most consistent of all the Maya eras, sharing similar forms and styles from south to north. This homogenization appears to have its roots in at least the Terminal Classic, and is perhaps related to a relatively constant population movement that may be even older (Graham 1994:325). By the Late Postclassic it seems reasonable to speak of a Postclassic "world system" in which styles and motifs were shared widely across Mesoamerica, and the few people left in the Belize Valley were full participants in this phenomenon.

By the Middle and Late Postclassic the Belize Valley was sparsely populated and at least partially reclaimed by forest. After European contact and into the 19th century, the Belize Valley was a frontier and a region of refuge from the Spanish, with small settlements like Tipu sited in densely forested areas and along rivers. Jones (1989:21) notes that in frontier locations like Tipu there is "movement of ideas, individuals, goods, and activities back and forth between places, a movement often hidden from the watchful eyes of those who seek to monitor it." Today we have just begun to recognize the Maya of this spatial and temporal frontier.

Acknowledgments

Almost every archaeologist working in the Belize Valley contributed to this research, but I am particularly grateful to Jaime Awe for over a decade of support and encouragement. I would also like to thank Elizabeth Graham for her generosity with the Tipu data and her assistance with this research generally.

20

Polities, Politics, and Social Dynamics

"Contextualizing" the Archaeology
of the Belize Valley and Caracol

Arlen F. Chase

What constitutes a Maya "political system?" How large were Maya polities? And how were they organized? Mayanists are currently wrestling with these questions with opinions ranging from centralized states to balkanized polities to hegemonic empires (Ball 1993, 1994; Ball and Taschek 1991; A. Chase and D. Chase 1992a, 1996c, 1998a; D. Chase et al. 1990; Culbert 1991, 2000; Fox et al. 1996; Marcus 1993; Martin and Grube 1995; Sanders and Webster 1988). Basic to this topic is a consideration of how archaeologists define political and cultural units and the interactions among them (e.g., "boundaries," "areas of influence," and "cultural spheres").

This chapter seeks to briefly examine the archaeological relationships between two geographically and environmentally distinct regions: the upper Belize Valley and Caracol, the valley's huge and influential neighbor to the south. It is clear—based on ceramics, burial patterns, and settlement—that the upper Belize Valley and Caracol are archaeologically different. Yet it is also evident, based on the known epigraphic data, that Caracol must have had a great impact on the upper Belize Valley, probably even at the level of having included this area within the Caracol political sphere for a substantial period of time following A.D. 631, when Caracol subsumed Naranjo into its political orbit (A. Chase and D. Chase 1998a, 2000). Through comparing and contrasting what is known about the archaeology of Caracol with that of the Belize Valley, it is possible to make some comments regarding the interpretation of archaeological data with regard to polities, political boundaries, and their changing nature over time.

Interpreting Ancient Settlement and Politics

Settlement archaeology in the Maya area had its recognized beginnings in the upper Belize Valley (Willey et al. 1965). Thus, it is a fitting locale from which to digress briefly into an assessment of the current state of settlement research in the Maya area—and of the relationship between settlement and political organization.

The primary goal of settlement archaeology has been to understand how humans have distributed themselves over a given landscape (e.g., Ashmore 1981). For the most part, settlement archaeology has incorporated an ecological approach that examines the relationship of environment or natural landscape factors to the physical location and density of human settlement. This, in turn, has led to the development of predictive models for the location of settlement (e.g., Ford 1986) and even terraces (Fedick 1994) based on factors such as terrain, soil, and water. A cultural approach also has been a part of settlement archaeology in the Maya area; attempts are made to place the settlement area under investigation into a wider social system, often with a focus on political economy or political hierarchy. However, most settlement work has not pursued wider issues, instead focusing on the function of specific buildings or groups (e.g., Becker 1982) and/or the proposed nature of the household unit (Wilk and Ashmore 1988) or other corporate group (Gillespie 2000). The visibility of ancient constructions on the settlement landscape has contributed largely to such interpretations.

Although the relationship between environment and settlement may be relatively easy to define, understanding social dynamics confronts practitioners of settlement archaeology with a host of perplexing problems on both methodological and theoretical levels: ancient populations must be reconstructed for numbers and status, excavation methodology must match stated goals, and functional interpretations must be incorporated into broader theory (A. Chase and D. Chase 1990, 2003). While it may be simple to identify nodal settlements in the Maya area—the kinds of sites that came to be called "major" or "minor" centers (Bullard 1960)—the unanswered, and sometimes unasked, question is, Do such nodes fit into a larger regional picture? And if they do, how? This in turn raises the question of whether what is defined as a region in terms of settlement archaeology (e.g., A. Chase 1979; A. Chase et al. 2001; Willey et al. 1965:25) or as a polity in terms of epigraphy (e.g., Martin and Grube 1995; Mathews 1991) represents an actual cultural or political entity. How does the settlement system being investigated fit into a larger context? Or, does it?

Settlement archaeology results in maps of visible constructions and other remains, but there is a major debate over the degree to which all is visible on the ground surface of a Maya site (e.g., Culbert and Rice 1990). For if all is not visible on the surface, how can social interpretations be made? The simplest solution to this problem is to assume that all archaeological remains are visible on the ground surface—an assumption that is patently false. Alternatively, one could assume that all "hidden structures" pertained to a single lower level of society—an assumption that is, at best, undocumented, especially given the vicissitudes of time and landscape. To be fair, most researchers in the Maya area currently attempt to test for hidden structures as part of their research designs. Further complicating the interpretation of mapped surface remains, however, is the difficulty of identifying the function of structures based solely on surface form without excavation. Buildings are often arbitrarily designated as "domestic" and "ceremonial" because of the general difficulty in inferring more complex functions without extensive (and intensive) excavation. Even if extensive excavations are undertaken, this does not necessarily guarantee that absolute function can be determined (D. Chase and A. Chase 2000a).

Certain typically utilized methodological aspects of settlement pattern research are unfortunately ill-equipped to deal with questions of social organization or social variability (A. Chase and D. Chase 1990). A test pit, the standard mode of excavation in settlement research, usually provides only an idea of chronology and of the kinds of remains that may be found at a given locus; this kind of investigation often does not provide the kind of information that lends itself to making interpretations of status and social variability, let alone economic organization.[1] The intensive investigation of entire groups—involving both widespread horizontal stripping and deeper penetration, such as has been done at Tikal (M. Becker 1999; W. Coe 1990; Haviland et al. 1985; Jones 1996), Copan (Webster 1989; Webster and Gonlin 1988; Webster et al. 2000), Caracol (A. Chase and D. Chase 2001b; Jaeger 1991), Seibal (Smith 1982; Tourtellot 1988), and Santa Rita Corozal (D. Chase and A. Chase 1988)—is more rarely undertaken often because of financial constraints. Yet it is generally only through combining these intensive investigations with other archaeologically gathered data that social questions can be answered.

To model a social system, one needs to define relationships among groups at a single site and among neighboring sites, and thus, one needs to undertake settlement archaeology. However, the identification of political units and their boundaries is not a simple matter. While mapping may reveal settlement drop-off and, therefore, the presumed physical boundaries of a given settlement, it does not necessarily identify the boundaries of social, political, or economic interaction. Thus, survey, excavation, and detailed analyses of material remains (from ceramics to hieroglyphic writing) are critical to this endeavor.

Heuristically useful models, adapted to settlement situations, can result in caricatures of the Maya political situation. For instance, the application of central place theory to Maya occupational concentrations or architectural nodes can produce a perception of equal geographical polities or units with little horizontal integration. Some archaeologists (e.g., Blanton et al. 1993:164), in fact, see each Maya political unit as having "a radius of thirty-three kilometers, roughly a one-day journey on foot," meaning that each polity is conceived as centering about a single major or minor architectural site. Military theory related to warfare suggests a slightly larger unit of maximum territorial control in the Maya case—60 km beyond any central node, given considerations of terrain and foot transport (A. Chase and D. Chase 1998a). However, a focus on territorial control centered on major or minor centers can mask other potential polity forms, such as the hegemonic empire of the pre-Conquest period Aztec (Hassig 1985, 1988).

Hieroglyphs are also commonly used to make interpretations about the nature of Maya political units. A version of central place theory employs "emblem glyphs" to demarcate polities (Mathews 1991). Epigraphically based models of Maya political organization have, with few exceptions (Marcus 1976; Martin and Grube 1995), been directly adapted to a Greek-like city-state model (Mathews 1991). An assumption is generally made that each emblem glyph represents an independent polity (a postulate that is not necessarily true). Because emblem glyphs are generally associated with specific sites, these sites have been advanced as focal points for separate Maya polities. As the distribution of any specific emblem glyph is relatively limited (usually corresponding to a single site), the areal extent of interpolated polities is also viewed as being limited. Interpretations of Maya social boundaries based on this view of emblem glyphs and on postulated evolutionary processes have produced a "balkanization" model that sees the fragmentation of the Maya lowlands into increasingly smaller polities as the Late Classic era progresses (Dunham 1990). However, it is now evident that some sites share emblem glyphs (e.g., Tikal and Dos Pilas; Houston 1993), that a single site can have more than one emblem glyph (e.g., Yaxchilan; Mathews 1988), and that one emblem can potentially control another (Martin and Grube 1995). Thus, no one-to-one correspondence between emblem glyph and polity can be assumed. In fact, the real meaning of an emblem glyph—whether it was kinship-based, religious, territorial, or something else—remains to be determined.

Just as certain Maya political models derived solely from epigraphy or general theory have their problems, so too do those political models derived from a cursory examination of archaeological data alone. Attempts have been made to organize the Maya politically based on considerations of plaza group or "courtyard" counts (Adams and Jones 1981) as well as architectural scale (Adams 1981). Such archaeologically based schemes, however, are handicapped by unequally mapped (and excavated) Maya sites and thus can lead to simplistic and, usually, incorrect conclusions. Adams's (1986) version of large regional Maya polities, while probably correct in a broad sense for limited periods of time, needs modification given new epigraphic and archaeological data that suggest the possibilities of both larger and smaller political units.

Conceptions of Classic Maya polities are sometimes cast in potentially inappropriate Western modes of thought. For instance, Maya polities often are viewed as comprising contiguous territory. Yet the composition of the Aztec empire demonstrates that Pre-Columbian polities may not always have been so easily bounded (Hassig 1988). Thus, following the Aztec model, some Mesoamerican polities could have presented a patchwork appearance of loosely joined units, which hop-scotched over other independent states but expanded to include areas far removed from any central core. And there is no reason that Maya polities could not be similarly constituted.

Often, models for social, political, and economic organization are borrowed from outside the Maya area. Examples found in Maya archaeology include the use of temperate zone feudalism (Adams and Smith 1981), tropical zone galactic polities (Demarest 1992), and Western-style urbanization (Sanders and Webster 1988). The categorization of Maya sites as "regal-ritual centers" or "regal-ritual cities" (Ball and Taschek 1991; Sanders and Webster 1988; Taschek and Ball 1999) has been lauded by some and extensively critiqued by others (A. Chase and D. Chase 1996c; D. Chase and A. Chase 1992b; Marcus 1993, 1995). Particularly telling are that differing interpretations have resulted from the use of the same data framework by separate researchers. While there is nothing overtly wrong with this, it does clearly indicate the need for more refined data collection; it also may indicate that the database is not appropriate for the models being used and the questions being asked.

In spite of half a century of professing interest in settlement studies, we actually know very little about Maya settlement and the organizational systems that must have defined it (A. Chase and D. Chase 2003). Central architecture has been mapped and excavated, and long-distance transects have been laid out and tested according to sampling designs (Ford 1986; Puleston 1983). But large areas of non-epicentral architecture are rarely mapped in their entirety and archaeologically tested. We need this kind of archaeological data to be gathered first before we deign to understand Maya political systems and their relationships. Otherwise, we will continue to use preconceived models and solutions without knowing or understanding the full extent of our database.

Unlike much of the Maya area, both Caracol and the Belize Valley have been blessed by years of continuous and widespread research. Thus, reasonable databases are available from each area and it should be theoretically possible to make some statements relative to the political interdependence or independence of these two regions.

The Caracol Polity

To understand the Caracol polity, one needs to look at the epigraphic and archaeological data that have been recovered from Caracol (fig. 20.1), its outlying region, and neighboring sites. The boundaries and relationships of the Maya who inhabited Caracol can be explored through an examination of the archaeological record in terms of ceramics, architectural plans, settlement layout, burial practices, epigraphy, and the distribution of certain goods and features. Obviously, this is a complicated set of factors to be considered. But the conjunction of a multitude of variables is necessary to interpret the past situation, for a single focus view is likely to warp any conclusions that are offered.

Caracol is blessed with numerous hieroglyphic texts as well as carved and plain stone monuments. These texts have significantly enriched our understanding of Caracol's past in ways that archaeology alone cannot. We can talk about a dynastic history stretching back to A.D. 331 (A. Chase and D. Chase 1996b:table 1, 2000b; Grube 1994; Houston 1987). We can talk about the accomplishments of different rulers and attempt to relate them to the archaeological record. We can understand Caracol's rise during the transition between the Early and Late Classic eras through

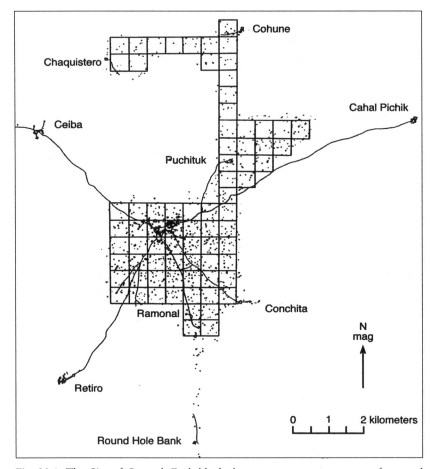

Fig. 20.1. The City of Caracol. Each blocked square represents an area of mapped settlement 500 × 500 m. Lines that cross the grid blocks are causeways that integrate Caracol's settlement by connecting several rings of outlying termini groups directly to the site epicenter.

its success in warfare (A. Chase and D. Chase 1989; D. Chase and A. Chase 2000b). We also can tentatively begin to understand some of the interpolity intrigue involving Tikal, Guatemala and Site Q (Calakmul?) that characterized Caracol's rise to power (A. Chase and D. Chase 1998a, 2000; Grube 1994; Martin and Grube 2000). We can examine Caracol's intense relationship with the Guatemalan site of Naranjo. All of this wealth of political information and propaganda can be garnered from the site's texts.

Epigraphy alone cannot provide the full story of Caracol. Hieroglyphic texts primarily record dynastic details pertaining to the site's "royal" echelon, yet little information is gained from this database that pertains to the vast majority of Caracol's population, and even less is gained from the epigraphy concerning how the site was organized politically or economically. Even when the epigraphy can be clearly read, it does not fully answer questions of royal relationships or, perhaps, even mirror political reality. For instance, Caracol rulers are named in monuments both at Naranjo and at La Rejolla, but does this mean that Kan II "lived" at Naranjo or that Smoke Skull "lived" at La Rejolla? That hieroglyphic texts focusing on Caracol individuals and dynastic events occur at Naranjo is fact. But could such texts have been moved there from Caracol? And for what purpose? Obviously, other information is necessary to consider these questions. It is only when other archaeological data are combined with epigraphic information that we understand the impact that the "Naranjo wars" (A.D. 626–636) had not only on Caracol but also on Naranjo and, by extension, the upper Belize Valley. The dates for the Naranjo wars are correlated with a burst of monument activity at Caracol and a general lack of stone monuments at Naranjo (other than those that deal with Caracol individuals). When the Naranjo epigraphic record burst forth again, it was under the auspices of a foreign female who gave birth to an heir that established a new dynastic line. Thus, a break in the textual record of a site can be conjoined with other information to interpret meaning more fully. Major war events at Naranjo and earlier at Tikal correlate with an extended lack of stone monuments at both sites following the respective events. This has been interpreted as meaning that the political orders of both sites may have been subject to external control. Yet a lack of stone monuments cannot be directly correlated with subjugation and war events as can be seen in the Late Classic excavation record of Caracol, where such an absence is correlated with substantial population and prosperity—and, potentially, an internal change in political organization (D. Chase and A. Chase 2000b). Nor can epigraphic statements of alliance and authority be assumed to be entirely accurate without other confirmation, especially as such statements are, after all, pronouncements intended to mollify, control, and impress in the arenas of politics and propaganda. However, epigraphy can provide a framework that can be revised and augmented by other archaeological data.

Likewise, not all connections among sites are indicated in stone monuments. Epigraphic texts must be conjoined with a wide variety of data sets to interpret relationships within and among sites more completely. For instance, although few texts directly link Caracol and the southeast Petén around Ixkun and Ixtutz, the burial practices and settlement information recovered by Juan Pedro Laporte (1991, 1994) and his cohorts (Laporte et al. 1989) place this entire area within the Caracol archaeological tradition. Both areas share a settlement emphasis on eastern focus plaza groups and the widespread use of tombs; ceramically, the areas are also similar. Thus, even though epigraphic data are lacking, the archaeological data are highly suggestive of the direct connection of this region with Caracol. A consideration of site hierarchy and spatial proximity are also indicative of control of this area by Caracol, especially when viewed in terms of scale and intrasite integration. In the future, the detailed settlement data currently being collected by Laporte (1996, 2001) for the southeast Petén may possibly be used to fix the southern and eastern boundaries for a Classic era Caracol polity.

Certain goods and features also can prove to be useful in interpreting boundaries and relationships. I have previously demonstrated that tomb volume can be used in the Caracol region as a way of inferring both status and site hierarchy (A. Chase 1992). Other archaeological indicators are also useful. Caracol has specific ritual traditions that can be used to archaeologically identify its populations. These traditions include an east structure focus in over 60 percent of the site's residential groups, the widespread use of tombs associated with the eastern structure, and residential caching practices that use specially formed ceramic containers, called "face" caches and "finger" caches (A. Chase 1994:174; A. Chase and D. Chase 1994; D. Chase and A. Chase 1996, 1998). Such ritual practices are either infrequent or unknown from Tikal, Copan, Coba, and other excavated Maya sites outside the Caracol area. However, finger caches have been recovered at Cahal Pech (Awe, personal communication 1994; chapter 8). Thus, it is possible that the ritual occurrence of this caching complex at this Belize Valley site is part of a Caracol connection. Similarly, while minimal terracing is known from the Belize Valley (Fedick 1994), the distribution of widespread agricultural terracing appears to have centered on Caracol (A. Chase and D. Chase 1998b). Extrapolating from this fact, it is possible that the practice of terraced agriculture in the southern lowlands may further provide some spatial indication of Caracol's sphere of influence during the Late Classic era.

Lack of certain objects may also be significant. Caracol does not share in the widespread pattern of ceremonially depositing eccentric flints, a practice that is found throughout many lowland sites (Coe 1959, 1965) and especially in the Belize Valley (Morris, personal communication; Willey et al. 1965; chapter 5). Rather, one finds the fairly regular use of crude obsidian eccentrics both in the site epicenter and in the residential groups located in the extensive site core (D. Chase and A. Chase 1998). Also, as noted above, other excavated sites do not apparently share in Caracol's proclivity for specialized cache vessels, especially associated with eastern structures in residential plaza groups. Presumably such ritual differences may prove significant in any determination of relationships. Conversely, multiple and/or disarticulated burials found at a number of Belize Valley sites may suggest further ties with Caracol. However, exactly how these associations reflect sociopolitical relationships is unclear, for it is conceivable that different distributions may reflect a combination of an intentionally created identity and increased prosperity at Caracol.

Caracol and the Belize Valley

Where, then, does this leave us in any attempt to understand relationships between Caracol and the upper Belize Valley during the Classic period? For the most part, there is little in the way of Belize Valley epigraphic texts that can guide such a consideration. This is understandable given the differences in scale between the two areas. Caracol is at the summit of any hierarchical arrangement while the sites in the Belize Valley, for the most part, comprise the middle and lower end of any defined hierarchy. Caracol was one of the major players in the Late and Terminal Classic eras, while most of the sites in the upper Belize Valley were either small independent units or pawns within other polities. Although Xunantunich erected some stone monuments, these all date to the last part of the Classic period and unfortunately contain little information that can be related directly to dynasty or political connections.

It has been argued based on ceramic affiliation and proximity that Belize Valley sites were under the control of Naranjo for most of their history (e.g., Ball and Taschek 1991). This assumption, however, cannot be tested without excavation at Naranjo. The epigraphic evidence, though, indicates that Naranjo was under the direct sway of Caracol for approximately 50 years from A.D. 631 to 680 (A. Chase and D. Chase 1998a). Thus, if Naranjo were in control of the upper Belize Valley, then epigraphic interpretation would suggest that Caracol was in fact the valley's ultimate overseer for at least a similar period of time. This assumption, however, also requires further archaeological testing and support.

Even though methodological questions remain over the degree to which uniformity in material remains (including settlement) can be used to suggest cultural and political boundaries, certain things can be said about the archaeological relationships expressed between the upper Belize Valley and Caracol. The upper Belize Valley was never a full participant in the Caracol cultural tradition. It may have been under Caracol control, but the settlement pattern, architectural layouts, ceramic subcomplexes, and burial practices all place it as an area culturally peripheral to or distinct from the Caracol archaeological tradition. Based on archaeological data recovered by Paul Healy (1990, 1999), Pacbitun (located 40 km from Caracol's epicenter) may represent the northernmost known extension of the complete Caracol tradition (as represented primarily by ceramics and burial patterns). Excavations by the Department of Archaeology at Ponces (Morris, personal communication) to the northeast of Pacbitun suggest that this area was beyond the direct Caracol ritual sphere in the Late Classic era, given the eccentric flints recovered in the site's caches. Further to the west, epigraphic evidence suggests that Ucanal, Guatemala was a border town between the Late Classic Naranjo and Caracol spheres; Late and Terminal Classic individuals from Ucanal are discussed as prisoners on both the monuments of Naranjo (Schele and Freidel 1990) and Caracol (A. Chase et al. 1991). Recent excavations at Ucanal have revealed ceramic assemblages that are consistent with those found at Caracol, but a surprising lack of burials in its excavated residential groups, something inconsistent with both the Caracol and southeast Petén archaeological data (Laporte and Mejia 2002). However, epigraphic texts suggest that Ucanal must have spent much time under direct Caracol administration; its distance from Caracol, some 28 km, make this plausible. Preliminary publication of archaeological data from Arenal (Las Ruinas, 35 km north of epicentral Caracol) suggest that it was outside of the Caracol sphere in the Late Classic era and had only minimal Terminal Classic overlap (Taschek and Ball 1999). However, the more northern site of Cahal Pech exhibits part of the Caracol cultural tradition in having finger bowl caches; thus, some direct relationship between Caracol and Cahal Pech during the early part of the Late Classic period is archaeologically plausible. For the most part, the Late Classic ritual patterns recovered from Arenal and the other sites of the Belize Valley differ from those known from Caracol (Taschek and Ball 1999:227), potentially indicating Naranjo's control of the upper Belize Valley after A.D. 680 in accord with its epigraphic resurgence.

Ceramics have often been used to suggest cultural affiliations. Analysis of available ceramic data suggests that there is no simple relationship among Naranjo, Caracol, and the upper Belize Valley. Like the Belize Valley, Caracol has a widespread and common distribution of Belize Red wares throughout its Late Classic history; in fact, Belize Red is one of the more common mortuary types at Caracol and may have ultimately been manufactured somewhere in the Caracol political system (A. Chase 1994). Yet the rest of Caracol's ceramic assemblages are divergent from those found in the Belize Valley (Gifford 1976; LeCount 1999). How, then, is this to be interpreted in terms of social relationships between the two areas?

A variant of Holmul style red-and-orange-on-white pottery may have been manufactured at Buenavista in the Belize Valley for distribution either locally or to other locales further afield (Reents-Budet 1994). Taschek and Ball (1992) suggest that such pottery was within the purview of the elite, arguing that more elaborate examples, such as the "Jauncy Vase" from Buenavista del Cayo, were distributed by the Naranjo royal elite as special gifts to loyal local lords (chapter 9). Houston et al. (1992) point out that the artist of the Buenavista cylinder, on which the name of Smoking Squirrel of Naranjo appears, also named an Ucanal lord on another of his cylinders; Reents-Budet (personal communication 1994) has shown, however, that the pastes on these two cylinders are different, implying they were made (if not painted) by different individuals. Taschek and Ball (1992, 1999:231) would see the presence of such epigraphic vases at sites as direct gifts of owned possessions by a royal ruler to either a peer or a lesser noble, thus implying political affiliation (see also Grube and Schele 1990). To me, however, this is too direct an application of a presentation or gift-giving model to what was likely a much more complex situation. Indeed, the naming of individuals on this pottery may not have been a mark of personal possession by a given ruler at all, but rather a form of advertising or support, much like the modern-day possession of a Walt Disney World "Mickey Mouse" hat. We need to know much more about the distribution and manufacture of these goods before we take the hiero-glyphic readings literally. The archaeological record at Caracol also proves potentially instructive on this point, for it indicates that Holmul-style red-on-orange-on-white pottery was locally available to a broad portion of Maya society during the Late Classic era. At Caracol, although limited in amount, it has a wide distribution at the site and is not restricted to the elite. In fact it is usually encountered in outlying residential groups in cist or crypt burials, but not in tombs. Individuals buried with these ceramics also are not characterized by the "palace diet" as determined by stable isotope studies of bone (e.g., A. Chase and D. Chase 2001a). Thus, the inferred social associations of such pottery and the overarching application of any presentation models are called into question by the Caracol archaeological data.

The recovered settlement data and site layouts of the upper Belize Valley are also different from that of Caracol and are suggestive of the distinctive political history of this area. However, the site plans of both Cahal Pech (Healy and Awe 1996; chapter 8) and Xunantunich (chapter 10) exhibit the use of causeways; those at Cahal Pech are more dendritic than those at Xunantunich and thus similar to those found at Caracol. The limited amount of terraces reported from this region (Fedick 1994) is also suggestive of "filtered" Caracol contact.

Caracol's settlement is continuous and evenly spaced over a huge area (A. Chase and D. Chase 2001a). The placement of its plaza groups implies both bureaucratic control of these residential settings (A. Chase and D. Chase 1998b) and a population who did not consider themselves to be militarily threatened. This continuous settlement amid extensive terrace systems has been followed for almost 10 km to the north of the Caracol epicenter. This evenly spaced and continuous Caracol settlement (see fig. 20.1) contrasts greatly with that thus far recorded in the upper reaches of the Belize Valley.

In the foothills above and around the modern town of Cayo and beyond the fertile river valley investigated by Gordon Willey so long ago, the settlement is concentrated in small nodes with only a sparse scattering of outlying plazuela groups. Even the site of Buenavista del Cayo, argued as being "open" by Ball and Taschek (1991), shares this concentrated settlement pattern. Xunantunich is placed on what is a militarily defensible summit. Based on the spacing seen between architectural centers and the noncontinuous nature of the residential settlement, it may be suggested that the upper Belize Valley was not well integrated politically. As the land in this region is generally quite fertile (e.g., Ford and Fedick 1992), there is no agricultural reason that its settlement should be so sparse and yet so nodal in appearance. The main settlements in the upper Belize Valley—Cahal Pech, Buenavista del Cayo, and Xunantunich—are fairly compact and situated on ridges or promontories with concentrated surrounding residential settlement. I would argue that what is being seen in the settlement of the upper Belize Valley is exactly what one might expect for a border area—a settlement response to a contested region. Control of the upper Belize Valley presumably switched back and forth between different polities and, at certain times in its history, it probably formed the first line of defense for an area that was subjected to extensive raiding by groups attempting to commandeer trade goods coming up the Belize River. The central Belize Valley, with its almost continuous settlement in the riverine alluvial terraces, was seemingly less affected by any political maneuvering and, in fact, may have prospered the most when the region was left to its own political devices.

Conclusion

In spite of differences of scale, it is useful to compare the archaeology of Caracol with that of the upper Belize Valley. Strikingly apparent are the differences that exist between the two areas. When such variability is explored, it becomes clear that Maya settlement and ritual patterns were often directly related to political or social situations. At Caracol the settlement distribution provides a situation of uniform spacing almost as if zoning laws were in effect, presumably indicative of a well-integrated political system (A. Chase and D. Chase 2001a; A. Chase et al. 2001). In the upper Belize Valley, settlement location was also dictated by political and social exigencies; the many smaller nodes that exist indicate that the area was probably not well integrated politically. Caracol also enjoys a ritual unification of its Late Classic population (A. Chase and D. Chase 1994, 1996b) that is not evident at other excavated Maya centers but that, at least partially, permeated the upper Belize Valley in the early part of the Late Classic period. In my estimation, the volume of work that has been undertaken in the upper Belize Valley and neighboring areas like Caracol, especially since settlement archaeology was formally started in the Belize Valley some forty years ago, is finally permitting settlement research to move beyond the simple ecological correlations and functional identifications that have dominated the field. With the amount of settlement work that has been carried out in western Belize we are finally poised to move beyond speculation and to use a solid body of archaeological data to examine questions of political and social relationships and their reflection in Maya antiquity in a way that is not possible elsewhere in the Maya area.

Notes

1. It should be noted, however, that test-pitting is preferable to solely using surface collections as a basis for higher order interpretations.

Acknowledgments

The research at Caracol, Belize, has been funded by a multitude of sources, including the University of Central Florida, the government of Belize, the United States Agency for International Development, the Harry Frank Guggenheim Foundation, the Dart Foundation, the Ahau Foundation, the Stans Foundation, FAMSI, the National Science Foundation (Grants Nos. BNS-8619996; SBR-9311773; SBR-9708637; DBI-0115837), and private donors.

21

Diverse Voices

Toward an Understanding of Belize Valley Archaeology

Diane Z. Chase

The archaeological research that has been undertaken in the Belize Valley and the chapters included in this volume provide a snapshot of lowland Maya settlement archaeology. This is appropriate, as the Belize Valley was the site of Gordon Willey's seminal settlement archaeology at the site of Barton Ramie, the first project intentionally focused on Maya settlement archaeology and the nonelite segments of Maya society.

While the focus of research in the region may have varied over the years, the Belize Valley is one of the longest and most intensively worked regions in the Maya lowlands. It is distinct from other long-term research—such as that at Tikal, Copan, or Palenque—in that the focus of the majority of the investigation has been on settlement as well as on minor or intermediate-sized sites rather than on major centers. This research emphasis is related to both the nature of the settlement in the Belize Valley and to the ease of working south of the Belize River and in the area near the modern town of San Ignacio.

This volume and the investigations in it focus on many different topics related to settlement pattern studies and Maya archaeology. They also raise many questions. The chapters run the full gamut from culture history to methodology and theory. Terminological differences are also apparent, especially as seen in the multiplicity of architectural typologies (e.g., major centers, minor centers, ceremonial centers, regal-ritual centers) that are used and in the varying opinions about what is considered to be "royal" and about which sites housed royalty as opposed to elite inhabitants. Topics considered here include all time periods and both the origins and "collapse" of Maya civilization. Several chapters focus on the earliest remains in the valley and the degree of internal and external involvement in these early remains, especially as expressed in ceramics. A number of chapters also discuss the Terminal Classic period, some noting the existence of incomplete construction efforts. Still other chapters focus on the Classic and Postclassic occupation of the valley.

Functional interpretations are also raised. Authors concern themselves with difficult questions such as the determination of ethnicity. Potentially problematic interpretations and topics include the identification of ritual feasting as well as dedication and termination events in opposition to more neutral functional inferences based on use-related on-floor debris or refuse. Middens are discussed but are not always clearly distinguished from redeposited structure fill or more temporally distinctive refuse. Not all authors are in agreement with regard to these functional interpretations. And it would seem that more effort should be expended in clearly identifying and operationalizing the distinctions among the various interpretations.

The chapters in this volume incorporate the use of different kinds of analysis, ranging from iconography (chapter 11) to specific material remains such as ceramics (chapter 19). And some chapters attempt to include all of the separate reports synthetically, while others are more specialized. There are different research approaches in this volume. Some authors have had a predominantly regional perspective (chapter 15). Others have focused on differences within and between minor centers and larger centers (chapters 17 and 18). Researchers also have varied in their approach to sampling. The scale of survey varies substantially from region to site. Likewise excavations vary in size and scale from test pits to trenches to larger areal clearing. No single project covers the entire Belize Valley area, yet there is enough information from the different research projects to attempt synthetic interpretations. There is, however, some disagreement among these syntheses (for example, see chapters 10 and 12).

Of particular interest is the interpretation of the political integration of the Belize Valley. There are differing interpretations offered by volume participants. It is necessary to consider variations in researchers' databases in assessing differences in interpretations. One impediment to the assessment of site integration in the valley is the sparse monument record. The majority of sites and the majority of the occupation in the valley existed without any significant use of hieroglyphic texts, leaving much of the Belize Valley outside of strict Maya historical perspective. Thus, there is heavy emphasis on both stratigraphy and ceramic associations. Other questions that arise include the definition of "community." How tightly integrated was the valley settlement? And what was the relationship between the Belize Valley settlement and the areas beyond it? Given the nature of the archaeological remains in the Belize Valley, can these data help us assess the different models of Maya social and political organization that are now in use? These topics will be returned to following a brief discussion of the individual chapters.

The Voices of Belize Valley Archaeology

Arlen Chase and James Garber (chapter 1) provide a summary of the history of settlement research in the Belize Valley. They further subdivide the valley into headwaters (upper Belize Valley) and valley proper (middle Belize Valley) and define significant geographical and settlement differences between these two areas. The settlement in the headwater area is formed by definable sites, such as Cahal Pech, Buenavista del Cayo, and Xunantunich, that are all characterized by sparse intersite settlement. The settlement that follows the Belize River is more continuously and densely spread along the bank of the Belize River, as Willey and his colleagues (1965) originally noted. Both Blackman Eddy and Baking Pot comprise larger architectural nodes within the alluvial lands that immediately flank the river.

Gordon Willey's wonderful retrospective essay (chapter 2) provides historical perspective to the volume. He describes the earliest attempts to do settlement archaeology and the difficulty of cutting transects through the jungle. He also demonstrates how important opportunistic sampling and survey was to settlement archaeology at Barton Ramie, for he conjoined his archaeological research program with the clearing of the site of overgrowth for agricultural purposes. In describing his work with Linton Satterthwaite and William Bullard, his chapter makes it clear how successful archaeological research is often based on the interactions and good relations among field researchers. He also makes it evident that there is historical tradition even in watering holes for Belize's archaeologists. Willey found out about the site of Barton Ramie in the social setting of the Western Club. Both the Western Club and the Stork Club have been relocated since Willey's times. The Stork Club, now located in the San Ignacio Hotel, is still a popular place for the exchange of news and ideas for Belize's archaeological community on Friday evenings.

James Garber and his colleagues write about the Middle Formative period occupation at the site of Blackman Eddy (chapter 3). They focus on their salvage investigations of a mound partially destroyed by a bulldozer cut in the 1980s. These investigations encountered Middle Formative (Middle Preclassic) occupation that they date to between 1100 and 850 B.C.; the authors further suggest that this material predates the early Jenney Creek materials at Barton Ramie. The authors then enter into a discussion concerning the local versus nonlocal origin of these early ceramics and what this might mean for considerations about the ethnic composition of the earliest Maya in the Belize Valley—a topic previously considered in some depth by Joseph Ball and Jennifer Taschek (2000). However, more archaeological data (other than ceramics alone) need to be obtained to resolve this complex issue. Garber and his colleagues also describe what they interpret to be ceremonial ritual that resulted from feasting. While problematic for later eras in Maya prehistory, their interpretation of ritual feasting may be appropriate for this time horizon, location, and evidence.

James Garber and his colleagues also discuss the broader project at Blackman Eddy, one of the major architectural nodes in the Belize Valley proper (chapter 4). They present a map of the site's core. An area measuring 200 m × 95 m formed the focus of their investigations, resulting in the partial excavation of 12 structures. As indicated in their initial article, the earliest occupation at Blackman Eddy dates to the Middle Formative (1100 B.C.); occupation, however, continued through the Late Classic period. The authors plausibly suggest that Blackman Eddy was the administrative center for Barton Ramie, which is located only 2 km distant. The excavations at Blackman Eddy produced typical Belize Valley remains as well as some surprises, such as a non-lowland Maya style eighth-cycle monument. However, an Early Classic interment (of approximately the same date as the monument) encountered in Structure A4 indicates that Blackman Eddy interments are consistent with broader patterns seen at both Caracol and Tikal in that this interment consisted of a primary individual combined with secondarily interred individuals.

James Conlon and Terry Powis report on their investigations of the Bedran Group, located 2.27 km southwest of the architectural concentration known as Baking Pot (chapter 5). Unfortunately, it was not possible to survey the area between these two groups to determine if there was continuity in settlement. A variety of burials and caches were recovered from excavations in the Bedran Group. Notable burial offerings include one ceramic vessel that exhibits hieroglyphs that form a "primary standard sequence." Burials 9 and 11 in the Bedran Group include both primary and secondary human skeletal remains, the latter interpreted as being the result of sacrifice. A cache in front of Structure 2 included chert and obsidian like that found earlier by Bullard in the center of Baking Pot. This clearly significant group is described both as a "minor center" and as a "larger plazuela group," thus reinforcing the problematic nature of the architectural typologies used in the Belize Valley. Differing opinions on architectural typologies constitute a recurring topic in many of the articles in the volume.

Lisa Lucero and her colleagues (chapter 6) use the land evaluation model originally established for the Belize Valley by Scott Fedick (1996). They look at the relationship between settlement and land classification types in a study area of 308 km² (although their project did not attempt to survey this entire area but, instead, considered known sites). Of the sites in the survey area, Saturday Creek served as a focus for their archaeological investigation. They confirmed a general correlation between good soil and settlement location in this study area. Just as interesting as the correlation of land types and settlement, however, are the exceptions that they note, such as Cara Blanca, a site that was likely situated for reasons other than agriculture. The study also shows that many areas with soils well suited for farming were not settled, suggesting that the Belize Valley area as a whole had additional room for population growth.

Paul Healy and his colleagues (chapter 7) describe the Early and Middle Formative at Cahal Pech, a medium-sized Maya center first occupied between 1100 and 1000 B.C. They define the various material culture remains associated with these excavations and indicate that the earliest ceramics at Cahal Pech are similar to those of the Jenney Creek complex at Barton Ramie. Among the more distinctive remains recovered at Cahal Pech are over 300 figurine fragments from assorted secondary contexts. Their analysis also suggests a change in lithic production from spar flakes to blades at some point between 650 and 330 B.C. Stable isotope analysis of human remains suggests that there was a diverse diet at Cahal Pech with less reliance on maize than in the succeeding Classic period. The authors use stable isotope data to suggest the existence of social distinctions by sometime during the Middle Formative period. There is cranial deformation and inlays in interments during this time along with a series of pathologies; however, the authors suggest that porotic hyperostosis, indicative of anemia, is more common in the subsequent Classic period. Discussion of ritual activity focuses on both burials and caches as well as on circular platforms thought to have been used for public performance.

David Cheetham (chapter 8) discusses the Zopilote terminus group, located 750 m south of the Cahal Pech site core at the end of the Martinez

Causeway. He attempts to place the Zopilote group within a broader context of other known terminus groups. However, Cheetham only focuses on one potential terminus pattern, arguing that "terminus groups represent the fusion of two disparate classes of architecture—distant temple buildings and causeways" and that causeways were not cosmological because there are not standard causeway directions (based on angles). However, his generalizations are not always matched by comparative data. His Caracol examples represent only residential plazuela groups and do not account for different kinds of known termini or their diverse functions (e.g., A. Chase 1998, A. Chase and D. Chase 1996c:fig. 3). Another source of comparative data on causeways and terminus groups is an issue of Ancient Mesoamerica (2001) dedicated to the topic. Cheetham also focuses on the excavation of Structure A-1, outlining its occupation history and defining the contents of Tomb 1 (which he ties to warfare because of iconographic representations of warriors on one vessel and the presence of a skull) and Tomb 2 (with its associated and ritually repositioned early stela). Significantly, this structure contains evidence of some ritual patterning similar to that found at Caracol, including multiple finger-bowl caches as well as the secondary interment of individuals.

Joseph Ball and Jennifer Taschek (chapter 9) provide an overview of the occupation of Buenavista del Cayo. It is located on the Mopan River within 5 km of Cahal Pech and 6 km of Xunantunich. It is 13 km from El Pilar and 14 km from Naranjo. The site is a medium-sized center covering 18 hectares. Ball and Taschek call it a "level 9" site, following an earlier typology of centers proposed by Hammond (1975). Buenavista del Cayo's earliest occupation dates to the Middle Preclassic. Ball and Taschek believe, based on the Buenavista data and comparisons to other sites covered in this volume, that there was not a smooth development from the Preclassic to the Classic period; they argue for discontinuities in ceramic types. Further changes took place during the Late Classic period. Three caches in Structures 2, 3, and 4 are suggested as having "activated and empowered the Buenavista Central Plaza complex as the sacral heart of the center." Tikal and Caracol ritual data have similarly been used to suggest the centering functions of certain epicentral caches (D. Chase and A. Chase 1998:325–326). They also further document the existence of a "palace school" of decorating polychrome ceramics at Buenavista (see also Ball and Taschek 2001). Interestingly, Terminal Classic household occupation at Buenavista contains ceramic vessels and types that Ball views as being similar to northern coastal Yucatec ceramics.

Richard Leventhal and Wendy Ashmore (chapter 10) write about the importance of using a large-scale broad regional approach in settlement archaeology. They focus on Xunantunich and on their five years of archaeological research at that site. Their Xunantunich Archaeological Project employed a strategy of both intensive excavations and survey transects, one of which reached a length of 8 km. They argue that the predominant occupation of Xuanantunich occurred between A.D. 650 and A.D. 1000, when the site occupied a preeminent position in the valley. In arguing for the predominance of Xunantunich and its hierarchical overshadowing of both Cahal Pech and Buenavista, the authors significantly disagree with Ball and Taschek (1991; chapter 12) over the social and political ordering of the upper Belize Valley.

Virginia Fields writes about the iconography of Xunantunich using the modeled stucco from Structure A-6 (chapter 11). Her analysis indicates both the local style of Xunantunich and the relationships of aspects of the stucco friezes to iconography elsewhere in the Maya world. She shows that the symbolism at Xunantunich focuses on rulership, particularly on the ruler as the axis mundi of the community and on the relationship of the ruler to the Maya gods and the acts of creation. Her detailed iconographic study is unique to the volume and shows the value of conjoined interdisciplinary approaches to ancient Maya remains.

Jennifer Taschek and Joseph Ball discuss the relationships that must have existed between the sites of Buenavista del Cayo, Cahal Pech, and Xunantunich (chapter 12). They suggest how these sites, each with their own distinct occupation history, were at the same time part of a single system. They review the Late and Terminal Classic occupation at each site before attempting a synthetic interpretation. They elaborate on previous interpretations that Cahal Pech and Buenavista were occupied by the same high elite or royal group with one site (Cahal Pech) serving a more private function and the other (Buenavista) serving a more public function; they further suggest the possibility of varying seasonal occupation. They suggest that Xunantunich was established as a holy place during the reorganization of the valley following the 7th-century defeat of Naranjo by Caracol. They believe that Xunantunich superceded Buenavista and became a year-round residence during the eighth and ninth centuries. While at odds with interpretations made by Leventhal and Ashmore, Taschek and Ball indicate that their interpretations are only hypotheses that require additional testing.

Paul Healy and his colleagues describe the archaeology of Pacbitun (chapter 13). This site is not in the Belize Valley but in the distant foothills that bound the south side of the valley. Healy and his colleagues suggest that the site has ties both to the Belize Valley (especially given the predominance of head to the south interments) and to Caracol (in terms of burials containing multiple individuals). They suggest that the site had a population of between 4,000 and 8,000 people circa A.D. 700–900; looking at their settlement data, I suspect that this number may be high. The site has an E Group that was previously identified as relating to cosmic geomancy rather than to astronomical factors (Aimers 1993). The possible non-astronomical functions of E Groups have been explored previously by others (Aveni and Hartung 1989; A. Chase 1985; A. Chase and D. Chase 1995).

Healy and his colleagues also describe a Late Classic "royal" burial at Pacbitun (chapter 14). This chapter goes hand in hand with two earlier chapters by M. Coe (1988) and A. Chase (1992) that define royal interments at larger sites. Those chapters, along with the current one, bring to the forefront a consideration of what "royal" means. Characteristics of this interment include a bed of chert flakes over the chamber's slate slab roofing as well as a large number of burial offerings. Included in the tomb were 19 ceramic vessels as well as beads, earflares, complete spondylus shells, and cinnabar. The head of the individual was placed to the south. The tomb measured 3 m in length by 1 m in width. Although not overly spacious in terms of Caracol or Tikal standards, the burial offerings included in the chamber are plentiful. Moreover, this variation in tomb size is consistent with concepts of site hierarchy; Pacbitun is a center smaller than Caracol or Tikal and, thus, potentially had a lesser "nobility." Slate tomb roofing is not common at Caracol, but was used for an early chamber at one of the outlying elite groups (Tulakatuhebe) near the Pajaro-Ramonal terminus; like Pacbitun, this chamber likely housed a member of the site's lesser nobility.

Anabel Ford writes about El Pilar, a site first occupied in 700 B.C. in the Middle Preclassic period. El Pilar ceased to be occupied between A.D. 900–1000, as indicated by an incomplete Terminal Classic construction (chapter 15). She estimates that the site occupies 50 hectares of land and that the core of the site exhibits a density of 200 structures per square kilometer. Her settlement survey indicates differential occupation in three major resource zones; settlement density is higher in the valley and ridge-lands but low in the foothills. Her work is important for understanding production and consumption activities in the Belize Valley and for an examination of hierarchical relationships among sites both within and bordering the Belize Valley.

Heather McKillop's chapter on the trading port of Moho Cay is an excellent reminder of the importance of trade in the Maya lowlands (chapter 16). Moho Cay is strategically located in the mouth of the Belize River, with access to both coastal and riverine trade. It would have formed a transshipment point for materials going upriver to be off-loaded in the Belize Valley headwaters or for materials coming out of the interior. Excavations confirm participation in both coastal and riverine trade during the Late Classic period, relating to both long distance and more local Belize trade. Moho Cay had access to marine resources as well as goods from more distant locations. Artifactual remains indicate extensive contact with both northern Belize and the Belize Valley. The temporal occupation on the island matches the occupation recorded inland and it is certain that this important node played a long-term role in the trade going to and through the Belize Valley.

Gyles Iannone's chapter is concerned with the variability in middle-level settlement in the Belize Valley (chapter 17). He reviews the various terminology that has been used to describe settlement, beginning with the work of Willey (1956a; Willey et al. 1955) and Bullard (1960). He suggests that there is a continuum of settlement in the valley and recommends using the terms "lower-," "middle-," and "upper-level" settlement and then dividing these groupings by subtypes. Again, the issue of consistent terminology is a significant one for the overall Belize Valley area.

David Driver and James Garber (chapter 18) also discuss Willey and Bullard's three-tiered hierarchy of sites (Bullard 1960:352; Willey et al 1965:561). They further review Garber et al.'s (1993) earlier work on settlement patterning in the valley. They suggest that major centers along the Belize River (Xunantunich, Cahal Pech, Baking Pot, Blackman Eddy, and Camelote) are 9.9 km apart. They then discuss what they call "Type 1" sites, those located within 2 km of a major center, "Type 2" sites, those beyond the 2-km range, and "Type 3" sites (Floral Park, Esperanza, Nohoch Ek, Ontario, and Warrie Head), those located equidistant between major centers. Their typology works well for most of the Late Classic settlement along the south bank of the Belize River. The pattern is altered, not surprisingly, in the upland area between the Macal and Mopan Rivers, specifically around Xunantunich, Buenavista del Cayo, and Las Ruinas. This is an excellent attempt to define the functional distinctions among the various kinds of sites noted in the valley. More work on the intermediate sites equidistant between major centers would be of interest and would further refine their typological distinctions.

James Aimers uses ceramic data to discuss the Terminal Classic to Postclassic transition in the Belize Valley (chapter 19). He indicates the widespread nature of Terminal Classic occupation as opposed to the more limited nature of Postclassic settlement (with focal areas in Barton Ramie, Baking Pot, and caves). He reviews the Postclassic ceramics and agrees with previous authors that the Late Postclassic ceramics are a break in the ceramic tradition with ties to both the Petén and the northern Maya area. Key to his discussion is the idea that the Belize Valley is a zone of interaction with increased influence from the northern Maya lowlands, the Gulf Coast, and Central Mexico over time.

Arlen Chase examines the role of settlement archaeology in discussing Maya social organization (chapter 20). He provides a different context for the Belize Valley by comparing and contrasting it with patterns from the site of Caracol. He raises the question of how the major and minor sites of the Belize Valley fit into broader settlement reconstruction, considering the problem of different research methodologies as well as the relationships of Belize Valley sites with settlements exterior to the valley. He notes the need to combine epigraphic and settlement data when both are available and points to the very different interpretations about polity size and organization that can be garnered from these two very different databases. In describing the Caracol polity, he refers to a Caracol cultural and ritual tradition involving the use of eastern buildings for burials and caches that extends into the southeastern Petén, but that was never fully shared by the Belize Valley. Instead of viewing the Belize Valley as a separate entity composed of one or more smaller political units, he views the Belize Valley as a "border area," likely varying its political allegiances over time from Caracol to Naranjo and, ultimately, to Xunantunich.

Concluding Thoughts on the Belize Valley: Toward a Uniform Language

The importance of the long-term archaeology that has been undertaken in the Belize Valley cannot be overstressed. In fact, because of the quantity of work, much of it reflected in this volume, the Belize Valley can ideally be viewed as comprising some of the most comprehensive settlement work that has been done in the Maya area. Settlement transects have been undertaken in the upper Belize Valley around Xunantunich (chapter 10), in the terrain southeast of the valley proper (chapter 6), and to the northwest of the valley (chapter 15). Nodal, architecturally significant archaeological remains and settlement have also seen extensive work at Xunantunich (chapters 10 and 11), Buenavista del Cayo (chapter 9), Nohoch Ek (Coe and Coe 1956), Cahal Pech (chapters 7, 8, and 12), Baking Pot (Bullard and Bullard 1965; chapter 5), and Blackman Eddy (chapters 3 and 4). Immediately outside the valley, excavation has been undertaken at Arenal (Las Ruinas; Taschek and Ball 1999), El Pilar (chapter 15), Negoman-Tipu (Graham et al. 1985), and Pacbitun (chapters 13 and 14). When combined with Willey et al.'s (1965) initial work at Barton Ramie, this continuous archaeological effort makes the Belize Valley one of the most intensively investigated areas in Mesoamerica.

But what do we know from all of the data that has been collected? And what new insight have we gained on the ancient Maya? One of the most glaring points that can be gleaned from the collected archaeological data is that there is no top-tier site in the Belize Valley. Thus, there has been an archaeological focus on intermediate-sized sites without a corresponding focus on any primate center. From the Belize Valley archaeological data we know a great deal about what happens in mid-level centers, but without knowing anything specific about higher-level integration. And while archaeologists undertaking settlement research at nonprimate centers traditionally point to the fact that their work reveals more about day-to-day Maya life and avoids relying on any elite focus, these chapters suggest that even settlement work on minor centers and outlying groups can provide substantial variation that raise questions very similar to those found in archaeological work at larger sites. For instance, the data from the Bedran Group (chapter 5) show how the social system is not easily broken down into presupposed elite and nonelite complexes based on the presence of hieroglyphic writing and cylinder tripods. There is a clear need for viewing the broader patterns.

Thus, a key question is how the different parts of the Belize Valley are related to each other and to neighboring areas. It would be a mistake to consider the Belize Valley settlement in isolation. Importantly, this volume appropriately includes data from outside the valley itself at sites like Caracol, Pacbitun, and Moho Cay. Undoubtedly, all these sites and areas interacted with and both conditioned and were conditioned by the ancient inhabitants of the Belize Valley. However, the exact nature of these interactions is still not well known.

To some extent, different models and researcher perceptions color interpretations, as may differences in the varied data themselves. Arlen Chase, writing from the vantage point of the larger Vaca Plateau site of Caracol, suggests that the Belize Valley is a border area, variously under either direct or indirect control of larger order centers such as Naranjo or Caracol within some sort of a hierarchically arranged political order. In contrast,

Ball and Taschek, writing from the vantage point of their excavations in the Belize Valley, view Cahal Pech and Buenavista del Cayo as regal-ritual cities, modeling these sites with Xunantunich as part of the same heterarchical social system. Viewing the Belize Valley in isolation, it could well be the case. With the addition of more massive sites like Caracol and Naranjo and considering the limits of the Belize Valley, it becomes evident that the overall Maya political landscape was more complex. Perhaps a better understanding of Buenavista del Cayo's "palace school" that produced distinctive polychrome pottery will eventually shed more light on the broader political, economic, and social interactions that once existed. Partially due to differences of opinion over social and political models, there is also significant controversy over the positioning of Xunantunich temporally and politically in the Belize Valley; no matter what position is taken, however, it certainly represents a Late to Terminal Classic move to a more defensive location.

From a temporal standpoint the archaeology undertaken in the Belize Valley has confirmed, and amplified, the unique character of its earliest remains. The Jenney Creek materials from Barton Ramie were initially viewed as being within their own ceramic sphere and separate from early ceramic development seen in the neighboring Guatemalan Petén (Willey et al. 1967). Excavations at Cahal Pech and Blackman Eddy have recovered a host of other intriguing early materials, which again stress the unique ceramic development of this area, perhaps representative of an early "non-Maya" settlement (Ball and Tashek 2000). Yet thus far all of this early material derives from redeposited fill. It is only when associated constructions and special deposits containing de facto materials of this early date are eventually uncovered in the Belize Valley that we will be able to better contextualize these materials.

The archaeology of the Belize Valley also promises to better inform us about the transition from the Classic to Postclassic periods. Virtually all researchers note the presence of Terminal Classic occupation at their respective sites. But the nodal architectural concentrations in the valley all suffer the "Maya collapse." Some researchers indicate the existence of incomplete construction efforts, suggesting relatively rapid events. Yet Postclassic occupation is plentiful, if not ubiquitous, in the valley-bottom alluvial areas, something noted by Willey and his colleagues (1965) for Barton Ramie and also well documented in the outlying Baking Pot settlement (J. Awe, personal communication 2002). Thus, without doubt further research in the Belize Valley should help resolve longstanding questions over the nature of the transition between the Classic and Postclassic periods and help to explain the visible shift in settlement patterns seen not only here, but also elsewhere in the Maya southern lowlands.

The Belize Valley is an excellent place to consider scale in relation to population, land use, and social relationships. Willey and his colleagues (1965:577) estimated that the Belize Valley housed approximately 24,000 individuals within a 600-km² area (60-mile strip of land along the river extending 5 km to either side); the work reported on in this volume does not appear to significantly modify Willey's original estimate. Although the original research at Barton Ramie did not focus on land use and social relationships, the more recent archaeological work permits both of these questions to be tentatively addressed. With regard to land use, the survey work that has been undertaken by Fedick and Lucero clearly shows that there was far more arable land in and around the valley than there was population available to use it. Perhaps the lack of pressure on available agricultural land explains why there are not extensive terrace systems in the Belize Valley, like those at Caracol (A. Chase and D. Chase 1998b). However, the fecundity of the alluvial soils may have been amplified to some extent by irrigation via canal systems, as indicated in the data from Baking Pot.

Even more intriguing are the spatial patterns that are inherent in the Belize Valley settlement. David Driver and James Garber report that there are an average of 9.9 km between major architectural nodes in the Belize Valley and that other smaller architectural nodes are located at the midpoints between the large architectural concentrations. Thus, there appear to be architectural nodes equidistantly spaced every 5 km. These spatial relationships are to some extent reflected in architectural concentrations that are embedded in other mapped settlement areas—such as Caracol (A. Chase and D. Chase 2001a), Tikal (Puleston 1983), Coba (Folan et al. 1983), and even the wider Dos Pilas area (Demarest 1997)—but the linear Belize River really emphasizes the regularity and the possibility of water transportation likely conditioned distances, at least to some degree. Thus, there would appear to be general patterns and principles of Maya nodal settlement location that may have been established in the southern lowlands as early as the Late Preclassic period. Whereas the astronomical "E Group" became the focus in the southern Petén (A. Chase and D. Chase 1995; Laporte 1996a), this was not necessarily the strict focus within the Belize Valley. However, the regularity of spacing seen in the Belize Valley settlements must be related to specific social or political factors that were once operational.

Researchers seeking answers to broader questions in the Belize Valley archaeological data remain challenged by the diverse data and research projects. After 50 years, we are not yet in a position to answer some of the questions originally posed by Gordon Willey regarding the nature and integration of the ancient Maya community. As in other parts of the Maya lowlands, the research sample has been skewed toward architectural concentrations with very little vacant terrain actually being investigated; however, many architectural concentrations are of a much smaller size than normally would be investigated elsewhere. Although the database has grown substantially and many more sites and groups within and adjacent to the valley have received some excavation, much of the raw archaeological data is not fully analyzed, "digested," or published—and, outside of this volume, there are no focal books or series that focus on Belize Valley research. And even though the Belize Valley has been more extensively studied than most parts of the Maya lowlands, there is still a need for more survey between centers and in upland areas, especially on the north side of the river away from the Western Highway (see chapter 1). There are also a plethora of different models and theoretical perceptions that can be and have been applied to the ancient Maya, often in conjunction with differing archaeological methodologies, techniques, strategies, and standards. In truth, the multiple projects and multiple researchers in the Belize Valley make it difficult to synthesize the extant data to answer broader questions. Each project operates to a large degree as a microcosm, focusing on specific questions that vary from site to site and excavation to excavation. Each project also seeks to emphasize the importance of their specific database. It is only by collecting these diverse data and voices into one place, as has been done in this volume, that one can begin to understand and appreciate the complexity of the archaeological record that comprises our interpretation of the ancient Maya.

The Belize Valley was chosen long ago by Gordon Willey to start the process of understanding how the Maya comprised their society and settlement; the chapters in this volume valiantly continue this tradition.

References Cited

Adams, R.E.W.

1971 *The Ceramics of Altar de Sacrificios.* Papers of the Peabody Museum of Archaeology and Ethnology 63 (1). Harvard University, Cambridge.

1973 "Maya Collapse: Transformation and Termination in the Ceramic Sequence at Altar de Sacrificios." In *The Classic Maya Collapse,* edited by T. P. Culbert, 133–163. School of American Research, University of New Mexico Press, Albuquerque.

1977 "Rio Bec Archaeology and the Rise of Maya Civilization." In *The Origins of Maya Civilization,* edited by R.E.W. Adams, 77–99. University of New Mexico Press, Albuquerque.

1981 "Settlement Patterns of the Central Yucatan and Southern Campeche Regions." In *Lowland Maya Settlement Patterns,* edited by W. Ashmore, 211–258. University of New Mexico Press, Albuquerque.

1986 "Rio Azul." *National Geographic* 169:420–451.

Adams, R.E.W., and R. C. Jones

1981 "Spatial Patterns and Regional Growth among Classic Maya Cities." *American Antiquity* 46:301–332.

Adams, R.E.W., and W. D. Smith

1981 "Feudal Models for Classic Maya Civilization." In *Lowland Maya Settlement Patterns,* edited by W. Ashmore, 335–449. University of New Mexico Press, Albuquerque.

Aimers, J. J.

1993 "Messages from the Gods: An Hermeneutic Analysis of the Maya E-Group Complex." Master's thesis, Trent University, Peterborough, Ontario.

2002a "The Terminal Classic to Postclassic Transition in the Belize Valley." Ph.D. diss., Tulane University, New Orleans.

2002b "Abandonment and Non-Abandonment at Baking Pot." In *Abandonment of Centers and Villages in Prehispanic Middle America,* edited by T. Inomata and R. Webb. Westview Press, Boulder, Colo.

Aimers, J. J., T. G. Powis, and J. J. Awe

2000 "Preclassic Round Structures of the Upper Belize River Valley." *Latin American Antiquity* 11 (1):71–86.

References Cited

Andrews, A. P., and R. Corletta
1995 "A Brief History of Underwater Archaeology in the Maya Area." *Ancient Mesoamerica* 6:101–117.

Andrews V, E. W.
1990 "The Early Ceramic History of the Lowland Maya." In *Vision and Revision in Maya Studies,* edited by F. S. Clancy and P. D. Harrison. University of New Mexico Press, Albuquerque.

Andrews V, E. W. and J. A. Sabloff
1986 "Classic to Postclassic: A Summary Discussion." In *Late Lowland Maya Civilization: Classic to Postclassic,* edited by J. A. Sabloff and E. W. Andrews V, 433–456. School of American Research, University of New Mexico Press, Albuquerque.

Aoyama, K.
1995 "Microwear Analysis in the Southeast Maya Lowlands: Two Case Studies at Copan, Honduras." *Latin American Antiquity* 6:129–144.

Arendt, C., R. Song, and P. F. Healy
1996 "The 1995 Excavations in Plaza C, Pacbitun, Belize: A Middle Preclassic Burial and a Late Classic Stela." In *Belize Valley Preclassic Maya Project: Report on the 1995 Field Season,* edited by P. F. Healy and J. J. Awe, 128–138. Occasional Papers in Anthropology no. 12. Trent University, Peterborough, Ontario.

Arie, J. C.
2001 "Sun Kings and Hierophants: Geocosmic Orientation and the Classic Maya." Master's thesis, New Mexico State University, Las Cruces.

Ashmore, W.
1981 "Some Issues of Method and Theory in Lowland Maya Settlement Archaeology." In *Lowland Maya Settlement Patterns,* edited by W. A. Ashmore, 37–69. University of New Mexico Press, Albuquerque.
1989 "Construction and Cosmology: Politics and Ideology in Lowland Maya Settlement Patterns." In *Word and Image in Maya Culture: Explorations in Language, Writing, and Representation,* edited by W. F. Hanks and D. S. Rice, 272–286. University of Utah Press, Salt Lake City.
1991 "Site-Planning Principles and Concepts of Directionality among the Ancient Maya." *Latin American Antiquity* 2:199–226.
1992 "Deciphering Maya Architectural Plans." In *New Theories on the Ancient Maya,* edited by E. Danien and R. J. Sharer, 173–184. University of Pennsylvania, Philadelphia.
1998 "Monumentos Politicos: Sitio, Asentamiento, y Paisaje Alrededor de Xunantunich, Belice." In *Anatomía de una Civilizacíon—Aproximaciones Interdisciplinarias a la Cultura Maya,* edited by A. Ciudad Ruiz, J.M.G. Campillo, Y. F. Marquínez, J. I. Ponce de León, A. L. García-Gallo, and L.T.S. Castro, 161–183. Sociedad Española de Estudios Mayas, Madrid.

Ashmore, W., and R. R. Wilk
1988 "Household and Community in the Mesoamerican Past." In *Household*

350

Community in the Mesoamerican Past, edited by R. R. Wilk and W. Ashmore, 1–28. University of New Mexico Press, Albuquerque.

Ashmore, W., J. Yaeger, and C. Robin

2000 "Commoner Sense: Late and Terminal Classic Social Strategies in the Xunantunich Area." In *Collapse, Transition, and Transformation: New Views of the End of the Classic Period in the Maya Lowlands,* edited by D. S. Rice, P. M. Rice, and A. A. Demarest. Westview Press, Boulder, Colo.

Aveni, A. F., and H. Hartong

1989 "Uaxactun, Guatemala, Group E and Similar Assemblages: An Archaeoastronomical Reconsideration." In *World Archaeoastronomy,* edited by A. F. Aveni, 441–461. Cambridge University Press, Cambridge.

Awe, J. J.

1984 "The Valley of Peace Maya Site." *Belizean Studies* 12:1–5.

1992 "Dawn in the Land between the Rivers: Formative Occupation at Cahal Pech, Belize and Its Implications for Preclassic Occupation in the Central Maya Lowlands." Ph.D. diss., University of London.

Awe, J. J., and N. Grube

2001 "La estela 9 de Cahal Pech: un monumento preclásico del Valle del Río Belice." In *Los Investigadores de la Cultura Maya* 9 (II), 55–64. Los Investigadores de la Cultura Maya 9 (II). Centro Cultural y Deportivo Universitario, Universidad Autonoma de Campeche, México.

Awe, J. J., and P. F. Healy

1994 "Flakes to Blades? Middle Formative Development of Obsidian Artifacts in the Upper Belize River Valley." *Latin American Antiquity* 5 (3):193–205.

Awe, J., and H. Topsey

1984 "Excavations at the Valley of Peace." *Belizean Studies* 12:6–9.

Awe, J. J., J. J. Aimers, and C. Blanchard

1992 "A Preclassic Round Structure at Cahal Pech, Belize." In *Progress Report of the Fourth Season (1991) of Investigations at Cahal Pech, Belize,* edited by J. J. Awe and M. D. Campbell, 119–140. Department of Anthropology, Trent University, Peterborough, Ontario.

Awe, J. J., M. D. Campbell, and J. M. Conlon

1991 "Preliminary Spatial Analysis of the Site Core at Cahal Pech, Belize and Its Implications for Lowland Maya Social Organization." *Mexicon* 8 (2):25–30.

Awe, J. J., D. Cheetham, and N. Grube

1995 "Comentario sobre la Estela 9 de Cahal Pech: Un Monumento Preclassico del Valle del Rio Belice." Paper presented at the 3d Congreso Internacional de Mayistas, Chetumal.

Awe, J. J., C. Bill, M. D. Campbell, and D. Cheetham

1990 "Early Middle Formative Occupation in the Central Maya Lowlands: Recent Evidence from Cahal Pech, Belize." Institute of Archaeology Papers 1: 1–6. University College, London.

Awe, J. J., P. F. Healy, C. Stevenson, and B. Hohmann

1996 "Preclassic Maya Obsidian in the Belize Valley." In *Belize Valley Preclassic Maya Project: Report on the 1995 Field Season,* edited by P. F. Healy and J. J. Awe, 153–174. Occasional Papers in Anthropology no. 12. Trent University, Peterborough, Ontario.

Baker, P.

1988 "Pacbitun 1987: Faunal Report." Manuscript on file, Department of Anthropology, Trent University, Peterborough, Ontario.

Ball, J. W.

1982 "A Note on the Ceramic History of Moho Cay, Belize, Central America." *Ceramica de Cultura Maya* 12:49–55.

1984 "Provisional Inventory of Ceramic Units from Moho Cay, Belize." *Ceramica de Cultura Maya* 13:74–75.

1989 "Pots and Prehistory: Some Ceramics-based Insights into Eighth Century Maya Civilization." Paper presented at the Annual Dumbarton Oaks Pre-Columbian Studies Symposium "On the Eve of the Collapse—Ancient Maya Societies in the Eighth Century." Dumbarton Oaks, Washington, D.C.

1993a "Cahal Pech, the Ancient Maya, and Modern Belize: The Story of an Archaeological Park." Albert W. Johnson University Lecture Series. San Diego State University Press, San Diego.

1993b "Pottery, Potters, Palaces, and Polities: Some Socioeconomic and Political Implications of Late Classic Maya Ceramic Industries." In *Lowland Maya Civilization in the Eighth Century A.D.,* edited by J. A. Sabloff and J. S. Henderson, 243–272. Dumbarton Oaks Research Library and Collection, Washington, D.C.

1994 "Northern Maya Archaeology: Some Observations on an Emerging Paradigm." In *Hidden among the Hills: Maya Archaeology of the Northwest Yucatan Peninsula,* edited by H. J. Prem, 389–396. Acta Mesoamericana 7. Verlag von Flemming Mockmuhl.

1997 "Ceramics, Culture History, and the Puuc Tradition: Some Alternative Possibilities." In *The Puuc: New Perspectives,* edited by L. Mills. Scholarly Studies in the Liberal Arts, no. 1. Central College, Pella, Iowa.

Ball, J. W., and J. T. Taschek

1986 "Settlement System and Community Organization in a Classic Realm: The 1984–85 SDU-NSF Northwestern Cayo Archaeological Project." Second Preliminary Report. Manuscript on file, Department of Anthropology, San Diego State University.

1991 "Late Classic Lowland Maya Political Organization and Central-Place Analysis: New Insights from the Upper Belize Valley." *Ancient Mesoamerica* 2 (2):149–166.

2000 "Pioneering the Belize Valley in the Early Middle Preclassic: Ceramics, Settlement, Interaction, and Culture History at a Maya-Zoque Interface." Paper presented at the Annual Meeting of the Society for American Archaeology, Philadelphia.

2001   "The Buenavista–Cahal Pech Court: A Multi-Palace Royal Court from a Petty Lowland Maya Kingdom." In *Royal Courts of the Ancient Maya*, edited by T. Inomata and S. Houston, 165–200. Westview Press, Boulder, Colo.

2003   "Reconsidering the Belize Valley Preclassic: A Case for Multiethnic Interactions in the Development of a Regional Cultural Tradition." *Ancient Mesoamerica* 12 (4):169–207.

Bawden, G.

1982   "Community Organization Reflected by the Household: A Study of Pre-Columbian Social Dynamics." *Journal of Field Archaeology* 9:165–181.

Becker, M. J.

1971   "The Identification of a Second Plaza Plan at Tikal, Guatemala, and Its Implications for Ancient Maya Social Complexity." Ph.D. diss., University of Pennsylvania, Philadelphia.

1982   "Ancient Maya houses and Their Identification: An Evaluation of Architectural Groups at Tikal and Inferences Regarding Their Function." *Revista Espanola de Antropologia Americana* 12:111–129.

1983   "Kings and Classicism: Political Change in the Maya Lowlands during the Classic Period." In *Highland-Lowland Interaction in Mesoamerica: Interdisciplinary Approaches,* edited by A. Miller, 159–200. Dumbarton Oaks, Washington, D.C.

1993   "Earth Offerings among the Classic Period Lowland Maya: Burials and Caches as Ritual Deposits." In *Perspectiveas Antropologicas in el Mundo Maya,* edited by J. I. Ponce de Leon and F. L. Perramon, 45–74. Sociedad Espanola de Estudios Maya, Madrid.

1999   *Excavations in Residential Areas of Tikal: Groups with Shrines.* Tikal Report no. 21. The University Museum, University of Pennsylvania, Philadelphia.

Bell, E. E., L. P. Traxler, D. W. Sedat, and R. J. Sharer

1999   "Uncovering Copan's Earliest Royal Tombs." *Expedition* 41 (2):29–35.

Benavides, C. A.

1981   *Los Cambios de Coba y sus Implicaciones Sociales.* Instituto Nacional de Antropologia e Historia, Mexico.

Bey, G. J., C. A. Hanson, and W. M. Ringle

1997   "Classic to Postclassic at Ek Balam, Yucatan: Architectural and Ceramic Evidence for Defining the Transition." *Latin American Antiquity* 8 (3): 237–254.

Bill, C. R.

1987   "Excavation of Structure 23: A Maya 'Palace' at the Site of Pacbitun, Belize." Master's thesis, Trent University, Peterborough, Ontario.

1997   "Patterns of Variation and Change in Dynastic Period Ceramics and Ceramic Production at Copan, Honduras." Ph.D. diss., Tulane University New Orleans.

Birchall, C. J., and R. N. Jenkin

1979   *The Soils of the Belize Valley, Belize.* Supplementary Report no. 15. Overseas Development Centre, Surbiton, England.

Bishop, R. L., E. V. Sayre, and J. Mishara
1993 "Compositional and Structural Characterization of Maya and Costa Rican Jadeites." In *Precolumbian Jade,* edited by F. W. Lange, 30–60. University of Utah Press, Salt Lake City.

Black, S. L.
1990 "The Carnegie Uaxactun Project and the Development of Maya Archaeology." *Ancient Mesoamerica* 1 (2):257–276.

Blanton, R. E., S. A. Kowalewski, G. M. Feinman, and L. M. Finsten
1993 *Ancient Mesoamerica: A Comparison of Change in Three Regions.* 2d edition. Cambridge University Press, Cambridge.

Blom, F.
1924 "Report on the Preliminary Work at Uaxactun, Guatemala." *Carnegie Institution of Washington Yearbook* 23:217–219.
1935 "Notes: The Pestac Stela." In *Maya Research* 2:189–194.

Borhegyi, S. F. de
1956 "Settlement Patterns in the Guatemala Highlands: Past and Present." In *Prehistoric Settlement Patterns in the New World,* edited by G. R. Willey, 101–106. Viking Fund Publications in Anthropology no. 23. New York.
1959 "Underwater Archaeology in Guatemala." *Scientific American* 200:100–113.

Boserup, E.
1965 *Conditions of Agricultural Growth.* Aldine, Chicago.

Brady, J. E., J. W. Ball, R. L. Bishop, D. C. Pring, N. Hammond, and R. A. Housley
1998 "The Lowland Maya 'Protoclassic': A Reconsideration of its Nature and Significance." *Ancient Mesoamerica* 9 (1):17–38.

Braswell, J. B.
1998 "Archaeological Investigations at Elite Group D, Xunantunich, Belize." Ph.D. diss., Tulane University, New Orleans.

Bricker, V. R.
1981 *The Indian Christ, the Indian King: The Historical Substrate of Maya Myth and Ritual.* University of Texas Press, Austin.

Brown, M. K., and J. F. Garber
1998 "The Origin and Function of Late Preclassic Mask Facades in the Maya Lowlands." Paper presented at the Annual Meeting of the Society for American Archaeology, Seattle.
2003 "Evidence of Conflict During the Middle Preclassic in the Maya Lowlands: A View from Blackman Eddy, Belize." In *Ancient Mesoamerican Warfare,* edited by M. K. Brown and T. W. Stanton. Altamira Press, California.

Bullard, W. R., Jr.
1960 "The Maya Settlement Pattern in Northwestern Peten, Guatemala." *American Antiquity,* 25:255–272.
1973 "Postclassic Culture in Central Peten and Adjacent British Honduras." In *The Classic Maya Collapse,* edited by T. P. Culbert, 221–241. University of New Mexico Press, Albuquerque.

Bullard, W. R., and M. R. Bullard

1965 *Late Classic Finds at Baking Pot, British Honduras.* Art and Archaeology Occasional Papers no. 8. Royal Ontario Museum, Toronto.

Bullard, W., Jr., and G. R. Willey

1965 "Baking Pot." In *Prehistoric Maya Settlements in the Belize Valley,* by F. R. Willey, W. R. Bullard, Jr., J. B. Glass, and J. C. Gifford, 301–308. Papers of the Peabody Museum of Archaeology and Ethnology, vol. 54. Harvard University, Cambridge.

Burmeister, S.

2000 "Archaeology and Migration." *Current Anthropology* 41 (3):539–567.

Campbell-Trithart, M. J.

1990 "Ancient Maya Settlement at Pacbitun, Belize." Master's thesis, Trent University, Peterborough, Ontario.

Carr, S. H.

1986 "Fauna at Cerros." In *Archaeology at Cerros, Belize, Central America,* edited by R. A. Robertson and D. A. Freidel, 127–146. Southern Methodist University, Dallas.

Carrasco Vargas, R., S. Boucher, P. Alvarez G., V. Tiesler B., V. Garcia V., R. Garcia M., and J. Vasquez N.

1999 "A Dynamic Tomb from Campeche, Mexico: New Evidence on Jaguar Paw, a Ruler of Calakmul." *Latin American Antiquity* 10 (1):47–58.

Cecil, L. G.

2001 "Technological Styles of Late Postclassic Slipped Pottery from the Central Peten Lakes Region, El Peten, Guatemala." Ph.D. diss., Southern Illinois University, Carbondale.

Chadwick, R.

1971 "Postclassic Pottery of the Central Valleys." In *HMAI 10: Archaeology of Northern Mesoamerica, Part 1,* edited by G. F. Ekholm and I. Bernal, 229–257. University of Texas Press, Austin.

Chase, A. F.

1979 "Regional Development in the Tayasal-Paxcaman Zone, El Peten, Guatemala: A Preliminary Statement." *Ceramica de Cultura Maya* 11:86–119.

1982 "Con Manos Arriba: Archaeology and Tayasal." *American Antiquity* 47: 167–171.

1985 "Archaeology in the Maya Heartland: The Tayasal-Paxcaman Zone, Lake Peten, Guatemala." *Archaeology* 38 (1):32–39.

1986 "Time Depth or Vacuum: The 11.3.0.0.0 Correlation and the Lowland Maya Postclassic." In *Late Lowland Maya Civilization: Classic to Postclassic,* edited by J. A. Sabloff and E. W. Andrews V, 99–140. School of American Research, University of New Mexico Press, Albuquerque.

1992 "Elites and the Changing Organization of Classic Maya Society." In *Mesoamerican Elites: An Archaeological Assessment,* edited by D. Z. Chase and A. F. Chase, 30–49. University of Oklahoma Press, Norman.

1994 "A Contextual Approach to the Ceramics of Caracol, Belize." In *Studies in the Archaeology of Caracol, Belize,* edited by D. Z. Chase and A. F. Chase, 157–182. Pre-Columbian Art Research Institute Monograph 7. Pre-Columbian Art Research Institute, San Francisco.

1998   "Planeacion Civica e Intergracion de Sitio en Caracol, Belice: Definiendo una Economia Administrada del Periodo Clasico Maya." *Los Investigadores de la Cultura Maya* 6 (1):26–44 (Universidad Autonoma de Campeche, Campeche).

Chase, A. F., and D. Z. Chase

1983   "La Ceramica de la Zona Tayasal-Paxcaman, Lago Peten Itza, Guatemala." Privately bound and distributed by The University Museum, University of Pennsylvania, Philadelphia.

1987   *Investigations at the Classic Maya City of Caracol, Belize: 1985–1987.* Pre-Columbian Art Research Institute, Monograph 3. Pre-Columbian Art Research Institute, San Francisco.

1989   "The Investigation of Classic Period Maya Warfare at Caracol, Belize." *Mayab* 5:5–18.

1990   "Los Sistemas Mayas de Subsistencia y Patron de Asentamiento: Pasado y Futuro" In *Los Mayas: El Esplendor de Una Civilizacion,* edited by L. Yanez-Barnuevo Garcia and A. Ciudad Ruiz, 38–48. Sociedad Estatal Quinto Centenario, Turner Libros, S.A., Madrid.

1992   "Mesoamerican Elites: Assumptions, Definitions, and Models." In *Mesoamerican Elites: An Archaeological Assessment,* edited by D. Z. Chase and A. F. Chase, 3–17. University of Oklahoma Press, Norman.

1994   "Maya Veneration of the Dead at Caracol, Belize." In *Seventh Palenque Round Table, 1989,* edited by M. Robertson and V. Fields, 55–62. Pre-Columbian Art Research Institute, San Francisco.

1995   "External Impetus, Internal Synthesis, and Standardization: E Group Assemblages and the Crystalization of Classic Maya Society in the Southern Lowlands." In *The Emergence of Lowland Maya Civilization: The Transition from the Preclassic to Early Classic. Acta Mesoamericana* 8:87–101 (Berlin).

1996a "A Mighty Maya Nation." *Archaeology* 49 (5):66–72.

1996b "The Organization and Composition of Classic Lowland Maya Society: The View from Caracol, Belize." In *Eighth Mesa Redonda de Palenque, 1993,* edited by M. Robertson and M. Macri. Pre-Columbian Art Research Institute, San Francisco.

1996c "More than Kin and King: Centralized Political Organization among the Ancient Maya." *Current Anthropology* 37 (5):803–810.

1998a "Late Classic Maya Political Structure, Polity Size, and Warfare Arenas." In *Anatomia de una Civilizacion: Aproximaciones Interdiscipliarias a la Cultura Maya,* edited by A. Ciudad Ruiz et al., 11–29. Sociedad Espanola de Estudios Mayas, Madrid.

1998b "Scale and Intensity in Classic Period Maya Agriculture: Terracing and

Settlement at the 'Garden City' of Caracol, Belize." *Culture and Agriculture* 20 (2/3):60–77.

2000 "Sixth Century Change and Variation in the Southern Maya Lowlands: Integration and Disbursement at Caracol, Belize." In *The Years Without Summer: Tracing A.D. 536 and Its Aftermath,* edited by J. D. Gunn, 55–65. BAR International Series 872, Archaeopress, Oxford.

2001a "Ancient Maya Causeways and Site Organization at Caracol, Belize." *Ancient Mesoamerica* 12 (2):1–9.

2001b "The Royal Court of Caracol, Belize: Its Palaces and People." In *Royal Courts of the Ancient Maya.* Vol. 2, *Data and Case Studies,* edited by T. Inomata and S. D. Houston, 102–137. Westview Press, Boulder, Colo.

2003 "Minor Centers, Complexity, and Scale in Lowland Maya Settlement Archaeology." In *Rural Complexity in the Maya World,* edited by G. Iannone and S. Connell. Institute of Archaeology, University of California, Los Angeles.

Chase, A. F., and P. M. Rice, editors

1985 *The Lowland Maya Postclassic.* University of New Mexico Press, Albuquerque.

Chase, A. F., D. Z. Chase, and C. White

2001 "El Paisaje Urbano Maya: La Integracion de los Espacios Construidos y la Estructura Social en Caracol, Belice." In *Reconstruyendo la Ciudad Maya: El Urbanismo en las Sociedades Antiguas,* edited by A. Ciudad Ruiz, M. Josefa Iglesias Ponce de Leon, and M. Del Carmen Martinez Martinez, 95–122. Sociedad Espanola de Estudios Mayas, Madrid.

Chase, A. F., N. Grube, and D. Z. Chase

1991 "Three Terminal Classic Monuments from Caracol, Belize." *Research Reports on Ancient Maya Writing* 36:1–18.

Chase, D. Z.

1981 "The Maya Postclassic at Santa Rita Corozal." *Archaeology* 34:25–33.

1992 "Postclassic Maya Elites: Ethnohistory and Archaeology." In *Mesoamerican Elites: An Archaeological Assessment,* edited by D. Z. Chase and A. F. Chase, 118–135. University of Oklahoma Press, Norman.

Chase, D. Z., and A. F. Chase

1982 "Yucatec Influence in Terminal Classic Northern Belize." *American Antiquity* 47 (3):597–613.

1988 *A Postclassic Perspective: Excavations at the Maya site of Santa Rita Corozal, Belize.* Pre-Columbian Art Research Institute Monograph 4. Pre-Columbian Art Research Institute, San Francisco.

1989 "Routes of Trade and Communication and the Integration of Maya Society: The Vista from Santa Rita Corozal." In *Coastal Maya Trade,* edited by H. McKillop and P. F. Healy, 19–32. Occasional Papers in Anthropology no. 8. Trent University, Peterborough, Ontario.

1992a "An Archaeological Assessment of Mesoamerican Elites." In *Mesoamer-*

ican Elites: An Archaeological Assessment, edited by D. Z. Chase and A. F. Chase, 303–317. University of Oklahoma Press, Norman.

1992b *Mesoamerican Elites: An Archaeological Assessment,* edited by D. Z. Chase and A. F. Chase. University of Oklahoma Press, Norman.

1996 "Maya Multiples: Individuals, Entries, and Tombs in Structure A34 at Caracol." *Latin American Antiquity* 7 (1):61–79.

1998 "The Architectural Context of Caches, Burials, and Other Ritual Activities for the Classic Period Maya (as Reflected at Caracol, Belize)." In *Function and Meaning in Classic Maya Architecture,* edited by Stephen D. Houston, 299–332. Dumbarton Oaks Research Library and Collection, Washington, D.C.

2000a "Inferences about Abandonment: Maya Household Archaeology and Caracol, Belize." *Mayab* 13:67–77.

2000b "La Guerra Maya del Periodo Clasico desde la Perspectiva de Caracol, Belice." In *La Guerra entre los Antiguos Mayas,* edited by Silvia Trejo, 53–72. CONACULTA-INAH, Mexico.

Chase, D. Z., A. F. Chase, and W. A. Haviland
1990 "The Classic Maya City: Reconsidering The Mesoamerican Urban Tradition." *American Anthropologist* 92:499–506.

Chase, S. M.
1993 "South Group Plaza 1 and Nabitunich Plaza Group." In *Xunantunich Archaeological Project: 1992 Field Season,* edited by R. M. Leventhal, 35–55. Department of Anthropology, University of California, Los Angeles.

1994 "Ancient Roadways, Elite Ritual, and Settlement Patterns of the Maya: Recent Evidence from Cahal Pech, Cayo, Belize." Paper presented at the Annual Meeting of the Society for American Archaeology, Anaheim.

Cheetham, D. T.
1995 "Excavations of Structure B-4, Cahal Pech, Belize: 1994 Operations." In *Belize Valley Preclassic Maya Project: Report on the 1994 Field Season,* edited by P. F. Healy and J. J. Awe, 18–44. Occasional Papers in Anthropology no. 10. Trent University, Peterborough, Ontario.

1996 "Reconstruction of the Formative Period Site Core of Cahal Pech, Belize." In *Belize Valley Preclassic Maya Project: Report on the 1994 Field Season,* edited by P. F. Healy and J. J. Awe, 1–33. Occasional Papers in Anthropology no. 12. Trent University, Peterborough, Ontario.

1998 "Interregional Interaction, Symbol Emulation, and the Emergence of Socio-Political inequality in the Central Maya Lowlands." Master's thesis, University of British Columbia, Vancouver.

2002 "Formative Period Pottery Figurines of the Southern Maya Lowlands." Manuscript on file, Department of Anthropology, Trent University, Peterborough, Ontario.

Cheetham, D. T., and J. J. Awe
1996 "The Early Formative Cunil Ceramic Complex at Cahal Pech, Belize." Pa-

per presented at the Annual Meeting of the Society for American Archaeology, New Orleans.

2002 "The Cunil Ceramic Complex, Cahal Pech, Belize." Manuscript on file, Department of Anthropology, Trent University, Peterborough, Ontario.

Cheetham, D., D. Forsyth, and J. E. Clark

2002 "La Ceramica Pre-Mamom de la Cuenca del Rio Belice y del Peten Central: Las Correspondencias y sus Implicaciones." Paper presented at the XVI Simposio de Investigaciones Arquelogicas en Guatemala, Guatemala City.

Clancy, F. S.

1985 "Maya Sculpture." In *Maya Treasures of an Ancient Civilization*, edited by C. Gallenkamp and R. E. Johnson, 58–70. Harry N. Abrams, New York.

1990 "A Genealogy of Freestanding Maya Monuments." In *Vision and Revision in Maya Studies*, edited by F. S. Clancy and P. D. Harrison, 21–31. University of New Mexico Press, Albuquerque.

Clark, J. E.

1987 "Politics, Prismatic Blades, and Mesoamerican Civilization." In *The Organization of Core Technology*, edited by K. K. Johnson and C. A. Morrow, 259–284. Westview Press, Boulder, Colo.

1988 *Lithic Artifacts of La Libertad, Chiapas, Mexico: An Economic Perspective*. New World Archaeological Foundation, Brigham Young University, Provo, Utah.

1989 "Obsidian Tool Manufacture." In *Ancient Trade and Tribute: Economies of the Soconusco Region of Mesoamerica*, edited by B. Voorhies, 215–228. University of Utah Press, Salt Lake City.

Clark, J. E., and D. Cheetham

2003 "Mesoamerica's Tribal Foundations." In *Tribal Tempos: Time and Social Organization in So-Called Middle Range Societies*, edited by W. Parkinson and S. Fowles. International Monographs in Prehistory, Ann Arbor.

Clark, J. E., and R. Hansen

2001 "The Architecture of Early Kingship: Comparative Perspectives on the Origins of the Maya Royal Court." In *The Maya Royal Court*, edited by T. Inomata and S. D. Houston, 1–45. Westview Press, Boulder, Colo.

Clark, J. E., and T. A. Lee Jr.

1984 "Formative Obsidian Exchange and the Emergence of Public Economies in Chiapas, Mexico." In *Trade and Exchange in Early Mesoamerica*, edited by K. Hirth, 235–274. University of New Mexico Press, Albuquerque.

Clark, J. E., R. D. Hansen, and T. Perez Suarez

2000 "La Zona Maya en el Preclasico." In *Historia Antigua de Mexico*. Bolumen 1, *El Mexico Antiguo, sus Areas Culturales, los Origenes y el Horizonte Preclasico*, edited by L. Manzanilla and L. Lopez Lujan, 437–510. INAH, Mexico City.

Clowery, S., and J. W. Ball

2001 "Continuity and Disjunction in the Western Belize Valley Ceramic Tradition: The Early Classic Ahcabnal Complex at Buenavista del Cayo." Paper presented at the Annual Meeting of the Society for American Archaeology, New Orleans.

Cobos, R.

1989 "Shelling In: Marine Mollusca at Chichen Itza." In *Coastal Maya Trade,* edited by H. McKillop and P. F. Healy, 49–58. Occasional Papers in Anthropology no. 8. Trent University, Peterborough, Ontario, Canada.

Coe, M. D.

1956 "The Funerary temple among the Classic Maya." *Southwestern Journal of Anthropology* 12 (4):387–394.

1975 "Death and the Ancient Maya." In *Death and the Afterlife in Pre-Columbian America,* edited by E. P. Benson, 87–104. Dumbarton Oaks, Washington, D.C.

1988 "Ideology of the Maya Tomb." In *Maya Iconography,* edited by E. P. Benson and G. G. Griffin, 222–235. Princeton University Press, Princeton, New Jersey.

Coe, M. D., and K. V. Flannery

1967 *Early Cultures and Human Ecology in South Coastal Guatemala.* Contributions to Anthropology vol. 3. Smithsonian Institution, Washington, D.C.

Coe, W. R.

1959 *Piedras Negras Archaeology: Artifacts, Caches, and Burials.* Museum Monograph 18. University of Pennsylvania, Philadelphia.

1965 "Caches and Offertory Practices of the Maya Lowlands." In *Handbook of Middle American Indians,* vol. 2, edited by G. Willey, 462–468. University of Texas Press, Austin.

1967 *Tikal: A Handbook of the Ancient Maya Ruins.* University Museum, University of Pennsylvania, Philadelphia.

1990 *Excavations in the Great Plaza, North Terrace and North Acropolis of Tikal.* Tikal Report no. 14. The University Museum, University of Pennsylvania, Philadelphia.

Coe, W. R., and M. D. Coe

1956 "Excavations at Nohoch Ek, British Honduras." *American Antiquity* 21: 370–382.

Coe, W. R., and W. A. Haviland

1966 Review of *Prehistoric Maya Settlements in the Belize Valley,* by G. R. Willey, W. R. Bullard Jr., P. Glass, and J. C. Gifford. *American Journal of Archaeology* 70:309–311.

Coe, W. R., and J. J. McGinn

1963 "Tikal: The North Acropolis and an Early Tomb." *Expedition* 5 (2):25–32.

Coggins, C.

1975 "Painting and Drawing Styles at Tikal: An Historical and Iconographic Reconstruction." Ph.D. diss., Harvard University.

Cohen, M. N.

1989 *Health and the Rise of Civilization.* Yale University Press, New Haven.

Cohen, M. N., K. O'Connor, M. E. Danforth, K. P. Jacobi, and C. Armstrong
1997 "Archaeology and Osteology of the Tipu Site." In *Bones of the Maya,* edited by S. L. Whittington, and D. M. Reed, 78–86. Smithsonian Institution, Washington, D.C.

Cohen, N. C.
1977 *Food Crisis in Prehistory: Overpopulation and the Origins of Agriculture.* Yale University Press, New Haven.

Conlon, J., and J. Ehret
2002 "Time and Space: The Preliminary Ceramic Analysis for Saturday Creek and Yalbac, Cayo District, Belize, Central America." In *Results of the 2001 Valley of Peace Archaeology Project: Saturday Creek and Yalbac,* edited by L. J. Lucero, 8–17. Department of Anthropology, New Mexico State University, Las Cruces.

Connell, S. V.
2000 "Were They Well Connected? An Exploration of Ancient Maya Regional Integration from the Middle-Level Perspective of Chaa Creek, Belize." Ph.D. diss., University of California, Los Angeles.

Costin, C. L., and M. B. Hagstrum
1995 "Standardization, Labor Investment, Skill, and the Organization of Ceramic Production in Late Prehispanic Highland Peru." *American Antiquity* 60 (4):619–639.

Covarrubias, M.
1947 *Mexico South: The Isthmus of Tehuantepec.* Cassell, London.

Craig, A. K.
1966 *Geography of Fishing in British Honduras and Adjacent Coastal Areas.* Coastal Studies Institute Technical Report 22(66). Louisiana State University, Baton Rouge.

Crumley, C. L.
1995 "Heterarchy and the Analysis of Complex Societies." In *Heterarchy and the Analysis of Complex Societies,* edited by R. M. Ehrenreich, C. L. Crumley, and J. E. Levy, 1–5. Archaeological Papers of the American Anthropological Association, no. 6. American Anthropological Association, Washington, D.C.

Culbert, T. P.
1973 "The Maya Downfall at Tikal." In *The Classic Maya Collapse,* edited by T. P. Culbert, 63–92. School of American Research, University of New Mexico Press, Albuquerque.
1974 *The Lost Civilization: The Story of the Classic Maya.* Harper and Row, New York.
1977 "Early Maya Development at Tikal, Guatemala." In *Origins of Maya Civilization,* edited by R.E.W. Adams, 27–43. University of New Mexico Press, Albuquerque.
1988 "The Collapse of Classic Maya Civilization." In *The Collapse of Ancient States and Civilizations,* edited by N. Yoffee and G. L. Cowgill, 69–101. University of Arizona Press, Tucson.

1991 *Classic Maya Political History: Hieroglyphic and Archaeological Evidence,* edited by T. P. Culbert. Cambridge University Press, Cambridge.

Culbert, T. P., and D. S. Rice, editors

1990 *Precolumbian Population History in the Maya Lowlands.* University of New Mexico Press, Albuquerque.

Dahlin, B. H.

1984 "A Colossus in Guatemala: The Preclassic Maya City of El Mirador." *Archaeology* 37 (5):18–25.

D'Altroy, T. N., and T. K. Earle

1985 "Staple Finance, Wealth Finance, and Storage in the Inka Political Economy." *Current Anthropology* 26:187–206.

Danforth, M. E.

1999 "Stature and Nutrition in the Southern Lowlands." In *Reconstructing Ancient Maya Diet,* edited by C. D. White, 103–109. University of Utah Press, Salt Lake City.

Demarest, A. A.

1986 *The Archaeology of Santa Leticia and the Rise of Maya Civilization.* Middle American Research Institute Publication 52. Tulane University Press, New Orleans.

1987 "Recent Research on the Preclassic Ceramics of the Southeastern Highlands and Pacific Coast of Guatemala." In *Maya Ceramics: Papers from the 1985 Maya Ceramic Conference,* edited by P. M. Rice and R. J. Sharer, 329–339. BAR International Series 345(ii). Oxford, England.

1992 "Ideology in Ancient Maya Cultural Evolution: The Dynamics of Galactic Polities." In *Ideology and Pre-Columbian Civilizations,* edited by A. A. Demarest and G. W. Conrad, 135–57. School of American Research Press, Santa Fe, N.M.

1997 "The Vanderbilt Petexbatun Regional Archaeological Project 1989–1994: Overview, History, and Major Results of a Multidisciplinary Study of the Classic Maya Collapse." *Ancient Mesoamerica* 8:209–227.

Demarest, A. A., and R. J. Sharer

1986 "Late Preclassic Ceramic Spheres, Culture Areas, and Cultural Evolution in the Southeastern Highlands of Mesoamerica." In *The Southeast Maya Periphery,* edited by P. A. Urban and E. M. Schortman, 194–223. University of Texas Press, Austin.

Dillon, B. D., L. Brunker, and K. O. Pope

1985 "Ancient Maya Autoamputation? A Possible Case from Salinas de los Nueve Cerros, Guatemala." *Journal of New World Archaeology* 5 (4): 24–38.

Dreiss, M. L.

1988 *Obsidian at Colha, Belize: A Technological Analysis and Distributional Study Based on Trace Element Data.* Papers of the Colha Project vol. 4. University of Texas at Austin, Texas Archaeological Laboratory, and University of Texas–San Antonio, Center for Archaeological Research, Austin and San Antonio.

1989 "An Obsidian Distribution Model for the Belize Periphery." In *Coastal Maya Trade,* edited by H. I. McKillop and P. F. Healy, 79–90. Occasional Papers in Anthropology no. 8. Trent University, Peterborough, Ontario.

Dunham, P. S.

1990 "Coming Apart at the Seams: The Classic Development and the Demise of Maya Civilization: A Segmentary View from Xnaheb, Belize." Ph.D. diss., State University of New York at Albany.

Earle, T. K.

1991a "Paths and Roads in Evolutionary Perspective." In *Ancient Road Networks and Settlement Hierarchies in the New World,* edited by C. D. Trombold, 10–16. Cambridge University Press, Cambridge.

1991b *Chiefdoms: Power, Economy, and Ideology,* edited by T. K. Earle. Cambridge University Press, Cambridge.

Eaton, J., and B. Kunstler

1980 "Excavations at Operation 2009: A Maya Ballcourt." In *The Colha Project: Second Season, 1980 Interim Report,* edited by T. R. Hester, J. D. Eaton, and H. J. Shafer, 121–32. Center for Archaeological Research, University of Texas, San Antonio.

Elson, M. D.

1996 "An Ethnographic Perspective on Prehistoric Platform Mounds of the Tonto Basin, Central Arizona." Ph.D. diss., University of Arizona.

Emery, K.

1987 "Faunal Report: Pacbitun, Belize, Central America." Manuscript on file, Department of Anthropology, Trent University, Peterborough, Ontario.

1991 "The Secular/Ritual Dichotomy in Animal Use: Final Faunal Analysis, Pacbitun, Belize." Manuscript on file, Department of Anthropology, Trent University, Peterborough. Ontario.

Fash, B. W.

1992 "Late Classic Architectural Sculpture Themes in Copan." *Ancient Mesoamerica* 3 (1):89–104.

Fash, W. L.

1983 "Deducing Social Organization from Classic Maya Settlement Patterns: A Case Study from the Copan Valley." In *Civilization in the Ancient Americas: Essays in Honor of Gordon R. Willey,* edited by R. M. Leventhal and A. L. Kolata, 261–288. University of New Mexico Press, Albuquerque.

1991 *Scribes, Warriors and Kings: The City of Copán and the Ancient Maya.* Thames and Hudson, New York.

Fedick, S. L.

1988 "Prehistoric Maya Settlement and Land Use Patterns in the Upper Belize River Area, Belize, Central America." Ph.D. diss., Arizona State University, Tempe.

1989 "The Economics of Agricultural Land Use and Settlement in the Upper Belize Valley." In *Research in Economic Anthropology: Prehistoric Maya Economies of Belize,* edited by P. A. McAnany and B. L. Isaac, 315–354. JAI Press, Greenwich, Conn.

1994 "Ancient Maya Agricultural Terracing in the Upper Belize River Area: Computer-Aided Modeling and the Results of Initial Field Investigations." *Ancient Mesoamerica* 5 (1):107–127.

1995 "Land Evaluation and Ancient Maya Land Use in the Upper Belize River Area, Belize, Central America." *Latin American Antiquity* 6:16–34.

1996 "An Interpretive Kaleidoscope: Alternative Perspectives on Ancient Maya Agriculture and Resource Use." In *The Managed Mosaic: Ancient Maya Agriculture and Resource Use,* edited by S. L. Fedick, 107–131. University of Utah Press, Salt Lake City.

Fedick, S. L., and A. Ford
1990 "The Prehistoric Agricultural Landscape of the Central Maya Lowlands: An Examination of Local Variability in a Regional Context." *World Archaeology* 22:18–33.

Feinman, G. M., S. Kowalewski, and R. E. Blanton
1984 "Modeling Ceramic Production and Organizational Change in the Prehispanic Valley of Oaxaca, Mexico." In *The Many Dimensions of Pottery,* edited by S.v.d. Leeuw and A. C. Pritchard, 295–337. Albert Egges van Giffen Instituut vor Prae-en Protohistorie, CINGLVA VII, Universiteit van Amsterdam, Amsterdam.

Ferguson, J., T. Christensen, and S. Schwake
1996 "The Eastern Ballcourt at Cahal Pech, Belize: 1995 Excavations." In *Belize Valley Preclassic Maya Project: Report on the 1995 Field Season,* edited by P. F. Healy and J. J. Awe, 34–58. Occasional Papers in Anthropology no. 12. Trent University, Peterborough, Ontario.

Flannery, K. V.
1972 "The Cultural Evolution of Civilizations" In *Annual Review of Ecology and Systematics,* edited by R. F. Johnson, P. W. Frank, and C. D. Michener, 399–426. Annual Reviews, Palo Alto, California.

Folan, W. J.
1983 "Urban Organization and Social Structure of Coba." In *Coba: A Classic Maya Metropolis,* edited by W. J. Folan, E. R. Kintz, and L. A. Fletcher, 49–63. Academic Press, London.

1991 "Sacbes of the Northern Maya." In *Ancient Road Networks and Settlement Hierarchies in the New World,* edited by C. D. Trombold, 222–228. Cambridge University Press, Cambridge.

Folan, W. J., E. R. Kintz, and L. A. Fletcher
1983 *Coba: A Classic Maya Metropolis.* Academic Press, New York.

Folan, W. J., L. A. Fletcher, J. May Hau, and L. F. Folan
2001 *Las Ruinas de Calakmul, Campeche, Mexico, Un lugar central y su paisaje cultural.* Universidad Autonoma de Campeche, Campeche.

Ford, A.

1981 "Conditions for the Evolution of Complex Societies: The Development of the Central Lowland Maya." Ph.D. diss., University of California, Santa Barbara.

1985 "Maya Settlement Pattern Chronology in the Belize River Area and the Implications for the Development of the Central Maya Lowlands." *Journal of Belizean Affairs* 4 (2):13–31.

1986 *Population Growth and Social Complexity: An Examination of Settlement and Environment in the Central Maya Lowlands.* Anthropological Research Papers no. 35. Arizona State University, Tempe.

1988 "The Future of El Pilar: The Integrated Research and Development Plan for the El Pilar Archaeological Reserve for the Maya Flora and Fauna, Belize-Guatemala." Bureau of Oceans and International Environmental and Scientific Affairs, Washington, D.C.

1990 "Maya Settlement in the Belize River Area: Variations in Residence Patterns of the Central Maya Lowlands." In *Precolumbian Population History in the Maya Lowlands,* edited by T. P. Culbert and D. S. Rice, 167–181. University of New Mexico Press, Albuquerque.

1991a "Evidence of Economic Variation of Ancient Maya Residential Settlement in the Upper Belize River Area." *Ancient Mesoamerica* 2:35–45.

1991b "Problems in the Evaluation of Population from Settlement Data: An Examination of Residential Unit Composition in the Tikal-Yaxha Intersite Area." *Estudios de Cultura Maya,* UNAM 18:157–186.

Ford, A., and S. L. Fedick

1992 "Prehistoric Maya Settlement Patterns in the Upper Belize River Area: Initial Results of the Belize River Archaeological Settlement Survey." *Journal of Field Archaeology* 19:35–49.

Ford, A., and K. Olson

1989 "Aspects of Ancient Maya Household Economy: Variation in Chipped Stone Production and Consumption." In *Prehistoric Maya Economies of Belize, Research in Economic Anthropology, Supplement 4,* edited by P. McAnany and B. L. Isaac, 185–214. JAI Press, Greenwich, Conn.

Ford, A., D. C. Werneke, and M. Grzybowski

1995 "Archaeology at El Pilar: A Report on the 1995 Field Season." CA:BRASS/ MesoAmerican Research Center, University of California, Santa Barbara.

Ford, A., D. C. Wernecke, M. Grzybowski, and R. Larios

1997 "Interpreting the Past to Protect the Future: BRASS/El Pilar Program— 1997 Field Report." CA:BRASS/MesoAmerican Research Center, University of California, Santa Barbara. www.marc.ucsb.edu/field reports/1997 report/1997_report.html

Forsyth, D. W.

1989 *The Ceramics of El Mirador, Peten, Guatemala.* New World Archaeological Foundation Paper no. 63. Brigham Young University, Provo, Utah.

1993 "The Ceramic Sequence at Nakbe, Guatemala." *Ancient Mesoamerica* 4 (1):31–53.

2000 "A Survey of Terminal Classic Ceramic Complexes and Their Socioeconomic Implications." Paper presented at the Society for American Archaeology Annual Meeting on "Terminal Classic Socioeconomic Processes in the Maya Lowlands Through a Ceramic Lens," Philadelphia.

Fox, J. G.

1980 "Lowland to Highland Mexicanization Processes in Southern Mesoamerica." *American Antiquity* 45 (1):43–54.

1987 *Maya Postclassic State Formation: Segmentary Lineage Migration in Advancing Frontiers.* Cambridge University Press, Cambridge.

1996 "Playing with Power: Ballcourts and Political Ritual in Southern Mesoamerica." *Current Anthropology* 37 (3):483–509.

Fox, J., G. Cook, A. F. Chase, and D. Z. Chase

1996 "Questions of Political and Economic Integration: Segmentary versus Centralized States among the Ancient Maya." *Current Anthropology* 37 (5): 795–801.

Franks, A. W.

1876 "On Stone Implements from Honduras, and Turks and Caicos Islands." *Journal of the Royal Anthropological Institute* (Liverpool) 6:37–40.

Freidel, D. A.

1977 "A Late Preclassic Monumental Mask at Cerros, Northern Belize." *Journal of Field Archaeology* 4:488–491.

1978 "Maritime Adaptation and the Rise of Maya Civilization: The View from Cerros, Belize." In *Prehistoric Coastal Adaptations,* edited by B. Stark and B. Voorhies, 239–265. Academic Press, New York.

1979 "Culture Areas and Interaction Spheres: Contrasting Approaches to the Emergence of Civilization in the Maya Lowlands." *American Antiquity* 44 (1):36–54.

1981 "Civilization as a State of Mind: The Cultural Evolution of the Lowland Maya." In *The Transition to Statehood in the New World,* edited by G. Jones and R. Kautz, 188–228. Cambridge University Press, Cambridge.

1983 "New Light on the Dark Age: A Summary of Major Themes." In *The Lowland Maya Postclassic,* edited by A. F. Chase and P. M. Rice, 286–309. University of Texas Press, Austin.

1985 "Polychrome Facades of the Lowland Maya Preclassic." In *Painted Architecture and Polychrome Monumental Sculpture in Mesoamerica,* edited by E. Boone, 5–30. Dumbarton Oaks Research Library and Collection, Washington, D.C.

1986a "Terminal Classic Lowland Maya: Successes, Failures, and Aftermaths." In *Late Lowland Maya Civilization: Classic to Postclassic,* edited by J. A. Sabloff and E. W. Andrews V, 409–430. School of American Research, University of New Mexico Press, Albuquerque.

1986b "The Monumental Architecture." In *Archaeology at Cerros, Belize, Central America*. Vol. 1, *An Interim Report*, edited by R. Robertson and D. Freidel, 1–22. Southern Methodist University Press, Dallas.

1986c "Maya Warfare: An Example of Peer Polity Interaction." In *Peer Polity Interaction and Socio-Political Change*, edited by C. Renfrew and J. F. Cherry, 93–108. Cambridge University Press, New York.

1992 "Children of the First Father's Skull: Terminal Classic Warfare in the Northern Maya Lowlands and the Transformation of Kingship and Elite Hierarchies." In *Mesoamerican Elites: An Archaeological Assessment*, edited by D. Z. Chase and A. F. Chase, 99–118. University of Oklahoma Press, Norman.

Freidel, D. A., and L. Schele

1988a "Symbol and Power: A History of the Lowland Maya Cosmogram." In *Maya Iconography*, edited by E. P. Benson and G. G. Griffin, 44–93. Princeton University Press, Princeton.

1988b "Kingship in the Late Preclassic Maya Lowlands: the Instruments and Places of Ritual Power." *American Anthropologist* 90:547–567.

1989 "Dead Kings and Living Temples: Dedication and Termination Rituals among the Ancient Maya." In *Word and Image in Maya Culture: Explorations in Language, Writing, and Representation*, edited by W. F. Hanks and D. S. Rice, 233–243. University of Utah Press, Salt Lake City.

Freidel, D. A., L. Schele, and J. Parker

1993 *Maya Cosmos: Three Thousand Years on the Shaman's Path*. William Morrow, New York.

Fried, M.

1967 *The Evolution of Political Society*. Random House, New York.

Friedman, J., and M. J. Rowlands

1977 "Notes Towards an Epigenetic Model of the Evolution of 'Civilisation.'" In *The Evolution of Social Systems*, edited by J. Friedman and M. J. Rowlands, 201–276. University of Pittsburgh Press, Pittsburgh.

Fry, R. E.

1989 "Regional Ceramic Distributional Patterning in Northern Belize: The View from Pulltrouser Swamp." In *Prehistoric Maya Economies of Belize*, edited by P. A. McAnany and B. L. Isaac, 91–114. Research in Economic Anthropology, Supplement 4. JAI Press, Greenwich, Conn.

1990 "Disjunctive Growth in the Maya Lowlands." In *Precolumbian Population History in the Maya Lowlands*, edited by T. P. Culbert and D. S. Rice, 167–181. University of New Mexico Press, Albuquerque.

Gann, T.

1911 "Exploration Carried on in British Honduras During 1908–1909." *Liverpool University Annals of Archaeology and Anthropology* 4:72–87.

1917 "Notes on Excavations at Indian Church, Wild Cane Cay, Kendal, Corozal, and San Antonio." Saville Files, American Museum of Natural History, New York.

1918   *The Maya Indians of Southern Yucatan and Northern British Honduras.* Bureau of American Ethnology, Bulletin 64. Smithsonian Institution, Washington, D.C.

1925   *Mystery Cities: Exploration and Adventure in Lubaantun.* Duckworth, London.

Garber, J. F.

1983   "Patterns of Jade Consumption and Disposal at Cerros, Belize." *American Antiquity* 48 (4):800–807.

1989   *Archaeology at Cerros, Belize, Central America.* Vol. 2, *The Artifacts.* Southern Methodist University Press, Dallas.

Garber, J. F., and M. K. Brown, editors

2001   *The Belize Valley Archaeology Project: Results of the 2000 Field Season.* Department of Anthropology, Southwest Texas State University, San Marcos.

Garber, J. F., W. D. Driver, and L. A. Sullivan

1993   "Medium Sized Ceremonial Centers in the Belize Valley: The Blackman Eddy Example." Paper presented at the Annual Meeting of the Society for American Archaeology, St. Louis.

Garber, J. F., W. D. Driver, L. A. Sullivan, and D. M. Glassman

1998   "Bloody Bowls and Broken Pots: The Life, Death, and Rebirth of a Maya House." In *The Sowing and the Dawning: Termination, Dedication, and Transformation in the Archaeological Record of Mesoamerica,* edited by S. Mock, 125–133. University of New Mexico Press, Albuquerque.

Garber, J. F., D. M. Glassman, W. D. Driver, and P. Weiss, editors

1994   *The Belize Valley Archaeology Project: Results of the 1993 Field Season.* Department of Anthropology, Southwest Texas State University, San Marcos.

Gellner, E.

1983   *Nations and Nationalism.* Basil Blackwell, Oxford.

Gerhardt, J. Cartwright, and N. Hammond

1991   "The Community of Cuello: The Ceremonial Core." In *Cuello an Early Maya Community in Belize,* edited by N. Hammond. Cambridge University Press, Cambridge.

Gifford, J. C.

1970   "The Earliest and Other Intrusive Population Elements at Barton Ramie." *Ceramica de Cultural Maya* 6:1–10.

1976   *Prehistoric Pottery Analysis and the Ceramics of Barton Ramie in the Belize Valley.* Memoirs of the Peabody Museum of Archaeology and Ethnology, vol. 18. Harvard University, Cambridge.

Gillespie, S. D.

1991   "Ballgames and Boundaries." In *The Mesoamerican Ballgame,* edited by V. L. Scarborough and D. R. Wilcox, 317–345. University of Arizona Press, Tucson.

2000 "Rethinking Ancient Maya Social Organization: Replacing Lineage with House." *American Anthropologist* 102 (3):468–484.

Glassman, D. M., J. M. Conlon, and J. F. Garber

1995 "Survey and Excavations at Floral Park." In *The Belize Valley Archaeology Project: Results of the 1994 Season,* edited by J. F. Garber and D. M. Glassman, 58–70. Department of Anthropology, Southwest Texas State University, San Marcos.

Gonlin, N.

1994 "Rural Household Diversity in Late Classic Copan, Honduras." In *Archaeological Views from the Countryside: Village Communities in Early Complex Communities,* edited by G. M. Schwartz and S. E. Falconer, 177–197. Smithsonian Institution, Washington, D.C.

Goodman, A. H., and R. Song

1999 "Sources of Variation in Estimated Ages at Formation of Linear Enamel Hypoplasias." In *Human Growth in the Past: Studies from Bones and Teeth,* edited by R. Hoppa and C. FitzGerald, 210–239. Cambridge University Press, Cambridge.

Gossen, G., and R. Leventhal

1993 "The Topography of Ancient Maya Religious Pluralism: A Dialogue with the Present." In *Lowland Maya Civilization in the Eighth Century A.D.: A Symposium at Dumbarton Oaks,* edited by J. Sabloff and J. Henderson, 185–217. Dumbarton Oaks, Washington, D.C.

Graham, E.

1984 "Excavations at Negroman-Tipu: The 1984 Season." Paper presented at the Annual Meeting of the Northeastern Anthropological Association, Hartford, Conn.

1987a "Terminal Classic to Early Historic Vessel Forms from Belize." In *Maya Ceramics: Papers from the 1985 Maya Ceramic Conference,* edited by P. M. Rice and R. J. Sharer, 73–98. BAR International Series 345(i), Oxford.

1987b "Resource Diversity in Belize and Its Implications for Models of Lowland Trade." *American Antiquity* 54:253–267.

1991 "Archaeological Insights into Colonial Period Maya Life at Tipu, Belize." In *Columbian Consequences,* edited by D. H. Thomas, 319–336. Smithsonian Institution, Washington, D.C.

1994 *The Highlands of the Lowlands: Environment and Archaeology in the Stann Creek District, Belize, Central America.* Monographs in World Prehistory no. 19. Prehistory Press, Madison.

Graham, E., and D. M. Pendergast

1989 "Excavations at the Marco Gonzalez Site, Ambergris Cay, Belize, 1986." *Journal of Field Archaeology* 16:1–16.

Graham, E., G. D. Jones, and R. R. Kautz

1985 "Archaeology and Ethnohistory on a Spanish Colonial Frontier: An Interim Report on the Macal-Tipu Project in Western Belize." In *The Lowland*

Maya Postclassic, edited by A. F. Chase and P. M. Rice, 206–214. University of Texas Press, Austin.

Graham, E., D. M. Pendergast, and G. D. Jones
1989 "On the Fringes of Conquest: Maya-Spanish Contact in Colonial Belize." *Science* 246:1254–1259.

Graham, I.
1967 *Archaeological Explorations in El Peten, Guatemala.* Middle American Research Institute, Publication 33. Tulane University, New Orleans.

Graham, J. A., R. F. Heizer, and E. M. Shook
1978 *Abaj Takalik 1976: Exploratory Investigations.* Contributions of the Archaeological Research Facility, vol. 6. University of California, Berkeley.

Grove, D. C., and S. D. Gillespie
1984 "Chalcatzingo's Portrait Figurines and the Cult of the Ruler." *Archaeology* 37 (4):27–33.

Grube, N.
1994 "Epigraphic Research at Caracol, Belize." In *Studies in the Archaeology of Caracol, Belize,* edited by D. Chase and A. Chase, 83–122. Pre-Columbian Art Research Institute, Monograph 7, San Francisco.

Grube, N., and L. Schele
1990 *Royal Gifts to Subordinate Lords,* Copan Notes 87. Copan Acropolis Project and Instituto Hondureno de Antropologia, Tegucigalpa.

Guderjan, T. H., and J. F. Garber, editors
1995 *Maya Maritime Trade, Settlement, and Population on Ambergris Caye, Belize.* Labyrinthos Press, Culver City, California.

Hall, G. D.
1989 "Realm of Death: Royal Mortuary Customs and Polity Interaction in the Classic Maya Lowlands." Ph.D. diss., Harvard University.

Hall, G., S. Tarka, W. Hurst, D. Stuart, and R.E.W. Adams
1990 "Cacao Residues in Ancient Maya Vessels from Rio Azul, Guatemala." *American Antiquity* 55 (1):138–143.

Hamblin, N.
1984 *Animal Use by the Cozumel Maya.* University of Arizona Press, Tucson.

Hammond, N.
1972 "Obsidian Trade Routes in the Maya Area." *Science* 178:1092–1093.

1974 "The Distribution of Late Classic Maya Major Ceremonial Centres in the Central Area." In *Mesoamerican Archaeology: New Approaches,* edited by N. Hammond, 313–334. University of Texas Press, Austin.

1975 "Maya Settlement Hierarchy in Northern Belize." In *Studies in Ancient Mesoamerica,* edited by J. A. Graham, 40–55. Contributions of the University of California Archaeological Research Facility 27. University of California Archaeological Research Facility, Berkeley.

1976 "Mayan Obsidian Trade in Southern Belize." In *Maya Lithic Studies: Papers from the 1976 Belize Field Symposium,* edited by T. R. Hester and N.

Hammond, 71–81. Center for Archaeological Research, Special Report 4. University of Texas, San Antonio.

1977 "British Archaeology in Belize: 1976." *Archaeology* 51:61–64.

1978 "Cacao and Cobaneros: An Overland Trade Route between the Maya Highlands and Lowlands." In *Mesoamerican Communication Routes and Cultural Contacts,* edited by T. A. Lee and C. Navarette, 19–25. New World Archaeological Foundation, Publication no. 40. Brigham Young University, Provo, Utah.

1982 "Colha in Context." In *Archaeology at Colha Belize: The 1981 Interim Report,* edited by T. R. Hester, H. J. Shafer, and J. D. Eaton, 65–71. Center for Archaeological Research, University of Texas, San Antonio.

1985 "The Emergence of Maya Civilization." *Scientific American* 255 (2):106–115.

1986 "New Light on the Most Ancient Maya." *Man* 21:399–413.

1989 "The Function of Maya Middle Preclassic Figurines." *Mexicon* 11:112–114.

1991a "Obsidian Trade." In *Cuello: An Early Maya Community in Belize,* edited by N. Hammond, 197–198. Cambridge University Press, Cambridge.

1992 "Preclassic Maya Civilization." In *New Theories on the Ancient Maya,* edited by E. C. Danien and R. J. Sharer, 137–144. University Museum Monograph no. 77. University of Pennsylvania, Philadelphia.

Hammond, N., editor

1991b *Cuello: An Early Maya Community in Belize.* Cambridge University Press, Cambridge.

Hammond, N., A. Clarke, and C. Robin

1991 "Middle Preclassic Buildings and Burials at Cuello, Belize: 1990 Investigations." *Latin American Antiquity* 2:352–363.

Hammond, N., A. Aspinall, S. Feather, J. Hazelden, T. Gazard, and S. Argell

1977 "Maya Jade: Source Location and Analysis." In *Exchange Systems in Prehistory,* edited by T. Earle and J. Ericson, 35–67. Academic Press, New York.

Hansen, R.

1990 *Excavations in the Tigre Complex, El Mirador, Peten, Guatemala.* El Mirador Series, Part 3. New World Archaeological Foundation Paper no. 62. Brigham Young University, Provo, Utah.

1991a "The Maya Rediscovered: The Road to Nakbe." *Natural History* 91 (5): 8–14.

1991b *An Early Maya Text from El Mirador, Guatemala.* Research Reports on Ancient Maya Writing 37. Center for Maya Research, Washington, D.C.

1998 "Continuity and Disjunction: The Pre-Classic Antecedents of Classic Maya Architecture." In *Function and Meaning in Classic Maya Architecture,* edited by S. D. Houston. Dumbarton Oaks, Washington, D.C.

Harrison, E.

1996 "The Ruler's Residential Plaza at Xunantunich, 1996 Excavations." In

Xunantunich Archaeological Project: 1996 Field Season, edited by R. M. Leventhal and W. Ashmore, 71–89. Department of Anthropology, University of California, Los Angeles.

Harrison, P.

1981 "Some Aspects of Preconquest Settlement in Southern Quintana Roo, Mexico." In *Lowland Maya Settlement Patterns,* edited by W. Ashmore, 259–286. University of New Mexico Press, Albuquerque.

1990 "The Revolution of Ancient Maya Subsistence." In *Vision and Revision in Maya Studies,* edited by F. Clancy and P. Harrison, 99–113. University of New Mexico Press, Albuquerque.

Hassig, R.

1985 *Trade, Tribute, and Transportation: The Sixteenth-Century Political Economy of the Valley of Mexico.* University of Oklahoma Press, Norman.

1988 *Aztec Warfare: Imperial Expansion and Political Control.* University of Oklahoma Press, Norman.

Haviland, W. A.

1968 *Ancient Lowland Maya Social Organization.* Middle American Research Institute 26:93–117. Tulane University, New Orleans.

1970 "Tikal, Guatemala, and Mesoamerican Urbanism." *World Archaeology* 2: 186–198.

1981 "Dower Houses and Minor Centers at Tikal, Guatemala: An Investigation into the Identification of Valid Units in Settlement Hierarchies." In *Lowland Maya Settlement Patterns,* edited by W. Ashmore, 89–117. University of New Mexico Press, Albuquerque.

1982 "Where the Rich Folks Lived: Deranging Factors in the Statistical Analysis of Tikal Settlement." *American Antiquity* 47 (2):427–429.

1988 "Musical Hammocks at Tikal: Problems with Reconstructing Household Composition." In *Household and Community in the Mesoamerican Past,* edited by R. R. Wilk and W. Ashmore, 124–134. University of New Mexico Press, Albuquerque.

Haviland, W. A., and H. Moholy-Nagy

1992 "Distinguishing the High and Mighty from the Hoi Polloi at Tikal, Guatemala." In *Mesoamerican Elites: An Archaeological Assessment,* edited by D. S. Chase and A. F. Chase, 50–60. University of Oklahoma Press, Norman.

Haviland, W. A., M. J. Becker, A. Chowning, K. A. Dixon, and K. Heider

1985 *Excavations in Small Residential Groups of Tikal: Groups 4F-1 and 4F-2.* Tikal Report no. 19. The University Museum, University of Pennsylvania, Philadelphia.

Hayden, B.

1994 "Village Approaches to Complex Societies." In *Archaeological Views from the Countryside: Village Communities in Early Complex Communities,* edited by G. M. Schwartz and S. E. Falconer, 198–206. Smithsonian Institution, Washington, D.C.

Healy, P. F.

1988 "Music of the Maya." *Archaeology* 41:24–31.

1990a "The Excavations at Pacbitun, Belize: Preliminary Report on the 1986 and 1987 Investigations." *Journal of Field Archaeology* 17 (3):247–262.

1990b "An Early Classic Maya Monument at Pacbitun, Belize." *Mexicon* 12 (6): 109–110.

1992 "The Ancient Maya Ballcourt at Pacbitun, Belize." *Ancient Mesoamerica* 3: 229–239.

1999 *Belize Valley Preclassic Project: Report on the 1996 and 1997 Field Seasons,* edited by P. F. Healy. Occasional Papers in Anthropology no. 13. Trent University, Peterborough, Ontario.

Healy, P. F., and J. J. Awe

1995a "Radiocarbon Dates from Cahal Pech, Belize: Results from the 1994 Field Season." In *Belize Valley Preclassic Maya Project: Report of the 1994 Field Season,* edited by P. F. Healy and J. J. Awe, 198–215. Occasional Papers in Anthropology no. 10. Trent University, Peterborough, Ontario.

Healy, P. F., and J. J. Awe, editors

1995b *Belize Valley Preclassic Maya Project: Report on the 1994 Field Season.* Occasional Papers in Anthropology no. 10. Trent University, Peterborough, Ontario.

1996 *Belize Valley Preclassic Maya Project: Report on the 1995 Field Season,* Occasional Papers in Anthropology no. 12. Trent University, Peterborough, Ontario.

Healy, P. F., J. J. Awe, and H. Helmuth

1998 "An Ancient Maya Multiple Burial at Caledonia, Cayo District, Belize." *Journal of Field Archaeology* 25 (3):261–274.

Healy, P. F., K. Emery, and L. E. Wright

1990 "Ancient and Modern Maya Exploitation of the Jute Snail (Pachychilus)." *Latin American Antiquity* 1 (2):170–183.

Healy, P. F., H. I. McKillop, and B. Walsh

1984 "Analysis of Obsidian from Moho Cay, Belize: New Evidence on Classic Maya Trade Routes." *Science* 255:414–417.

Healy, P. F., C. van Waarden, and T. J. Anderson

1980 "Nueva evidencia de antigua terrazas mayas en Belice." *America Indigena* 40:773–796.

Healy, P. F., J. J. Awe, G. Iannone, and C. Bill

1995 "Pacbitun (Belize) and Ancient Maya Use of Slate." *Antiquity* 69:337–348.

Healy, P. F., J.D.H. Lambert, J.T. Arnason, and R. J. Hebda

1983 "Caracol, Belize: Evidence of Ancient Maya Agricultural Terraces." *Journal of Field Archaeology* 10:397–410.

Hegmon, M.

1998 "Technology, Style, and Social Practice: Archaeological Approaches." In *The Archaeology of Social Boundaries,* edited by M. T. Stark, 264–280. Smithsonian Institution, Washington, D.C.

Hendon, J. A.

1991 "Status and Power in Classic Maya Society: An Archaeological Study." *American Anthropologist* 93:894–918.

1992 "The Interpretation of Survey Data: Two Case Studies from the Maya Area." *Latin American Antiquity* 3 (1):22–42.

Hendon, J. A., and R. A. Joyce

1993 "Questioning 'Complexity' and 'Periphery': Archaeology in Yoro, Honduras." Paper presented at the Annual Meeting of the Society of American Archaeology, St. Louis.

Hester, T. R., H. J. Shafer, and D. Potter

1983 "Preclassic Communities at Colha, Belize." Paper presented at the 11th ICAES conference, Vancouver, British Columbia.

Hintzman, M. W.

2000 "Scarce-Resource Procurement and Use: The Technological Analysis of an Obsidian Blade Workshop in the Lowlands of Belize." Master's thesis, University of California, Riverside.

Hirth, K.

1992 "Interregional Exchange as Elite Behavior: An Evolutionary Perspective." In *Mesoamerican Elites: An Archaeological Assessment,* edited by D. Z. Chase and A. F. Chase, 18–29. University of Oklahoma Press, Norman.

Hohmann, B.

2002 "Preclassic Maya Shell Ornament Production in the Belize Valley, Belize." Ph.D. diss., University of New Mexico, Albuquerque.

Hohmann, B., and M. D. Glascock

1996 "Formative Period Obsidian from the Belize River Valley: A View from Pacbitun and Cahal Pech." Paper presented at the Annual Meeting of the Society for American Archaeology, New Orleans.

Hohmann, B., and T. Powis

1996 "The 1995 Excavations at Pacbitun, Belize: Investigations of the Middle Formative Occupation in Plaza B." In *Belize Valley Preclassic Maya: Report on the 1995 Field Season,* edited by P. F. Healy and J. J. Awe, 98–127. Occasional Papers in Anthropology no. 12. Trent University, Peterborough, Ontario.

1999 "The 1996 Excavations of Plaza B at Pacbitun, Belize." In *Belize Valley Preclassic Maya Project: Report on the 1996 and 1997 Field Seasons,* edited by P. F. Healy, 1–18. Occasional Papers in Anthropology no. 13. Trent University, Peterborough, Ontario, Canada.

Hohmann, B., T. G. Powis, and C. Arendt

1999 "The 1997 Investigations at Pacbitun, Belize." In *Belize Valley Preclassic Maya Project: Report on the 1996 and 1997 Field Seasons,* edited by P. F. Healy, 19–29. Occasional Papers in Anthropology no. 13. Trent University, Peterborough, Ontario.

Houston, S. D.

1987 "Notes on Caracol Epigraphy and Its Significance." In *Investigations at the Classic Maya City of Caracol, Belize: 1985–1987, Appendix 2,* edited by A.

Chase and D. Chase, 85–100. Pre-Columbian Art Research Institute Monograph 3, Pre-Columbian Art Research Institute, San Francisco.

1993 *Hieroglyphs and History at Dos Pilas: Dynastic Politics of the Classic Maya.* University of Texas Press, Austin.

Houston, S. D., D. Stuart, and K. A. Taube

1992 "Image and Text on the 'Jauncy Vase.'" In *The Maya Vase Book,* vol. 3, edited by J. Kerr, 499–512. Kerr Associates, New York.

Hurst, W. J., S. M. Tarka Jr., T. G. Powis, F. Valdez Jr., and T. R. Hester

2002 "Cacao Usage by the Earliest Maya Civilization." *Nature* 418:289.

Iannone, G.

1992 "Ancient Maya Eccentric Lithics: A Contextual Analysis." Master's thesis, Trent University, Peterborough.

1996 "Problems in the Study of Ancient Maya Settlement and Social Organization: Insights from the 'Minor Center' of Zubin, Cayo District, Belize." Ph.D. diss., Institute of Archaeology, University of London.

Iannone, G., and J. M. Conlon

1993 "Elites, Eccentrics, and Empowerment in the Maya Area: Implications for the Interpretation of a Peripheral Settlement Cluster near Cahal Pech, Cayo District, Belize." *Papers of the Institute of Archaeology* 4:77–89.

Iannone, G., and D.F.H. Lee

1996 "The Formative Period Chipped Stone Assemblage from Cahal Pech, Belize: A Preliminary Comparative Analysis." Paper presented at the Annual Meeting of the Society for American Archaeology, New Orleans.

Inomata, T.

2001 "The Power and Ideology of Artistic Creation: Elite Craft Specialists in Classic Maya Society." *Current Anthropology* 42 (3):321–333.

Jackson, L. J., and H. McKillop

1989 "Defining Coastal Maya Trading Ports and Transportation Routes." In *Coastal Maya Trade,* edited by H. McKillop and P. F. Healy, 91–110. Occasional Papers in Anthropology no. 8. Trent University, Peterborough, Ontario.

Jaeger, S.

1987 "The Conchita Causeway & Associated Settlement." In *Investigations of the Classic Maya City of Caracol, Belize: 1985–1987,* edited by Arlen F. Chase and Diane Z. Chase, 101–106 (Appendix 3). Pre-Columbian Art Research Institute, San Francisco.

1991 "Settlement Pattern Research at Caracol, Belize: The Social Organization in a Classic Maya Center." Ph.D. diss., Southern Methodist University, Dallas.

Jamison, T.

1996 "Excavations on the West Side of Plazas A-I and A-II." In *Xuantunich Archaeological Project: 1996 Field Season,* edited by R. M. Leventhal and W. Ashmore, 59–70. Department of Anthropology, University of California, Los Angeles.

Jamison, T. R., and G. Wolff
1994 "Excavations In and Around Plaza A-I and Plaza A-II." In *Xunantunich Archaeological Project: 1994 Field Season,* edited by R. M. Leventhal and W. Ashmore, 25–47. Department of Anthropology, University of California, Los Angeles.

Jenkin, R. N., R. R. Innes, J. R. Dunsmore, S. H. Walker, C. J. Birchall, and J. S. Briggs
1976 *The Agricultural Development Potential of the Belize Valley.* Land Resources Study no. 24. Land Resources Division, Ministry of Overseas Development, Surbiton, England.

Johnson, A., and T. Earle
1987 *The Evolution of Human Societies from Foraging Group to Agrarian State.* Stanford University Press, Palo Alto.

Jones, C.
1977 "Inauguration Dates of Three Late Classic Rulers of Tikal, Guatemala." *American Antiquity* 53:28–60.
1991 "Cycles of Growth at Tikal." In *Classic Maya Political History: Hieroglyphic and Archaeological Evidence,* edited by T. P. Culbert. Cambridge University Press, Cambridge.
1996 *Excavations in the East Plaza of Tikal.* Tikal Report no. 16. The University Museum, University of Pennsylvania, Philadelphia.

Jones, C., and L. Satterthwaite
1982 *The Monuments and Inscriptions of Tikal: The Carved Monuments.* Tikal Report no. 33, Part A. University Monograph 44. The University Museum, University of Pennsylvania, Philadelphia.

Jones, G. D.
1989 *Maya Resistance to Spanish Rule: Time and History on a Spanish Colonial Frontier.* University of New Mexico Press, Albuquerque.

Jones, G. D., R. B. Kautz, and E. Graham
1986 "Tipu: A Maya Town on the Spanish Colonial Frontier." *Archaeology* 39: 40–47.

Joyce, R., and J. S. Henderson
2001 "Beginnings of Village Life in Eastern Mesoamerica." *Latin American Antiquity* 12 (1):5–24.

Kidder, Alfred V.
1947 *The Artifacts of Uaxactun, Guatemala.* Carnegie Institution of Washington, Publication 576. Washington, D.C.

King, E., and D. Potter
1994 "Small Sites in Prehistoric Maya Socioeconomic Organization: A Perspective from Colha, Belize." In *Archaeological Views from the Countryside: Village Communities in Early Complex Communities,* edited by G. M. Schwartz and S. E. Falconer, 64–90. Smithsonian Institution, Washington, D.C.

Kinkella, A.

2000 "Settlement at the Sacred Pools: Preliminary Archaeological Investigations at the Late Classic Maya Site of Cara Blanca, Belize." Master's thesis, California State University, Northridge.

Kirke, C. M.

1980 "Prehistoric Agriculture in the Belize River Valley." *World Archaeology* 2 (3):281–286.

Knapp, A. B., and W. Ashmore

1999 "Archaeological Landscapes: Constructed, Conceptualized, Ideational." In *Archaeologies of Landscape: Contemporary Perspectives,* edited by W. Ashmore and A. B. Knapp, 1–30. Blackwell Publishers, Oxford.

Kolb, C. C.

1985 "Demographic Estimates in Archaeology: Contributions from Ethnoarchaeology on Mesoamerican Peasants." *Current Anthropology* 26 (5):581–599.

Koontz, R. A.

1994 "The Iconography of El Tajin, Veracruz, Mexico." Ph.D. diss., University of Texas at Austin.

Kosakowski, L. J.

1987 *Preclassic Maya Pottery at Cuello, Belize.* Anthropological Papers of the University of Arizona no. 47. University of Arizona Press, Tucson.

Kosakowski, L. J., and D. C. Pring

1998 "The Ceramics of Cuello, Belize—A New Evaluation." *Ancient Mesoamerica* 9:55–66.

Kowalewski, S. A., G. M. Feinman, and L. Finsten

1992 "'The Elite.'" In *Mesoamerican Elites: An Archaeological Assessment,* edited by D. Z. Chase and A. F. Chase, 259–277. University of Oklahoma Press, Norman.

Kurjack, E. B.

1974 *Prehistoric Lowland Maya Community and Social Organization: A Case Study at Dzibilchultun, Yucatan, Mexico.* Middle American Research Institute, Publication 38. Tulane University, New Orleans.

Kurjack, E. B., and E. W. Andrews V

1976 "Early Boundary Maintenance in Northwest Yucatán, México." *American Antiquity* 41:318–325.

Kurjack, E. B., and S. Garza T.

1981 "Pre-Columbian Community Form and Distribution in the Northern Maya Area." In *Lowland Maya Settlement Patterns,* edited by W. Ashmore, 287–311. University of New Mexico Press, Albuquerque.

Lambert, J.

1980 "Moho Cay Soil Report." Appendix in "Moho Cay, Belize: Preliminary Investigations of Trade, Settlement, and Marine Resource Exploitation," by H. McKillop, 287–289. Master's thesis, Trent University, Peterborough, Ontario.

Landeen, E. S.
1986   "Excavations on a Late Preclassic Plaza Unit at El Mirador." Master's thesis, Brigham Young University, Provo.

Laporte, J. P.
1991   "Reconocimiento Regional en el Noroeste de las Montanas Mayas, Guatemala: Segundo Reporte." *Mexicon* 13 (2):30–36.

1993   "Architecture and Social Change in Late Classic Maya Society: The Evidence from Mundo Perdido, Tikal." In *Lowland Maya Civilization in the Eighth Century A.D.: A Symposium at Dumbarton Oaks,* edited by J. Sabloff and J. Henderson, 299–320. Dumbarton Oaks, Washington, D.C.

1994   *Ixtonton, Dolores, Peten: Entidad Politica del Noroeste de las Montanas Mayas, Atlas Arqueologico de Guatemala no. 2.* Escuela de Historia, Universidad de San Carlos, Guatemala.

1996a *Organizacion Territorial y Politica Prehispanica en el Sureste de Peten, Atlas Arqueologico de Guatemala no. 4.* Escuela de Historia, Universidad de San Carlos, Guatemala.

1996b "La Cuenca del Río Mopan-Belice: Una Sub-Región Cultural de las Tierras Bajas Mayas Centrales." In *IX Simposio de Investigaciones Arqueologicas en Guatemala,* edited by J. P. Laporte and H. L. Escobido, 253–279. Museo Nacional de Arqueologia y Etnologia, Guatemala City.

2001   "Dispersion y Estructura de las Ciudades del Sureste de Peten, Guatemala." In *Reconstruyendo la Ciudad Maya: El Urbanismo en las Sociedades Antiguas,* edited by A. Ciudad Ruiz, M. Josefa Iglesias Ponce de Leon, and M. Del Carmen Martinez, 95–122. Sociedad Espanola de Estudios Mayas, Madrid.

Laporte, J. P., and V. Fialko
1990   "New Perspectives on Old Problems: Dynastic References for the Early Classic at Tikal." In *Vision and Revision in Maya Studies,* edited by F. Clancy and P. D. Harrison, 33–66. University of New Mexico Press, Albuquerque.

1993   El Preclasico de Mundo Perdido: Algunos Sobre los Origenes de Tikal." In *Tikal y Uaxactun en el Preclasico,* edited by J. P. Laporte and J. A. Valdes, 4–96. Universidad Nacional Autonoma de Mexico, Mexico City.

Laporte, J. P., and H. E. Mejia
2002   Ucanal: Una Ciudad del rio Mopan en Peten, Guatemala. *U tz'ib: Serie Reportes* 1 (2):1–71 (Association Tikal).

Laporte, J. P., and R. Torres
1987   "Los Senores de Sureste de Peten." *Mayab* 3:7–22.

Laporte, J. P., and J. A. Valdes, editors
1993   *Tikal y Uaxactun en el Preclasico.* Universidad Nacional Autonoma de Mexico, Mexico City.

Laporte, J. P., R. Torres, and B. Hermes
1989   "Ixtonton: Evolucion de un Asentamiento en el Alta Mopan, Peten, Guatemala." *Mayab* 5:19–29.

Lawlor, E. J., A. J. Graham, and S. L. Fedick

1995 "Preclassic Floral Remains from Cahal Pech, Belize." In *Belize Valley Preclassic Maya Project: Report on the 1994 Field Season,* edited by P. F. Healy and J. J. Awe, 150–172. Occasional Papers in Anthropology no. 10. Trent University, Peterborough, Ontario.

LeCount, L. J.

1996 "Pottery and Power: Feasting, Gifting, and Displaying Wealth among the Late and Terminal Classic Lowland Maya." Ph.D. diss., University of California, Los Angeles.

1999 "Polychrome Pottery and Political Strategies in Late and Terminal Classic Lowland Maya Society." *Latin American Antiquity* 10 (3):239–258.

2002 "Like Water for Chocolate: Feasting and Political Ritual among the Late Classic Maya at Xunantunich, Belize." *American Anthropologist* 103 (4): 935–953.

LeCount, L. J., J. Yaeger, R. M. Leventhal, and W. Ashmore

2002 "Dating the Rise and Fall of Xunantunich: A Late and Terminal Classic Maya Center." *Ancient Mesoamerica* 13 (1):41–63.

Lee, D.

1996 "Nohoch Na (The Big House): The 1995 Excavations of the Cas Pek Group, Cahal Pech, Belize." In *Belize Valley Preclassic Maya Project: Report on the 1995 Field Season,* edited by P. F. Healy and J. J. Awe, 77–97. Occasional Papers in Anthropology no. 12. Trent University, Peterborough, Ontario.

Lee, D. and J. J. Awe

1995 "Middle Formative Architecture, Burials, and Craft Specialization: Report on the 1994 Investigations at the Cas Pek Group, Cahal Pech, Belize." In *Belize Valley Preclassic Maya Project: Report on the 1994 Field Season,* edited by P. F. Healy and J. J. Awe, 95–115. Occasional Papers in Anthropology no. 10. Trent University, Peterborough, Ontario.

Lehmann, W.

1926 "Reisebrief aus Puerto Mexico." *Zeitschrift fur Ethnologie* 126:171–177.

Lentz, D. L.

1990 "Acrocomia Mexicana: Palm of the Ancient Mesoamerican." *Journal of Ethnobiology* 10 (2):183–194.

1991 "Maya Diets of the Rich and Poor: Paleoethnobotanical Evidence from Copan." *Latin American Antiquity* 2:269–287.

Leventhal, R. M.

1981 "Settlement Patterns in the Southeast Maya Area." In *Lowland Maya Settlement Patterns,* edited by W. Ashmore, 187–211. University of New Mexico Press, Albuquerque.

1983 "Household Groups and Classic Maya Religion." In *Prehistoric Settlement Patterns: Essays in Honor of Gordon R. Willey,* edited by E. Z. Vogt and R. Leventhal, 55–76. University of New Mexico Press, Albuquerque.

Leventhal, R. M., editor
1992 *Xunantunich Archaeological Project: 1992 Field Season.* Department of Anthropology, University of California, Los Angeles.

Leventhal, R. M., and W. Ashmore
1997 "Xunantunich: An Ancient and Modern City." Paper presented at the Third Belize Interdisciplinary Conference, Belize City, Belize.

Leventhal, R. M., S. Zelenik, T. Jamison, L. LeCount, J. McGovern, J. Sanchez, and A. Keller
1993 "Xunantunich: A Late and Terminal Classic Center in the Belize Valley." Paper presented at the Palenque Mesa Redonda, Aniversario Katun, 1973–1993, Palenque, Mexico.

Lincoln, C. E.
1985 "Ceramics and Ceramic Chronology." In *A Consideration of the Early Classic Period in the Maya Lowlands,* edited by G. R. Willey and P. Mathews, 55–94. Institute for Mesoamerican Studies, State University of New York, Albany.

Looper, M. G.
1993 "The Three Stones of Maya Creation Mythology at Quiriguá." *Mexicon* 17 (2):24–30.

1994 "The Iconography of North-Face Scenes of Quiriguá Stelae A and C." Manuscript.

Low, S. M.
1995 "Indigenous Architecture and the Spanish American Plaza in Mesoamerica and the Caribbean." *American Anthropologist* 97 (4):748–762.

Lowe, G. W.
1962 "Algunos Resultados de la Temporada 1961 en Chiapa de Corzo, Chiapas." *Estudios de Cultura Maya* 2:185–196.

Lucero, L. J.
1994 "Household and Community Integration among Hinterland Elites and Commoners: Maya Residential Ceramics of the Belize River Area." Ph.D. diss., University of California, Los Angeles.

2001 *Social Integration in the Ancient Maya Hinterlands: Ceramic Variability in the Belize River Area.* Anthropological Research Paper no. 53. Arizona State University, Tempe.

MacKie, E.
1961 "New Light on the End of Classic Culture at Benque Viejo, British Honduras." *American Antiquity* 27 (2):216–224.

1985 *Excavations at Xunantunich and Pomona, Belize, in 1959–1960.* BAR International Series 251. Oxford: British Archaeological Reports.

Magnoni, A.
1999 "Relative Sea-Level Rise and Excavations at Crown Conch Mound, a Partially-Submerged Ancient Maya Mound, Frenchman's Cay, Belize." Master's thesis, Louisiana State University, Baton Rouge.

Mallory, J. K.

1984 "Late Classic Economic Specialization: Evidence from the Copan Obsidian Assemblage." Ph.D. diss., Pennsylvania State University, Pittsburgh.

Marcus, J.

1976 *Emblem and State in the Classic Maya Lowlands.* Dumbarton Oaks, Washington, D.C.

1983a "On the Nature of the Mesoamerican City." In *Prehistoric Settlement Patterns: Essays in Honor of Gordon R. Willey,* edited by E. Z. Vogt and R. Leventhal, 195–242. University of New Mexico Press, Albuquerque.

1983b "Lowland Maya Archaeology at the Crossroads." *American Antiquity* 48: 454–482.

1989 "Zapotec Chiefdoms and the Nature of Formative Religions." In *Regional Perspectives on the Olmecs,* edited by R. J. Sharer and D. C. Grove, 148–197. Cambridge University Press, Cambridge.

1993 "Ancient Maya Political Organization." In *Lowland Maya Civilization in the Eighth Century A.D.,* edited by J. A. Sabloff and J. S. Henderson, 111–184. Dumbarton Oaks, Washington, D.C.

1995 "Where Is Lowland Maya Archaeology Headed?" *Journal of Archaeological Research* 3 (1):3–53.

1998 *Women's Ritual in Formative Oaxaca: Figurine Making, Divination, Death and the Ancestors.* Memoirs of the Museum of Anthropology no. 33. University of Michigan, Ann Arbor.

Martin, S., and N. Grube

1995 "Maya Super-States." *Archaeology* 48 (6):41–46.

2000 *Chronicle of the Maya Kings and Queens: Deciphering the Dynasties of the Ancient Maya.* Thames & Hudson, London.

Mason, G.

1940 *South of Yesterday.* New York.

Masson, M. A.

1997 "Cultural Transformation at the Maya Postclassic Community of Laguna de On, Belize." *Latin American Antiquity* 8 (4):293–316.

Matheny, R. T.

1986a "Investigations at El Mirador, Peten, Guatemala." *National Geographic Research* 2:332–353.

1986b "Early States in the Maya Lowlands: Edzna and El Mirador." In *City States of the Maya: Art and Architecture,* edited by E. Benson, 1–44. Rocky Mountain Institute of Pre-Columbian Studies, Denver.

1987 "El Mirador: An Early Maya Metropolis Uncovered." *National Geographic* 172 (3):317–339.

Mathews, P.

1988 "The Sculpture of Yaxchilan." Ph.D. diss., Yale University, New Haven.

1991 "Classic Maya Emblem Glyphs." In *Classic Maya Political History,* edited by T. P. Culbert, 19–29. Cambridge University Press, Cambridge.

Maxwell, D.

2000 "Beyond Maritime Symbolism: Toxic Marine Objects from Ritual Contexts at Tikal." *Ancient Mesoamerica* 11:91–98.

McAnany, P. A.

1995 *Living with the Ancestors: Kinship and Kingship in Ancient Maya Society.* University of Texas Press, Austin.

1998 "Ancestors and the Classic Maya Built Environment." In *Function and Meaning in Classic Maya Architecture,* edited by S. D. Houston, 271–298. Dumbarton Oaks Research Library and Collection, Washington, D.C.

McDonald, A. J.

1983 "Tzutzuculi: A Middle Preclassic Site on the Pacific Coast of Chiapas, Mexico." In *Papers of the New World Archaeological Foundation no. 47.* Brigham Young University, Provo, Utah.

McGee, R. J.

1990 *Life, Ritual, and Religion among the Lacandon Maya.* Wadsworth, Belmont, Calif.

McGovern, J. O.

1992 "1992 Study of Actuncan (Cahal Xux)." In *Xunantunich Archaeological Project: 1992 Field Season,* edited by R. M. Leventhal, 74–83. Department of Anthropology, University of California, Los Angeles.

1994 "Survey and Excavation at Actuncan." In *Xunantunich Archaeological Project: 1993 Field Season,* edited by R. M. Leventhal, 100–126. Department of Anthropology, University of California, Los Angeles.

McKillop, H.

1980 "Moho Cay, Belize: Preliminary Investigations of Trade, Settlement, and Marine Resource Exploitation." Master's thesis, Trent University, Peterborough, Ontario.

1984 "Prehistoric Maya Reliance on Marine Resources: Analysis of a Midden from Moho Cay, Belize." *Journal of Field Archaeology* 11:25–35.

1985 "Prehistoric Exploitation of the Manatee in the Maya and Circum-Caribbean Areas." *World Archaeology* 16:337–353.

1987 "Wild Cane Cay: An Insular Classic Period to Postclassic Period Maya Trading Station." Ph.D. diss., University of California, Santa Barbara.

1989 "Coastal Maya Trade: Obsidian Densities from Wild Cane Cay, Belize." In *Prehistoric Maya Economies of Belize,* edited by P. McAnany and B. Isaac, 17–56. Research in Economic Anthropology, Supplement 4. JAI Press, Greenwich, Conn.

1994 "Ancient Maya Tree-Cropping: A Viable Subsistence Alternative for the Island Maya." *Ancient Mesoamerica* 5:129–140.

1995 "Underwater Archaeology, Salt Production, and Coastal Maya Trade at Stingray Lagoon, Belize." *Latin American Antiquity* 6:214–228.

1996a "Ancient Maya Trading Ports and the Integration of Long-Distance and

Regional Economies: Wild Cane Cay in South-Coastal Belize." *Ancient Mesoamerica* 7:49–62.

1996b "Prehistoric Maya Use of Native Palms: Archaeobotanical and Ethnobotanical Evidence." In *The Managed Mosaic: Ancient Maya Agriculture and Resource Use,* edited by S. L. Fedick, 278–294. University of Utah Press, Salt Lake City.

1998 "Environmental Impact Assessment of Wild Cane Cay, Port Honduras, Belize." Report on file, Ministry of Natural Resources, Belmopan, Belize.

2002 *Salt, White Gold of the Ancient Maya.* University Press of Florida, Gainesville.

McKillop, H., and P. F. Healy

1989 *Coastal Maya Trade.* Occasional Papers in Anthropology no. 8. Trent University, Peterborough, Ontario.

Michaels, G. H.

1989 "Craft Specialization in the Early Postclassic of Colha." In *Prehistoric Maya Economies of Belize,* edited by P. A. McAnany and B. L. Isaac, 139–183. JAI Press, Greenwich Conn.

1993 "Evidence for Lithic Craft Specialization by the Classic Period Maya of the Upper Belize River Valley, Belize." Ph.D. diss., University of California, Santa Barbara.

Miksicek, C. H.

1991 "The Natural and Cultural Landscape of Preclassic Cuello." In *Cuello: An Early Maya Community in Belize,* edited by N. Hammond, 70–84. Cambridge University Press, Cambridge.

Miller, A. G.

1976 "The Little Decent: Manifest Destiny from the East." *Actes du XLII Congrès des Americanistes* (Paris, Société des Americanistes), 8:231–236.

1977 "The Maya and the Sea: Trade and Cult at Tancah and Tulum, Quintana Roo, Mexico." In *The Sea in the Pre-Columbian World,* edited by E. Benson, 97–140. Dumbarton Oaks, Washington, D.C.

Miller, M.

1986 *The Murals of Bonampak.* Princeton University Press, Princeton, N.J.

1995 "Maya Masterpiece Revealed at Bonampak." *National Geographic* 187 (2):50–69.

Miller, M. E., and S. D. Houston

1987 "The Classic Maya Ballgame and Its Architectural Setting: A Study of Relations between Text and Image." *RES* 14:47–65.

Miller, V. E.

1991 *The Frieze of the Palace of the Stuccoes, Acanceh, Yucatan, Mexico.* Studies in Pre-Columbian Art and Archaeology 31. Dumbarton Oaks. Washington, D.C.

Mitchum, B. A.

1991 "Lithic Artifacts from Cerros, Belize: Production, Consumption, and Trade."

In *Maya Stone Tools: Selected Papers from the Second Maya Lithic Conference,* edited by T. R. Hester and H. J. Shafer, 45–53. Monographs in World Archaeology no. 1. Prehistory Press, Madison.

Moholy-Nagy, H.

1978 "The Utilization of Pomacea at Tikal, Guatemala." *American Antiquity* 43: 65–73.

1985 "The Social and Ceremonial Uses of Marine Molluscs at Tikal." In *Prehistoric Lowland Maya Environment and Subistence Economy,* edited by M. Pohl, 147–154. Papers of the Peabody Museum of Archaeology and Ethnology no. 77. Harvard University, Cambridge.

Moore, A. F.

1997 "Investigaciones Preliminares en un Grupo de la Periferia de Baking Pot, Belice." *Los Investigadores de la Cultura Maya* 5: 145–154.

1999 "Micro-Settlement Analysis in the Belize River Valley: Archaeological Investigations at Atalaya, a Formal Patio Group at Baking Pot." Ph.D. diss., Institute of Archaeology, University College, London.

Morley, F. R., and S. G. Morley

1938 *The Age and Provenance of the Leyden Plate.* Carnegie Institution of Washington, Publication 509. Washington, D.C.

Morris, J.

1984 "Ceramic Analysis of Valley of Peace." *Belizean Studies* 12:15–20.

Muhs, D. R., R. R. Kauts, and J. J. MacKinnon

1985 "Soils and the Location of Cacao Orchards at a Maya Site in Western Belize." *Journal of Archaeological Science* 12:121–137.

Nelson, F. W.

1985 "Summary of Results of Analysis of Obsidian Artifacts from the Maya Lowlands." *Scanning Electron Microscopy* 11:631–649.

Nicholson, H. B.

1981 "The Mixteca-Puebla Concept in Mesoamerican Archaeology: A Re-examination." In *Ancient Mesoamerica: Selected Readings,* edited by J. A. Graham, 253–258. Peek Publications, Palo Alto, Calif.

Norman, V. Garth

1976 *Izapa Sculpture.* Part 2, *Text.* Papers of the New World Archaeological Foundation, no. 30. Brigham Young University, Provo, Utah.

O'Day, S. J., and W. F. Keegan

2001 "Expedient Shell Tools from the Northern West Indies." *Latin American Antiquity* 12:274–290.

Olson, K.

1994 "Inclusive and Exclusive Mechanisms of Power: Obsidian Blade Production and Distribution among the Ancient Maya of the Belize River Area." Master's thesis, University of California, Los Angeles.

Orrego, C. M.

1990 *Investigaciones Arqueologicas en Abaj Takalik, El Asintal, 1988.* Reporte no. 1. Proyecto Nacional Abaj Takalik, IDAEH, Ministerio de Cultura y Deportes, Guatemala.

1995 *Investigaciones Arqueologicas in la Estructura EP7 El Pilar, Belice: Una Interpretacion Preliminar de los Sistemas Constructivos y Arquitectonicos del Sitio Arqueologico de El Pilar, Belice.* BRASS/El Pilar Program, Meso-American Research Center. University of California, Santa Barbara.

Osterholtz, A.

1999 "Underwater Archaeology of the Maya Area: A History and Study of the Methodological Approaches for the Recovery and Treatment of Cultural Materials Recovered from a Freshwater Environment." Honors thesis, New Mexico State University, Las Cruces.

Otto, B. E.

1995 "The Eccentrics of Buenavista: Typology, Terminology, and Meaning." Master's thesis, San Diego State University.

Pendergast, D. M.

1969 *Altun Ha, British Honduras (Belize): The Sun God's Tomb.* Occasional Paper 19. Royal Ontario Museum, Toronto.

1979 *Excavations at Altun Ha, Belize, 1964–1970,* vol. 1. Royal Ontario Museum Archaeology Monograph. Alger, Toronto.

1986 "Stability Through Change: Lamanai, Belize, from the Ninth to the Seventeenth Century." In *Late Lowland Maya Civilization: Classic to Postclassic,* edited by J. A. Sabloff and E. W. Andrews V, 223–249. School of American Research, University of New Mexico Press, Albuquerque.

1992 "Noblesse Oblige: The Elites of Altun Ha and Lamanai, Belize." In *Mesoamerican Elites: An Archaeological Assessment,* edited by D. Z. Chase and A. F. Chase, 61–79. University of Oklahoma Press, Norman.

Pendergast, D. M., and E. Graham

1981 "Fighting a Looting Battle: Xunantunich, Belize." *Archaeology* 34 (4):12–19.

Pendergast, D. M., G. D. Jones, and E. Graham

1993 "Locating Maya Lowlands Spanish Colonial Towns: A Case Study from Belize." *Latin American Antiquity* 4 (1):59–73.

Piehl, J. C.

1997 "The Burial Complexes of Baking Pot: Preliminary Report on the 1996 Field Season." In *Belize Valley Archaeological Reconnaissance Project: Progress Report of the 1996 Field Season,* edited by J. J. Awe and J. M. Conlon, 21–45. Department of Anthropology, Trent University, Peterborough, Ontario.

Pohl, M.

1976 "Ethnozoology of the Maya: An Analysis of the Fauna from Five Sites in the Peten, Guatemala." Ph.D. diss., Harvard University.

1977 "Hunting in the Maya Village of San Antonio, Rio Hondo, Orange Walk District, Belize." *Journal of Belizean Affairs* 5:52–97.

1983 "Maya Ritual Faunas." In *Civilization in the Ancient Americas: Essays in Honor of Gordon R. Willey,* edited by R. M. Leventhal and A. L. Kolata, 55–103. University of New Mexico Press, Albuquerque, and the Peabody Museum of Archaeology and Ethnology, Harvard University, Cambridge.

Potter, D. R.

1985 "Settlement." In *A Consideration of the Early Classic Period in the Maya Lowlands,* edited by G. R. Willey and P. Mathews, 135–144. Institute for Mesoamerican Studies, State University of New York, Albany.

1991 "A Descriptive Taxonomy of Middle Preclassic Chert Tools at Colha, Belize." In *Maya Stone Tools: Selected Papers from the Second Maya Lithic Conference,* edited by T. R. Hester and H. J. Shafer, 21–29. Monographs in World Archaeology no. 1. Prehistory Press, Madison.

Powis, T. G.

1996 "Excavations of Middle Formative Round Structures at the Tolok Group, Cahal Pech, Belize." Master's thesis, Trent University, Peterborough, Ontario.

Powis, T., and B. Hohmann

1995 "From Private Household to Public Ceremony: Middle Formative Occupation at the Tolok Group, Cahal Pech, Belize." In *Belize Valley Preclassic Maya Project: Report on the 1994 Field Season,* edited by P. F. Healy and J. J. Awe, 45–94. Occasional Papers in Anthropology no. 10. Trent University, Peterborough, Ontario.

Powis, T., B. Hohmann, and C. Arendt

1996 "Preliminary Report on the 1995 Excavations at the Ch'um Group, Cahal Pech, Belize." In *Belize Valley Preclassic Maya Project: Report on the 1995 Field Season,* edited by P. F. Healy and J. J. Awe, 59–76. Occasional Papers in Anthropology no. 12. Trent University, Peterborough, Ontario.

Powis, T., J. J. Awe, P. F. Healy, and N. Stanchly

2000 "La Explotacion de Recursos Animales por los Antiguos Maya del Periodo Formativo Medio: Nueva Evidencia del Grupo Tolok en Cahal Pech, Belice." In *III Congreso Internacional de Mayistas, 1995,* edited by A. L. Izquierdo y de la Cueva, Tomo 2:225–241. Centro de Estudios Maya del Instituto de Investigaciones Filologicas de la Universidad Autonoma de Mexico (UNAM), Chetumal, Quintana Roo.

Powis, T., B. Hohmann, J. J. Awe, and P. F. Healy

1996 "Las Estructuras Circulares del Grupo Tolok en Cahal Pech, Belice: Nueva Informacion Sobre la Complejidad de Plataformas Redondas de Periodo Formativo." In *IX Simposio de Investigaciones Arqueologicas en Guatemala, 1995,* edited by J. P. LaPorte and H. L. Escobedo, 281–294. Museo Nacional de Arqueologia y Etnologia-Guatemala, Ministerio de Cultura y Deportes, Instituto de Antropologia e Historia, y Asociacion Tikal, Guatemala City.

Powis, T. G., F. Valdez Jr., T. R. Hester, W. J. Hurst, and S. M. Tarka Jr.
2002 "Spouted Vessel and Cacao Use among the Preclassic Maya. *Latin American Antiquity* 13 (1):85–106.

Powis, T., N. Stanchly, C. D. White, P. F. Healy, J. J. Awe, and F. Longstaffe
1999 "A Reconstruction of Middle Preclassic Maya Subsistence Economy at Cahal Pech, Belize." *Antiquity* 73 (280):364–376.

Proskouriakoff, T.
1962 "Civic and Religious Structures of Mayapan." In *Mayapan Yucatan Mexico,* edited by H.E.D. Pollock, 87–164. Carnegie Institution of Washington, Publication 619. Washington, D.C.

Puleston, D. E.
1973 "Ancient Settlement Patterns and Environment at Tikal, Guatemala: Implication for Subsistence Models." Ph.D. diss., University of Pennsylvania, Philadelphia.
1974 "Intersite Areas in the Vicinity of Tikal and Uaxactun." In *Mesoamerican Archaeology: New Approaches,* edited by N. Hammond, 303–311. University of Texas Press, Austin.
1983 *The Settlement Survey of Tikal.* Tikal Report Number 13, University Museum Monograph 48, W. A. Haviland, vol. ed. University of Pennsylvania, Philadelphia.

Rands, Robert L., and B. C. Rands
1965 "Pottery Figurines of the Maya Lowlands." In *Handbook of Middle American Indians,* vol. 2, *Archaeology of Southern Mesoamerica,* Part 1, edited by G. R. Willey, 535–560. University of Texas Press, Austin.

Reed, D. M.
1992 "Ancient Maya Diet at Copan, Honduras, as Determined through the Analysis of Stable Carbon and Nitrogen Isotopes." Paper presented at the conference on "Paleonutrition: Diet and Health of Prehistoric Americans." Center for Archaeological Investigations, Southern Illinois University, Carbondale.

Reents, D. J.
1985 "The Late Classic Maya Holmul-Style Polychrome Pottery." Ph.D. diss., University of Texas at Austin.

Reents-Budet, D.
1994 *Painting the Maya Universe: Royal Ceramics of the Classic Period.* Duke University Press, Durham, N.C.

Reents-Budet, D., R. L. Bishop, and B. MacLeod
1994 "Painting Styles, Workshop Locations, and Pottery Production." In *Painting the Maya Universe: Royal Ceramics of the Classic Period,* edited by D. J. Reents, 164–233. Duke University Press, Durham, N.C.

Reents-Budet, D., R. L. Bishop, J. T. Taschek, and J. W. Ball
2000 "Out of the Palace Dumps: Ceramic Production and Use at Buenavista del Cayo." *Ancient Mesoamerica* 11 (1):99–121.

Rice, D. S.

1976 "The Historical Ecology of Lakes Yaxh and Sacnab, Peten, Guatemala." Ph.D. diss., Pennsylvania State University, Pittsburgh.

1986 "The Peten Postclassic: A Settlement Perspective." In *Late Lowland Maya Civilization: Classic to Postclassic,* edited by J. A. Sabloff and E. W. Andrews V, 301–345. School of American Research, University of New Mexico Press, Albuquerque.

Rice, D. S., and D. E. Puleston

1981 "Ancient Maya Settlement Patterns in the Peten, Guatemala." In *Lowland Maya Settlement Patterns,* edited by W. Ashmore, 121–156. University of New Mexico Press, Albuquerque.

Rice, P. M.

1983 "Serpents and Styles in Peten Postclassic Pottery." *American Anthropologist* 85:866–880.

1984 "Obsidian Procurement in the Central Petén Lakes Region, Guatemala." *Journal of Field Archaeology* 11:181–194.

1985 "Postclassic and Historic-Period Pottery from Negroman-Tipu, Belize." Paper presented at the Annual Meeting of the Society for American Archaeology, Denver.

1986 "The Peten Postclassic: Perspectives from the Central Peten Lakes." In *Late Lowland Maya Civilization: Classic to Postclassic,* edited by J. A. Sabloff and E. W. Andrews V, 251–299. School of American Research, University of New Mexico Press, Albuquerque.

1987 *Macanche Island, El Peten, Guatemala: Excavations, Pottery, and Artifacts.* University of Florida Press, Gainesville.

1999 "Rethinking Classic Lowland Maya Pottery Censers." *Ancient Mesoamerica* 10:25–50.

Richie, C.

1990 "Ancient Maya Settlement and Environment of the Eastern Zone of Pacbitun, Belize." Master's thesis, Trent University, Peterborough, Ontario.

Ricketson, O. G.

1925 "Burials in the Maya Area." *American Anthropologist* 27 (3):381–401.

1929 *Excavations at Baking Pot, British Honduras.* Contributions to American Archaeology no. 1. Carnegie Institution of Washington, Publication 403. Washington, D.C.

1931 *Excavations at Baking Pot, British Honduras.* Contributions to American Archaeology, 1 (1). Carnegie Institution of Washington, Washington, D.C.

1937 "Part I: The Excavations." In *Uaxactun, Guatemala: Group E: 1926–1931,* 1–180. Carnegie Institution of Washington, Publication 407. Washington, D.C.

Ricketson, O. G., Jr., and E. B. Ricketson

1937 *Uaxactun, Guatemala: Group E: 1926–1931.* Carnegie Institution of Washington, Publication 477. Washington, D.C.

Robertson, D.

1970   "The Tulum Murals: The International Style of the Late Postclassic." *Verhandlungen des XXXVIII Internationalen Amerikanisten Kongresses* 2: 77–88.

Robertson, M. G.

1977   "Painting Practices and Their Change through Time of the Palenque Stucco Sculptors." In *Social Process in Maya Prehistory: Studies in Honour of Sir Eric Thompson,* edited by N. Hammond, 297–326. Academic Press, London.

Robin, C.

1999   "Towards an Archaeology of Everyday Life: Maya Farmers of Chan Noohol and Dos Chombitos Cik'in, Belize." Ph.D. diss., University of Pennsylvania, Philadelphia.

Robin, C., and J. R. Yaeger

1996   "Ancient Maya Royalty and Expressions of Power at Xunantunich." *ECO-Journal of Environmental Information* 1 (3):32–36.

Rovner, I., and S. M. Lewenstein

1997   *Maya Stone Tools of Dzibilchaltún, Yucatán, and Becán and Chicanná, Campeche.* Middle American Research Institute, Publication 65. Tulane University, New Orleans.

Ruppert, K.

1940   "A Special Assemblage of Maya Structures." In *The Maya and Their Neighbors,* edited by C. L. Hay, R. L. Linton, S. K. Lothrop, H. L. Shapiro, and G. C. Vaillant. Appleton-Century, New York.

Ruz Lhuillier, A.

1965   "Tombs and Funerary Practices in the Maya Lowlands." In *Handbook of Middle American Indians,* vol. 2, edited by G. R. Willey, 331–361. University of Texas Press, Austin.

1968   *Costumbres Funerarias de los Antiguos Mayas.* Universidad Nacional Autonoma de Mexico, Mexico.

1973   *El Templo de las Inscripciones, Palenque.* Coleccion Cientifica, Arqueologia 7. Instituto Nacional de Antropologia e Historia, Mexico.

Sabloff, J. A.

1973   "Major Themes in the Past Hypotheses of the Maya Collapse." In *The Classic Maya Collapse,* edited by T. P. Culbert, 35–40. School of American Research, University of New Mexico Press, Albuquerque.

1975   "Ceramics." In *Excavations at Seibal, Department of Peten, Guatemala, no. 2.,* edited by G. R. Willey. Memoirs of the Peabody Museum of Archaeology and Ethnology, Harvard University, Cambridge.

1983   "Classic Maya Settlement Pattern Studies: Past Problems, Future Prospects." In *Prehistoric Settlement Patterns,* edited by E. Z. Vogt and R. M. Leventhal, 413–422. University of New Mexico Press, Albuquerque.

1994   "The New Archaeology and the Ancient Maya." In *The New Archaeology and the Ancient Maya*. Scientific American Library, New York. Distributed by W. H. Freeman, New York.

Sabloff, J. A., and W. L. Rathje

1975 "The Rise of a Maya Merchant Class." *Scientific American* 233:72–82.

Sabloff, J. A., and G. R. Willey

1967 "The Collapse of Maya Civilization in the Southern Lowlands: A Consideration of History and Process." *Southwestern Journal of Anthropology* 23 (4):311–336.

Sackett, J.

1977 "The Meaning of Style in Archaeology: A General Framework." *American Antiquity* 42 (3):369–380.

Sanchez, J.

1993 "1993 Excavations on El Castillo, Xunantunich, Belize." In *Xunantunich Archaeological Project: 1993 Field Season*, edited by R. M. Leventhal, 56–64. Department of Anthropology, University of California, Los Angeles.

Sanders, W. T.

1960 *Prehistoric Ceramics and Settlement in Patterns in Quintana Roo, Mexico*. Contributions to American Archaeology no. 60. Carnegie Institute of Washington, Publication 606. Washington, D.C.

1981 "Classic Maya Settlement Patterns and Ethnohistoric Analogy." In *Lowland Maya Settlement Patterns*, edited by W. Ashmore, 351–369. University of New Mexico Press, Albuquerque.

1992 "Ranking and Stratification in Prehispanic Mesoamerica." In *Mesoamerican Elites: An Archaeological Assessment*, edited by D. Z. Chase and A. F. Chase, 278–291. University of Oklahoma Press, Norman.

Sanders, W. T., and D. Webster

1978 "Unilinealism, Multilinealism, and the Evolution of Complex Societies." In *Social Archaeology: Beyond Subsistence and Dating*, edited by C. L. Redman, 245–302. Academic Press, New York.

1988 "The Mesoamerican Urban Tradition." *American Anthropologist* 90:521–546.

Satterthwaite, L.

1950 "Plastic Art on a Maya Palace." *Archaeology* 3 (4):215–222.

1951 "Reconnaissance in British Honduras." *University Museum Bulletin* 16 (1): 21–37.

Saturno, W.

2002 "Proyecto Aqueologico Regional San Bartolo: Resultados de la Primera Temporada de Campo 2002." Paper presented at the XVII Simposio de Investigaciones Arqueologicas en Guatemala, Guatemala City.

Saul, F. P.

1972 *The Human Skeletal Remains from Altar de Sacrificios, Guatemala: An Osteobiographic Analysis*. Papers of the Peabody Museum of Archaeology and Ethnology no. 63 (2). Harvard University, Cambridge.

Saul, F. P., and J. M. Saul
1991 "The Preclassic Population of Cuello." In *Cuello: An Early Maya Community in Belize,* edited by N. Hammond, 134–158. Cambridge University Press, Cambridge.

Scarborough, V. L.
1991 "Courting the Southern Maya Lowlands: A Study in Pre-Hispanic Ballgame Architecture." In *The Mesoamerican Ballgame,* edited by V. L. Scarborough and D. R. Wilcox, 129–144. University of Arizona Press, Tucson.
1993 "Water Management in the Southern Maya Lowlands: An Accretive Model for the Engineered Landscape." In *Research in Economic Anthropology, Supplement 7: Economic Aspects of Water Management in the Prehispanic New World,* edited by V. L. Scarborough and B. L. Isaac, 17–69. JAI Press, Greenwich, Conn.

Scarborough, V. L., and R. A. Robertson
1986 "Civic and Residential Settlement at a Late Preclassic Maya Center." *Journal of Field Archaeology* 13:155–177.

Scarborough, V. L., and D. R. Wilcox, editors
1991 *The Mesoamerican Ballgame.* University of Arizona Press, Tucson.

Scarborough, V. L., B. Mitchum, S. Carr, and D. A. Freidel
1982 "Two Late Preclassic Ballcourts at the Lowland Maya Center of Cerros, Northern Belize." *Journal of Field Archaeology* 9 (1):21–34.

Schele, L.
1985 "Color on Classic Architecture and Monumental Sculpture of the Southern Maya Lowlands." In *Painted Architecture and Polychrome Monumental Sculpture in Mesoamerica,* edited by E. Hill Boone, 31–49. Dumbarton Oaks, Washington, D.C.

Schele, L., and D. A. Freidel
1990 *A Forest of Kings.* Morrow, New York.

Schele, L., and P. Mathews
1998 *The Code of Kings: The Language of Seven Sacred Maya Temples and Tombs.* Scribner, New York.

Schele, L., and J. H. Miller
1983 *The Mirror, the Rabbit, and the Bundle: "Accession" Expressions from the Classic Maya Inscriptions.* Studies in Pre-Columbian Art and Archaeology no. 25. Dumbarton Oaks, Washington, D.C.

Schele, L., and M. E. Miller
1986 *The Blood of Kings: Dynasty and Ritual in Maya Art.* Kimbell Art Museum, Fort Worth, and Braziller, New York.

Schmidt, P.
1976/77 "Postclassic Finds in the Cayo District, Belize." *Estudios de Cultura Maya* 10:103–114.

Scholes, F. B., and E. Thompson
1977 "The Francisco Perez Probanza of 1654–1656 and the Matricula of Tipu

(Belize)." In *Anthropology and History in Yucatan,* edited by G. D. Jones, 43–68. University of Texas Press, Austin.

Schwartz, G. M., and S. E. Falconer

1994 "Rural Approaches to Social Complexity." In *Archaeological Views from the Countryside: Village Communities in Early Complex Communities,* edited by G. M. Schwartz and S. E. Falconer, 1–9. Smithsonian Institution, Washington, D.C.

Service, E.

1975 *Origins of the State and Civilization: The Process of Evolution.* W. W. Norton, New York.

Shafer, H. J.

1991 "Late Preclassic Formal Stone Tool Production at Colha, Belize." In *Maya Stone Tools: Selected Papers from the Second Maya Conference,* edited by T. R. Hester and H. J. Shafer, 31–44. Monographs in World Archaeology no. 1. Prehistory Press, Madison.

Shafer, H. J., and T. R. Hester

1983 "Ancient Maya Chert Workshops in Northern Belize, Central America." *American Antiquity* 48:519–543.

Sharer, R. J.

1976 "The Jenney Creek Ceramic Complex at Barton Ramie." In *Prehistoric Pottery Analysis and the Ceramics of Barton Ramie Belize,* by J. C. Gifford, 61–63. Memoirs of the Peabody Museum of Archaeology and Ethnology 16. Harvard University, Cambridge.

1992 "The Preclassic Origin of Lowland Maya States." In *New Theories on the Ancient Maya,* edited by E. C. Danien and R. J. Sharer, 131–136. University Museum Monograph no. 77. University of Pennsylvania, Philadelphia.

1999 "Archaeology and History in the Royal Acropolis, Copan, Honduras." *Expedition* 41 (2):8–15.

Sharer, R. J., and A. F. Chase

1976 "The New Town Ceramic Complex." In *Prehistoric Pottery Analysis and the Ceramics of Barton Ramie,* edited by J. C. Gifford, 420–445. Memoirs of the Peabody Museum of Archaeology and Ethnology. Harvard University, Cambridge.

Sharer, R. J., and J. C. Gifford

1970 "Preclassic Ceramics from Chalchuapa, El Salvador and Their Relationships with the Maya Lowlands." *American Antiquity* 35 (4):441–462.

Sharp, R.

1981 *Chacs and Chiefs: The Iconology of Mosaic Stone Sculpture in Pre-Conquest Yucatán, Mexico.* Studies in Pre-Columbian Art and Archaeology 24. Dumbarton Oaks, Washington, D.C.

Shaw, L.

1991 "The Articulation of Social Inequality and Faunal Resource Use in the Preclassic Community of Colha, Northern Belize." Ph.D. diss., University of Massachusetts, Amherst.

Shennan, S. J., editor
1989   *Archaeological Approaches to Cultural Identity.* Unwin Hyman, London.
Shook, E. M.
1960   "Tikal Stela 29." *Expedition* 2 (2):28–35.
Shook, E. M., and A. V. Kidder II
1961   "The Painted Tomb at Tikal." *Expedition* 4 (2):2–7.
Simmons, S. E.
1995   "Maya Resistance, Maya Resolve: The Tools of Autonomy from Tipu, Belize." *Ancient Mesoamerica* 6:135–146.
Smith, A. L.
1950   *Uaxactun, Guatemala: Excavations of 1931–1937.* Carnegie Institution of Washington, Publication 588. Washington, D.C.
1961   "Types of Ball Courts in the Highlands of Guatemala." In *Essays in Pre-Columbian Art and Archaeology,* edited by S. K. Lothrop and others, 100–125. Harvard University Press, Cambridge.
1962   "Residential and Associated Structures at Mayapan." In *Mayapan Yucatan Mexico,* edited by H.E.D. Pollock, 165–320. Carnegie Institution of Washington, Publication 619. Washington, D.C.
1972   *Excavations at Altar de Sacrificios: Architecture, Settlement, Burials and Caches.* Papers of the Peabody Museum of Archaeology and Ethnology no. 62 (2). Harvard University, Cambridge.
1982   *Excavations at Seibal, Department of Peten, Guatemala: Major Architecture and Caches.* Peabody Museum of Archaeology and Ethnology Memoirs vol. 15 (1). Harvard University, Cambridge.
Smith, M. E., and C. Heath-Smith
1980   "Waves of Influence in Postclassic Mesoamerica? A Critique of the Mixteca-Puebla Concept." *Anthropology* 4 (2):15–50.
Smith, R. E.
1937   *A Study of Structure A-1 Complex at Uaxactun, Guatemala.* Contributions to American Archaeology, no. 19. Carnegie Institution of Washington, Publication 456. Washington, D.C.
1955   *Ceramic Sequence at Uaxactun, Guatemala.* 2 vols. Middle American Research Institute, Publication 20. Tulane University, New Orleans.
1971   *The Pottery of Mayapan.* Peabody Museum of Archaeology and Ethnology vol. 66. Harvard University, Cambridge.
Song, R.
1995   "Bones and Bowls of the Formative Maya: A Preliminary Report on the Human Skeletal Remains from Cahal Pech, Belize, and the Implications for Mortuary Behavior." In *Belize Valley Preclassic Maya Project: Report on the 1994 Field Season,* edited by P. F. Healy and J. J. Awe, 173–197. Occasional Papers in Anthropology no. 10. Trent University, Peterborough, Ontario.
1996   "The Formative Period Skeletal Assemblage at Cahal Pech." Paper presented at the Annual Meeting of the Society for American Archaeology, New Orleans.

1997 "Developmental Defects of Enamel in the Maya of Altun Ha, Belize: Implications for Ancient Maya Childhood Health." Master's thesis, Trent University, Peterborough, Ontario.

Spence, M. W.
1996 "Commodity or Gift: Teotihuacan Obsidian in the Maya Region." *Latin American Antiquity* 7 (1):21–39.

Spencer, C. S., E. M. Redmond, and M. Rinaldi
1994 "Drained Fields at La Tigra, Venezuelan Llanos: A Regional Perspective." *Latin American Antiquity* 5 (2):119–143.

Stanchly, N. W.
1992 "An Analysis of the Faunal Remains from Structure B-4, Cahal Pech, Belize." Appendix in "Dawn in the Land between the Two Rivers," by J. J. Awe, 338–403. Ph.D. diss., Institute of Archaeology, University of London.

1995 "Formative Period Maya Faunal Utilization at Cahal Pech, Belize: Preliminary Analysis of the Animal Remains from the 1994 Field Season." In *Belize Valley Preclassic Maya: Report on the 1994 Field Season,* edited by P. F. Healy and J. J. Awe, 124–149. Occasional Papers in Anthropology no. 10. Trent University, Peterborough, Ontario.

1999 "Preliminary Report on the Preclassic Faunal Remains from Pacbitun, Belize: 1995 and 1996 Field Seasons." In *Belize Valley Preclassic Maya: Report on the 1996 and 1997 Field Seasons,* edited by P. F. Healy, 41–52. Occasional Papers in Anthropology no. 13. Trent University, Peterborough, Ontario.

Steinberg, J. M.
1992 "Labor in Maya Architecture: A Theory of Consumption." Master's thesis, University of California, Los Angeles.

Stirling, M. W.
1940 "An Initial Series from Tres Zapotes, Veracruz, Mexico." *Contributed Technical Papers Mexican Archaeology Series* 1 (1). National Geographic Society, Washington, D.C.

Stone, A.
1989 "Disconnection, Foreign Insignia, and Political Expansion: Teotihuacan and the Warrior Stelae of Piedras Negras." In *Mesoamerica after the Decline of Teotihuacan A.D. 700–900,* edited by R. A. Diehl and J. C. Berlo, 153–171. Dumbarton Oaks, Washington, D.C.

1992 "From Ritual in the Landscape to Capture in the Urban Center: The Recreation of Ritual Environments in Mesoamerica." *Journal of Ritual Studies* 6 (1):109–132.

Strelow, D., and L. J. LeCount
2001 "Regional Interaction in the Formative Southern Maya Lowlands: Evidence of Olmecoid Stylistic Motifs in a Cunil Ceramic Assemblage from Xunantunich." Poster session at the Annual Meeting of the Society for American Archaeology, New Orleans.

Stuart, D.

1987 *Ten Phonetic Syllables.* Research Reports on Ancient Maya Writing 14. Center for Maya Research, Washington, D.C.

Stuart, G.

1997 "The Royal Crypts of Copan." *National Geographic* 192 (6):68–93.

Sunahara, K. S.

1994 "Ancient Maya Settlement: The Western Zone of Pacbitun, Belize." Master's thesis, Trent University, Peterborough, Ontario.

Sutro, L. D., and T. E. Downing

1988 "A Step Towards a Grammar of Space: Domestic Space Use in Zapotec Villages." In *Household and Community in the Mesoamerican Past,* edited by R. R. Wilk and W. Ashmore, 29–50. University of New Mexico Press, Albuquerque.

Tainter, J. A.

1988 *The Collapse of Complex Societies.* Cambridge University Press, Cambridge.

1994 *The Artifacts of Dzibilchaltun, Yucatan, Mexico: Shell, Polished Stone, Bone, Wood, and Ceramics.* Middle American Research Institute, Publication 50. Tulane University, New Orleans.

Taschek, J. T., and J. W. Ball

1992 "Lord Smoke-Squirrel's Cacao Cup: The Archaeological Context and Socio-Historical Significance of the Buenavista 'Jauncy Vase.'" In *The Maya Vase Book,* vol. 3, edited by J. Kerr, 490–498. Kerr Associates, New York.

1999 "Las Ruinas de Arenal, Belize—Preliminary Report on a Subregional Major Center in the Western Belize Valley (1991–1992 Excavations)." *Ancient Mesoamerica* 10 (2):215–235.

Taube, K.

1983 "The Teotihuacan Spider Woman." *Journal of Latin American Lore* 9: 107–189.

1986 "The Teotihuacan Cave of Origin: The Iconography and Architecture of Emergence Mythology in Mesoamerica and the American Southwest." *RES* 12:51–82.

1994 "The Birth Vase: Natal Imagery in Ancient Maya Myth and Ritual." In *The Maya Vase Book,* vol. 4, edited by J. Kerr, 650–685. Kerr Associates, New York.

Taylor, W. W.

1948 *A Study of Archaeology,* Memoirs of the American Anthropological Association no. 69. Reprinted 1967 by Southern Illinois University Press, Carbondale.

Tedlock, D.

1985 *Popul Vuh: The Mayan Book of the Dawn of Life.* Simon and Schuster, New York.

Thomas, P. M., Jr.

1981 *Prehistoric Maya Settlement Patterns at Becan, Campeche, Mexico.* Middle

American Research Institute, Publication 45. Tulane University, New Orleans.

Thompson, J.E.S.

1931 *Archaeological Investigations in the Southern Cayo District, British Honduras*. Publication 301, Anthropological Series vol. 17 (3). Field Museum of Natural History, Chicago.

1939 *Excavations at San Jose, British Honduras*. Carnegie Institution of Washington, Publication 506. Washington, D.C.

1940 *Late Ceramic Horizons at Benque Viejo, British Honduras*. Carnegie Institution of Washington, Publication 528. Washington, D.C.

1970 *Maya History and Religion*. University of Oklahoma Press, Norman.

Tourtellot, G.

1970 *The Peripheries of Seibal, an Interim Report*. Papers of the Peabody Museum of Archaeology and Ethnology, vol. 16: 405–421. Harvard University, Cambridge.

1988 *Excavations at Seibal, Department of Peten, Guatemala: Peripheral Survey and Excavation, Settlement and Community Patterns*. Peabody Museum of Archaeology and Ethnology Memoirs, vol. 16. Harvard University, Cambridge.

Tourtellot, G., J. A. Sabloff, and K. Carmean

1992 "Will the Real Elites Please Stand Up? An Archaeological Assessment of Maya Elite Behavior in the Terminal Classic Period." In *Mesoamerican Elites: An Archaeological Assessment,* edited by D. Z. Chase and A. F. Chase, 80–98. University of Oklahoma Press, Norman.

Tozzer, A. M.

1913 *A Preliminary Study of the Prehistoric Ruins of Nakum, Guatemala*. Papers of the Peabody Museum of Archaeology and Ethnology, vol. 5 (3). Harvard University, Cambridge.

1941 *Landa's Relacion de las Cosas de Yucatan*. Papers of the Peabody Museum of Archaeology and Ethnology 2. Harvard University, Cambridge.

Trik, A. A.

1963 "The Splendid Tomb of Temple 1, Tikal Guatemala." *Expedition* 6 (1):2–18.

Valdés, J. A.

1987 "Uaxactun: Recientes Investigaciones." *Mexicon* 8 (6):125–128.

1988 "Los Mascarones Preclassicos de Uaxactun: el Caso del Grupo H." In *Primer Simposio Mundial Sobre Epigraphia Maya,* 165–181. Asociacion Tikal, Guatemala City.

Villa Rojas, A.

1934 *The Yaxuna-Coba Causeway*. Carnegie Institution of Washington, Publication 436, Contribution 9. Washington, D.C.

Vogt, E. Z.

1969 *Zinacantan: A Maya Community in the Highlands of Chiapas*. Belknap Press of Harvard University Press, Cambridge.

1976 *Tortillas for the Gods: A Symbolic Analysis of Zinacanteco Rituals.* University of Oklahoma Press, Norman.

1983 "Ancient and Contemporary Maya Settlement Patterns: A New Look from the Chiapas Highlands." In *Prehistoric Settlement Patterns: Essays in Honor of Gordon R. Willey,* edited by E. Z. Vogt and R. M. Leventhal, 89–114. University of New Mexico Press, Albuquerque.

von Falkenhausen, L.

1985 "Architecture." In *A Consideration of the Early Classic Period in the Maya Lowlands,* edited by G. R. Willey and P. Mathews, 111–134. Institute for Mesoamerican Studies, State University of New York, Albany.

Walker, D. S.

1990 "Cerros Revisited: Ceramic Indicators of Terminal Classic and Postclassic Settlement and Pilgrimage in Northern Belize." Ph.D. diss., Southern Methodist University, Dallas.

Washington, H. S.

1922 "The Jade of the Tuxtla Statuette." *Proceedings of the U.S. National Museum* 60 (14):1–14.

Waterman, T. T.

1924 "On Certain Antiquities in Western Guatemala." *Bulletin of the Pan American Union.* Washington, D.C.

Wauchope, R.

1934 *Housemounds of Uaxactun, Guatemala.* Contributions to American Archaeology no. 7. Carnegie Institution of Washington, Publication 436. Washington, D.C.

Webb, M. C.

1973 "The Peten Maya Decline Viewed in the Perspective of State Formation." In *The Classic Maya Collapse,* edited by T. P. Culbert, 367–404. School of American Research, University of New Mexico Press, Albuquerque.

1975 "The Flag Follows Trade: An Essay on the Necessary Interaction of Military and Commercial Factors in State Formation." In *Ancient Civilization and Trade,* edited by T. A. Sabloff and C. C. Lamberg-Karlovsky, 155–209. University of New Mexico Press, Albuquerque.

1987 "Broader Perspectives on Andean State Origins." In *The Origins and Development of the Andean State,* edited by J. Haas and T. Pozorski, 161–167. Cambridge University Press, Cambridge.

Webster, D. L.

1977 "Warfare and the Evolution of Maya Society." In *The Origins of Maya Civilization,* edited by R.E.W. Adams, 335–372. University of New Mexico Press, Albuquerque.

1985 "Surplus, Labor, and Stress in Late Classic Maya Society." *Journal of Anthropological Research* 41:375–399.

1989 *The House of the Bacabs, Copan, Honduras,* edited by D. L. Webster. Dumbarton Oaks, Washington, D.C.

1992   "Maya Elites: The Perspective from Copan." In *Mesoamerican Elites: An Archaeological Assessment,* edited by D. Z. Chase and A. F. Chase, 135–156. University of Oklahoma Press, Norman.

1993   "The Study of Maya Warfare: What It Tells Us about the Maya and What It Tells Us about Maya Archaeology." In *Lowland Maya Civilization in the Eighth Century A.D.,* edited by J. A. Sabloff and J. S. Henderson, 415–455. Dumbarton Oaks, Washington, D.C.

1998   "Warfare and Status Rivalry: Lowland Maya and Polynesian Comparisons." In *Archaic States,* edited by G. M. Feinman and J. Marcus, 311–351. School of American Research Press, Santa Fe.

Webster, D. L., and N. Gonlin

1988   "Household Remains of the Humblest Maya." *Journal of Field Archaeology* 15:169–190.

Webster, D. L., A. C. Freter, and N. Gonlin

2000   *Copan: The Rise and Fall of an Ancient Maya Kingdom.* Harcourt Brace, Fort Worth.

Webster, G. S.

1990   "Labor Control and Emergent Stratification in Prehistoric Europe." *Current Anthropology* 31 (4):337–366.

Welsh, W.B.M.

1988   *An Analysis of Classic Lowland Maya Burials.* BAR International Series, no. 409. Oxford.

Wernecke, D. C.

1994   "Aspects of Urban Design in an Ancient Maya Center: El Pilar, Belize." Master's thesis, Florida Atlantic University, Boca Raton.

White, C. D.

1986   "Paleodiet and Nutrition of the Ancient Maya at Lamanai, Belize: A Study of Trace Elements, Stable Isotopes, Nutritional and Dental Pathologies." Master's thesis, Trent University, Peterborough, Ontario.

White, C. D., editor

1999   *Reconstructing Ancient Maya Diet.* University of Utah Press, Salt Lake City.

White, C. D., P. F. Healy, and H. P. Schwarcz

1993   "Intensive Agriculture, Social Status, and Maya Diet at Pacbitun, Belize." *Journal of Anthropological Research* 49:347–375.

White, C. D., F. Longstaffe, and R. Song

1996   "Preclassic Maya Diet at Cahal Pech, Belize: The Isotopic Evidence." Paper presented at the Annual Meeting of the Society for American Archaeology, New Orleans.

Wiesen, A., and D. L. Lentz

1999   "Preclassic Floral Remains at Cahal Pech and Pacbitun, Belize: Summary Report." In *Belize Valley Preclassic Maya Project: Report on the 1996 and 1997 Field Seasons,* edited by P. F. Healy, 53–67. Occasional Papers in Anthropology no. 13. Trent University, Peterborough, Ontario.

Wiessner, P.

1990 "Is There a Unity to Style?" In *The Uses of Style in Archaeology*, edited by M. W. Conkey and C. A. Hastorf, 105–121. Cambridge University Press, Cambridge.

Wilk, R. R., and W. Ashmore, editors

1988 *Household and Community in the Mesoamerican Past*. University of New Mexico Press, Albuquerque.

Willey, G. R.

1953 *Prehistoric Settlement Patterns in the Viru Valley, Peru*. Bulletin 155, Bureau of American Ethnology, Smithsonian Institution, Washington, D.C.

1956a "The Structure of Ancient Maya Society: Evidence from the Southern Lowlands." *American Anthropologist* 58 (5):777–782.

1956b "Problems Concerning Prehistoric Settlement Patterns in the Maya Lowlands." In *Prehistoric Settlement Patterns in the New World*, edited by G. R. Willey, 107–114. Viking Fund Publications in Anthropology no. 23. New York.

1973 "Certain Aspects of the Late Classic to Postclassic Periods in the Belize Valley." In *The Classic Maya Collapse*, edited by T. P. Culbert, 93–106. School of American Research, University of New Mexico Press, Albuquerque.

1976 "Foreword." In *Prehistoric Pottery Analysis and the Ceramics of Barton Ramie in the Belize Valley*, by J. Gifford, vii–viii. Memoirs of the Peabody Museum 18. Harvard University, Cambridge.

1981 "Maya Lowland Settlement Patterns: A Summary Review." In *Lowland Maya Settlement Patterns*, edited by W. Ashmore, 385–415. University of New Mexico Press, Albuquerque.

1988 *Portraits in American Archaeology. Remembrances of Some Distinguished Americanists*. University of New Mexico Press, Albuquerque.

Willey, G. R., and W. Bullard Jr.

1956 "The Melhado Site: A House Mound Group in British Honduras." *American Antiquity* 22:29–44.

1965 "Prehistoric Settlement Patterns in the Maya Lowlands." In *Handbook of Middle American Indians*, vol. 2, edited by G. R. Willey, 360–377. University of Texas Press, Austin.

Willey, G. R., and J. C. Gifford

1961 "Pottery of the Holmul I Style from Barton Ramie, British Honduras." In *Essays in Pre-Columbian Art and Archaeology*, edited by S. K. Lothrop et al., 152–170. Harvard University Press, Cambridge.

Willey, G. R., and R. M. Leventhal

1979 "Prehistoric Settlement at Copan." In *Maya Archaeology and Ethnohistory*, edited by N. Hammond and G. R. Willey, 75–102. University of Texas Press, Austin.

Willey, G. R., and D. B. Shimkin
1973 "The Maya Collapse: A Summary View." In *The Classic Maya Collapse*, edited by T. P. Culbert, 457–501. School of American Research, University of New Mexico Press, Albuquerque.

Willey, G. R., W. R. Bullard Jr., and J. B. Glass
1955 "The Maya Community of Prehistoric Time." *Archaeology* 8 (1):18–25.

Willey, G. R., T. P. Culbert, and R.E.W. Adams
1967 "Maya Lowland Ceramics: A Report from the 1965 Guatemala City Conference." *American Antiquity* 32:289–315.

Willey, G. R., W. R. Bullard Jr., J. B. Glass, and J. C. Gifford
1965 *Prehistoric Maya Settlements in the Belize Valley*. Papers of the Peabody Museum of Archaeology and Ethnology 54. Harvard University, Cambridge.

Winfield Capitaine, F.
1988 *La Estela 1 de La Mojarra, Veracruz, Mexico*. Research Reports on Ancient Maya Writing no. 16. Center for Maya Research, Washington, D.C.

Wing, E. S., and D. Steadman
1980 "Vertebrate Faunal Remains from Dzibilchaltun." In *Excavations at Dzibilchaltun, Yucatan, Mexico*, edited by E. W. Andrews IV and E. W. Andrews V, 326–331. Middle American Research Institute, Publication 48. Tulane University, New Orleans.

Wobst, M. H.
1977 "Stylistic Behavior and Information Exchange." In *For the Director: Research Essays in Honor of James B. Griffin*, edited by C. Clelland, 317–342. Anthropological Papers no. 61. Museum of Anthropology, University of Michigan, Ann Arbor.

Wren, L. H., and P. Schmidt
1991 "Elite Interaction During the Terminal Classic Period: New Evidence from Chichen Itza." In *Classic Maya Political History: Hieroglyphic and Archaeological Evidence*, edited by T. P. Culbert, 199–225. Cambridge University Press, Cambridge.

Wright, A.C.S., D. H. Romney, R. H. Arbuckle, and V. E. Vial
1959 *Land Use in British Honduras: Report of the British Honduras Land Use Survey Team*. Colonial Research Publication 24. Colonial Office, London.

Wright, H. T.
1984 "Prestate Political Formations." In *On the Evolution of Complex Societies: Essays in Honor of Harry Hoijer*, edited by T. K. Earle, 41–77. Undena, Malibu.

Wright, L. E.
1990 "Stresses of Conquest: A Study of Wilson Bands and Enamel Hypoplasias in the Maya of Lamanai, Belize." *American Journal of Human Biology* 2:25–35.

Yadeun, J.
1992 *Tonina*. El laberinto del Inframundo. Gobierno del Estado de Chiapas, Mexico.
Yaeger, J. R.
1997 "The 1997 Excavations of Plaza A-III and Miscellaneous Excavation and Architectural Clearing in Group A." In *Xunantunich Archaeological Project—1997 Field Season,* edited by R. M. Leventhal, 24–55. Department of Anthropology, University of California, Los Angeles.
2000a "Changing Patterns of Social Organization: The Late and Terminal Classic Communities at San Lorenzo, Cayo District, Belize." Ph.D. diss., University of Pennsylvania, Philadelphia.
2000b "The Social Construction of Communities in the Classic Maya Countryside: Strategies of Affiliation in Western Belize." In *The Archaeology of Communities: A New World Perspective,* edited by M. A. Canuto and J. Yaeger, 123–142. Routledge, London.

Contributors

James Aimers, assistant professor, Southern Illinois University, has worked at sites in the Belize Valley, Mexico, and Honduras. His research concerns Maya architecture and Postclassic ceramics.

Joseph W. Ball, professor, San Diego State University, has conducted research at several sites throughout the Maya area, including Becan, Kamilnaljuyu, Buenavista del Cayo, Cahal Pech, Las Ruinas, and Nohoch Ek. He has published articles and book chapters on Maya archaeology and is a leading authority on ceramics.

Arlen F. Chase is professor and interim director of Latin American area studies at the University of Central Florida. His research focuses on archaeological method and theory in the Maya area with particular emphasis on urbanism and ethnicity, hieroglyphic interpretation, settlement patterns, and ceramic and contextual analysis. Since 1985 he has codirected annual research at the Classic period site of Caracol, Belize. He has published articles and half a dozen monographs and books, many with his wife, Diane Z. Chase.

Diane Z. Chase is professor and interdisciplinary coordinator for academic affairs at the University of Central Florida. Her research interests focus on complex societies and hermeneutics, ethnohistory, and ceramic and mortuary analysis. For the last two decades, she has codirected excavations at Caracol, Belize; before that she directed a seven-year project at Santa Rita Corozal, also in Belize. She has written scores of articles as well as several monographs and books.

David Cheetham is a research associate at the New World Archaeological Foundation, Brigham Young University, and a Ph.D. candidate at Arizona State University. He has worked at several sites in Mexico, Guatemala, and

Belize. His current research includes an extensive study of early Maya pottery, ethnicity, and the role of long-distance contact with neighboring regions in the rise of social and political complexity.

James M. Conlon, Ph.D. candidate at the University of London, has worked at several sites in the Belize Valley over the past decade and is currently engaged in an investigation of the site of Saturday Creek.

W. David Driver, a Ph.D. candidate at Southern Illinois University, has worked on many excavations, including sites in the United States, Belize, and Saudi Arabia. In Belize he served as field director for the Blackman Eddy and Blue Creek projects. He has contributed to site reports, serving as senior editor for the Blue Creek reports, and has written articles in several journals.

Virginia M. Fields, curator of pre-Columbian art, Los Angeles County Museum of Art, has been active in the fields of pre-Columbian and Native American art for over twenty years, organizing exhibitions and publishing articles and essays.

Anabel Ford, research anthropologist at the Institute of Social Behavioral and Economic Research and director of the Meso-American Research Institute at the University of California at Santa Barbara, has worked at several sites in Belize and Guatemala and is currently directing a large project at the site of El Pilar. She has published several articles and book chapters.

James F. Garber, professor of anthropology and field school director, Texas State University–San Marcos, has been active in Maya archaeology for twenty-five years. His research interests include the investigation of the role of trade in sociopolitical development, reconstructing ritual, and the rise of complex society. He has conducted research at several sites in Belize since 1976 and is the author of *Archaeology at Cerros Belize, Central America*, vol. 2, *The Artifacts*, in addition to numerous articles and book chapters.

Paul F. Healy, professor, Trent University (Ontario, Canada), is director of the Trent University Archaeological Research Centre. Since 1976, he has directed archaeological projects at the lowland Maya sites of Moho Cay, Caracol, Mountain Cow, Caledonia, Pacbitun, and Cahal Pech in Belize.

He is the author of over forty publications on the pre-Columbian archaeology of Mesoamerica and lower Central America.

Gyles Iannone, assistant professor, Trent University (Ontario, Canada), currently directs a project in western Belize and has written several articles and reports. He is the senior editor of a recently published volume on settlement systems.

Richard M. Leventhal, director, School of American Research, Santa Fe, N.M., has directed research at several sites in the Maya lowlands, including a large project at the site of Xunantunich. He has written numerous reports, articles, and book chapters.

Lisa Lucero, associate professor, New Mexico State University, has worked at several sites in the Belize Valley and currently directs a project in the lower end of the valley. She is interested in the emergence of Maya rulership and has written many articles and reports.

Heather McKillop, William G. Haag Professor of Archaeology, Louisiana State University, has carried out fieldwork on the coast of Belize since 1979 and has published articles on the ancient coastal Maya and a book, *Salt: White Gold of the Ancient Maya* (UPF, 2002).

Jennifer T. Taschek, adjunct professor, San Diego State University, has conducted research on a variety of topics associated with Maya archaeology, including architecture, site layout, and use of public space. She has published a book and articles and reports.

Gordon R. Willey (deceased) held the prestigious Bowditch Chair at Harvard University. He had been active in the field of Maya studies for fifty years and wrote many books, articles, book chapters, and reports. He is generally regarded as one of the most important scholars of Maya archaeology in particular and New World archaeology in general.

Index

Page numbers for illustrations are in italics.

Actuncan, 48, 153, 177, 205n3, 289; Preclassic, 4, 68, 138, 156, 199; stela, 138, 170

Adams, R.E.W., 125, 233, 249, 255, 262, 305, 315, 324

agouti, 199, 221, 224

aguada, 253, 288

Aimers, J. J., 110, 153, 163, 209, 210, 223, 229, 305, 306, 311, 315, 342, 343

Alta Vista, 283

Altar de Sacrificios: ceramics, 262, 315; skeletal remains, 120; stone tools, 116; tomb, 233

Altun Ha, 134, 233, 262, 270

Ambergris Cay, 260

ancestor: shrines, 281; veneration, 62, 202, 301; worship, 233

Ancestor Mountain, 153, 193, 194, 200, 202

Anderson, H., 12, 18, 20–22, 261

Andrews, A. P., 100

Andrews V, E. W., 31, 125, 257, 305

Aoyama, K., 211

Archaic valley populations, 30

Arenal, 199. See also Las Ruinas

Arendt, C. 215

Arie, J. C., 91

Armadillo, 40, 221, 224

Ashmore, W., 10–12, 54, 55, 72, 75, 76, 79, 125, 126, 130, 141, 168, 171, 176, 178, 225, 255, 278–282, 287, 299, 301, 321, 340

atlatl, 311

Audet, C., 306

Aveni, A. F., 342

avian-serpent, 31

Awe, J. J., 12, 13, 25, 30, 31, 33, 34, 40, 44–46, 52, 67, 75, 81, 87, 103, 104, 107, 109, 110, 112–116, 122, 132, 133, 136, 138, 145, 153, 156, 165n3, 169, 170, 171, 207, 208, 224, 225, 228, 229, 306, 317, 328, 332, 346

axe-eye, 185, 186, 187

axis mundi, 175, 189, 229, 341

Aztec, 323, 324

bajo, 288, 303n2

Baker, P., 219

Baking Pot, 4, 289, 292, 294; and Bedran, 70–86; history of research, 12, 13, 22; Late Classic, 305; location in valley, 5, 24, 49; site plan, 71; Terminal Classic, 31. See also Bedran

Ball, J. W., 7, 12, 13, 30–32, 41, 43, 45, 48, 72, 103, 122, 139, 149, 153, 156–161, 168–171, 181, 191, 192, 198, 200, 205n4, 236n4, 261, 262, 278, 282, 283, 290, 296, 297, 303n1, 306, 317, 320, 324, 329, 330, 331, 332, 338, 340, 341, 345, 346

Banana Bank, 9, 94

barkbeater, 301

barrier reef, 260

Barton Ramie, 6, 10, 274; and Blackman Eddy, 50; chronology, 7, 40–41, 42, 50; in historical perspective, 5–6; Postclassic, 8–9, 310; settlement, 9, 10, 49; Willey's work at, 21–23, 283

Bawden, G., 284

bead: bone, 39; ceramic, 117; greenstone, 40; jade, 52, 116, 133, 216; shell, 25, 38, 39, 110, 116, 216, 224; stone, 133

bean, 91, 118, 119, 123

Becan, 164*n*2

Becker, M. J., 72, 77, 78, 300, 321, 322

Bedran, *71, 73;* agricultural ditch system, 79–80, 293; and Baking Pot, 292, 297; chronology, 74–75; investigations at, 70–85, 283. *See also* Baking Pot

Bell, E. E., 233

Benavides, 125

Benque Viejo. *See* Xunantunich

Bey, G. J., 310

Bill, C. R., 308, 314

Birchall, C. J., 87

Bishop, R. L., 216

Black, S. L., 4

Blackman Eddy, 48–69, 199, 289; and Barton Ramie, 10, 338; early ceramics, 7; Middle Formative, 25–47, 153, 165*n*4, 337–338; site plan, *50;* stratified sequence, 25, *51. See also* Kanocha

Blanton, R. E., 144, 323

Blom, F., 64, 210

bloodletter: Middle Formative, 39; in tombs, 234, 235; personified, 169*n*9

bloodletting: at Bonampak, 52; bowls, 58; royal ritual, 199; trade 258

bola, 311

Bonampak, 52

Borhegyi, S. F. de, 100, 278

Boserup, E., 254

Bowditch, C. P., 15

Brady, J. E., 7, 156, 158, 165*n*7

Braswell, J. B., 171, 173, 175, 205*n*1

Bricker, V. R., 308

Brown, M. K., 25, 42, 45, 48

Buenavista, 4, 8, 289; chronology, 151, 191–192, 196–197; device, 159–160, 165*n*8; investigations, 149–167; and Naranjo, 331; site plan, *150, 151,* 332. *See also* palace school

Bullard, M. R., 12, 70, 75, 78, 287, 288, 291, 345

Bullard, W. R. Jr., 5, 8, 12, 17, 20, 22, 23, 70–73, 75, 78, 83*n*2, 125, 275–279, 281–283, 289, 292, 300–302, 305, 312, 321, 337, 343, 345

Burmeister, S., 308

cacao, 77, 84*n*6, 98, 100, 122, 317. *See also* kakaw

Cahal Pech, 4, 289; and Buenavista, 198–204; chronology, 194–196; finger cache, 328; history of work, 12–13; Middle Formative, 103–129; site plan, *104, 105, 195,* 332; Terminal Classic, 306; Willey's work at, 19–20; and Xunantunich, 202–204. *See also* Cunil; Zopilote

calabash, 118

Calakmul: alliances, 140, 326; settlement, 11; tomb, 233

Callar Creek, 177, 283

Camelote, 49, 292, 293

Campbell-Trithart, M. J., 217, 218

cannibalism, 121

Caracol, 320–334; and Belize Valley, 329–333; burial patterns, 215; causeways, 128; finger caches, 137; and Naranjo, 140, 341; and Pacbitun, 225; polity, 325–329, 344; site map, *326;* site morphology, 126–130; terminus groups, 291

Carr, J., 94

Carr, S. H., 219

Carrasco Vargas, R., 233

Cas Pek, 110

causeways, 281; Baking Pot, 70; Cahal Pech, 103, 111, 332; El Pilar, 242, 250; functions, 125, 141; Pacbitun, 209; Xunantunich, 332; Yalbac, 96

cave, 95, 100, 234, 306

Cayo Y, 4, 283

Cecil, L. G., 8

cedar, 133

ceiba, 159

censor, 78, 313, 314

central place theory, 13, 323

Cerros: ballcourt, 212; mask, 56, 58, 180, 212; submerged deposits, 260

Chaa Creek, 12; survey, 177, 283

Chadwick, R., 309

Chalcedony, 224

Chalchuapa, 31

Chambers, M., 21

Chan site, 176

Chase, A. F., 1, 4, 9–11, 71, 72, 79–81, 82n1, 83n4, 137, 140, 170, 215, 221, 225, 226, 233, 258, 291, 308, 314, 317, 318, 320–333, 337, 340, 342, 344, 347

Chase, D. Z., 3, 9–11, 24, 71, 72, 78–81, 82n1, 83n4, 125, 137, 140, 170, 215, 221, 225, 226, 257, 258, 278, 291, 317, 320, 321, 323–329, 331–333, 335, 340, 342, 347

Chase, S. M., 75

Cheetham, D. T., 31, 32, 40, 45, 46, 103–105, 107–109, 113, 114, 116, 118, 122, 125, 132, 136, 138, 152, 165n3, 208, 339, 340

chert: honey-brown, 217; plano-convex points, 216, 260, 268; tool production, 251

Chiapa de Corzo, 67

Chiapas, 31, 114

Chichen Itza, 16, 100

chile-grinding bowl, 315

Chontal, 307, 310, 312, 313

Chultun, 35, 110

cinnabar, 78; in tombs, 228, 231, 234, 235, 242, 342

clams, 118, 119, 225

Clancy, F. S., 135, 213

Clark, J. E., 114, 115, 122, 247

cloth, 163, 182, 185

Clowery, S., 157

Coba, 328, 347

Cobos, R., 269

Cocos Bank, 3, 67, 86, 94, 287, 303n1

codex, 133, 186, 234, 301

Coe, M. D., 38, 71, 81, 115, 154, 234, 283, 296, 297, 342, 345

Coe, W. R., 9, 38, 70, 81, 125, 154, 233, 283, 296, 297, 322, 328, 345

Coggins, C., 160

Cohen, M. N., 122, 163

Cohen, N. C., 254

colander, 27, 35, 36

Colha, 34, 116; ballcourt, 212; chert, 216,

269, 270; early ceramics, 41, 121

Conlon, J., 70, 77, 78, 83n4, 97, 141, 145, 283, 292, 338

Connell, S. V., 12, 176, 177, 283

copal, 121, 234

Copan: cache patterns, 328; coyol use, 118; diet, 222; elite residence, 79; North Group themes, 54; royal tombs, 233; sacbes, 146, 172; sculpture, 175

Copan Valley, 31

coral, 159

Corletta, R., 100

Costin, C. L., 308

cotton, 98, 100, 118, 306

Covarrubias, M., 67

Cozumel, 310

craft specialization, 44, 68. See also chert, tool production; obsidian production; shell, ornament production; slate workshop

Craig, A. K., 261

creation, 57, 182, 183, 185, 188, 341; reenactment, 54, 58, 175, 189

crocodile, 121, 221

Crumley, C. L., 285

Cuello, 34, 41, 116, 225

Culbert, T. P., 25, 72, 73, 81, 170, 278, 305–307, 320, 322

cult of the dead, 228, 233

Cunil, 7, 113, 141, 165n4, 208; architecture, 107; dating, 28, 105; description, 31, 113; incised designs, 113, 114; residential units, 108

curassow, 220

Dahlin, B. H., 104

D'Altroy, T. N., 255

Danforth, M. E., 236n3

deer, 39, 40, 117, 118, 119, 221, 224

Demarest, A. A., 7, 31, 80, 139, 324, 347

Dillon, B. D., 137

ditched fields, 75, 79–80, 84n6

dog, 40, 234

Dos Chombitos, 176, 283

Dos Pilas, 236n1, 324, 347

Downing, T. E., 300

Dreiss, M. L., 114, 116, 301

Driver, W. D., 5, 48, 283, 287, 347, 434
Dunham, P. S., 323
dwarf, 158, *159*
Dzibilchaltun, 100

earflare, 56, 133, 213, 321, 341
Earle, T. K., 126, 254, *255*
earplug, 262, 271
Eaton, J., 40, 212
eccentrics, 328–329; Bedran, 75, 77, 78;
  Buenavista, 158; elite context, 83*n*4;
  Ontario, 301; Ponces, 330
E-Group: Bedran, 75; Buenavista, 83*n*3;
  Cahal Pech, 109, 138; Pacbitun, 209–
  210, 229, 341, 347
Ehret, J., 97, 283
Ek Balam, 175
El Baul, 67
El Castillo, 173, 174, 181, 193, 202. *See
  also* Ancestor Mountain
El Chayal, 115, 224, 271
El Mirador, 180
El Pilar, 5, 13, 24, 48; construction history,
  242; investigations, 238–256; palaces,
  203; Preclassic expansion, 68, 138, 153;
  resource zones, 243; site plan, *242, 250*
El Salvador, 7, 31
elite residence, 59, 79, 242, 245, 255, 277
Elson, M. D., 40
emblem glyph, 171, 323
Emery, K., 219–221
enamel hypoplasia, 120
Epstein, J., 17
Esperanza, 292, 300, 303, 343; excava-
  tions, 294–296; site plan, *295*

facade, stucco, 54, 144. *See also* mask,
  facade; Xunantunich frieze
Falconer, S. E., 284
Fash, B. W., 186
Fash, W. L., 31, 125, 146, 172, 175, 187,
  288
fauna, 117, 219, 220
feasting, 36–40, 121, 285, 297, 301, 338
Fedick, S. L., 10, 13, 45, 48, 86–88, 98,
  110, 112, 119, 169, 171, 176, 225, 226,
  240, 241, 243, 244, 253, 255, 290, 321,
  328, 332, 347
Feinman, G. M., 309
Ferguson, J., 83*n*3, 103
Fialko, V., 78, 109
Fields, V. M., 180, 341
fig, wild, 119
figurines: Blackman Eddy, 31, *32*, 38;
  Cahal Pech, 31, 114, *115*, 117, 122,
  339; Saturday Creek 93
finger-bowl cache, 137, 330, 340
finger cache, 328. *See also* phalange
flame eyebrow, 113, 116, 122
Flannery, K. V., 115, 290
Floral Park, 3, 49, 274, 283, 289, 292,
  300, 303, 306, 343; ceramic complex,
  7; early ceramics, 28; excavations, 293–
  294; site map, *294*; termination ritual,
  52
Folan, W. J., 11, 126, 130
Ford, A., 10, 13, 23, 45, 48, 71–73, 81, 87,
  88, 98, 110, 112, 169, 171, 176, 238,
  240, 241, 243–245, 247, 250–255, 277,
  280, 281, 283, 290, 303*n*1, 321, 325,
  332, 342
Forsyth, D. W., 104
Fox, J. G., 301, 302, 312, 316, 320
Franks, A. W., 260
Freidel, D. A., 54, 56–58, 83*nn*3,4, 123,
  125, 138, 140, 144, 145, 180, 182, 185,
  186, 188, 189, 257, 260, 301, 305, 308,
  310, 318, 330
Freidman, J., 254
Frenchman's Cay, 266, 271
Fried, M., 82
Fry, R. E., 10, 315

Gann, T., 205*n*1, 259–261
Garber, J. F., 1, 4, 5, 13, 24, 25, 37, 42, 45,
  48, 49, 52, 54, 75, 83*n*3, 257, 283, 287,
  288, 291, 337, 338, 343, 347
Garza T., S., 125
gastropod, 221, 266, 267
Gellner, E., 308
Gerhardt, J. C., 34
Gibson, C., 259

Gifford, J. C., 6–8, 28, 41, 45, 75, 77, 88, 105, 113, 162, 207, 224, 262, 270, 305, 306, 309, 313, 318, 331

Gillespie, S. D., 122, 301, 321

Glascock, M. D., 115, 224

Glassman, D. M., 48, 294

God K, 185

Gonlin, N., 284, 285, 322

Goodman, A. H., 120

Gossen, G., 80

Graebner, S. M., 86

Graham, E., 4, 8, 9, 12, 171, 177, 260, 270, 305, 311, 316, 318, 345

Graham, I., 125

Graham, J. A., 64, 66, 67

green obsidian, 165n7, 216, 301. *See also* Pachuca

greenstone: Kanocha phase (Blackman Eddy), 32, 33, 35, 36; Jenney Creek phase (Blackman Eddy), 41, 44; Pacbitun, 215

grater bowl, 301, *309*, 311, 317. *See also* jade; jadeite

griddle, 309, 310, 317

Grove, D. C., 122

Grube, N., 12, 52, 67, 136, 140, 156, 161, 202, 320–326

Guderjan, T. H., 257

Gulf Coast, 116, 307, 311, 317

Hagstrum, M. B., 308

Hall, G. D., 77, 233–235, 236n2

Hamblin, N., 219

Hammond, N., 7, 35, 71, 72, 104, 116, 119, 122, 150, 212, 213, 216, 257, 261, 276, 277, 279–283, 288, 290, 303n1, 305, 311, 317, 340

Hansen, R., 35, 38, 44, 104, 122, 136, 138, 144, 147n3

Harrison, E., 205n1

Harrison, P., 79, 290, 291

Hartman, C. J., 25, 48

Hartong, H., 342

Hassig, R., 323, 324

Haviland, W. A., 9, 71, 78, 80, 81, 83n4, 144, 284, 287, 300, 322

Hayden, B., 282

Healy, P. F., 3, 12, 45, 48, 103, 114, 116, 118, 121, 170, 207, 210–218, 220, 221, 224–226, 228, 271, 330, 332, 339, 341, 342

Heath-Smith, C., 312

Hegmon, M., 308

Helmuth, H., 228

hematite, 95. *See also* ochre

Henderson, J. S., 27

Hendon, J. A., 76, 81, 284, 301

hero twins, 68

Hester, T. R., 25, 216

Hintzman, M. W., 241, 247

Hirth, K., 82n1

historic period, 4, 305

Hohmann, B., 34, 38, 44, 110, 115, 116, 209, 216, 223, 224

Holmul style, 331

Hondo River, 3

Hopun, L. C., 18, 19

Houston, S. D., 139, 170, 181, 301, 324, 325, 331

hummingbird, 165n9

Hurst, W. J., 122

hydraulic engineering, 108. *See also* water management

Iannone, G., 71, 77, 78, 83n4, 110, 116, 273, 278, 281, 283, 284, 302, 343

iguana, 221

incense, 139

Initial Series, 61, 66, 67

Initial Series Introducing Glyph, 63, 213

Inomata, T., 211

Itza, 307, 311, 312, 318

Ixtepeque, 115, 224, 271

Jackson, L. J., 4

jade: dental inserts, 133; Pacbitun, 216, 217, 224, 228, 231; royal tombs, 234, 235; Moho Cay, 257, 261, 271. *See also* greenstone; jadeite

jadeite: Buenavista, 194; Cahal Pech, 120, 121; royal tombs, 234. *See also* greenstone; jade

Jaeger, S., 128, 322
jaguar pelts, 234
Jamison, T., 173, 205n1
Jauncy Vase, 331
Jenkin, R. N., 87
Johnson, A., 254
Jones, C., 136, 170, 322
Jones, G. D., 305, 317, 319
Jones, R. C., 249, 255, 324
Joyce, R., 27, 81
Jute, 37, 39, 217, 224, 225

Kakaw, 161. *See also* cacao
Kamp, K., 251
kan cross, 31, 122
Kanocha, 7, 27–36, 165n4; buildings, 35; dating, 27, 46; incised designs, 31; origins, 27–31; phase, 27–36
K'awil, 185, 186, 187
Keegan, W. F., 269
Keller, A., 171
Kichpanha, 40
Kidder, Alfred V., 133, 233
k'in, 185
King, E., 284, 285
Kinkella, A., 86, 89
Kirke, C. M., 79, 293
Knapp, A. B., 301
Kolb, C. C., 218
Koontz, R. A., 301
Kosakowski, L. J., 31
Kowalewski, S. A., 82n1
Kunstler, B., 212
Kurjack, E. B., 75, 125, 126, 287

La Mojarra, 67
Lacandon, 58
Lamani: architecture, 310, 317; ceramics, 306, 314, 316; diet, 222; stucco masks, 180
Lambert, J., 259
Landeen, E. S., 147n3
Laporte, J. P., 11, 78, 83n3, 104, 109, 171, 328, 330, 347
Las Ruinas, 12, 48, 193, 330. *See also* Arenal

Lawlor, E. J., 118, 119
LeCount, L. J., 7, 12, 28, 113, 169, 173, 178, 205nn1,2, 225, 305, 311, 313, 331
Lee, D., 110, 116
Lee, T. A. Jr., 115
Lehmann, W., 67
Lentz, D. L., 118, 119, 223, 224
Leventhal, R. M., 12, 80, 146, 168, 181, 225, 278, 301, 311, 340
Lewenstein, S. M., 151
Leyden Plaque, 64
Lincoln, C. E., 81
Long Count, 64, 66, 213
long-distance exchange, 114
long-distance trade, 270, 343; Belize River, 4; Blackman Eddy, 33; ceramics, 30; at Moho Cay, 271; Pacbitun, 225
Looper, M. G., 185, 187, 188
Low, S. M., 310
Lowe, G. W., 67
Lubaantun, 282
Lucero, L. J., 86, 93, 98, 241, 245, 339, 347

macro-blade, 32, 268
Magnoni, A., 271
maize, 79, 84n6, 118, 119, 120, 222; god, 58, 68
MacKie, E. W., 12, 174, 205n1
Mallory, J. K., 247
mamiform tetrapod, 262
Mamom, 7, 31, 32, 44, 113, 142
manatee, 257, 260, 267, 268, 269
mandibular periodontis, 120
Marco Gonzalez (site), 260
Marcus, J., 122, 141, 142, 146, 282, 290, 291, 320, 323, 324
Martin, S., 140, 161, 170, 202, 320, 322–324, 326
mask, 183; facade, 42, 55, 56, 58, 180
Mason, G., 12
Masson, M. A., 308, 311
Matheny, R. T., 104, 147n3
Mathews, P., 317, 322–324
Maxwell, D., 258
Maya Mountains, 3, 103, 207, 294

Mayapan, 16, 17, 306, 311
McAnany, P. A., 229, 236, 280, 284, 300, 301
McDonald, A. J., 58
McGee, R. J., 58
McGinn, J. J., 144
McGovern, J. O., 49, 83n3, 138, 154, 156, 170, 177, 205n1
McKillop, H., 3, 4, 119, 257, 258, 260–262, 264–270, 342
Mejia, H. E., 330
Melhado settlement group, 110
Melongena, 267
Michaels, G. H., 245
Miksicek, C. H., 118
Miller, A. G., 258, 317
Miller, J. H., 234
Miller, M. E., 52, 64, 301
Miller, V. E., 180
Mirador Basin, 104, 147n3
mirror, 52, 58, 231, 234, 235
Mitchum, B. A., 114
Mixe-Zoque, 31
Moho Cay, 4, 257–272, 342
Moholy-Nagy, H., 225, 233, 234, 236nn2,3, 247
Moore, A. F., 12, 13, 70
Morelos, 31
Morley, F. R., 64
Morley, S. G., 18, 64
Morris, J., 13, 329, 330
Motogua Valley, 46, 216, 271
Mountain Cow, 9
Muhs, D. R., 317
musical instrument, 215, 221, 234

Nakbe, 34–35, 38, 44
Naranjo, 170; and the Belize Valley, 139–140, 168, 331; and Buenavista, 161; and Caracol, 320, 326, 327; polity, 181, 202, 329
Nelson, F. W., 116
net sinker, 260, 268, 315. *See also* potsherd, notched
New River, 4
Nicholson, H. B., 312

Nohmul, 283, 317
Nohoch Ek: architecture, 32, 81, 82; function, 296–297, 303, 343; settlement, 300
Norman, V. G., 136, 138

Oaxaca, 31
obsidian production, 247–248
ocarina, 32
ochre, 231. *See also* hematite
O'Day, S. J., 269
Olmec, 58, 113, 116, 122
Olson, K., 241, 245, 247, 248, 251
Ontario: excavations, 283, 297–302; function, 292, 343; termination ritual, 52; site plan, *298, 299*
Orrego, C. M., 136, 252, 253
osteoarthritis, 120
Osterholtz, A., 89, 96
Otto, B. E., 192

Pacbitun, 207–227, 330, 341; chronology, 207–208; Middle Formative, 28, 38, 223–225; royal burial, 228–237, 342; site plan, 209, 211; stela, 64, *214*
Pachuca, 95. *See also* green obsidian
Pacific Coast, 31, 58, 136
palace school, 160, *161*, 340, 346
Palenque: royal tomb, 233; scaffolds, 56; smoking axe, 186; stone panel, 183; stucco relief, 56, 181, 183, 186, 233; Tablet of the Cross, 189; Tablet of the Foliated Cross, 189; Tablet of the Sun, 189
Pan-mesoamerican symbol system, 31, 36, 46, 113
paper, 119
Pasion River, 113
Pax god, 183, 186, 187, 188
peccary, 40, 121, 220, 221, 224
pendant, 32, 121
Pendergast, D. M., 12, 79, 81, 134, 233, 260, 262, 270, 314
Peru, 1, 15
phalange, 52, 137, 201
Piedras Negras, 17

Piehl, J. C., 70, 76
pine, 118, 207, 223
Pohl, M., 40, 219, 221
Pollock, H., 16–18
Pomacea, 37, 225
Ponces, 13, 330
Popul Vuh, 37, 189, 301
porotic hyperostosis, 120, 339
potsherd, notched, 117, 264, 265, 268. *See also* net sinker
Potter, D. R., 80, 81, 114, 284, 285
Powis, T. G., 28, 34, 38, 70, 103, 110, 119, 120, 122, 209, 223–225, 292, 338
preceramic, 30, 107
Primary Standard Sequence, 77, 338
Pring, D. C., 32
Proskouriakoff, T., 16, 311
Puerto Escondido, 27
Puleston, D. E., 9, 11, 255, 283, 284, 287, 291, 292, 300, 303n2, 325, 349
pumice, 270
Putun, 307, 312
Puuc, 180
pyrite, 120, 228, 231, 234

Quiche Maya, 37, 189
Quintana Roo, 290, 291
Quiriqua, 187, *188, 189*

rabbit, 40, 118, 224
radiocarbon dates: Blackman Eddy, 27, 28, 29; Cahal Pech; 105, 106; Pacbitun, 207, 224; southern Belize, 260
ramon, 119, 223
Rands, B. C., 122
Rands, R. L., 122
Reed, D. M., 222
Reents, D. J., 160
Reents-Budet, D., 160, 331, 236n1
Reilly, F. K. III, 48
reservoir, 103, 110, 253, 293
Rathje, W. L., 257, 258, 307
Rice, D. S., 255, 284, 310
Rice, P. M., 9, 78, 248, 305, 312, 315, 318
Richie, C., 217, 218
Ricketson, E. B., 9, 287

Ricketson, O. G. Jr., 9, 12, 18, 22, 70, 142, 233, 287, 310
Rio Azul, 170, 234, 236n2
Rio Bec, 164n2
Roaring Creek, 289
Robertson, D., 312
Robertson, M. G., 181
Robertson, R. A., 81
Robin, C., 176, 177, 205n1
roller seal, *32,* 40; stamp, 117
Rovner, I., 151
Rowlands, M. J., 254
Ruppert, K., 209, 229
Ruz Lhuillier, A., 233

Sabloff, J. A., 11, 83n4, 188, 257, 258, 262, 305–307
sacbe, 70, 125, 171
Sackett, J., 307
salt, 258, 268
salt-making, 119, 268
San Esteban, 270
San Jose, 9, 17, 100, 101, 270
San Lorenzo, 177, 283
San Martin Jilotepeque, 115, 224
Sanders, W. T., 82, 254, 277, 278, 300, 320, 324
Santa Rita, 78, 322
Satterthwaite, L., 12, 17–22, 103, 136, 174, 182, 297, 337
Saturday Creek, 3, 89, *92, 339*; bound captive, 317; investigations, 91–93; sacred area, 101; soils and settlement, 98
Saturno, W., 144
Saul, J. M., 120, 225
Saul, F. P., 120, 225
scaffold, 55, 185
Scarborough, V. L., 81, 125, 211, 212, 301
Schele, L., 64, 123, 125, 138, 140, 144, 145, 161, 180, 181, 234, 301, 317, 330, 331
Schmidt, P., 164n1, 305, 306, 310
Scholes, F. B., 318
Schwartz, G. M., 284
Service, E., 255
settlement: archaeology, 274, 321–323,

333, 337; density, 3, 86, 99, 100, 218, 241, 245, 251, 293, 300, 303, 303*n*2, 342, 344; hierarchy, 70, 82; pattern, 1, 10, 17, 98, 101, 217, 241, 254, 274, 287–289, 335, 343, 347; system, 86

Shafer, H. J., 114, 216

Sharer, R. J., 7, 9, 45, 122, 144, 147*n*3, 233

Sharp, R., 180

Shaw, L., 40

shell: disk, 300; ornament production, 110, 116, 224. *See also* bead, shell

Shennan, S. J., 308

Shimkin, D. B., 307

Shook, E. M., 64, 233

Siebal: architecture, 310; ceramics, 187, 262, 313, 317; elite residences, 79

Simmons, S. E., 305

skyband, 183, 185, 187

skybearer, 183, 185, 186

slab-foot cylinder, 52

slash-and-burn, 87. *See also* swidden cultivation

slate: Cahal Pech, 116; Caracol, 342; Pacbitun, 213, 216, 217, 224, 226, 228; workshop, 211

Smith, A. L., 9, 125, 133, 142, 211, 233, 311, 322

Smith, M. E., 312

Smith, R. E., 6, 7, 142, 262

Smith, W. D., 324

snails, 118, 119, 216, 225

Song, R., 120, 225

Spanish Lookout, 10, 274, 283, 292

Spence, M. W., 216

Spencer, C. S., 83*n*5

spindle whorl, 166*n*10, 268

spondylus, 133, 216, 231, 234, 235, 341

spouted vessel, 121. *See also* stirrup spouted vessel

squash, 118, 119

Stanchly, N. W., 40, 118, 119, 219, 220

Steadman, D., 219

Steinberg, J. M., 241

stelae: Abaj Takalik, 66, 67; Actuncan, 138; Blackman Eddy, 63–67; Cahal Pech, 200–210; Hauberg, 64; Pacbitun,

213–214; Pestac (Tonina), *63*, 64; Xunantunich, 170–171; Zopilote, 135–137, *201,* 340

Steward, J., 1

stingray spines: Blackman Eddy, 32; Buenavista, 159; Moho Cay, 257, 262, 269, 270; Pacbitun, 216; royal tombs, 234, 235

Stirling, M. W., 67

stirrup spouted vessel, *36,* 40

Stone, A., 301, 308

stone bowl, 32

Strelow, D., 28, 113

strombus, 133, 216, 224, 268, 269

Stuart, D., 185

Stuart, G., 233

Sullivan, L. A., 48

sun god, 133, 187

Sunahara, K. S., 217, 218

Sutro, L. D., 300

Swazey Complex, 31

sweatbath, 157

swidden cultivation, 91, 119. *See also* slash-and-burn

Tainter, J. A., 306

tapir, 224

Taschek, J. T., 7, 12, 30–32, 40, 43, 45, 48, 72, 103, 122, 139, 149, 153, 156, 158–161, 166*n*10, 168–171, 181, 191, 192, 198, 200, 205*n*4, 278, 282, 283, 290, 296, 297, 303*n*1 320, 324, 329–332, 338, 340, 341, 345, 346

Taube, K., 58, 183, 186, 187

Tayasal, 314, 317, 318

Taylor, W. W., 8

tecomate, 27, 32, 35

Tedlock, D., 37

Tehuacan Valley, 307

temper, volcanic ash, 27, 162, 316

Teotihuacan, 313, 317

termination: ritual, 37, 38, 52, 75; offerings, 121

terminus group, 125–148; Caracol, 128, 291; Pacbitun, 130; Zopilote, 130–137, 340. *See also* causeways

terrace, agricultural, 91, 221, 296, 297, 347
textile, 118
Thomas, P. M. Jr., 277, 278, 280, 281
Thompson, J.E.S., 6, 9, 12, 16, 17, 22, 72, 100, 171, 173, 205n1, 287, 307, 309, 318
three stone place, 57
Tikal, 170, 276; chipped stone, 116; excavations, 322; minor centers, 291; polity, 326; royal tombs, 233; settlement, 9, 347; stela, 66; stucco masks, 180; warfare, 327
Tipu, 4, 163, 305; ceramics, 313, 314, 315, 319; ethnohistory 318; side-notched points, 311
Tolok, 110, *111, 112,* 119
Tonina, 64, 185, 186
Topsey, H., 13, 87
Torres, R., 171
Tourtellot, G., 80, 310, 313, 322
Tozzer, A. M., 15, 16, 18, 78, 287
trace element analysis, 115
trading port, 257, 258, 268
transshipment, 257, 260, 343
Tres Zapotes, 67
Trik, A. A., 233
tripod cylinder, 158
trumpet, 258
Tulum, 306, 318
turkey, 221
turtle, 224
Tuxtla Statuette, 64, 67
Twin Pyramid Complex, *54, 55,* 282
Tzinic, 110, 141, 145–146
Tzutzuculi, 58

Uaxactun, 18, 276; facade masks, 58, 180; Middle Formative, 142; settlement density, 292
Ucanal, 149
underworld, 76, 100, 180, 234. *See also* Xibalba
Uxmal, 310

Valdés, J. A., 104, 144
Valley of Mexico, 31

Valley of Peace, 86–101
Valliant, G., 18
Venus, 183
Villa Rojas, A., 125
Viru Valley, 1, 273
vision serpent, 58
Vogt, E. Z., 216, 288
von Falkenhausen, L., 83n3

Walker, D. S., 305
warfare, 32; and ballcourts, 301, 302; Cahal Pech, 139, 140, 145, 340; ethnohistoric, 311; Middle Formative, 42, 44; Terminal Classic, 307, 318; Xunantunich, 185
Warrie Head, 49, 292, 300, 303, 343
Washington, H. S., 67
Waterman, T. T., 67
water management, 125, 285
Wauchope, R., 9, 287
Webb, M. C., 254, 255, 305
Webster, D. L., 81, 82n1, 84n7, 142, 255, 320, 322, 324
Webster, G. S., 254
Welsh, W.B.M., 76–78, 214, 230, 233, 234
Wernecke, D. C., 250, 251
Whitaker, J., 251
White, C. D., 120, 221, 222
Wiesen, A., 118, 119, 223, 224
Wiessner, P., 307, 308
Wilcox, D. R., 211
Wild Cane Cay, 258, 266, 270
Wilk, R. R., 79, 321
Willey, G. R., 1, 3, 5–13, 15, 16, 23, 25, 41, 45, 46, 48, 49, 67, 70–73, 79–81, 83n6, 86, 94, 101, 110, 112, 125, 163, 168–171, 207, 215, 236n4, 269, 273–275, 277, 278, 281, 283, 287, 288, 291–293, 298, 300, 302, 305–307, 310, 312, 321, 322, 329, 335, 337, 343, 346–348
Wing, E. S., 219
Winfield Capitaine, F., 67
witz-monster, 187
Wobst, M. H., 307
Wolff, G., 205n1
world tree, 183, 185, 187
Wren, L. H., 310

Wright, A.C.S., 261
Wright, H. T., 254
Wright, L. E., 120

Xibalba, 100, 234. *See also* underworld
Xunantunich, 4, 168–190, 191, 289, 329,
    332, 341; architecture, 8, 174; ceramics,
    28, 234; chronology, 169, 173, 176, 192–
    194, 197–198, 205*n*2; frieze, 174–175,
    180, *183*, 341; history of work, 12; Late
    Classic florescence, 7, 171; settlement
    survey, 176–178; site plan, *172, 193. See
    also* El Castillo; Ancestor Mountain

Yadeun, J., 185, 186
Yaeger, J. R., 176, 177, 205*n*1, 283
Yalbac, 89, 96, 99, 101
Yalbac Creek, 96, *97, 99*
Yaxchilan, 324
Yaxha, 282
Yaxox, 110

Zopilote, *131,* 291, 339; investigations,
    130–137, 283; Middle Formative, 110
Zoque, 138
Zotz, 110, 305
Zubin, 110, 283